Michał Lubina

Russia and China

A political marriage of convenience – stable and successful

Barbara Budrich Publishers
Opladen • Berlin • Toronto 2017

Proofreading of this book was supported by the Faculty of International and Political Studies, Jagiellonian University, Krakow, Poland.

A CIP catalogue record for this book is available from
Die Deutsche Bibliothek (The German Library)

ISBN 978-3-8474-2045-3
eISBN 978-3-8474-1072-0

Die Deutsche Bibliothek – CIP-Einheitsaufnahme
Ein Titeldatensatz für die Publikation ist bei der Deutschen Bibliothek erhältlich.

Verlag Barbara Budrich Barbara Budrich Publishers
Stauffenbergstr. 7. D-51379 Leverkusen Opladen, Germany

86 Delma Drive. Toronto, ON M8W 4P6 Canada
www.barbara-budrich.net

Jacket illustration by Bettina Lehfeldt, Kleinmachnow – www.lehfeldtgraphic.de
Copy-Editing: Máiréad Collins, Belfast, UK
Type-Setting: Anja Borkam, Jena – kontakt@lektorat-borkam.de
Printed in Europe on acid-free paper by
paper&tinta, Warsaw

Contents

Preface

Everything that needs to be said has already been said.
But since no one was listening, everything must be said again.
André Gide

Sino-Russian relations have recently become much discussed, even popular, if not trendy. There is a certain logic in this fact. Because of objective reasons, such as the giant territories of the two countries, their position and political influence, geographical location, and economic and military potential, Sino-Russian relations are one of the most important global political issues. However, since their spectacular rapprochement in 2014, Sino-Russian relations drew even closer attention which increases the interest in researching the Moscow-Beijing dynamics.

The aim of this publication is to depict the sophisticated relationship between Russia and China from the USSR's dissolution (1991) to the Silk Road Forum in Beijing (2017), and to present the growing asymmetry in their relations. It shows that the Russia-China relationship is pragmatic, a political "marriage of convenience" which serves as a means to increase their global influence. Russia and China are two different worlds, maybe even two different civilizations. They do do not trust each other; however, that does not stop them from developing relations and doing business together. Thus, they constitute a paradoxical relationship based on convience, yet successful and stable at the same time.

The last two decades were decisive for the character of Moscow-Beijing relations. For the first time in contemporary history, Russia faces a China stronger than itself – Beijing achieved a multidimensional advantage and became the senior partner. This book shows the origins of this process, presents how it happened and gives prognoses for the future. It explains that Beijing is implementing what may be described with a paradoxical phrase as "the asymmetric win-win" agenda: both sides gain, but it is China that wins more, much more. The book shows the possible consequences of this situation – "a return to the past" – and claims that despite this asymmetry, Sino-Russian relations will remain strong.

This book is a continuation of my PhD dissertation ("Growing asymmetry. Sino-Russian relations in 1991-2011"), published in Polish with the title "Niedźwiedź w cieniu smoka" (*The Bear Overshadowed by the Dragon*)[1]. This monograph, however, has undergone such major changes compared to the Polish edition that it has become a distinct book – around 35% of this book is

1 M.Lubina, *Niedźwiedź w cieniu smoka. Rosja-Chiny 1991-2014* [The Bear Overshadowed by the Dragon. Russia-China 1991-2014], Kraków 2014.

entirely new. I supplemented the description for the period between 2015 and 2017, and I had to shorten this book from its initial 623 pages, which forced me to systematize and synthesize the contents and to highlight the most important aspects. Presenting the book to international readers deprived me of one of my assets – contrary to the Polish edition, this is not the first book on contemporary Sino-Russian relations. Thus, I needed to transform the contents, to eliminate many aspects well-known to international readers and to emphasize my original thesis: the "return to the past", to the 17th century model of Sino-Russian relations.

Therefore, in this book I will present Sino-Russian relations as *the return to the past.* Although the conditions and political decorum changed, a roughly similar model exists today. If one compares the 17th century relations between the two countries with the current ones, one can trace some striking similarities. The most important one being that China is much stronger in this relationship (like it used to be in the 17th century) and Russia accepts this fact (albeit quietly) and adheres to this situation by taking as many opportunities as possible. China's policy towards Russia today is a pragmatic equivalent of the 17th century Manchu politics, focused on having a long-lasting deal with Moscow in order to have it not endanger China's policies. This deal was made on Chinese terms, though with some benefits for Russia as well. Therefore, this is an adaptation of the 17th century model of relations: both countries benefit from their mutual relations, however, it is China that benefits more.

I am fully aware that some may not find this idea particularly innovative; it is a platitude to say that history repeats itself. Yet, I believe that applying this very obvious idea to contemporary Russia-China relations is something new – to my best knowledge nobody did this before, at least not in a book or in a peer-review journal article. And in my book, I will try to prove the hypothesis that Russia-China relations came back to its initial stage. After all, I believe – as many Asians do – that the world is spherical and historical periods come around in cycles.

This book is a result of my fourteen years of study on Russia-China relations: first at Jagiellonian University at the faculties of the Russian Studies and the Far Eastern Studies, then at a scholarship in Beijing in 2009-2010, as well as during many visits to Russia (over a dozen since 2004) and China (annually since 2006), and innumerous discussions with Russian, Chinese and Western specialists in the field. That is why the list of acknowledgments would be too long, so I will limit myself to the people who supported me with this edition.

Writing this book would have been impossible without the support of my family, friends, and colleagues. I would like to thank especially Professor Salvatore Babones from University of Sydney who convinced me to publish this book in English and who helped me intellectually and technically with this work; to Barbara Budrich, my publisher, who has trusted an internationally unknown young Polish researcher and to Marcin Grabowski from Jagiellonian

University, whose support was instrumental in making the publication of this book possible. I would also like to express my gratitude to the Jagiellonian University's Faculty of International and Political Studies for providing some sources for proofreading of this book, to Małgorzata Kmita who proofread it and to the three anonymous reviewers whose comments on my work helped me to improve it.

In my research career at Jagiellonian University, I benefitted from the support of Professor Adam W. Jelonek and the mentorship of Professor Bogdan Góralczyk from University of Warsaw. I owe my gratitude to Professor Roman Bäcker, Professor Joachim Diec and Professor Mieczysław Smoleń, too. Conversations with Jacek Bartosiak, Andrzej Bolesta, Adrian Brona, Łukasz Fyderek, Stefan Hejnowicz, Robert Krzesaj, Marcin Kaczmarski, Piotr Leszczewicz, Aleksandra Łopińska, Patrycja Pendrakowska, Tomasz Pugacewicz, Radosław Pyffel, Jacek Raś, Karolina Schab, Chen Yurong, Li Fengling, Zhou Hong, Jiang Shixue, Chong Pin Lin, Kong Tianping, Chen Xin, Shen Wei, Cheng Yuchin, Li Zengwei, Deng Ketang, Cho Byoung-se, Fyodor Lukyanov, Oleg Timofeev, Luka Ezerski, Sanat Kushkumbaev, as well as my faculty colleagues at Jagiellonian University, had significant impact on the way I see Russia-China relations. Finally, I benefitted from the insights from researchers and individuals from Moscow, St. Petersburg, Vladivostok, Beijing, Harbin, Guangzhou, Shanghai, Hong Kong, Seoul, Astana, Ashgabat, Prague, Paris, Oxford and Washington D.C.

Writing this book, as well as my entire career, would have been impossible without my wife, Magdalena Kozłowska, my great supporter, who remains my ultimate source of inspiration of what it means to be a world-class researcher.

Michał Lubina

This book has been completed in 2016, with last adjustments in May 2017

Introduction

I. Theoretical Introduction

This publication is an analysis of Russia-China relations from the point of view of political science and international relations theory. This chapter describes the present literature in the field and its theoretical findings. It uses tools of three approaches – political neorealism, social constructivism and asymmetry theory – and tries to combine these three. The most important argument is that the present model of Russia-China relations is a contemporary equivalent of their relations in the 17th century.

The official narrative in Russia and China about their relations follows the pattern of what can be called "official optimism", something that the Chinese would call *gei mianzi,* or "granting face", "showing respect" in public, "complimenting somebody in an exaggerated manner". In general, the official narrative "testifies to extraordinary transformation" in Russia-China relations: "ancient antagonisms and suspicions appear to have given way to an unparalleled convergence across multiple policy agendas".[2] The development of Russia-China relations then is "a rare case of two neighbouring great powers improving their relations and then keeping them on an even keel, despite the fact that one has risen in importance while the other has gone through a difficult and painful post-imperial adjustment."[3] This official "strategic partnership" narrative presents Russia-China relations as being of "a qualitatively distinct nature" from the previous periods based on "collection of Russia's and China's shared interests."[4] This "official optimism" has naturally evoked reactions from international academic circles (though, equally naturally, not from Russian and Chinese academic circles which follow the "official optimism" line of their governments to lesser or greater extent), where a much different picture of China-Russia relations dominates. In the mainstream international academic narrative of Russia-China relations, the pessimistic approach built on neorealistic assumption still dominates, yet it is naturally challenged by other points of view.

---

2 B. Lo, *Axis of Convenience. Moscow, Beijing and the New Geopolitics*, London, Chatham House, 2008, p. 1.

3 D. Trenin, *From Greater Europe to Greater Asia? The Sino-Russian Entente*, Carnegie Center, 09.04.2015.

4 M. Kaczmarski, *Russia-China Relations in the Post-Crisis International Order*, London-New York, Routledge, 2015, p. 24.

1. Between Neorealism and Constructivism

Among the main schools in international relations theory – liberalism, institutionalism, realism and constructivism (including the English School) – it is very easy to tell which one does not apply to Russia-China relations: liberalism. Although both Russia and China use phrases from a liberal understanding of international relations (interdependency, mutual benefits, win-win, etc.) this is merely a smoke screen. Chinese and especially Russian policymaking may serve as an archetypical antithesis to the liberal and institutional approach, with Moscow and Beijing vehemently rejecting the idea of transformative developments such as globalization, democratization, and the proliferation of international institutions that are all – according to liberal and institutional schools – offering the possibility of an enduring peace.[5] That leaves room for neorealism and constructivism only.

Despite its criticism in the Western academia ("no one loves a political realist")[6], neorealism remains the dominant school of political thinking in researching Russia-China relations; foreign policy of Russia and China is usually viewed through the bluntly realist lens of immediate material interests and military security. This is somehow natural. A neorealistic approach seems perfectly adequate to Russia and China: "the ruling elites in Moscow and Beijing have been brought up in a realist strategic culture that emphasizes the element of struggle in an often viciously competitive world, where power relations dominate at the expense of allegedly universal values."[7] *Realpolitik* remains the dominant school of political thinking in Russia, though naturally embodied in local understanding, wording and discourse.[8] Russian political thinking, no matter with which ideological screen, "functions inclusively within *Realpolitik* framework" – the Russians consider others' actions almost only in geopolitical terms.[9] Putin and his team, like their Soviet predecessors, perceive the world as a zero-sum game (contest between communism and capitalism gave way to the one between authoritarian traditionalism and democratic liberalism) and believe in the "timeless character of international politics": the worldview according to Kremlin is, as Bobo Lo calls it, "a Neo-Hobbesian vision". The world "is an alien and often hostile place, in which the strong prosper and the weak get beaten"; it is "a dog-eat-dog" world where the Leninist rule "who will beat whom" dictates the rules of the game and where one "cannot trust in the good intentions of others, but must concentrate on building up its own

5 R. O. Keohane, *Theory of World Politics: Structural Realism and Beyond* [in:] *Neorealism and Its Critics*, ed. R. O. Keohane. New York: Columbia University Press, 1986, p. 198.
6 R. Giplin, *No One Loves a Political Realist*, "Security Studies" 1996, no 5(1), p. 3-26.
7 B. Lo, *The Axis of Convenience*...p. 176.
8 J. Collins et. all, *Is Russia Ready for Change?* Carnegie Moscow Center 2010, 6 II.
9 M. Kaczmarski, *Rosja na rozdrożu. Polityka zagraniczna Władimira Putina* [Russia at the crossroads. The foreign policy of Vladimir Putin], Warszawa 2006, p. 168.

strength"; a world defined "as much by competition as cooperation; the primacy of hard power; the centrality of the great powers; and the abiding importance of geopolitics", where great power poses a "divine right."[10] Certainly, the perception of China lies within this realistic perspective as well.[11]

As for the Chinese, having such traditions as the ideas of Sun Zi and Han Feizi, they could be called Godfathers of realism. In China, as in Russia, political realism remains the dominant school of political thinking, though naturally it is expressed in their own language and local wording[12]: "China is a realistic country"[13], but its realism (best seen in Chinese strategic culture with its zero-sum approach to international order in general and to the USA in particular[14]) – is specific, embedded in the past[15], emphasizing moral leadership ("moral realism")[16] and China's uniqess (even in IR theory).[17] Moreover, traditionally China has acted according to realist assumptions in international relations, but based not on the objective structure of the international system, but rather on a specific historical strategic culture – the roots of *Realpolitik* in China are ideational and not predominantly structural.[18] Although China "does not fit" into the Western understanding of realism[19] as there are important differences between the Chinese and Western understanding of realism (e.g. dominance of hierarchy in Chinese thinking in opposition to "anarchy" in classic Western IR

---

10 B. Lo, *Russia and The New World Disorder*, London, Chatham House 2015, pp. xviii-xx, 14, 20 and 47.

11 М. Титаренко, *Геополитическое значение Дальнего Востока. Россия, Китай и другие страны Азии* [The Geopolitical importance of the Far East. Russia, China and the other Asian countries], Москва 2008, p. 246.

12 Though not unrivalled, see: F. Godement, *Contemporary China: Between Mao and Market*, Rowman & Littlefield Publishers 2016, p. 217.

13 Shen Dingli, *Russian cooperation with China is tactical, not strategic*, "Global Times", 27.06.2016.

14 F. Godement, *Introduction*, [in:] *China And Russia: Gaming the West?*, ECFR, 05.11.2016. G. Rozman, *The Sino-Russian Challenge to the World Order. National Identities, Bilateral Relations, and East Versus West in the 2010s*, Woodrow Wilson Center, Stanford University Press 2014, pp. 149 and 168.

15 Yan Xuetong, *Ancient Chinese Thought, Modern Chinese Power*, Princeton University Press, 2010.

16 Yan Xuetong, *Shijie quanli de zhuanyi: Zhengzhi lingdao yu zhanlue jingzheng* [The Transition of World Power: Political Leadership and Strategic Competition], Beijing 2015; for English overview (interview with Yan), see: *Yan Xuetong Urges China to Adopt a More Assertive Foreign Policy*, "New York Times", 09.02.2016.

17 B. Creutzfeld, *Qin Yaqing on Rules vs Relations, Drinking Coffee and Tea, and a Chinese Approach to Global Governance*, Tsingua Theory Talk #45, 2011.

18 A. I. Johnston, *Cultural Realism: Strategic Culture and Grand Strategy in Chinese History*, Princeton University Press Princeton 1998.

19 Zheng Yongdian, *Preface*, [in]: *China and International Relations. The Chinese view and the contribution of Wangu Gungwu*, London-New York, Routledge 2010, p. xiii.

works)[20], or preference to achieve dominance via political/economic/other means rather than by military power; and the difference between Chinese and Russian understanding, too (the Chinese have less pessimism than Russians "regarding human nature and the capacity to realize an ideal order"; while the latter are skeptical about that, the former make "the repeated appeal to Datong – Great Harmony")[21]; nevertheless, despite all these reservations, Chinese policy making can be classified as generally realistic, too.

Furthermore, even with all these differences, there is a meta-understanding between Russia and China on the philosophical level: in the perception of the nature of politics, China and Russia understand each other without words in such issues as political philosophy as the principle on which the international order should be based (such as non-intervention and the unconditional respect for sovereignty).[22] In the Chinese vision of *Realpolitik*, as in the Russian one, the world is characterized by a constant struggle for power, and the USA remains China's main adversary.[23]

The neorealist approach to Sino-Russian relations has been brilliantly summarized by Bobo Lo in his seminal and much-quoted book *"The Axis of Convenience"*. According to him: *Axis of Convenience* "combines tactical expediency with strategic calculus and long views (…) This is not, however, "an axis in the sense of being a budding political-military alliance" for the conflicting reasons (…) this is an axis born of necessity, real and perceived, not natural inclination (…) the relationship works precisely because it is based on expediency, pragmatism, and no small degree of cynicism."[24]

According to this narrative, Russia-China rapprochement is based not on a common strategic vision or mutual values, but on common interests, both political and economic. Dmitri Trenin writes that contrary to rhetoric, there is no friendship between Russia and China: "There has never been a spirit of camaraderie about Russo-Chinese summits (…) but the summits are invariably business-like and results-orientated (…) In the Sino-Russian official intercourse, politeness is the norm, while candor is a rare and precious quality."[25] In the absence of mutual trust, the China-Russia relations are "an example of pragmatic and opportunistic co-operation – real, but shallow."[26] Thus they are

20 James C. Hsiung, *A re-appraisal of Abrahamic values and neorealist IR theory: from a Confucian-Asian perspective*, [in:] Ibid., p. 18.

21 G. Rozman, *The Sino-Russian Challenge…*, p. 64.

22 M. Kaczmarski, *Russia-China Relations…*, p. 6.

23 See writings of Yan Xuetong, for example *Ancient Chinese Thought…*, p. 199-223; 229-252.

24 B. Lo, *The Axis of Convenience…*, pp. 54-55 and 131.

25 Д. Тренин, *Верные друзья? Как Россия и Китай воспринимают друг друга*, Carnegie, 1 VI 2012, (for English version, see: *True Partners? How Russia and China see each other*).

26 L. Jakobsen, P. Holtom, D. Knox, and Jingchao Peng, *China's Energy and Security Relations with Russia. Hopes, Frustrations and Uncertainties*, SIPRI policy paper 29, Stockholm 2011, pp. 3-5.

even, perhaps, "frienemies": friends and enemies at the same time, as Minxin Pei put it.[27]

The "axis of convenience", or pessimistic narrative, claims that this relationship is convenient for Russia and China alike: for both domestic and international reasons. For Russia, it answers security interests and global geopolitical ambitions. It strengthens the security of the Russian Far East, ("keep your friends close, keep your enemies closer") and "in its most primitive (...) sense it is an 'anti-relationship' driven by the urge to neutralize or negate."[28] In general, however, this narrative claims that this partnership, even after its 2014 rapprochment, is limited: it is a "partnership of strategic convenience – pragmatic, calculating and constrained."[29]

Although in the pessimistic narrative Russia is considered by China as an important, though secondary and limited partner – "generally speaking, Chinese attitude toward Russia combines Middle Kingdom hauter, pragmatism, and cynicism"[30] – nevertheless, it claims that the Chinese are very "careful not to irritate Russia" because "they do not want to encourage it to become more aggressive towards China."[31] For all the inadequacies in their bilateral ties, "Russia and China are each other's strategic rear."[32] This approach suits China's general policy of "peace on the borders" well: maintaining friendly relations with neighbours. Thanks to this, China secures its northern flank, and does not need to worry about security issues from this area and may concentrate on the most important issues, such as Taiwan, the South China Sea or the relations with the USA. That is why on both sides the axis of convenience is based on interests, not ideology.[33] This "axis of convenience narrative" implicitly, or sometimes explicitly, emphasizes the neorealist explanations of Russia-China relations.

This dominant, neorealist perspective on Russia-China relations has been challenged by researchers who used the tools of social constructivist perspective (that pays attention to values and ideas that influence actions and choices).[34] Craig Nation writes that "Sino-Russian relationship should be perceived as something more than 'an axis of convenience' plagued by 'fear, anx-

---

27 Minxin Pei, *China and Russia: Best Frenemies Forever?*, "Fortune", 28.03.2013.
28 B. Lo, *The Axis of Convenience...*, pp. 3-44.
29 Idem, *A Wary Embrace. What the China-Russia relationship means for the world*, Iowy Institute Papers, 03.04.2017.
30 Idem, *The Axis of Convenience...*, p. 3.
31 Д. Тренин, *Верные друзья...*, p. 20.
32 Yu Bin, *Russia Says "No" to the West and "Sort of" to China*, "Comparative Connections" 2007, vol. 9, no 1.
33 B. Lo, *The Axis of Convenience ...*, p. 6.
34 More on constructivism, see: A. Wendt, *Social Theory of International Politics*, Cambridge University Press 2000, Idem, *Constructing international politics*, "International Security" 20, p. 71-81.

iety and mistrust' which is ultimately 'of secondary importance'; if convenience is defined as the pragmatic pursuit of interests, we have in fact arrived at the essence of statecraft – the Sino-Russian relationship is not a sacramentally consecrated marriage."[35] The Chinese elites point out the fact that, as Yu Bin put it, "frequent disagreements and even contractions" between Russia and China do not influence the general good mood in their relations: "temporary inability to conclude talks on specific cooperation or difficulty in implementing something will not shake the overall bilateral relationship."[36] Dmitri Trenin writes that Russia and China accepted the formula "never being against each other, but not necessarily always with each other"; which allows them to "put a premium on a solid partnership where their interests meet, eschew conflicts where they don't, and allow a lot of flexibility where interests overlap only partially; Russia and China will probably never become full allies; the important thing is that they abhor mutual hostility, and have mastered their differences."[37] Alexander Gabuev echoes his words by calling Russia and China "friends with strategic benefits."[38] According to Marcin Kaczmarski, in the post 2008-crisis period "Russia-China relations have diverged from the expected pattern and failed to conform to the logic of power politics; rather than reversing or collapsing, rapprochement between Moscow and Beijing flourished and collaboration expanded to encompass new areas"; moreover, Russia has not hedged against China or balanced its rise, but chose instead closer co-operation and an even more unequal relationship – "breakthroughs in co-operation have transformed the relationship too much to be dismissed as 'geopolitical convenience.'"[39] This argument points out the fact that despite the growing asymmetry and widening the material power in favour of Beijing after the 2008 crisis, this did not lead to tensions or restrictions of the co-operation; instead it only accelerated the rapprochement of the two countries – Moscow and Beijing "avoided the Thucydides trap."[40] That is why an analysis of Russia-China relations only in terms of strategic interactions (national interests, geopolitical response to the USA or power projection) is insufficient – it "does not explain how Moscow and Beijing managed to come to terms with an increasingly balance of power; *Realpolitik* considerations cannot account for Russia's mounting dependence on China (…) they do not explain why Russia chose to adapt

35 R. C. Nation, *Russia in East Asia: Aspirations and Limitations*, [in:] *Russia's Prospects in Asia*, ed. S. Blank, Carlisle, PA, 2010, pp. 38-41.

36 Yu Bin, *Politics of "Reluctant Allies"*, "Comparative Connections", Vol. 18, No. 2, Sept. 2016, pp.129-144.

37 D. Trenin, *Russia, China Can Help Kashmir Tensions*, Carnegie Moscow, 10.10.2016.

38 A. Gabuev, *Friends with Strategic Benefits*, Carnegie Moscow, 07.07.2017.

39 M. Kaczmarski, *Russia-China Relations…*, pp. 3-8.

40 Idem, *How China and Russia avoided the Thucydides trap*, Iowy Institute, 11.04.2017.

to a new distribution of material power, nor do they explain why China decided to exercise strategic restraint towards its neighbour."[41]

Therefore, this opposite narrative proposes a term of "peaceful power transition" between Russia and China where "Russia gradually accommodated itself to the power shifts, while China exercised self-restraint."[42] This process, visible in energy cooperation, arms trade, "protectorate" in Central Asia and Moscow's Sinocentristic policy in East Asia, has in turn increased the already existent power asymmetry in favour of Beijing, and made Moscow a much more vulnerable partner. In a way, Russia had abandoned its attempts to balance the Chinese influence (evident before 2008) and came to terms with the reality of Chinese dominance. According to this narrative, the most important reason for this policy making lies in the social fact being the Russian elite's reading of China's intentions: "China appears to have convinced Moscow of its benign intentions by exercising self-restraint in policies implemented towards Russia"; although China may be a difficult partner in economic projects, Beijing refrains from using its advantage to obtain political concession from Moscow – this is how China was able to make Russian elite believe in its good intentions.[43] To conclude this narrative, Russia *nolens volens* accepted the Chinese privilege and has been trying to use it as much as possible to favour Russian interests.

Those two narratives (neorealist and constructivist) are not exactly contradictory, in fact they may be rather complementary than contradictory. This book tries to combine these two above mentioned narratives: the pessimistic neorealistic approach of "axis of convenience" with the moderate optimistic constructivist "power transition" one. This eclecticism is reflected in the very title of this book (a direct reference to "axis of convenience") and its subtitle (a reference to "optimistic narrative"), is done on purpose and intended to be, at least in a way, intellectually healthy. As in Taoism, where extremes meet and are complementary to one another, so here these two narratives on Russia-China relations can be combined. These two approaches, however, need to be complemented even further: by the asymmetry theory.

2. *The Asymmetric Win-Win*

The case study of Sino-Russian relations can be tackled using the asymmetry theory that explains the fundamental reality of unequal power amongst states and the impact of power's variables on states policies. Conceptually, in accordance with asymmetry theory, the asymmetry between China and Russia can be described in a few ways. The first one would naturally be the Lowell Dittmer's

41 Idem, *Russia-China Relations…*, p. 165.
42 Ibid..
43 Ibid., p. 169.

“positive asymmetry” model that is characterized by economic dependence, but not enmity (as in his “negative asymmetry”), where chief beneficiary (China) continuously deludes or coerces lesser beneficiary (Russia), while the lesser beneficiary turns a blind eye on it by believing that this is a temporary necessity.[44] Moreover, Ditmmer’s Cold War triangular model of “stable marriage” relationship between three great powers[45] can also be modified to present relations, as now there is amity between the two (Russia and China) players and enmity between each of them and the third party (Russia-USA, China-USA). Dittmer’s model has been modified to adjust it to the contemporary conditions by Brantly Womack who proposed his own asymmetric theory framework. According to him, “normal” relations between states are neither symmetric nor hegemonic, but rather constitute a comprehensive matrix of agreements with autonomy and deference being exchanged in increments rather than complete structural shifts. Here a “negotiated hierarchy” rather than dominance and subservience is the most frequent norm, whereas acknowledgment for deference (AFD) is a stable alternative to war between unequal states. This AFD paradigm works in accordance with the following logic: the stronger country (here: China) is more resourceful, but less committed to bringing about specific results in the bilateral relationship, while the weaker country (Russia) is more vulnerable and therefore more alert to threat and committed to survival.[46] That is why Russia and China would fit into Womack’s category of “normalized asymmetry”. Russia-China relations are asymmetrical (in favour of Beijing), but asymmetry in international relations does not necessarily mean that the more powerful partner dominates the less powerful one or that the weaker one is hopeless. In the Womack’s “normalized asymmetry”, the relationship is not harmonious, but both sides are confident of fulfilling their basic interests and expectations of mutual benefits.[47] Finally, Russia-China can be described by Krystof Kozáks’s Asymmetric Option Model. Both sides’ approach towards one another is “open”, which translates into resolving bilateral issues cooperatively. China as the stronger partner acts to promote a stable asymmetric relationship, knowing that this is Beijing’s responsibility as the stronger partner to minimize misperception and increase involvement in its relations to the weaker partner; and to promote voluntary deference instead of

44 L. Dittmer, *The Strategic Triangle: An Elementary Game-Theoretical Analysis*, “World Politics” 33, no. 4 (July 1981), p. 485.

45 Ibid., p. 488.

46 B. Womack, *China Among Unequals: Asymmetric Foreign Relations in Asia*, Singapore: World Scientific Publishing Company, 2010, p. 372-403.

47 The term “normalized asymmetry” is taken from Brantly Womack, Idem, *Asymmetry and Systemic Misperception: China, Vietnam and Cambodia*, “The Journal of Strategic Studies”, vol. 26, no. 2, June 2003, pp. 96-100.

facing resistance.[48] Thus, all these proposed categories emphasize the rather optimistic state of relations between Russia and China – despite being asymmetric, they are strong.

The expression "asymmetric win-win" is naturally a reference to a famous slogan of Chinese win-win diplomacy. China loves to portray its interactions with other countries as mutually beneficial relationship and cooperation among different countries, that is based on Five Principles of Peaceful Coexistence and mutual trust, mutual benefits, equality and cooperation, etc.[49] In reality, however, it is usually China that wins most (though their partners do not necessary lose, just gain less). The same story is true in case of Russia. As this book attempts to show, both sides gain, but it is China that wins more, much more. As China sets the agenda of bilateral relations, those relations reflect mostly the Chinese needs and visions. That is why China consequently pushes Russia, step-by-step, into being a raw material appendage to the Chinese economy. Although this is not detrimental to Russia – Moscow gets money for its resources – still China gains more from this relationship, thanks to Chinese-dominated agenda of bilateral, asymmetrical relations.

This asymmetry in favour of Beijing must be filtered through the Chinese strategic and political tradition that dates back to Sun Zi. The emphasis here is put on achieving victories by psychological methods and by avoidance of a direct clash. Building its own political and psychological position patiently is preferred, so as to persuade the opponent to conscious resignation (the biggest victory is to win without the need to fight). Victory does not mean armed forces triumph, but rather a final fulfillment of ultimate political goals. Instead of challenging the opponent, it is better to push him into an inconvenient position. The goal is to achieve victory indirectly, using against the opponent deception and manipulation in order to seize his resources with minimal losses and risks.

Russia, as the weaker state *vis-à-vis* the stronger partner, may respond by conducting two main policies: to bandwagon or to balance.[50] Moscow has been inconsistent in its approach towards China since 1991, switching from one policy to another; finally, however, after 2014, it chose the bandwagon strategy and decided that it must get as much as possible from cooperating with China on Chinese terms. Thus, Russia tacitly accepted the asymmetry of power

---

48 K. Kozák, *Facing Asymmetry: Understanding and Explaining Critical Issues in U.S.-Mexican Relations*, lecture, International Studies Association 2010 Annual Conference, New Orleans, LA, quoted in: R. J. Basaldú, *Two Eagles, One Dragon: Asymmetric Theory and the Triangular Relations between the U.S., China and Mexico*, unpublished MA thesis, Baylor University 2011, pp. 64-68 and 122.

49 The phrase win-win diplomacy appears in almost every Chinese statement; for recent usage of this slogan, see: *Xi's new diplomacy offers 'Chinese solutions'*, "China Daily" 11.05.2016.

50 S. Waltz, *Theory of International Politics*, Reading, Mas. 1979, p. 73; J.Mearsheimer 2001, *The Tragedy of Great Power Politics*, New York, pp. 162–163.

(though naturally in public both states display the illusion of equality), and adjusted accordingly.

3. *The Argument: 17th Century as the Model for Sino-Russian Relations*

The main argument of this book – that Russia-China relations came back to their past state of affairs – derives from the realistic tradition that "appeals to historical precedent rather that abstract principle" and dismisses "a modernistic prejudice that takes for granted the superiority of the present over the past."[51] On the other hand, this very argument is built on the historical precedent – the 17th century's Russia and China's *modus vivendi*, which prognosed a stable and peaceful relationship – a rather optimistic scenario in the very constructivist spirit. So, in other words, this book explains that the current Russia-China "power transition" is nothing new, but a return to the original situation from the 17th century.

China first learned about Russia in the 13th century. Then, the Mongols who had invaded Ruthenia earlier, brought Russian captives to Beijing, back then capital of the Yuan dynasty (1271-1368).[52] The first information about China reached Russia via circular route – through British merchants who wanted to find a shorter route to China. The pressure from the British and an awoken imagination for China's riches contributed to sending the first Russian reconnoiter mission to China lead by Cossak Ivan Petlin in 1618. It was more an intelligence mission than diplomacy – this explains why Petlin did not bring any gift and – as a result – was not received by the emperor.[53] Nevertheless, emperor Wangli wrote two letters to the tzar. Unfortunately, in the Kremlin nobody was able to read Chinese, so the letters were put to the archives and remained there for… 57 years.[54] The first chance of establishing bilateral relations failed. Nobody strived for it anyway.

The next contact took place in a much less friendly atmosphere: it was associated with Russian conquests in Siberia. Russian colonization of Siberia and

---

51 Ibid.

52 А. Д. Воскресенский, *Китай и Россия в Евразии. Историческая динамика политических взаимовлиянии* [China and Russia in Eurasia. Historical Dynamism of Political Interactions], Москва 2004, p. 405.

53 *Русско-китайские отношения в XVII в. т.1 1608-1683* [Russo-Chinese Relations in 17th Century, 1608-1683], ред. В. С. Мясников, Москва 1969, pp. 10-64; В.С.Мясников,*Договорными статьями утвердили.Дипломатическая история русско-китайской границы XVII-XX вв.*[The Treates Have Settled. The Diplomatic History of Russo-Chinese Border in 17-20centuries],Хабаровск 1997,pp.6-165.

54 M. Heller, *Historia Imperium Rosyjskiego* [The History of the Russian Empire], Warszawa 2000 (the Polish translation of: М. Я. Геллер, *История Российской империи. В трех томах*, Москва, «МИК» 1997), p. 245.

Amur lead to conflict with the Qing Dynasty, for whom Manchuria was their fatherland.[55] The leading role in colonizing Siberia was played by Yerofiei Khabarov – a Russian discoverer, colonizer, businessman, and conquistador. His expeditions mark the first clash of Russian and Chinese interests.[56] The first round was won by Beijing, which sent an army that destroyed troops of Khabarov's successor – Stepanov, and chased the Russians out of the Amur region. This, however, did not end the migration on these lands, simply the migration itself changed its character – it was now an activity of mostly individual adventurers, fugitives and explorers, including such extravagant figures as a Pole, Nicefor Czernichowski (Nikifor Chernigovsky).[57] The first failed diplomatic attempts between Moscow and Beijing were made in the meantime. The reason for failure was a difference in understanding of international relations. The Chinese based their view on the Sinocentric system *waifan* that excluded equality between states and assumed "natural" superiority of China over other states. The Russians, on their turn, tried to base their relations on the European tradition of equality of sides and horizontal relations between states. This is why the first official Ambassador to China, Baykov, failed to achieve recognition. He was sent off for rejecting to perform the *koutou* gesture. After a long stand-off, the Manchu court finally decided that Baykov "did not turn toward civilization" and his embassy failed completely.[58]

Trade relations were more successful. Merchant caravans from Russia brought mainly furs and exchanged them for gold, gems and tea. Initially, the Russian presence along the Amur did not disturb trade relations, until around 1670 "the Manchus failed to identify the Cossacs with the Moscow mission."[59]

---

55 В. С. Мясников, Н. Р. Шепелева, *Империя Цин и Россия в XVII – начале XX в.* [Qing Empire and Russia, 17th Century – Beginning of 20th century], [in:] *Китай и соседи в новое и новейшее время* [China and Its Neighbours in the Modern and Contemporary Times], ред. С. Л. Тихвинский, Москва 1982, pp. 34-89.

56 Khabarov's explorations have key meaning for further Russsian-Sino relations. Russian historitians claim that they resulted in inclusion of (what is nowadays) the Russian Far East to Russia; for the Chinese Khabarov's action constitute a foreign aggression to territories that belonged to the Empire. In reality, these land did not belong to anybody, but Beijing considered it its own. В. С. Мясников, Н. Р. Шепелева, op. cit., p. 38; А. Д. Воскресенский, op. cit., pp. 223, 408-410.

57 A Pole, Nicefor "Jaxa" Czernichowski (Chernigovsky) was a fascinating example of a European adventurer in the Far East; he established de facto independent duchy at the Russo-Chinese border with Albazin/Jaxa as its capital. With time, however, Czernichowski surrendered to the tzar; this led to Russian-Chinese conflict, E. Kajdański, *Długi cień Wielkiego Muru. Jak Polacy odkrywali Chiny* [The Long Shade of the Great Wall; How Poles Were Discovering China], Warszawa 2005, p. 218-225.

58 M. Mancall, *Russia and China. Their Diplomatic Relations to 1728*, Harvard University Press 1972, p. 51.

59 "Machu concepts of world geography were hazy at best (…)The Manchus, so conscious of the difference between continental and maritime power, must have been led to believe that the Cossacs' country was beyond the sea (…) Cossacs must have been a maritime power,

Only when the Manchu court discovered that Cossacs are tzar's subjects (it happened more less the same time when Albazin under Czernichowski switched to the Russian side), the trade relations were cut, while a prolonged Russian presence led to the decision of resolving the issue of the Russian colonization for good. In 1676, Moscow sent the Embassy to Beijing headed by Nikolai Milescu (known also as Spatharius or Spafari).[60] The Manchus made to him a proposal that resembled an ultimatum: trade and commercial benefits in return for withdrawal from the Amur region and giving Albazin back. Milescu tried to maneuver, but despite his diplomatic talent, the embassy ended in failure.[61] War became inevitable. In this confrontation Russia had no chance. A vast distance from Moscow, lack of communication, scarce population and most importantly – innumerous Cossacs' army were not a match to a long-planned and well prepared Chinese campaign. All of this led to China's victorious war in 1685-1686. Beijing's victory paved way to a compromise reached in 1689 in Nerchinsk.[62]

According to this treaty – signed between equal states (which in itself was a significant change from the Chinese policy toward European states; Russia was therefore the first foreign country to sign an equal treaty with China[63]) – the Amur basin was to remain in Manchu hands, while Albazin was to be destroyed and abandoned. Russia kept the Baikal region and the lands near the Okhotsk Sea.[64] In return for their concession, the Russians gained commercial privileges which they soon used effectively.[65] Thus, it was a forced compromise brokered on Chinese terms.

The Nerchinsk treaty, with its subsequent modification at Kyakhta (1727), initiated the so called "Nerchinsk order", or Nerchinsk/Kyakhta treaty system – a specific model of Sino-Russian relations. Its essence was that Russia,

---

the missions from Moscow, which came overland, must be continental in origin; there was no reason for Pekin to identify the two as related in any way", Ibid., p. 34.

60 Ibid., p. 50.

61 Ibid., p. 100.

62 It was, naturally, a forced compromised. Russian sources like to point out that Chinese delegation was accompanied by 12.000 soldiers, whereas Russian by 1400 only. This applied psychological and physical pressure that led to Russian concessions, *Русско-китайские отношения в XVII веке. Материалы и документы* [Russo-Chinese relations in 17th Century. Materials and Documents], Москва 1972, т. 2. 1686–1691, сост. Н. Ф. Демидова, В. С. Мясников, pp. 5-54; В. С. Мясников, *Сведения китайцев о России в XVII в.* [The Chinese People's Relations on Russia in 17th Century], "Вопросы истории" 1985, № 12, p. 90-101.

63 А. Д. Воскресенский, op. cit., p. 407.

64 *Русско-китайские отношения 1689-1916. Официалные документы* [Russo-Chinese Relations 1698-1916. Official Documents], сост. П. С. Скачков, В. С. Мясников, Москва 1958, pp. 9-11.

65 Trade with China was very profitable for Russia; it had been seling fur and lether (salt to lesser extend) and buying textiles, tea, porcelain, tobacco, emalia and other luxurious goods, M. Mancall, *Russia and China*..., pp. 134-150.

in exchange for trade profits, made a concession, and against the European tradition, accepted Chinese superiority. It ceded claims to the Amur basin and received concord for lucrative trade with China. Although Russia was weaker and less significant than China, and in the eyes of Beijing certainly not equal (this would be impossible by the very definition of their Sinocentric outlook on the world), it did not become a part of the Chinese vassal system. Moscow's position was better than that of the Western powers: "dealings with the Russians had been conducted not through the Ministry of Rituals, which handled the so-called tributary relations with such countries as Holland, Spain, and Portugal, but through a special bureau, the Lifan Yuan (...) by putting Russian affairs under this bureau, the Manchu tacitly admitted that their northern neighbour were a special case (...) required different handling from those in the southeast."[66] Russia's unique position in China was best illustrated by the presence of the orthodox mission in Beijing.[67] The Nerchinsk/Kyakhta treaty system turned out to be long-lasting (until the mid 19th century) because – according to Mark Mancall – it created "neutral institutions", which could be incorporated into the structure of assumptions of each society without infringing upon the prerogatives or sensibilities of the other: "the system established very narrow paths of access from each society into the other and permitted each to control those paths on its own side (free access might upset either side's internal socio-cultural equilibrium). At the same time, access was sufficient enough, so that neither party felt the need to go to war to obtain greater access to the other empire". The same model, although on a much lesser scale, worked in Canton (and in Deshima, Japan).[68]

With the exception of small amendments (in 1768 and 1792), the Nerchinsk/Kyaktha treaty system survived for a very long time – until the 19th century and regulated relations between Russia and China. The main reason why this system was so stable and lasted for so long was that it was based on what Mancall called "cultural neutrality". According to this researcher, until the late 18th century the European powers entering Asia behaved on a basis of Grotius's 'natural law' (*jus gentium*). The Russians, like the Dutch or the Portuguese, could begin to accept Chinese ceremonial practices such as *kowtow*, as a custom that did not imply anything more than recognition under the natural law of the Emperor's dignity in his own land.[69] In other words, it was a local equivalent of what today is called political culture whose patterns should be followed if a state wants to maintain successful relations with a host country. This attitude was followed by the Dutch at Dezhima and originated from the

66 Jonathan Spence, *In Search for Modern China*, London, Norton 2001, p. 67.

67 It was the first Russian permanent diplomatic mission abroad. Formally it started functioning after Kyakhta treaty in 1727 r., but in reality it started existing earlier. А. Д. Воскресенский, op. cit., p. 406.

68 M. Mancall, *Russia and China...*, pp. 265-275.

69 Ibid., p. 275.

objective fact that Europe then was neither central to the world nor was it the most important of continents and could not demand an imposition of its cultural patterns on others.

The Nerchinsk and Kyakhta treaties were based on this 'natural law of nations' and that is why the order lasted so long. It collapsed in the mid 19th century due to changes that were initiated by the intellectual revolution of the European Enlightenment in the late 18th century. The positivistic attitude put the concept of natural law outside the law entirely and instead introduced the construct of a "family of nations" in the center of political philosophy. Whereas under natural law, the family of nations was presumed to be a universal continuum, under the developing positive law it was redefined as those states that adhered to accepted international legal practices as proclaimed by the European states acting in concert – the entry into the family of nations was formalized and symbolized by 'recognition', a concept that is purely European and positivist. A 'modernization' in the sense of 'Europeanization' started to be required for the participation in the international community. This intellectual change was accompanied by a growth in Europe's technological ability to insist on, even by force (e.g. gunboat) to others' adherence to these new rules.[70] In other words, for a European Ambassador to China, a *kowtow* before the 18th century was not a problem; it was a recognition of the emperor's right (although, of course, in an extremely unpleasant way). Later, after this positivistic change, it was a violation of the rule he considered universal. Furthermore, the European powers in the 19th century were strong enough to follow their own way in international relations with China, the Westernocentric one that they considered universal. This, as a side effect, contributed to the collapse of the Nerchinks-Kyakhta model of Sino-Russian relations, as Russia had joined the Western powers and had begun exploiting China with them.

Although the conditions and political decorum changed, some of the most important aspects still remain today. If we compare the 17th century relations between the two countries with the current ones, we can trace some striking similarities. The most important one is that China is much stronger now in this relationship (as it used to be in the 17th century) and Russia accepts this fact (albeit quietly) and adheres to this situation by taking as many opportunities as possible. This leads to the predominance of trade in the economic sphere of the relations. Secondly, although Russia is weaker, it is still strong enough not to fit into the category of Chinese "modern vassals", such as Laos or Cambodia, thus it is again outside the China-centered world. China knows that Russia is still too strong, not to mention too proud, to be provoked or humiliated, and chooses to appease Moscow in order to keep it on Beijing's side. Russia plays a delicate role in China's relationships. If Russia tilted too much towards the

70 Ibid., p. 269.

United States, becoming a junior partner of Washington, China's overall strategic position would dramatically worsen. Russia would stop being the 'safe rear' for China, leading to Beijing's fears of a 'strategic encirclement' by the United States. This is a pragmatic equivalent of the 17th century Manchu politics, which wanted to have a long-lasting deal with Moscow not to make them endanger the Amur basin. This deal was made on Chinese terms, though with benefits for Russia as well. So, the modern "asymmetric win-win situation" is just an adaptation of the the 17th century model of the relations: both countries benefit from their relations, however, it is China that benefits more. Finally, with reference to Mancall's "cultural neutralism" in their 17th century relations, this can be matched with their axiological opposition against Western values, such as democracy and human rights. The limited communication between both societies is now being repeated and reflected in the famous sentence that "China-Russia relations are hot on the top, but cold at the bottom" which does not bother the Chinese nor Russian leaders who have more important issues on their agenda than taking care of the bilateral friendship between their societies. The most important common factor, however, is their pragmatism. In the 21st century, much like in the 17th century, China and Russia do not have much in common. They are two different worlds, maybe even two different civilizations. They do not like each other and do not trust one another; however, they want to do business and do it successfully.

II. The Domestic Determinants of Russia's and China's Policymaking

No political event takes part in a vacuum; the domestic context inevitably influences the process of decision making. Such aspects as historical tradition, heritage, mentality that influence the patterns of political culture, political preferences, interests and decisions, as well as political systems – they are all extremely important to understand the dynamics of Russia-China relations. Historical tradition should be presented first, as Russian and Chinese perceptions of international affairs take their roots from historical experiences.

1. *Historical and Cultural Determinants*

Ideas matter, even in societies notorious for their cynicism, such as Russian and Chinese ones.[71] Although national identities do not automatically dictate

71 Here I paraphrase Bobo Lo's words about Russian society; *Russia and The New World Disorder…*, p. 6; in my opinion this applies to China, too.

the destiny of a country, they signify "something deeply embedded in the way the country has evolved"; in the cases of China and Russia rising themes in their national identity are "Sinocentrism and Russocentrism" respectively.[72]

In the case of Russia, the most important historical and cultural determinant is first and foremost the imperial tradition, dating back to "collecting of Russian lands" and integrating history of both the Russian Empire and the USSR. That is why the USSR's dissolution was such an important event, shock and time *limes* (latin: boundary) for Russia: the state lost its superpower status. Since 1991, Russia's various foreign policy concepts are in fact just attempts to reply to a question: how to rebuild an empire in post-modern conditions?[73] In the case of China, three determinants dominate its foreign policy: 1) rebuilding the power status ("getting back the proper place in the world"), 2) self-perception of China as a victim of Western colonialism ("hundred years of national humiliation", *bai nian guo chi*), strongly emphasized in contrast to former glory (and apparent "peacefulness" of the Imperial China), and used to potray Western powers as denying China its due in the international system[74]; 3) a defensive approach towards the international community (fear of "China's encirclement").[75]

As for time *limes* in the contemporary conditions, for Russia, the USSR's fall marks the most important date. In the post-cold war world Russia as a "post-imperial power"[76] has been seeking a place for itself, being torn between bandwaggoning to the USA and balancing the USA hegemony. As for China, the proper time *limes* are Deng Xiaoping's reforms: the Chinese modernization and going out to the world combined with awareness of having peaceful international surroundings (without peace there would be no space for Chinese reforms). The famous Deng's 16 character formula best illustrates this way of thinking: out of all these sentences, two phrases are of particular importance: "hide your capabilities, wait for a proper moment" (*tao guang, yang hui*) and a warning frequently emphasized by Deng: "do not raise your heads" (*bu dan tou*) – China cannot provoke others with its actions to start a conflict, particularly with the present hegemon, the USA, because Beijing is still unprepared for such a clash[77]. China may accept conflict only when it is strong enough to be sure that it can win (in accordance with Sun Zi's advice).

---

72 G. Rozman, *The Sino-Russian Challenge…*, p. 1.

73 A. Bryc, *Cele polityki zagranicznej Federacji Rosyjskiej* [The goals of Russian Federation's foreign policy], Toruń 2004, pp. 30-32.

74 G. Rozman, *The Sino-Russian Challenge…*, p. 49.

75 K. Kozłowski, *Państwo Środka a Nowy Jedwabny Szlak* [The Middle Country and the New Silk Road], Toruń 2011, p. 40-50.

76 B. Lo, *Russia and The New World Disorder…*, p. xx.

77 Quoted in: D. Shambaugh, *China's Identity as a Major Power*, George Washington University, 09.07.2014, p. 5.

Beside historical experience, cultural and civilizational aspects also matter. Both Russia and China define their national interests using a "holistic" approach, typical for authoritarian and totalitarian regimes.[78] This cultural convergence is well seen in the light of business relations – both in China and Russia politics converges with economy: despite obvious differences (see: below), the model of state-to-business relations dominates, as well as a high scope of state integration with economy. Moreover, both Russia and China consider themselves something more than a state or a nation – a separate civilization (or civilization that became a nation state): "here originates their different ideas about the supreme values, domestic and international politics, assessment of tendencies in the international situation and existing contradictions."[79]

2. The "Russian Idea"

For Russia, the most important cultural (civilizational) aspect is the conviction about its own exceptionalism and uniqueness, literarily expressed by Tyutchev's famous poem that begins with the words "Russia cannot be understood with the mind alone (...) in Russia, one can only believe". Although these verses along with other classical Russian texts have been subject to "myth-making on an industrial scale" that led to "a host of trite simplifications and sometimes outright falsehoods" (many observers used this "cloud of mysticism" to tell that Russia cannot be explained in rational categories)[80], they nevertheless should not be dismissed in a "throwing the baby out with the bathwater" manner as they indicate sets of values and beliefs different than Western ones.[81] The conviction about its own uniqueness found its expression in the so-called "Russian idea" (*russkaya idea*), a term that "on the one hand means distinctiveness of the Russian culture and institutions and on the other – an ideal model of society based on an extrapolation of these elements. The former applied to the specific interpretation of the Russian history, the latter was associated with practical realization of state regime."[82] The so called "Russian idea" was based on the assumption that "Russia possesses [its] own, independent and

---

78 S. Bieleń, *Tożsamość międzynarodowa Federacji Rosyjskiej* [The international identity of Russian Federation], Warszawa 2006, p. 39.

79 T. Dmochowski, *Radziecko-chińskie stosunki polityczne po śmierci Mao Zedonga* [Soviet-Sino Political Relations after Mao Zedong's death], Gdańsk 2008, p. 29.

80 B. Lo, *Russia and The New World Disorder*..., p. 3.

81 И.Чубайс, *Как нам понимать свою страну. Русская идея и Российская идентичность. Прошлое, настоящее, будущее* [How should we understand our country. Russian Idea and Russian identity. Past, Present, Future] Москва 2014, p. 11-18.

82 S. Bieleń, op. cit., p. 55.

unique tradition that puts it aside from the West and enables future development."[83] It was the "essence of Russia's history."[84] Moreover, Russia introduces itself as a unique "organism", specific type of civilization, with its own culture, history and customs, not just a nation-state.[85] Specific understanding of community has been opposed to Western individualism, while orthodox spirituality – to Western materialism[86]; "thinking hostile to Western civilization had mixed cultural exceptionism insistent on the uniqueness of Russian civilization (*samobytnost*), claims to Russia's special role in international affairs, and dismissal of freedom at odds with Russian ideas of community (*sobornost*)."[87] The West itself plays an important role in Russian self-identification: "The Russians have defined themselves rather in opposition against others, while the 'Russian idea' did not create ground for synthesis, a process of adaptation based on compromise (like in Chinese or Japanese cultures); in Russian mentality the antithesis 'we' and 'them' have been rooted for centuries; this also applies to international relations (Russians-aliens)."[88] This contributed to a chronic feeling of discomfort based on a constant sense of threat; contradicting influences of West and East made Russia an alienated country that does not belong to any great "family of nations"[89]: Russia is in a way "a torn country"[90], or a "lonely power."[91] As Benjamin Disraeli aptly summarized it, "Russia has two faces: an Asiatic face which always looks towards Europe, and a European face which always looks towards Asia."[92] The claim on uniqueness and exclusiveness came in response to these anxieties: Russia, then, "is a civilization unto itself (…) may pick and choose as it sees fit, thereby preserving its independence."[93] It is telling that it was this uniqueness that made Russians proud of their country: "Russia's historic pride was more

---

83 A. Комаров, *О российской националной идее* [On Russian national idea], "Духовное наследе. Аналитика", 04.04.2014.

84 G. Rozman, *The Sino-Russian Challenge…*, p. 33.

85 J. H. Billington, *Russia in Search of Itself*, Woodrow Wilson Center and John Hopkins University Press 2004, pp. 51-77.

86 A. Валицкий, *По поводу «русской идеи» в русской философии* [On the issue of Russian idea in Russian philosophy], Вопросы философии 1994, № 1, [quoted in:] S. Bieleń, op. cit., p. 58.

87 G. Rozman, *The Sino-Russian Challenge…*, p. 121.

88 S. Bieleń, op. cit., p. 60.

89 *Russian Exeptionism: Is Russia Different?* "The Economist" 1996, 15 VI, , p. 21-23.

90 S. Huntington, *The Clash of Civilization and the Remaking of World Order*, Penguin Books, 1997, p. 39.

91 L. Shevtsova, *Lonely Power: Why Russia Has Failed to Become the West and the West Is Weary of Russia*, Washington D.C., Carnegie 2010.

92 Quoted in: A. Matveeva, *Return to Heartland: Russia's Policy in Central Asia*, "The International Spectactor. Italian Journal of International Affairs", Volume 42, 2007 - Issue 1.

93 B. Lo, *Russia and The New World Disorder…*, p. 17.

grounded in distinctiveness than in claims to superiority."[94] This belief in uniqueness in turn influenced the Russian politics.

One of the most important consequences of the "Russian idea" was that the Russians "consider their country in extraordinary categories. Ordinary inhabitants are not accustomed to think about their country as foreigners do. They tend to explain all disasters that have been falling on Russia via this magical form: we are not similar to anybody."[95] Russians see Russia as special: "as possessing a special status and aura—no longer an empire in the traditional sense, but certainly more than an 'ordinary' nation-state (…) Konstantin von Eggert once put it, 'all peoples are unique, but Russians think they are more unique than the others.'"[96] Messianism has been going hand in hand with this exceptionism: conviction about Russia's "mission" ("the Holy Rus", "the Third Rome", "the Slav's Defender") that combines metaphysical and theological features with great power and imperialism. The Soviet Union has continued the tradition of using the "uniqueness" factor in politics; so does the Russian Federation. Naturally, these claims do not have such ideological and emotional intensity as before (but state's power is much weaker than it used to be in the imperial or Soviet times), nevertheless they lie within the tradition described above. The lack of coherent, all-encompassing "new Russian idea" is the exclusion that makes the Russian Federation different from the Russian Empire or the Soviet Union; according to many, after the USSR's dissolution Russia "lost its idea": communism was compromised and nothing appeared to replace it. Since then, there has not been such a strong ideological and emotional vision. This somehow explains the failure of the Russian transformation in the 1990s: simple convergence to the West has been absolutely out of the question: this is one of the reasons why during Putin's terms Russia has "left the West" for good.[97]

Since the USSR's fall, Russia had been "searching for an idea": "many Russians are confident that without an idea similar to *The Great American Dream,* the country could not regain its status as one of global leading powers."[98] As Sergei Karaganov writes – "there is no new national idea with the exception of memory of the Great Patriotic War – we have not found anything that pushes country ahead."[99] Lack of a national idea translates somehow into foreign policy: Russia had real problems with defining its role on the world stage. Russia

94 G. Rozman, *The Sino-Russian Challenge…*, p. 41.

95 S. Bieleń, op. cit., p. 58.

96 Quoted in : B. Lo, *Russia and The New World Disorder…*, p. 17.

97 D. Trenin, *Russia Leaves the West*, "Foreign Affairs" 87, no. 4 (2006).

98 I. V. Podberezsky, *Between Europe and Asia: The Search for Russia's Civilisational Identity*, [in:] *Russia and Asia. The Emerging Security Agenda*, ed. G. Chufrin, Oxford 1999, p. 44.

99 С. Караганов, *Зачем нужна национальная идентичность* [Why a national identity is needed], Ria Novosti, 23.09.2013.

had problems with finding a successful way to fulfill its superpower need – it was torn between many concepts, without eventually choosing and consequently fulfilling any of them.[100] This explains political thrashing and tactical changes of alliances. Yeltsin was striving to identify a "new Russian idea" but he failed in establishing "Rossiskyaia" (state, supra ethnic) nationality "as a melting point"; it was only his successor who was able to merge the tsarist, (post)communist and neoimperial elements into one concept.[101]

When Putin came to power, this political-spiritual search has been simplified to a very easy message: being the great power for its own sake simply became the contemporary equivalent of the "Russian idea" – "the status of an independent global great power and a regional hegemon has been the core of the 'Russian idea' promoted by Vladimir Putin and the ruling elite; 'making great power' (*derzhavnost'*) the intristic element of the Russian identity helped to dilute tensions between Russian nationalism and the multi-ethnic character of the Russian Federation."[102] Putin's Russian idea "combines *gosudarstvennost* (identification with state), patriotism, collectivism, and solidarity" and the fact that his vision prevailed means that "statists had won the debate on the "Russian idea", even if they agreed on few specifics apart from sovereignty first, great power assertiveness in seeking multipolar world, and a defense of civilization against values imported from the West."[103] Putin's Russian idea, derived from writings of nationalist thinkers such as Konstantin Leontiev and Ivan Ilyin and expressed in aggressive self-confidence, is based on "conservative political and social values, free of the contaminating influence of Western liberalism", combined with "a resurgent nationalism that openly defies U.S. leadership" and the current international system.[104] Although one may argue that from the spiritual point of view, being a superpower just for being it would be too little for the Russians – Putin's vision of the "Russian idea" is a dramatic philosophical simplification of it – nevertheless, so far it has been working and Putin's regime enjoys support and legitimacy.

3. *Russia's Great Power Syndrome*

Putin's reinterpretation of the "Russian idea" is another reason why imperialism remains one of the keys to understand Russian politics. The conviction about Russia's cultural and moral superiority that predestinates it to become a

100 M. Nizioł, *Dylematy kulturowe międzynarodowej roli Rosji* [The Cultural Dilemmas of Russia's International Role], Lublin 2004, pp. 151-157.

101 G. Rozman, *The Sino-Russian Challenge*…, pp. 7 and 128.

102 M. Kaczmarski, *Russia-China Relations*…p. 45.

103 G. Rozman, *The Sino-Russian Challenge*…, pp. 109 and 120.

104 B. Lo, *Russia and The New World Disorder*…, p. xv-xvi and 6.

superpower is an imperative deeply rooted within Russian mentality. Even today, the ruling elite believes that to survive Russia must "be a great power; only on this basis can it (and its people) flourish"; hence, Russia's destiny as a great power and unique civilizational identity are accepted as self-evident truths, while resentment of Western policies and actions is evident across the political spectrum; it helps too that the wider population shares these sentiments."[105]

The historical process of creating Russian identity tied it inseparably to the imperial tradition; Russia existed not so much in time, as in space.[106] The Russian concept of nation-building was a concept of expansion: the Russians cared more about conquering more lands than about economic, political or cultural development.[107] This imperative is deeply rooted in the survival instinct of the Russians: by living in the state of a chronic threat (due to open, continental borders Russia has "a special sense of vulnerability",[108] while "Russian history is a chronicle of the agony of surviving invasion after invasion"[109]) they follow the simple rule that the best defence is an attack: "in short, for Russia to be secure it must create some kind of empire"[110]. Thus, "geography has nourished a security outlook dominated by threat perceptions and geopolitical calculus."[111]

Gaining new lands, however, led to a paradox situation. New territorial conquests create new challenges and stimulate further expansion – a never ending vicious circle is the result. That is why the Russian ideology is based on a "siege fortress" mentality. The feeling of permanent threat strengthens thinking in the imperial categories. And the giant territory itself helps to keep the imperial mindset: "Russia's vastness has also been critical in establishing and reinforcing its identity as an empire"[112]; "deeply embedded in Russian tradition was the notion that a vast, ever-expanding territory is essential to Russian power".[113] Thus happens what George Orwell once described: "an effect can become a cause, reinforcing the original cause and producing the same effect in an intensified form, and so on indefinitely. A man may take to drink because

---

105 Ibid., pp. 10 and 47.

106 M. Nizioł, op. cit., p. 67-71.

107 This comes from a specific attitute towards the land; territory here is almost sacred, R. Bäcker, *Rosyjskie myślenie polityczne czasów prezydenta Putina* [Russian political thinking during President Putin times], Toruń 2007, p. 18.

108 J. H. Ballington, *The Icon and the Axe: An Interpretative History of Russian Culture*, New York, Vintage Books, 1970, p. 303.

109 *The Geopolitics of Russia: Permanent Struggle*, Stratfor, 15.04.2012.

110 L. Goodrich, *Russia: Rebuilding Empire While it Can*, Stratfor, 31.10.2011.

111 Two most important elements of geography that have contributed to Russian political culture are the location of resources and the uneven distribution of population, B. Lo, *Russia and The New World Disorder*..., p. 18.

112 Ibid., p. 16.

113 G. Rozman, *The Sino-Russian Challenge*..., p. 128.

he feels himself to be a failure, and then fail all the more completely because he drinks".[114]

The territorial expansion has always played a compensation role, too: it compensated to the Russians their country's civilizational backwardness and authoritarian governance. Thinking in great power categories has been a tool used by the authorities to keep social coherence and integrity – a lack of civil liberties, subjectivity of the inhabitants, low standard of living – all this was compensated by the glory of belonging to an imperial power[115]: "war or the preparation for a new war became the way Russian civilization has survived"[116]. Being a superpower remains a key aspect in Russian mentality. But, as Dmitri Orieshkin noted, being a power is not understood as in political science (power as a state with force and resources) but rather "in reference to the 19th century's Tyutchev's vague metaphysical concepts of an empire as a global leader and an exclusive centre of culture, statehood and spirituality."[117]

The great power syndrome still has an important influence on how Russia is functioning politically. The very number of proper names that Russians has been trying to use to depict their country today –"liberal empire"[118], "Eurasian empire"[119], "post-Imperium"[120], "world's third greatest power",[121] etc. – is telling. Perhaps the most adequate description comes, however, from an outsider: Australian scholar Bobo Lo, who calls contemporary Russia "a postmodern empire". According to him "many of the physical features of empire have disappeared, but the imperial spirit is still present and even resurgent (…) the idea of empire is very much alive". Although Putin is not interested in rebuilding the Soviet Union ("oldstyle imperial dominion remains an unattractive proposition"), he is reluctant to recognize ex-Soviet republics as sovereign, let alone to accept Western involvement there. This vision of a "pax Rossica" in the post-Soviet area is "a version of empire tailored to a post-imperial era in international politics", an "indirect imperialism by bureaucrats", which is more "calculating than messianic" and is characterized by: "indirect control rather than direct rule", control of the strategic space ('what we (still) have, we hold'),

---

114 G. Orwell, *Politics and the English Language*, www.orwell.ru.

115 M. Nizioł, op. cit., p. 67- 71.

116 B. Lo, L. Shevtsova, *A 21th Century Myth. Authoritarian Modernization in Russia and China*, Carnegie Center Moscow 2012, p. 14. One can see a significant difference with China here; China traditionally prefers to achive its goals by non-military means.

117 D. Orieszkin, *Imperialny projekt Rosji – smutna perspektywa* [The Imperial Project of Russia – a Sad Perspective] , [in:] *Imperium Putina* [Putin's Empire], Warszawa 2007, p. 166.

118 *Выступление А.Чубайса "Миссия России" в Санкт-Петербургском государственном инженерно-экономическом университете* [Lecture of A. Chubayis 'the Mission of Russia' in St.Petersbourg State University], vodaspb.ru, 26.09.2003.

119 J. Fiedorow, *Rosyjskie supermocarstwo: mity i rzeczywistość (Russian Superpower: Myths and Reality*), [in:] *Imperium Putina*… p. 121.

120 D. Trenin, *Post-Imperium: Eurasian Story*, Washington D.C, 2011, pp. 13-18.

121 S. Karaganov, *Lucky Russia*, Russia in Global Affairs, March 29, 2011.

dominant influence without imperial burden ("control, not conquest"), and cultural mission civilisatrice.[122]

In short, Putin is not "collecting Soviet lands", he just wants other great powers to consider this area as a Russian zone of exclusive influence, as if politically following Oscar Wilde's maxim "there are many things that we would throw away if we were not afraid that others might pick them up".

Hence, the worldview of the contemporary Russian elites synthesizes the Russian Empire and the Soviet Union traditions and may be characterized, too, as "moderate neoimperialism", "post-imperialism", or "trans-imperialism": it promotes the zone of influence (CIS) and bases on the archetype of space and claim on geostrategic and cultural uniqueness of Russia.[123] Russia's pillars of "great power" (*derzhavnost'*) are traditional: the sheer geographic extent, a vast nuclear arsenal, and abundant natural resources: "Russian policy makers tend to view the world through Cartesian lens: 'we think we are a great power, therefore we are.'"[124]

Russian great power syndrome is associated, too, with the "need for recognition and respect", undermined by the USSR's fall.[125] The breakup was a "source of atavistic fears and humiliation", comparable to Mongol invasion or to Chinese "hundred years of humiliation" (see: below), and the real disaster "was the transformation of the world's second superpower into an impotent also-ran."[126] Due to these historical reasons, Russia possesses a great need for being recognized by other subjects. As Lilia Shevtsova put it, Russia in axious that others will not respect it.[127] Leonid Radzikhovsky went further by writing that the Russians have a giant need for respect but throughout the centuries, the fear was the only means of being respected, that they mastered.[128] As Bobo Lo put it, "here originates an almost pathological need for acceptance by others", "demand for 'respect' by others, meaning the respect due by right to one

---

122 B. Lo, *Russia and The New World Disorder…*, p. 101-105. When Bobo Lo writes about "indirect imperialism by bureaucrats" he echoes words of Dmitri Trenin, who wrote that Russia is "post-empire": the USSR's dissolution marked the fall of the last colonial empire and Russians started to care about individualistic projects without having to share the costs of empire-building. According to him imperial idea is so strong due to the trauma after the USSR's fall; nostalgia plays compensation role, but limits itself to rhetoric mostly, D. Trenin, *Post-Imperium…*pp. 233-243.

123 B. Lo, *Russia and The New World Disorder…*, p. 127; Idem, The Axis…, p. . 64-74 ; B. Lo, L. Shevtsova, op. cit., p. 139 ; G. Rozman, *The Sino-Russian Challenge…*, p. 130 ; C. Wallander, *Russian Transimperialism and Its Implications*, [in:] "Washington Quarterly", vol. 30, no. 2, 2007.

124 B. Lo, *The Axis of Convenience…*, p. 81.

125 S. Bieleń, op. cit., p. 31.

126 B. Lo, *Russia and The New World Disorder…*, p. 19.

127 L. Shevtsova, *Lonely power…*, pp. 53-55 and 167.

128 L. Radzichowski, *Traktat o szacunku* [The Treaty on Respect], Newsweek (Poland) 20.04.2007.

of the world's elite (...) respect is a state of mind rather than something quantifiable. It is measured by the extent of Western acceptance of Russia's 'special' interests in the post-Soviet space, of its privileged place in international decisionmaking, and of its right to manage its domestic affairs free from "interference."[129] This is where the need for a great power status and Putin's popularity is coming from: "Russia pays a lot of attention to being treated and perceived as an equal and as one of the key decision makers in the multipolar world order; this self-perception as a great power is closely related to the syndrome of humiliation that Russia feels it experienced at the end of the Cold War; by imagining the state as a great power, the Russian elite hopes to overcome and compensate for the period of *smuta* (or rather second *smuta* – M.L.) (trouble and depression) of the 1990s."[130] The great power status derives, too, from specific reading of Russian history "that has boasted great victories and achievements, along with tragedy and disaster; Russia has lost many battles, but few wars" which led its leaders to believe "that Russia generally finds itself on the right side of history" and the others will sooner or later be forced to accept its realities – it ends with "over-confidence and triumphalism."[131]

The current Russian leadership has been rather a traditional one in its nation-building based on rebuilding the Russian state's great power status. Most of the Russian population due to psychological determinants feel the need to be a part of an empire, so they widely accepted Putin's politics. Thanks to high prices of oil and gas in the 2000s, Putin was able to play on these moods.[132] Russia's "'energetic superpower'" is nothing more than yesterday's 'resources reservoir' but how commanding it sounds!"[133] During Putin's term "a historical revenge-ism", based on rebuilding state greatness and creating Eurasian empire, became the state ideology.[134]

Since Putin's first presidential term energy resources started to play a dual role: they delivered financial resources (oil and gas make up around 50% of export) and secured the improvement of Russia' strategic position.[135] Combination of vast natural resources and a rising global need for energy allowed Russia to play an influential role in world politics. Russia became a *petro-state*, with an economy based on resources and built on the idea of an "energy superpower" that "won the minds of Russian elites" – they imagined that Russia is a superpower again."[136] Kremlin elites were jubilating: "Russia is up, the USA

129 B. Lo, *Russia and The New World Disorder*..., pp. 48 and 216.
130 M. Kaczmarski, *Russia-China Relations*..., p. 44.
131 B. Lo, *Russia and The New World Disorder*..., pp. 20-21 and 56.
132 Idem, *The Axis of Convenience*..., p. 132.
133 D. Orieszkin, op. cit., p. 179.
134 J. Fiedorow, op. cit., p. 121.
135 M. Kaczmarski, *Russia-China Relations*..., p. 152.
136 J. Fiedorow, op. cit., p. 124.

is down and the EU is out" was the slogan of those days.[137] Energy became central to Russian policy not only as a revenue source but mostly as a tool of political pressure. Major energy concerns, such as Gazprom, have been active foreign policy players, at times more influential than conventional entities such as the MFA. It happened to such an extent that to "Kremlin.inc"[138], its own interest is equal to the state interest"[139], while the line between Putin's group interests and national interests is "completely blurred in Russia."[140] Improvement of the economic situation "led Russian elites to believe in the illusory conclusion that the 'time of chaos', so characteristic for the 1990s, has ended, while the country was gaining back its great power status."[141]

These hopes underwent a difficult fact check in 2014 and 2015 when energy prices hit low records. What had been the source of confidence became a "source of vulnerability", as "keeping the elite happy" and society calm is the key to the survival of the current system.[142] So far Putin's team was able to compensate society's lowered standards of living[143] by using a strengthened great power nationalistic agenda (regaining Crimea, defending against the West, upholding traditional values). He used an anti-Americanism, too, as not only his ideological challenge to the West and/or his personal revenge for supporting the protests in 2012, but also as a calculated strategy. Due to the fact that economic growth was over, and Putin could no longer rely on a "materialist 'social contract,'" he needed to find new sources of legitimacy and he exploited the old Russian tradition of "a Russia besieged by enemies abroad and traitors within"; thus "attacking Washington was no longer part of managing the United States, but became an extension of domestic politics by different means; the risk of a new crisis in bilateral relations paled into insignificance compared with the imperative of preserving power at all costs."[144] It works, at least for a while, domestically – society has bought into the Kremlin message and is happy to get Crimea back (though the spring 2017 youth protests showed first signs of crisis). In the circumstances of "a new world disorder"[145], and in growing social cynicism (like in late Brezhnev times)[146] that makes the people

137 D. Trenin, *Russia's Strategic Choices*, Moscow, Carnegie 2007.

138 M. Mandras, *Powrót do oblężonej twierdzy?* [A return to siege fortress?], [in:] *Imperium Putina…*, p. 150.

139 B. Lo, *The Axis of Convenience…*, pp. 135-147.

140 I. Torbakov, *'What Does Russia Want?'—Investigating the Interrelationship between Moscow's Domestic and Foreign Policy,* quoted in: Idem, *Russia and The New World Disorder…*, p. 6.

141 J. Fiedorow, op. cit., p. 119.

142 B. Lo, *Russia and The New World Disorder…*, p. 29.

143 J. Strzelecki, *Painful adaptation. The social consequences of the crisis in Russia*, OSW, Warsaw, 06.02.2017.

144 B. Lo, *Russia and The New World Disorder…*, p. 25.

145 Ibid., pp. xviii and 53-54.

146 С. Караганов, *Зачем нужна национальная идентичность…*

apathetic towards the rhetoric of the regime[147], however, it remains to be seen whether Kremlin will be able to find a new way to keep the Russia's position, regain great power status and control society.

4. *Russia in Asia*

Geography dictates Russia to be a part of Asia (it is "Asian-ness" – without it Russia would rather still be Muscovy).[148] Yet Russia understands Asia in narrow terms: as Asia-Pacific (East Asia) plus India, which are understood as "East"; this outlook excludes Central Asia and the Middle East (understood as "South").[149] Moreover, "Russia may be in Asia in a physical sense, but the historical and civilizational foundations for such an identity are flimsy (…) it has been said that "while Russia is in Asia, it is not of Asia"[150] and has an "East-West dilemma," where engagement with Asia is balanced by attachment to Europe.[151] It is best seen in the Russian Far East – "not a gateway to Asia, but a natural geographical border for expansion; a frontier and a barrier", "an extension of Europe" more than a part of Asia.[152] This translates to the issues of mentality, in psychological, cultural and emotional terms, Russians remain more tied to the West than to the East: "theories that try to find the "Asian soul" inside Russians are 'exotic.'"[153] Russians judge their successes and failures through Western points of view: as Chen Yu correctly observed, "in spite of Putin's (and all Kremlin's elite – M.L.) ideological contempt for Europe's liberalism, Russia's values are closest to Europe's."[154] Axiologically and mentally, Russia remains a European country and this makes logical its orientation towards the West. The Russians, as inhabitants of Europe, view the world via

---

147 G. Rozman, *The Sino-Russian Challenge…*, p. 203.

148 Д. Тренин, *Конец Евразии: Россия между геополитикой и глобализацей* [The End of Eurasia. Russia between Geoeconomics and Globalization] , Москва 2001, p. 227.

149 B. Lo, *Russia and The New World Disorder…*, p. 134. Throughout this book I will follow this Russian understanding of Asia-ness.

150 Quoted in: Idem, *The Axis of Convenience…*, p. 57.

151 V. Larin, *Russia's Eastern Border: Last Outpost of Europe Or Base for Asian Expansion?* "Russian Expert Review", vol. 18, no. 4, October 2006.

152 B. Lo, *The Axis of Convenience…*, p. 57. Д. Тренин, *Интеграция и идентичность. Россия как «новый Запад»* [Integration and Indentity. Russia as a 'New West'], Москва 2006, pp. 169-170.

153 А.В. Лукин, *Россия и Китай: четыре века взаимодействия. История, современное состояние и перспективы развития российско-китайских отношений* [RussiaChina Four Centuries of Interaction. History, Contemporary Situation and Perspectives of Development], Под ред А.В. Лукина, Москва 2013, p. 628.

154 Chen Yu, *E Zhuanxiang dongxiang ? Zhongguo duanqinei nanyi tidai xifang* [Russia's pivot to the East? China will not replace the West in the short term] quoted in: M. Duchâtel, *China and Russia: Towards an alliance treaty?*, [in:] *China and Russia. Gaming the West*, eds. by F. Godement and M. Duchâtel, ECFR.Eu, 02.11.2016.

Western lenses: "although the Russian eagle has two heads, out of habit it looks only to the West."[155] Unlike the West which represent "the known" ("a well-rehearsed repertoire of behaviors, negotiating tactics, and policy positions") for Russians the interaction with the Chinese and other Asians is "a more unfamiliar enterprise, requiring revised assumptions and different approaches. The Chinese have proved especially challenging partners, notwithstanding the upward trajectory of their relationship (…) with the Chinese, everything is so much more ambiguous (…) the reasons are not linguistic, but cultural in the wider meaning of the term."[156] For Russians, Chinese and other Asians are "the other": "at times threatening, at other times an object of contempt or puzzlement, but always alien"; despite more frequent visits to Asia, "this hardly signifies empathy, let alone identification. Asia represents exotica and difference— more accessible than before, but still a world apart."[157] Despite quarrels with the West, Russia considers itself a part of Europe and the West remains its main reference point. China and the East are good tactical points in political games with the West, but the East is certainly not a rival as an attractive civilization: for long "Asia has mattered in Russia's games with Europe; it was understood that being raw material appendage to Asia is bad, while being it to Europe is normal."[158] For centuries "the Russians regarded their East Asian neighbours with superiority and a pinch of contempt; the place accorded to China in their thinking was always secondary, at best."[159] Russia interest in Asian "has been uneven at best, often nonexistent and its focus overwhelmingly instrumental; if Asia has mattered, then it has largely been because of its relevance to Russia's interaction with the West, and, by extension, its position in the world"; cooperation with Asia "was frequently cast in revanchist terms (…) the accent was less on engaging with the East than withdrawing from the West (or teaching it a lesson)."[160] This is where the characteristic thinking that China is important not per se, but as an informal partner against USA, originates: "this logic is so simple, even primitive. Strong China and India appear on the horizon, they would inevitably clash with the United States, Russia

155 Ф. Лукьянов, *Мы и новая Азия* [We and the New Asia], SVOP.ru, 11.11.2013; the claim for Russian eagle to look to the East has been heard since 1990s, A.B. Лукин, *От нормализации к стратегическому партнерству. Россия и Китай после распада СССР* [From Normalization to Strategic Partnership. Russia and China after USSR's Fall], [in:] *Россия и Китай: четыре века…*, p. 326.

156 B. Lo, *Russia and The New World Disorder…*, p. 197.

157 Ibid., pp. 132 and 140.

158 *«Китайцы понимают, что Россия деградирует из-за коррупции и неэффективного управления»* [The Chinese understand that Russia degradates due to corruption and mismanagement], Lenta.Ru, 30.04.2015.

159 D. Trenin, *The China Factor: Challenge and Chance for Russia*, [in:] *Rapprochement or Rivalry? Russia – China Relations in a Changing Asia*, ed. S. W. Garnett, Washington D. C. 2000, p. 41.

160 B. Lo, *Russia and The New World Disorder…*, pp. 132-136.

would join them and enter the group of countries that would decide about the future of the world."[161] The condsideration of Asia as an extention of Europe led Russians to call Russia "a European civilization, but Eurasian empire" which emphasizes "both its distinctiveness and its geopolitical position as the heartland power" and implies that Russia is not "Asian as such, but rather an in- between—and independent—civilization; this self-identification is at the root of the popular notions of Russia as a bridge between civilizations, and geopolitical balancer between the United States and Chin."[162] Recently Russia has introduced a new term, "Euro-Pacific power" that highlights the changing international situation (decline of the West, the shift of global power to the East), and Moscow's ambitions: "Russia that has arrived as a Euro-Pacific power would combine the dynamism of East Asia with the still powerful trumps of Western culture and technology, and, of course, Russian tradition."[163]

It is very symptomatic, however, that Russian attempts to play the role "of a bridge between Europe and Asia"[164], being "like a bird and can only fly well if it uses both wings" (European and Asian)[165], "respecting European pragmatism and Eastern wisdom alike"[166], or building a Eurasian/Euro-Pacific identity are from Asian perspective – as well as from European – a failure. Russia "is not an Asia-Pacific nation by most criteria; historically and culturally, it is incontrovertibly a European civilization; and politically, economically, and in terms of strategic culture, it looks far more to the West than to the East (…) from Asian perspective, Russia is just an European country that happens, through historical and imperialist 'accident' to have some of its territory in Asia."[167] Seen from this perspective, Russia is the "third West" (after the USA and Western Europe); for Asians Putin's habits of practicing judo and eating Chinese food are examples of his "Asian superficiality" only[168]. Asians do not regard Russia as culturally Asian.[169] As one Chinese "old-Russia hand" put it, "Russia's heart is always with the West. Its biggest hope is to earn the respect from the West and integrate into the Western hemisphere."[170] Asian elites see

---

161 J. Fiedorow, op. cit., pp. 127-128.

162 B. Lo, *Russia and The New World Disorder…*, p. 134.

163 Ibid., p. 135.

164 Е. Стригин, *Эра Дракона* [The Dragon's Era], Москва 2008, 252-458, М. Титаренко, *Геополитическое…*, pp. 30-45 and 371-408.

165 *Putin's Asia Tour to boost Russia's Role in the Region*, Reuters 2000, 16 VII.

166 Путин В.В. *Интервью китайской газете «Жэньминь жибао», китайскому информационному агентству Синьхуа и телекомпании РТР* [Putin's Interview to Chinese Media], Kremlin.Ru, 16.07.2000,

167 B. Lo, *The Axis of Convenience…*, p. 126.

168 Yu Bin, *Guns and Games of August: Tales of Two Strategic Partners*, "Comperative Connections" vol. 10, no 3.

169 P.Salin, *Russia's Three Roads to Asia*, "Russia in Global Affairs", December 27, 2012.

170 Shen Dingli, *Russian cooperation…*

Russia as backward, non-atractive and non-modernizing country with "a sclerosis worse than anything seen in the West", and have a dismissive view of Russia's engagement in Asia, too: "Russia was rarely serious about cooperation for its own sake, but harbored ulterior motives born of an irredeemably Westerncentric outlook"; thus – they "view it as an outsider" which "will never be Asian except in the most literal sense of possessing" and "looks at Asia from the distorted perspective of an outside power."[171] Former Indonesian President Yudhoyono may sing for Putin "happy birthday" in public, but he does so not because he considers Putin as his follow Asian, but because he made good business with Russia (arms sales).

Russia belongs to Asia formally not only because of the independent international processes (a weak position of the RF in Asia), but also due to the Russian way of conducting foreign policy.[172] It "misunderstands the dynamics of regional political and economic processes."[173] Russia praises itself on making decisions alone without any consultations, let alone collective decision-making[174], while the latter is precisely the way politics is done in Asia. That is why it is difficult for Russia to find itself in Asian regional organizations – this would mean accepting the unpleasant fact that Moscow is an unimportant player in the region and that there is always the risk of being outvoted by smaller nations. For Russian policy makers it is difficult to accept – Moscow definitely prefers the realistic concept of the "great powers' concert"[175], which is currently impossible in Asia. First and foremost, during crises, "moments of truth" such as Georgian and Ukrainian crises, Russia behaves in the non-Asian way. Moscow's resolve to force earns respect in Asia, but at the same time, it deepens the perception of Russia's cultural and civilizational strangeness to Asia. Asians may feel respect for Russia, but its way of resolving matters reminds them of the worst patterns of the 19th century colonialism and imperialism – this alienates Russia like nothing else from its Asian partners.

This alienation is well seen in the example of the last Kremlin's Asian initiative – "turn to the East", internationally inaugurated during the APEC summit in Vladivostok in 2012. Choosing Vladivostok, however, showed Russia's detachment from the Asian reality: making this city the center of the "Russian turn to the East" was an implicit, perhaps even unwanted reference to the 19th century's imperialistic attempt to conquer the continent, best exemplified by city's symbolic name (Vladivostok = "the Ruler of the East"). This is how it was interpreted in Asia, where Russia is still being considered a European

171 B. Lo, *Russia and The New World Disorder* ..., pp. 136 and 207.

172 M. Kaczmarski, *Russia's turn towards Asia: more words than actions*, OSW, Warsaw 09.09.2012.

173 B. Lo, *Russia and The New World Disorder*..., p. 133.

174 А. Девятов, *Китай и Россия в двадьсать первом веке* [China and Russia in the 21th century], Москва 2002, p. 272.

175 M. Kaczmarski, *Russia's turn*...; D. Trenin, *Pivoting to Asia or Just to China?*...

power with colonial heritage: "For many Asians (…) Russia had 'pivoted' to the region at least a century and a half before when (…) Russia got its 'Treaty of Aigun' (1858) in the wake of the second Opium War."[176] Although the Asian states have tactically welcomed Russia's pivot to Asia (in hope of balancing China) this did not lead to reconsideration of Russia as the Asian state and it is unlikely in the future.

5. *China's Sinocentricism*

In China, the most important cultural factor is Sinocentricism: the claim that China is central to other countries. This has given China "cultural confidence (…) unity, strength, and resilience"[177]; it has given it, too, a "deep reservoir of cultural pride" and the feeling of superiority: "China's historic conceit centers on its superiority as a civilized state."[178]

In the traditional Sinocenctristic worldview, "the Chinese state was the administration of civilized society *in toto*" whereas the emperor was the "*paterfamilias* of all mankind."[179] The emperor has been given the "Mandate of Heaven", thus becoming chosen from chosen, the bearer of the supernatural permit to rule the world."[180] Chinese elites of power had "an absolute claim of superiority over 'barbarians' – all the other nations.[181] Chinese had considered their country "the only civilization."[182] The Chinese Empire was understood as "the only universalistic entity that covers all the world (…) beyond its borders other countries were, naturally, spotted, but were not considered as fully sovereign nor equal."[183] As Salvatore Babones writes, "to the extent that the political system of which China was the central state had a name, or at least a label, it might be identified with the Chinese word *tianxia* ('all under heaven')"; *tianxia* was "an abstract notion embodying the idea of a superior

176 Yu Bin, *Tales of Different 'Pivots'*, "Comparative Connections" 2012, vol. 14, no 3.
177 F.M. Mote, *Imperial China, 900-1800*, Cambridge, MA: Harvard University Press, 1999, p. 948.
178 G. Rozman, *The Sino-Russian Challenge…*, p. 37 and 85.
179 M. Mancall, *China at the Center: 300 Years of Foreign Policy*, New York 1984, pp. 3 and 38.
180 W. Olszewski, *Chiny. Zarys kultury* [China. The Outline of Culture], Poznań 2003, p. 58.
181 D. Landes, *The Wealth and Poverty of Nations. Why Some are so Rich and Some so Poor*, New York 1998, p. 335.
182 N. Sivin, *Science and Medicine*, [in]: *Heritage of China:Contemporary Perspectives on Chinese Civilisation*, ed. P. Ropp, Berkeley 1990, p. 166.
183 W. Olszewski, op. cit., p. 59.

moral authority that guided behaviour in a civilized world."[184] The main institutional mechanism through which the Chinese state managed their world-polity, was the tributary system in East Asia.[185] Foreign relations were regulated by the *waifan* doctrine ("the outer tributaries") based on a fundamental assumption of inequality of sides; each country that maintained diplomatic relations with China was automatically becoming its vassal (in Chinese eyes, certainly not in these countries' eyes). In this system, "the sovereigns of the other states (and quasi-states) of the East Asian world-polity regularly acknowledged the suzerainty of the Chinese emperor, who in exchange legitimized their rule over their various domains."[186] *Tianxia*'s system had put "primacy on harmony and order, not freedom" and was "premised on the notion that there is one all-inclusive order."[187] Although this Sinocentric world order "did not necessary involve any significant political control by China, it did require the lesser political entities to recognize a hierarchical structure with China at the apex."[188] Although is questionable whether China did indeed maintain such control, whether East Asian neighbours considered it as the center of the universe and even whether this vision is not entirely false[189]; what matters here is that this is the narrative Chinese elites believe in and it serves them as the idealized model for international relations, at least in East Asia.

With this Sinocentric historical legacy, China entered the world of the 19th and the 20th century international politics and, especially after 1949, followed the Sinocentric patterns, counciously or not (see e.g., "three circles" concept, exporting Mao's thought, or Deng's "teaching Hanoi a lesson" in 1979). This tradition remains strongly present in China even now as it represents the idealized vision of IR – "the Tianxia system is the key to China's ideal world order."[190] The emphasis, explicit or implicit, on hierarchy in the Chinese approach to international relations, or relations in East Asia, with China at the top, is a clear indicator of this tradition.[191]

---

184 S.Babones, *American Tianxia: Sovereignity in Millennial World-System*; IROWS papers; see also: Idem, *American Tianxia. Chinese Money, American Power and the End of History*, Policy Press 2017, p. iv.

185 J.K.Fairbank, *China: A New History*, Cambridge, MA: Belknap Press of Harvard University Press, 1992. Enlarged Edition, with Merle Goldman, 1998; Second Enlarged Edition, 2006, pp. 112-113.

186 S.Babones, *American Tianxia. Sovereignity...*

187 G. Rozman, *The Sino-Russian Challenge...*, p. 167-168.

188 Maung Aung Myo, *In the name of Pauk-Phaw. Myanmar's China Policy Since 1948*, Singapore University Press 2011, p. 1.

189 On this discussion, see e.g. H. W. French, *Everything Under the Heavens. How the Past Helps Shape China's Push for Global Power*, Knopf 2017; I. Johnston, *Xi Jinping: The Illusion of Greatness*, NYRB, 17.03.2017; *How Does China's Imperial Past Shape Its Foreign Policy Today?* A ChinaFile Conversation, 15.03.2017.

190 G. Rozman, *The Sino-Russian Challenge...*, p. 167.

191 James C. Hsiung, op. cit., p. 18.

The idealization of the *tianxia* period is even stronger given the fact how it has been destroyed: by Western colonialism. The "hundred years of national humiliation" (*bai nian guo chi*, 1842-1949), or the period of colonial dependence, is the central point in official Beijing's nationalistic narrative that portrays the road from past glory through defeat and failure to rejuvenation[192]; colonial defeat from the hands of Westerners came as a shock for the Chinese: "regarding their nation as chosen, close to heaven, and civilized beyond comparison, the Chinese were traumatized as all elements of their national identity were disrupted" by foreign "barbarians"; communism then, as in Russia, "turned the tables" enabling the Chinese to feel respect again – and to restart rebuilding the Sinocentric world: "CPP's revolution is steeped in heroic struggle against imperialism, layed foundation for Sinocentrism."[193] Legitimization of the ruling of the CPC has been so strong until now, because the communists were able to make the society believe that they gave China back the national pride, strained and humiliated by colonialism ("gave back the lost face"). Now, when they are "regaining the proper place" for China, they reach for the Sinocentristic patterns of relations with other countries. When admiral Yuan Yubai says that the South China Sea is the Chinese Sea "as the name indicates"[194], he follows this tradition. As does Xi Jinping with his "Chinese dream" (see below). In Sino-Russian relations one can find examples of Sinocentric approach, too. The most obvious example is the "Shanghai spirit" from the Shanghai Cooperation Organization – a clear hint to China's centrality; another one is the Chinese approach to the 2004 border agreement with Russia where Beijing, despite being stronger, finally compromised part of the disputed territory (according to international regulations it should have received all disputed islands, instead it agreed on a 50:50 share): "China proceeded from a position of strength as it recalled the Sinocentric tradition of benevolence."[195]

6. *China's (post)Confucianist Ideational Eclecticism*

It is a platitude to describe Chinese culture as dominated by Confucianism (along with the other two parts of the great triade: Taoism and Buddhism; and by legalism as well). The dramatic and transformative events of the 20th century, Maoist onslaught on Confucianism, post-1978 Westernization, consumptionism and many others factors, all challenged the traditional, pre-1911 patterns of Chinese culture. Yet Confucian tradition remains the background of

---

192 J.Wardęga, *Chiński nacjonalizm. Rekonstruowanie narodu w ChRL* [The Chinese nationalism. Reconstructing the nation in PRC], Krakow 2014, pp. 23-323.

193 G. Rozman, *The Sino-Russian Challenge…*, pp. 39-55.

194 *Chinese Admiral: South China Sea 'Belongs to China'*, "The Diplomat", 16.09.2015.

195 G. Rozman, *The Sino-Russian Challenge…* , pp. 260 and 261.

Chinese thinking in a similar way as Judeo-Christian tradition remains the core of Western thinking.

This is not a place to describe Confucianism per se or dwelve into the discussion over differences in Confucianism imperial, reformed or Neo. What is important here is to mention the most important assumptions as they influence Chinese policy making. Hence, in Confucian tradition the group (family, clan, society) takes priority over the individual, mind (reason) over emotions, obligations over preferences, norms over beliefs, pragmatism over ideology; duties over rights; rationalism, lack of interest in transcendental issues (ethics more important than religion, very little interest in the latter), admiration for knowledge is propagated, alongside with morality, discipline, respect for authority and elders, cult of the past, dislike for changes (uphold of the existing order); in Confucian idealized well-organized society every one should know his/her right place within the social and political structures and follow norms and obligations accordingly ("rectification of names"; that would lead to harmony; otherwise *luan,* chaos or anarchy ruins everything and society crumbles). The perfect state should be built on moral authority, governed by competent, moral rulers (*junzi*) and exercise its power by persuasion and "soft" means rather than by hard power and military means (naturally, in reality the Chinese Empire had functioned rather in accordance with means of legalism, as it ruthlessly exercised power against the *xiao ren*, poor, simple men; the theory of power came from Confucianism, practice – from Han Fezi and other legalism thinkers). Confucianism is a political philosophy of the rulers and ruling elites, as it propagates structure and order.[196]

Nonwithstanding other traditions and different interpretations of Confucian tradition, in general terms, Confucianism was the core of pre-1911 China political thinking. Then, however, came the "interesting times" in the proverbial Chinese curse understanding of these words, with wars, anarchy, divisions, Chiang Kai-shek's failed "conservative modernization" attempt and communist victory. Mao Zedong and his comrades despite being Confucian themselves in a sense undermined many aspects of the traditional Confucian approach (probably most importantly the Confucian dislike for change). Communists called for creating the New China (Xinhua) and indeed were able to mobilize society under communist slogans. PRC's shortcomings, however, most importantly the Great Leap Forward and the Cultural Revolution, combined with successful market reforms in the post-1978 period compromised communism as the source of authority. Although the exact moment when Chinese society ceased to believe in communism is difficult to spot[197] (perhaps the

196 C.P. Fitzgerald, *China: A Short Cultural History*, New York, 3rd ed, 1950 (I used the Polish edition, *Chiny. Zarys History Kultury*, Warszawa 1974, pp. 30-256).

197 For example, an Italian journalist, Tiziano Terzani, while visiting China in early 1990s has been mocked for using Maoist phrases, T. Terzani, *A Fortune Teller Told Me*, HarperCollins 1997, p. 276.

Tiananmen massacre is a good turning point), it is much easier to say what replaced it: an eclectic amalgam of (post)Confucianism, nationalism, pragmatism, cult of money, a surface Westernization and spiritual emptiness (widespread cynicism). Politically, since the early 1990s, communism was brushed aside in everyday governance, and as a source of legitimacy has been replaced by nationalism, pride of economic achievements and re-emerged Confucianism[198], yet the communist legacy is still acknowledged in public and the remnants of communist elements remain here and there, in concepts such as *tifa* (set phrases chosen to further ideological and identity objectives). Although most of Chinese apparatchiks, as most of society, do not believe in communist slogans[199], Bejing still "takes pride in the era of traditional communism, no matter what shortcomings have been acknowledged."[200] The lack of an official rejection of communism (with acceptance of the free market), makes it hard to categorize China[201], but does not especially bother the Chinese, culturally accustomed to syncretism, and serves the party as a means to maintain control over society. Culture plays an important role here: it is "the key to rebuilding pride" under the leadership of the CPC: "Chinese leaders take the offensive through a full-fledged effort to boost *minzu yishi* (national consciousness) and a sense of cultural sovereignty. Political identity is reinforced by *wenhua yishi* (cultural consciousness), interpreted to center on the state and the party."[202] Here originates "the permanent emphasizing – in opposition to the West – [of the] Chinese distinctness and specifics based on concepts deeply rooted in Confucian traditions and modification of Marxism-Leninism in the spirit of socialism with Chinese characteristics."[203] Seen from this perspective, Western influences are dangerous, as they may show that such unwanted ideas as democracy or human rights are not necessarily alien to the Chinese cultural context (Taiwan's example, with its vibrant democracy, is a particularly horryfing example for the PRC), seen from this angle, Westernization is "synonymous with cultural imperialism, splittism, disunity in China and even regime change."[204] Nevertheless, politically speaking, China is much better "equipped" to resist Western political and cultural influences than Russia. Although it is debatable which country, Russia or China, experienced the biggest spiritual onslaught in the transition period, in using ancient, communist and

---

198 J. Wardega, op. cit., pp. 246-276.

199 As one fomer Polish Ambassador told me, "each time I start singing 'the Internationale' while drinking with the Chinese officials I see that they are unsure whether it is not a provocation; but they keep singing anyway", private conversation, July 2016.

200 G. Rozman, *The Sino-Russian Challenge*..., p. 21.

201 For a list of numerous labels that try to explain Chinese phenomenos, see: Richard Baum, Elexei Shevchenko, *The 'State of the State'*, [in:] *The paradox of China's Post-Mao Reforms*, eds. Merle Goldman,Roderick MacFarquhar, Harvard,Cambridge 1999, pp. 333-334.

202 G. Rozman, *The Sino-Russian Challenge*..., pp. 157-159.

203 T. Dmochowski, op. cit., p. 30.

204 G. Rozman, *The Sino-Russian Challenge*..., p. 163.

post-communist ideas to keep the power, Chinese elites achieved better results than Russian elites: they "preserved much better than Russia the apparatus for coordinating and inculcating national identity (…) it had more clarity about premodern identity, a less complicated sense of anti-imperialist humiliation, more continuity with traditional communist identity, and a more elaborate orchestration of new identity construction."[205]

7. *War and Peace by China and Russia*

The substantial differences between China and Russia are seen in their approach to war and peace. Or to put it in more favourable light, to chaos and stability: "China benefits from stability (still has more to lose than to gain from chaos), while Russia benefits from disruption."[206]

China rejects war, but not out on moral grounds. Chinese pacifism, contrary to the European one, does not originate from rejection of war as political means, but derives from pure political rationale. It is a reference to classical Sun Zi thought that it is better not to make war, unless it is absolutely necessary – war is a risky, uncertain and dangerous means of politics. The essence of this approach is based on the following assumption: why use force and risk one's own casualties, if the same result may be achieved through diplomacy or intrigues? That is why "military adventurism is very far from the Chinese tradition."[207] China's rise is based on stability and peace around the world (or at least in China's neighbourhood). Although China will probably strive to change the international system in the future, currently it uses to the maximum the existing one according to its own needs. Establishing a stable geopolitical environment remains the top priority – China wants to have a secure and peaceful environment (neighbourhood) to modernize. China's policy is "subjugated to pragmatic goals of building the regional security and the development of economic cooperation without enforcing on partners any political ballast."[208] To fulfill these goals, China needs domestic and international, neighbourhood peace. That is why it stresses "peacefulness" and a "non-confrontational"[209] attitude, seen in such concepts as its "Peaceful rise/development" strategy, PRC's "forth generation" official agenda.[210] Peaceful development is not a

205 Ibid., pp. 8 and 25.

206 I. Bond, *Russia and China Russia and China Partners of choice and Partners of choice and necessity?* CFER Report 2016.

207 F. Godement, *Introduction* [in:] *China And Russia: Gaming…*

208 K. Kozłowski, *Państwo Środka a Nowy Jedwabny…* p. 315.

209 Pan Guang, *Chinese Perspective on the Shanghai Cooperation Organization* [in:] "The Shanghai Cooperation Organization", SIPRI Policy Paper, 2007 No 17 (May), p. 46; Zhao Huasheng, *Central Asia: Views from Washington, Moscow and Beijing*, ed. E. Rumer, D. Trenin, Zhao Huasheng, New York 2007 pp. 158-159.

210 *Full Text: China's Peaceful Development Road*, People's Daily Online 2005, 22 XII.

philosophical abstract idea, nor even a good propaganda slogan, but a practical political philosophy of China that originates from a realistic assumption of its limitations and possible implications for using force in order to improve its international position.[211] Although since Xi Jinping's "Chinese dream", China has become much more assertive, the most important principles mentioned above have not changed. This has well been seen recently, when China has been opposing Brexit, EU's dissolution, has been frightened by Trump's actions and defended (economic) globalization. Although China looked at it all with a mixture of schadenfreude (interpreting Western problems as "the ultimate proof of democracy's inherent weaknesses"), genuine concern prevailed: China still needs stability worldwide: open trade, stable markets and Western consumers and their demand for China's goods and capital.[212] In short, China still needs stability, order, or simply peace to continue its path to "regain the proper place".

With Russia, the opposite is true: its chosen element is war. "War or the preparation for a new war became the way Russian civilization has survived" wrote Bobo Lo and Lilia Shevtsova[213]; Chinese Academy of Military Science authors came to similar conclussions (Russia is a "warlike nation ... founded and strengthened by war" that has never hesitated to use military force to defend its interests).[214] During peace, Russia's weak potential and limited importance is best seen. That is why conflicts and crisis situations are so important for Russia. Then such aspects as diplomacy and the army, traditionally the areas in which Russia is strong, become most important, whereas the economy is being relegated to the secondary status and "the primacy of politics over economics" follows. This allows Russia to play beyond its position and achieve much more than its economic potential allows. That is why "Moscow's interests may be best served by a semi-permanent state of 'controlled tension' (...) in other words, a condition of 'neither peace nor war' (...) when other powers are in a state of 'controlled', but tense balance, even a modest Russia input can prove surprisingly effective."[215] Recent worldwide disorder is a good illustration. Moscow supports populist movements in the EU and hopes for its dissolution, Kremlin enjoys Brexit and had high hopes (that now waned a bit) for Trump. In general, Kremlin hopes to take advantage of the chaos in the West as it gives Russia another chance to play beyond its scale and to portray

211 With one exception – Taiwan, considered a domestic issue.

212 M. Kaczmarski, *Chaos or Stability*, "New Eastern Europe" 2/2017; Idem, *Russia-China and the West…*

213 B. Lo, L. Shevtsova, *A 21th Century Myth. Authoritarian Modernization in Russia and China*, Carnegie Center Moscow 2012, p. 14.

214 Quoted in: A. Sheldon-Duplaix, *Russia's military strategy: China's partner, model, or competitor?*, [in:] *China and Russia. Gaming…*

215 B. Lo, *The Axis of Convenience…*, p. 125.

the West as the scapegoat for Russia's own problems.[216] That is why Russia has much to win from chaos, instability and, indeed, war.

8. Two Different Authoritarianisms

Russian and Chinese quests for "authoritatianism on the basis of consent", their dislike for Western democracy, human rights, transparency, check and balances etc.[217] has led many to look for similarities in the Russian and Chinese political systems. Although there are some similarities, particularly on the level of the philosophical understanding of politics (see next chapter), they are too small to say that the two countries are ideologically or normatively convergent. As Bobo Lo has put it, "under Putin Russia remains a more democratic, pluralistic and liberal polity than China."[218] Some researchers even say that the Russian system "achieved a sort of equilibrium, located at an indeterminate point between democracy and authoritarianism", though they admit that "it has been sliding towards the authoritarian end of the spectrum."[219] Others say that the Russian and Chinese models "represent contrasting types of authoritarianism, characterized by various combinations of personalized and bureaucratic power", politically "Russia is a semi-authoritarian rather than authoritarian system, with substantial freedoms as well as restrictions"; the Russian system is based "on three fundamental principles borrowed from the past: personalized power, the fusion of power and property, and claims to great power status *(derzhavnichestvo)* and to "spheres of influence" in the post-Soviet space and even beyond"; it is a very eclectic system that includes, among other things: the imitation of Western institutions; the replacement of any coherent ideology by non-ideological "pragmatism"; bribing society; broad personal freedoms; selective repressions against opposition.[220] As for China's equivalent of post-comunistic authoritarianism, it has chosen the opposite to the Russian path: retained communist symbols but brushed aside economic policies of communism (the accent was on economy, not ideas) This produced a situation where there is much less freedom in China, but much more economic efficiency and therefore the system is more successful[221]: "For all its weaknesses, the Communist Party is a much more dynamic and modernizing enterprise than 'Kremlin Inc.'. It has largely absorbed the historical lesson that true legitimacy comes from responding to the imperatives of change, not fetishizing 'stability'

---

216 M. Kaczmarski, *Chaos or Stability...*

217 G. Rozman, *The Sino-Russian Challenge...*, p. 202.

218 B. Lo, *The Axis of Convenience...*, p. 52. Russian analysts echoe his statement, but add that Russia is "democratic", А.В. Лукин, *Россия и Китай...* p. 669.

219 M. Kaczmarski, *Russia-China Relations...*, p. 35.

220 B. Lo, L. Shevtsova, op. cit., p. 45 and 55-66.

221 G. Rozman, *The Sino-Russian Challenge...*, p. 21.

for its own sake."[222] This is very different from Russia which has "become an international anti-model— a byword for non-modernization (and even de-modernization), uncompetitiveness, and chronic corruption."[223] Hence, different transformation paths from communism contributed to the present character of Russian and Chinese authoritarianisms.[224] Thus, the claim for "normative convergence" between Russia and China is "a hoary myth, aimed at frightening Western policymakers into being more 'understanding' of (that is, compliant toward) Russian interests."[225]

9. Personalities in Russia-China Relations

Writing on individuals in politics is not advocated within academic political science. Focusing on institutions, rules, norms, etc. is much more expected and appreciated.[226] There are several arguments in favour of that, but the most important one is probably that transformative developments such as globalization or democratization have created a pattern where individuals matter much less than the rules and norms of the institution they work for or represent. This is certainly true in democracies where systems of check and balances have been intended to prevent a degeneration of authority from power-thirsty individuals. Therefore the importance of individuals in politics indeed decreases in democratic countries. In non-transparent and unaccountable authoritarian states like Russia and China however, the importance of individuals still cannot be overestimated. The culture of confidentiality is pervasive here and input is limited to the selected few; the decision making process is being carried out by a small group of policy makers with their leader to the detriment of official state structures that are legally responsible for legislation and execution.[227] There is "primacy of personalities over institutions": they and their personal networks matter much more than formal institutions, or rather "individuals make institutions, not institutions the individual", influences of institutions "may wax and wane as individuals gain and lose favor", individuals, not institutions or big ideas, "are paramount" at the "court", be it Kremlin or Zhongnanhai; this "personalized model" is not limited to the leaders alone but "is replicated at all

222 B. Lo, L. Shevtsova, op. cit., pp. 45-66.

223 B. Lo, *Russia and The New World Disorder…*, p. 58.

224 The reasons for this state of affairs were perhaps cultural/philosophical: "Identity extremes also come easier to Russian intellectuals, who are known for sitting around the kitchen table pontificating on grand philosophical themes, as opposed to the Chinese, whose Confucian traditions avoid transcendental issues in favor of fine-tuning state-society relations." G. Rozman, *The Sino-Russian Challenge…*, p. 99.

225 B. Lo, *Russia and The New World Disorder…*, p. 65.

226 R. O. Keohane, *Theory of World Politics: Structural Realism and Beyond,* [in:] *Neorealism and Its Critics*,ed. R. O. Keohane, Columbia University Press, New York 1986, p. 198.

227 B. Lo, *The Axis of Convenience…*, p. 17.

levels of power."[228] The "strong culture of secrecy and informal networking" creates "two broad policy milieus— the real and the virtual (the latter is what outsiders see): the real policy world is exclusive and almost invisible. This is where the big decisions are made. The vast majority of the political class plays little role, and public input is minimal (... it) operates on the principle that 'fewer is better' —at once more cohesive, more secure, and more effective (...) without exceptionally privileged access it is often impossible to know who influenced whom, what, and how; it is often a case of 'those who know don't tell, and those who tell don't know.'"[229]

Thus, one can rarely be sure who initiated or influenced the decision making process and clarity emerges only with time, if ever. In these circumstances, a human factor, or an individual with his/her personality, is still having the predominant influence on history, behaviour and change of state policy. This happens because the real power still lies in the hands of an individual, or a group of individuals, instead of being checked and balanced by control mechanisms, so dominant in democracies. In authoritarian countries, official structures only formalize or accept the decisions already made. That is why the importance of personalities is higher in authoritarian systems. Here "the role and possibilities of the leader depends mostly on the scope of power based in his hand or in the hands of a narrow group that surrounds him."[230]

This is the case both of Russia and China, where the decision-making process is implemented by a small group of policy makers with the leader, in a narrow circle, often during informal meetings. That is why this book emphasizes the role of individuals – Yeltsin and Putin in Russia, Jiang Zemin, Hu Jintao and Xi Jinping in China.

10. Yeltsin's Russia and his Policy Concepts

Russian foreign policy has been particularly influenced by the personal features of its leaders. Yeltsin's character in the 1990s made an impact on Russia's foreign policy including its relations with China. Yeltsin governed via "controlled instability" which was characterized by an expansion of the presidential "court" and regional leaders' and oligarchs' "courts"; in this system, Yeltsin dreamed of the position of a "final judge", who often enough initiated conflicts

228 Idem, *Russia and The New World Disorder...*, pp. 10-11 and 19. Naturally, in the quoted (here and below) fragments Bobo Lo writes about Russia only, but I believe it can be generalized to China, too (with all cultural differences nonwithstanding).

229 Ibid., p. 5.

230 T. Dmochowski, op. cit., p. 62.

to strengthen his position.[231] To make matters worse, he governed with an unstable coalition.[232] This all led to chaos that Yeltsin was unable to control. This was true in foreign policy, too.[233] Yeltsin desperately wanted to keep the superpower status for Russia; he understood it, however, in prestigious terms, not as a new vision for the world. Worse still, he did not know how to achieve it, which deepened the chaos.

Yeltsin had two competitive schools of foreign policy to choose from. Initially "the reformers", or "atlantists", such as Yegor Gaidar or Andrei Kozyrev, took the upper hand. Particularly Kozyrev is important here. He was the face of the "Atlantic" concept of Russia's foreign policy from the early 1990s: its main features were common interests with the USA and Western Europe, and integration with the Western civilization.[234] Kozyrev's team dreamed of Russia's "normalization": its closer acquaintance with Western countries' standards. The "Antlantists" counted on substantial help, investments and strengthening of the democratic transformation in Russia as well.[235] Finally, the reformers hoped that closer cooperation with the United States and other developed democracies would lead to regaining Russia's lost status in the world.[236] They cared little about Asia and had cut ties with Asian communist countries[237], and considered China a "dangerous and vicious neighbour."[238] "Atlantists" dominated Russian political thinking (including that towards China) during Yeltsin's presidency's initial moments. With time, however, Eurasianist opposition grew. Supporters of this alternative approach (whose representatives quite often had a background in science, think tanks or secret service, and not rarely an Asian experience) were quite an eclectic group that represented a wide spectrum of formations (often nationalistic) disappointed with the pro-Western course. Eurasianists have claimed the necessity of departure from one-

231 M. Kaczmarski, *Rosja na rozdrożu*… p. 24.

232 G. Rozman, *The Sino-Russian Challenge*…, p. 105.

233 А.В. Лукин, *От нормализации к стратегическому партнерству* … p. 325.

234 *Основные положения концепции внешней политики Российской Федерации в редакции распоряжения Президента Российской Федерации от 23 IV 1993 № 284-рп* [The Basis Principles of Russia's Foreign Policy Concept] "Дипломатический вестник", 1993; А.Козырев, *преображенная Россия в новом мире* [Transformed Russia in the new world], "Международная жизнь". 1992. № 3–4., p. 92.

235 А.В. Лукин, *От нормализации к стратегическому партнерству*… p. 300.

236 A. Kuchins, *Russian Perspective on China: Strategic Ambivalence*, [in:] *The Future of China-Russia Relations*, ed. J. Ballacqua, Kentucky 2010, p. 33; S. Bieleń, *Tożsamość międzynarodowa*…, pp. 67-71; Li Jingjie, *From Good Neighbours to Strategic Partners*, [in:] *Rapprochement or Rivalry?*…, p. 73.

237 Е. Бажанов, *Эволуция внешней политики России 1991-1999* [The Evolution of Russia's Foreign Policy 1991-1999], Москва, Дипломатическая академия МИД 1999, p. 490.

238 Е. Гайдар, *Россия XXI века: не мировой жандарм, а форпост демократии в Евразии* [Russia: not a Gendarme of the World, but a Forepost of Democracy in Eurasia], "Известия", 18.05.1995.

sided, pro-Western "Atlantic" policy. They criticized the turn of Russian diplomacy towards the West and the negligence of other dimensions, such as the Eastern and Southern ones. They advocated political and economic consolidation of the "near abroad" and the CIS reintegration. Here relations with China were considered key to bring back the lost balance in the Russian foreign policy, which would give Russia more independence in dealing with the West. Eurasianists steadily gained more and more influence on Yeltsin and Moscow's foreign policy. Yevgeni Primakov's nomination for foreign minister in 1996 was the most visible sign of their growing importance. Yeltsin initially was favourable to the reformers, with time however, he started valuing Eurasianists more and more. Nevertheless, from the very beginning his politic was – as Bobo Lo put it – "erratic". "Sino-Russian relations became hostage to extraneous geopolitical considerations. The 'China card', not partnership with China, became Kremlin's priority, as strategic direction gave way to a series of *ad hoc* responses and a lowest common denominator to international relations (…) In these circumstances, China became Yeltsin's 'balancer' of choice – he envisaged, at a minimum, that the 'strategic partnership' would force the West to take greater account of Russian interests. Better still, Russia might aspire to become the 'swing power' between the United States and China (…) Unfortunately for the Kremlin, others refused to play Moscow's game (…) Yeltsin's clumsy use of the China card betrayed Russia as an awkward but weak 'partner', whose appetites greatly exceed its modest capacities."[239] Nonwithstanding Yeltsin's failures, to his defence must be said that he, as all Russian leaders, wanted to secure great power status for Russia but contrary to his predecessors and successor, the domestic and international situation didn't allow him to do much.[240]

11. Putin and Putinism

Putin's rise to power has strengthened Russia's position. He came to power with slogans of strengthening, stabilizing the state and bringing back its domestic and international authority and he achieved that. Since taking power, Putin has been trying to modernize Russia by maintaing a strong and dominant central authority. Putin represents "*gosudarstienniki*" (state-orientated governmental officials), people who assume that without the strong central authority, Russia would disintegrate; but with such strong central authority – would become a great power again. In this approach, what is good for the state is good for the country. Strong state is here contrasted with the anarchy of the 1990s: the state had to be rebuilt after the chaos of the Yeltsin era.[241] Putin "reinforced

239 B. Lo, *The Axis of Convenience…*, p. 33.
240 F. Lukyanov, *Vigor, Toughness and Tolerance*, "Russia in Global Affairs", 27.03. 2011.
241 А.В. Лукин, *От нормализации к стратегическому партнерству…* p. 326.

the view that the state takes precedence over the individual and that the prime task ahead was to strengthen the state."[242] The claim of Putin's team arose from a deep understanding of Russian history: the state must be strong to defend its inhabitants against each other and foreign enemies – this in turn implicates the great power status for Russia.[243] This is why the majority of Russian society welcomed or was indifferent to establishing new system that evoked national pride of bringing back the lost, imperial glory. Putin guaranteed stability, social peace and even a relative prosperity[244], finally, he brought back the dreams for a great power status. In short, he has been creating an image of Russia and him at top as the paternalistic state that is able to secure the population's needs, achieve development and become a great power again.[245] Apperently, he "considers Russian destiny to be in his personal hands" and "sees himself as a transformative figure in the tradition of Peter I and Peter Stolypin".[246]

From the point of view of the political system, since his coming to power, Putin has "attempted to establish his personal authority and control in the form of vertical power (*vertical vlasti*); this phrase encapsulated the top-down nature of political process, the 'rebuilding' of the Russian state and the concentration of power in the Kremlin."[247] He opted for a hierarchical model of the state, consolidated the central power and limited the powers of the regional "overlords", moved away the secession and dissolution threat and finally, instead of supporting the compromised ideas of democracy and liberalism, he advocated the centralization of power and establishing the half-autocratic system.[248] Particularly after 2003, when Putin launched a successful attack on Mikhail Khodorkovsky and since then limited the economic influence of the oligarchs and diminished their political capabilities, Putin has started establishing a new, hierarchical structure of power. He, with his group of friends, has been on the top ever since. Putin has been ruling thanks to the control of a variety of key political institutions, such as state bureaucracy, security services, law-enforcement agencies, the army (and its industrial complex), and two of the power

242 G. Rozman, *The Sino-Russian Challenge*..., pp. 110 and 122.

243 R. Pipes, *Flight from Freedom: What Russians Think and Want*, "Foreign Affairs", vol. 83, no 3 May/June 2004.

244 When Putin took the power in 1999, Russia's GDP was 195 bld USD; in 2013 r. it reached 2,113 mld USD. In 1999 GDP per capita was 1320 USD, while in 2013 – 14800 USD. J. Malczyk, *Rosja: Era Putina trwa już 15 lat i może potrwać jeszcze długo* [Putin's era lasts 15 years, and may last longer], Polska Agencja Prasowa [Polish Press Agency] 08.08.2014.

245 A. Lukin, *Russia's New Authoritarianism and the post-Soviet Polirtical Ideal*, "Post-Soviet Affairs" 25, no. 1/2009, p. 56-92.

246 G. Rozman, *The Sino-Russian Challenge*..., p. 118.

247 M. Kaczmarski, *Russia-China Relations*...p. 37. More about vertical power of Putin, see, F.Hill, C. Gaddy, *Mr. Putin: Operative in the Kremlin*, Brookings, 2nd ed. 2015, p. 219.

248 E. B. Rumer, C. A. Wallander, *Russia: Power in Weakness*, "Washington Quarterly", vol. 27, no 1 (winter 2003-2004), pp. 57-73.

holders with economic resources – Gazprom and Rosoboronexport (arms-exporting state monopoly). His most important inner circle of empowered individuals that supervised the particular state policies included: Igor Sechin, Dmitri Medvedev, Sergei Ivanov (until August 2016), Vladislav Surkov, Alexei Kudrin, Anatoliy Serdukov, Nikolai Patrushev and Sergei Shoigu. During the first two of Putin's terms, this group exercised "the pluralism of the powerful", coming back to the presidential office in 2012, however, Putin was able to "broaden his autonomy and diminish the overall importance of the inner circle."[249] He "had demonstrated heightened patrimonial activism."[250] Therefore, his personal power as well as his personal influence in 2016 is much wider and broader than in 2000, 2004 or 2008. Consequently, power has been relying "more heavily on the personality of the leader than on institutions; consequently the role of Vladimir Putin is instrumental for the stability of the contemporary political system in Russia."[251] He has created the "patronal presidentialism" system in Russia[252], where "everyone, no matter who, needs to check back with Putin or refer back to Putin to legitimate his own position, ideas, or general standing."[253] As Bobo Lo writes, Putin is now the "icon" ("his public self-confidence and unapologetic demeanor have become metaphors for a buoyant Russia— a far cry from the weak, humiliated nation of the 1990s, led by a disoriented Yeltsin"), "the supreme decisionmaker" via whom "all big decisions go through in some form or other" and "stands at the apex of a tall and thin pyramid of personalized power". "No single person in the six decades since the death of Stalin has been so intimately identified with power and policy in Russia. Such is his domination that he has engendered his own 'ism.' Putinism has emerged as a hybrid of centralized political power, economic rent-seeking, social materialism, conservative morality, and an assertive international posture"; it is Putin, too, who determines the fortunes, on the Russian side, of key relationships, including this with China (see gas contract in 2014).[254]

12. Putin and China

Putin, contrary to his predecessor, knows the world better, so from the very beginning he understood the implications of China's rise and realized that for Russia a "close partnership with Beijing is neither a luxury nor even a case of

---

249 Marcin Kaczmarski, *Russia-China Relations…*, p. 41.
250 B. Lo, *Russia and The New World Disorder …*, p. xx.
251 M. Kaczmarski, *Russia-China Relations…*, p. 37.
252 M. Mommsen, *Russia's Political Regime: Neo-Soviet Authoritarianism and Patronal Presidentialism*, [in:] *Presidents, Oligarchs and Bureaucrats. Forms of Rule in the Post-Soviet Space*, ed. Susan Stewart, et. all, Ashgate, Farnham 2012.
253 F. Hill, C. Gaddy, op. cit., p. 219.
254 B. Lo, *Russia and The New World Disorder…*, p. 7.

choice, but an absolute necessity in the long term."[255] Already in 2000 Putin wrote in the article "Russia: new eastern perspectives" that "we have never forgotten that the main part of our territory lies in Asia."[256] That is why, during his terms, Russian foreign policy has been more balanced and more concentrated on the Asian vector. Contrary to Yeltsin's decade, the relations with Beijing have not been entirely a function of Russia's relations with the West. During Yeltsin's time, there was little beyond geopolitics. During Putin's terms geopolitics remained dominant, but there was something more: economics, growing trade and developing cooperation in many areas: "the radical improvement of bilateral relationship was due mainly to changes on the Russian side (…) although Putin has remained faithful to the Westerncentric tradition of Russian foreign policy, he has pursued a genuinely multi-vector foreign policy, consistent with Russia's status and potential as a global power."[257]

During Putin's terms Sino-Russian relations improved. Their cooperation deepened and relations on many aspects normalized (demarcation of the border, increase of the volume of trade, cooperation in Central Asia, development of the Russian Far East and calming down the anti-Chinese resentments there). Simply, China steadily has become one of the Russia's most important partners, not only as an alternative to the West, real or imagined. Relations with the People's Republic of China touch upon many aspects of Russia's domestic and foreign policy – only the United States are more important to Russia in this aspect.

Strengthening the real ties with China meant that China became a factor in Russia's domestic policy consideration. It happened both institutionally and domestically. On the institutional level, before Russia's turn to Asia, the links with China were "primitive" – intergovernmental commission for preparing prime ministers' meetings and strategic dialogue on energy issues; after Russia's pivot, a new intergovernmental commission was formed, co-chaired by Russian First Deputy Prime Minister Igor Shuvalov, Putin's powerful point man for economic troubleshooting; this commission has become the key institution for negotiating large-scale bilateral projects. In addition to these institutions, Putin made his friend Gennady Timchenko chair the Russian-Chinese Business Council.[258] Additionally, from the intergovernmental commission separated the "Energy dialogue" and there is another commission on cultural (people to people) bilateral issues headed by Oleg Golodec; that creates a lot

---

255 S. Bieleń, op. cit., p. 320; Russia realized that so far there was too little attention paid to China, А.В. Лукин, *От нормализации к стратегическому партнерству…* p. 328.

256 *Статья Президента России Владимира Путина «Россия: новые восточные перспективы»* [Article of FR President Putin "Russia: New Eastern Perspectives], Kremlin.Ru, 09.11.2000.

257 B. Lo, *The Axis of Convenience…*, p. 39.

258 A. Gabuev, *Friends with Benefits? Russian-Chinese Relations After the Ukrainian Crisis*, Carnegie Moscow 29.06.2016.

of administrative bodies that deal with China which makes Russian policy prone to bureaucratic delays.[259] On the personal level, a strong advocate for Sino-Russian partnership had been Igor Rogachev, "a patriarch of Sino-Russian relations"[260] (Russia's Ambassador to China from 1992 to 2005); although he died in 2012, his legacy endured.[261] Since the late 2000s, those who advocated and benefitted from closer cooperation with China out of Putin's inner circle, were Igor Sechin, one of Putin's closests colleagues, responsible for the Russian energy sector and personally engaged in developing ties with China, Sergei Ivanov (until August 2016) and Dmitri Rogozin associated with the military-industrial sector; the energy sector in general has favoured cooperation with China, considering it a chance rather than threat, despite difficulties in negotiating with Beijing, the same can be said about bureaucracy for which the socio-political model of China seemed very appealing.[262] Gennadiy Timchenko is another example of the tendency of involvement of those closest to Putin in cooperating with China (and advocating stronger rapprochement).[263] The same can be said about Yuri Trutnev who does not belong to Putin's inner circle, but is Presidential permanent envoy to the Russian Far East and is influential in Sino-Russian joint commissions.[264] On the other hand, the army remained ambiguous, while secret services and law enforcement agencies were among the most critical actors of the cooperation with China. Nevertheless, those who supported the cooperation prevailed as there has been a general understanding among elites that China does not threaten Russia's regime position (and vice versa).[265] After Moscow's "pivot to Asia", or rather pivot to China, it turned out – as Alexander Gabuev put it – that China… has made "a pivot to Putin's friends". Due to a fall in commodity prices in 2015 and China's economic slowdown, Beijing has been reluctant to invest in Russia's economy. Instead, China has provided a small set of Putin's inner circle, such as Gennady Timchenko, with "favourable loans and sweetheart energy deals designed to keep Putin's clique both happy and looking east."[266]

Personal corruption, however, is not the only reason why Russian elites support cooperation with China. The Russian elites are aware of the growing asymmetry in favour of Beijing and its negative consequences ("resource ap-

259 «*Китайцы понимают, что*… Lenta.Ru, 30.04.2015.
260 А.В. Лукин, *От нормализации к стратегическому партнерству*…, p. 318.
261 B. Lo, *Russia and The New World Disorder*…, p. 6.
262 M. Kaczmarski, *Russia-China Relations*… p. 43.
263 I. Bond, op. cit.
264 «*Китайцы понимают, что*… Lenta.Ru, 30.04.2015.
265 M. Kaczmarski, *Russia-China Relations*…p. 43; Idem, *Russia-China Relations and the West*…
266 A. Gabuev, *China's Pivot to Putin's Friends*, "Foreign Policy", 25.06.2016.

pendage") and are aware that "Russia needs China more than China needs Russia."[267] Nevertheless, since the economic crisis of 2008, they have chosen to cooperate anyway – they consider the rising China a chance rather than a threat – for them China is "a benign superpower in the making."[268] Firstly, despite its attempts, Russia cannot balance the Chinese influence, so it prefers to bandwagon. Secondly, the rise of China is not threatening Russia (yet) because Moscow knows that – for now – the strategic ambitions of China are concentrated elsewhere. Thirdly, China respects Russia's ambitions in the post-Soviet area and has a lot of sympathy for Russian actions there, which tunes down the anxieties and eliminates the reason for competition. Fourthly, although Russians acknowledge the success of the Chinese (with a mixture of envy and fascination),[269] they remain rather distanced about the ultimate triumph of the reforms: they realize that the Chinese modernization is still unfinished; China still has a long way to go.[270] Russian elite chose bandwagoning to China not because they wanted to choose the "China-model" (that would require too many reforms which could undermine the Putin regime), but to diversify its commercial ties beyond the West to minimize risks from too much dependence on the global, Western-dominated economy: this is "about spreading the economic and geopolitical risk."[271] Five, China does not meddle in Russia's domestic affairs.[272] Six, a rising China weakens the United States and forms a more balanced international system, giving Moscow a place to manoeuver. Russia, although anxious about China, knows that Chinese historical resentments are focused on the West rather than on Russia. Finally, the Ukrainian crisis has added one more reason: emotional bonds with Chinese elites based on a common outlook, which "constituted a kind of group psychotherapy for the Russian leadership after the trauma of the Ukraine crisis. An uneasy sense of isolation and feelings of rage about what was viewed as betrayal by the West was combined with the sense of belonging to a resurgent great power after the incorporation of Crimea into Russia, and this created a strong need for international soul mates."[273]

Putin's achievements were recognized in Beijing. Until now, Putin has been very popular in China: "there is a brand in China: Vladimir Putin. The Chinese think he fights with corruption and against oligarchs and he is generally cool;

267 B. Lo, *The Axis of Convenience…*, p. 88. Dmitri Trenin writes that "first time since two and half century China is stronger". Д. Тренин, *Верные друзья…*; see also: А. Лукин, *Китай: опасный сосед или выгодный партнер* [China: dangerous neighbour or convenient partner], "Pro et Contra", Ноябрь– декабрь 2007

268 M. Kaczmarski, *Russia-China Relations…*pp. 47- 48.

269 Personal conversations, Moscow 2006-2013, Vladivostok 2006, Beijing 2009-2010.

270 G. Rozman, *The Sino-Russian Challenge…*, p. 248.

271 B. Lo, *Russia and The New World Disorder…*, p. 27.

272 А.В. Лукин, *Россия и Китай сегодня и завтра* [Russia and China. Today and Tomorrow], [in:] *Россия и Китай: четыре века…* p. 629.

273 A. Gabuev, *Friends with Benefits?…*

but this concerns ordinary people and is associated with its anti-Americanism; before Chinese looked at Putin, equalled it with their leaders and thought 'how nice to have someone like him'; but now its gone, since comrade Xi became very popular in China."[274] Putin still enjoys a very good press in China, too. The period of his role is seen as "having brought back stability and predictability to Russian politics."[275] His authoritarian and centralistic tendencies were welcomed in Beijing with understanding as something obvious – a "return to normality": "for Chinese political elites Russia quickly became the negative example of how democracy and glasnost do not pay off, as well as a confirmation of the hpyothesis that to modernize a country one needs a dictatorship, not a democratic experiment that under Russian conditions ended up as a pipe dream."[276] When Putin says that "freedom without moral foundation leads to anarchy"[277] the Chinese couldn't agree more. They understand that since perestroika, Russia "opened Pandora's box" of civil and ethnic societal identities and "spent the better part of a decade trying to put all the 'evils' back in it."; hence in Chinese eyes the Russian 1990s model was discreditated one.[278] Yeltsin's "democratic" era has a devastating opinion in China: it "was politically democratized and destabilized, economically shocked and confused, and strategically squeezed and eclipsed."[279] Chinese writings saw Russia as "being victimized by the West" which "sought to keep Russia weak, divided, and unable to resurrect its identity"; this narrative impicitely suggested that "this was also the fate planned for China" (by the West).[280] Unsurprisingly, "Putin the strongman's comeback was welcomed in Beijing not with hope but with understanding. Such leaders are being respected in China. If they kept the power it means that the Heaven supports them; in China one does not discuss with Heaven's decision."[281] For the Chinese, Putin was "clearly a pragmatic and nationalistic response out of dismay and frustration with the U.S. post-Cold War dominance."[282] From the Beijing's perspective, during his terms "Russia has gone from chaos to stability, fragmentation to recentralization, and poverty to initial prosperity", in contrast to Yeltsin's "shock therapy" – "meaning many shocks without therapy" – Russia has opted for a "development without any shocks"; Putinism "meaning political stability, economic statism, and a more

---

274 *«Китайцы понимают, что…* Lenta.Ru, 30.04.2015.

275 M. Kaczmarski, *Russia-China Relations…*p. 48.

276 R. Pyffel, *Chiny-Rosja: Kto kogo?* [China-Russia Who will Beat Whom], polska-azja.pl, 16.10.2009.

277 В.Путин, *Россия сосредотачивается — вызовы, на которые мы должны ответить* [Russia Concentrates: Challenges We Should Answer], "Известия" 16.01. 2012.

278 G. Rozman, *The Sino-Russian Challenge…*, pp. 190 and 224.

279 Yu Bin, *Crouching Missiles, Hidden Alliances*, "Comparative Connections" vol. 01, no 1.

280 G. Rozman, *The Sino-Russian Challenge…*, p. 143.

281 R. Pyffel, *Chiny-Rosja: Kto kogo…*

282 Yu Bin, *Crouching missiles…*

nationalistic and proactive foreign policy" was for the Chinese something easily understandable: "the Yeltsin malaise – decline, disorder, decay, albeit with a more democratic society – was over, and Russia may have finally found its own identity and path."[283] The regime mouthpiece Global Times has called Putin an "outstanding statesman" with qualities of a "great leader", such as decisiveness, wisdom, and ambition; "give me 20 years and I will make Russia strong and powerful again", the article recalled Putin's promise in the early days of his presidency."[284] The Chinese have no illusion, though: "an alliance with China is only a tactic, while Putin's goal is to restore the Russia's greatness."[285]

Admiration of Putin and official praise to Russia is part of the *gei mianzi* ("granting face" in Chinese) tactics, too: the Chinese learned how to tackle the Russians. They behave "nearly impeccably with regard to Russia: China is one of the few countries that spare Russia's injured vanity (…) Chinese leaders have learned to play up the remnants of Russian greatness."[286] Beijing in public shows Russia respect and praises Russia as the 'great power' – the Chinese elites know how to make use of the Russian megalomania; they tell the Russians exactly what they want to hear: "Chinese leaders and media flatter Russian sensibilities (by) extolling Sino-Russian partnership, inflating Russia's importance in the world, and praising the personal achievements of President Putin."[287] In short, the Chinese know they should not humiliate Russia. In reality, however, China considers Russia a fallen power that lost its confrontation with the West, even though the Chinese elites respect Putin as a strong leader who wants to bring back the lost glory. From the Chinese perspective, Russia is a backward, unorganized and non-attractive country that cannot be compared with developed Western countries (the countries which possess something truly priceless: high technologies).[288] Despite acknowledging that under Putin, Russia has "pull(ed) itself from the brink of the decline", the Chinese see it as a country whose "fundamental weakness has been revealed by economic crisis (…) (it) failed to modernize and integrate into global economy, property law is not guaranteed, its economy underwent a process of 'offshorisation' and lost its attraction for foreign investors."[289] To make matters worse, the Chinese elites do not trust Russia either. They have learned that Moscow cannot be counted on. Since the 1990s, China has realized that trusting Russia is unwise.

283 Idem, *From Election Politics to Economics Posturing*, "Comperative Connections" vol. 10, no 1; Idem, *Living with Putin Unfading Glory and Dream,* "Comparative Connections", vol. 9, No. 4

284 Idem, *Succession, Syria and the Search for Putin's Soul*, "Comparative Connections" 2012, vol. 14, no 1.

285 Ibid.

286 D. Trenin, *The China Factor*…, p. 47.

287 B. Lo, *Russia and The New World Disorder*…, p. 144.

288 Personal conversations, Beijing, 2009-2017.

289 M. Kaczmarski, *Russia-China Relations*…, p. 48.

Therefore, when dealing with Moscow, Beijing gives examples of the Chinese proverbial pragmatism: it takes what is to be taken, and does not care about a proclaimed 'friendship'.

13. China's Third and Fourth Generation of Leadership

As for Chinese leaders, both Jiang Zemin and Hu Jintao's "generations" continued the course set forth by Deng Xiaoping. Although they left their imprint on Chinese politics with their own concepts and actions, they did not change foundations laid by Deng. Until Xi Jinping's generation what differentiated China from Russia was that individual Chinese power holders were less influential than the corporate ones. The most important corporate power holder is the CPP which position, though dominant, is not monopolistic, especially in the economic sphere, where such state agencies as China National Petroleum Corporation (CNPC), Sinopec or the China National Offshore Oil Corporation also matter; the same can be said about big private business, regional economic actors, central administrative branches responsible for economic relations (Ministry of Commerce, Ministry of Finance, National Development and Reform Commission), provincial governments responsible for their regions' economic development, armed forces and internal security services.[290]

Jiang Zemin and his "third generation" have continued the concept of multipolarity based on "five principles of peaceful coexistence". According to this idea, China recognized the USA as the only superpower, but considered its position likely to weaken with time. This would lead to establishing a multipolar world; until this materializes, China would conduct an independent policy of not joining any alliances nor military blocks. Beijing's foreign policy goal since then has been to "develop and maintain good working relationships with both Washington and Moscow (…) Beijing should avoid two 'extreme' ends of the alliance-adversary spectrum in dealing with both countries; this maximizes China's flexibility in the timeless geopolitical game between major powers."[291] This approach was combined with the necessity of a prolonged contact with the external world to continue modernization and break away from social problems of transformation.

A normalization relation with Russia was Jiang's big asset. Jiang found a common language with Yeltsin (it was the Russian language, Jiang mastered it during his studies in Moscow in the 1950s) – he was patient and indulgent

290 Ibid., pp. 41-42.

291 Yu Bin, *China-Russia Relations: Trilateral Politics: Trump Style*, "Comparative Connections", Vol. 19, No. 1.

towards Yeltsin's extravagancies and waited for his initially anti-Chinese attitude to change. Their good personal relations[292] enabled normalization and development of Sino-Russian relations that ended in the "strategic partnership" in 1996. The success of rapprochement with Russia in the 1990s had wider meaning for China – "China-Russia relations can be viewed as the prototype of a new Chinese model of post-Cold War state-to-state relations", "many key tenets of Chinese foreign policy: peaceful development, win-win diplomacy aiming towards multipolarization, and the creation of a harmonious world based on the democratization of international relations (…) may be found in Sino-Russian partnership document."[293]. Nevertheless, despite their good relations and common, Russian language, there was a distance between them: "the Russian president never called his Chinese colleague 'friend', as he addressed former U.S. president Bill Clinton and former Japanese prime minister Ryutaro Hashimoto."[294]

In 2002/2003, the Chinese leadership changed. Jiang Zemin's team gradually gave way to the "forth generation" of Hu Jintao (Chairman of the CCP and the PRC) and Wen Jiabao (prime-minister of the PRC). This generation "has exercised power in a rather cautious manner, avoiding radical decisions"(his power was so limited that during his terms the party gradually weakened and its dominant position was replaced by the triangle of the party, the military and state-owned big companies)[295] this was reflected in Hu's major political slogan of a harmonious society.[296] The "forth generation" initially was an unknown for Sino-Russian relations. These leaders came from technocrat backgrounds and made careers in the party's regional structures. Contrary to the "third generation" they did not know Russia, did not study there nor speak Russian (they spoke English instead).[297] It seemed that Russia would have "its own 'who is Hu?' problem in that the incoming generation of leaders in China are not Russian-speaking nor able to sing 'Moscow Nights'"[298] with culturally alien Russians.[299] It turned out, however, that the pragmatic Chinese were able to find a common language with Russians. Although the leaders did not develop close relations (this might have been impossible given Hu Jintao's unemotional nature – "various interlocutors describe Hu as wearing the same inscrutable face

292 А.В. Лукин, *От нормализации к стратегическому партнерству…* p. 324.

293 E. Wishnick, *Why a Strategic Partnership?The Vew from China,* [in:] *The Future of China-Russia…*, p. 56-60.

294 A. Gabuev, *Friends with Benefits?...*

295 M. Kaczmarski, *Russia-China Relations…*, p. 37.

296 *Harmonious society*, "China Daily", 29.09.2007.

297 The forth generation was "the least Russified" generation of Chinese leaders, Yu Bin, *Presidential Politicking and Proactive Posturing,* "Comperative Connections" 2004,vol. 6,no 1.

298 Yu Bin, *One Year Later: Geopolitics or Geoeconomics?* "Comparative Connections" v.4 n.3.

299 А.В. Лукин, *От нормализации к стратегическому партнерству…*, p. 338.

in all situations"),[300] Sino-Russian relations developed during Hu Jintao's term, despite the lack of harmony in energy issues. Hu Jintao's team put its main emphasis on the security of supplies combining it with finishing China's modernization (crucial for CCP's stay in power). Unfortunately, the Chinese could not count on Russia here – this showed the limitations of the "strategic partnership" very well and led Beijing to diversify its supplies in Central Asia.

As for China's domestic actors, those who have supported cooperation with Putin's Russia since Hu Jintao's term have been state-owned energy agencies and all those who rely on natural resources, since Russia gave them a chance to access to these resources at a relatively low price and with little political strings attached; Chinese military also viewed Russia favourably (as a useful source of military equipment), as well as ruling party and bureaucracy as the Russian political model did not threat their position. There was no major political actor who would protest against closer cooperation with Russia.[301]

14. Xi Jinping and his "Chinese Dream"

A significant change in Chinese foreign policy occurred with Xi Jinping's rise to power in 2012. His presidency "brought the strengthening of the *primus inter pares* role" which was reflected in the shrinking size of the Standing Committee from nine to seven members, gaining immediate control over the army by becoming the chairman of the Central Military Commission and by creating a new institution – the National Security Council.[302] Xi has also embarked on a campaign to limit the influence of other power holders, by initiating the anti-corruption campaign.[303] Xi is different from not only Hu Jintao, but all Chinese leaders since Deng Xiaoping. From the very beginning he showed that he is a strong and confident leader. Xi "reinstated personal leadership instead of Hu's 'collective leadership', re-established the primacy of the party over half-hearted liberalization reforms, ignored statements about 'low-profile' foreign policy inherited from Deng Xiaoping and claims a role for China as a global power"; moreover, "his style differs from that of his predecessors: he speaks in the first person, emphasizes the greatness of China, and quotes Mao."[304] He is a strong leader: he "represents a new vigor in Chinese politics after Mr Hu's studied grayness."[305] He even starts to introduce his own personality cult ("Uncle Xi".)[306] In domestic policy, Xi's governance is an attempt to re-establish a

300 A. Gabuev, *Friends with Benefits?...*

301 M. Kaczmarski, *Russia-China Relations...*, p. 44.

302 Ibid., p. 37.

303 *Xi Calls for a China in 2016 Where 'Nobody Dares to Be Corrupt'*, "Bloomberg", 13.01.2016.

304 F. Godement, *Xi Jinping's China*, European Council on Foreign Affairs 2013, 17 VII.

305 *Chasing the Chinese dream*, "The Economist", 03.05.2013.

306 B. Góralczyk, *China under Uncle Xi*, "Aspen Review Central Europe" 2/2016.

party state as the effective model for nation-building; economically its "top-down approach" with stress on control and supervision.[307] There is no place for political liberalization in this vision – Xi was quoted as saying that "the reason for the Soviet Union's collapse was its straying from ideological orthodoxy."[308] As one researcher summarizes, Xi's action represent "hard-line modernization" that combines "nineteenth-century geopolitics with twentieth-century Leninist politics in order to gain the upper hand in a globalised twenty-first-century world" while Xi Jinping is "the Chinese Yuri Andropov."[309]

This explicit assessment must be nuanced by a domestic factor: the competition of three socio-political schools in China and a vivacious debate on "China's development model" (*Zhongguo Moshi*) that influences Xi's political agenda. The first school "the dreamers" (from the "Chinese dream", see below) claims that the world already entered the "post-American era". The USA is being considered as a declining superpower that sooner or later will give way to China. The second school, with Prof. Hu Angang, orientates itself on the bases Chinese heritage and Chinese civilizations. Representatives of this school do not search for patterns in the West, but look into Chinese tradition and culture, civilizational heritage instead: they call for a return to look for inspiration as regards solutions and the country's future in the Chinese tradition (*Guo Qing)*. The third school, with Professor Chi Fulian, claims that the first stage of transformation is over and calls for "the second reform" (*Di er ci gaige*). In this approach effectiveness already ended and the party must opt for social justice instead of development.[310]

Xi Jinping has been mostly influenced by the dreamers' school, whose name comes from the "Chinese dream" concept (*zhongguo meng*). According to the most popular version, it comes from Liu Mingfu's 2010 book "*The China Dream: Great Power Thinking and Strategic Posture in the Post-American Era*". Liu's main hypothesis is that China should regain its position as the most powerful nation in the world, a position it had held for thousands of years before its humiliation. To make it happen, China needs the "Chinese dream" thanks to which "China's era" would come – an era without hegemons, with China as the leader. To fulfill this vision, China needs to reform its economy, strengthen the state and the army and in foreign policy, to concentrate on relations with the weakening hegemon – the United States.[311] The "Chinese

307 F. Godement, *Xi Jinping's China…*

308 *Chasing the Chinese dream…*

309 F. Godement, *Xi Jinping's…*

310 B. Góralczyk, *W poszukiwaniu chińskiego modelu rozwojowego* [In Search of a Chinese Model of Development], "Sprawy Międzynarodowe" 2016, no. 1, pp. 40-61.

311 Liu Mingfu, T*he China Dream: Great Power Thinking and Strategic Posture in the Post-American Era,*CN Times Books 2015, pp. 69-73 and 103-124.

dream" became popular when Xi Jinping started using this concept ("great renewal of the Chinese nation", *Zhonghua minzu wei da fuxing*).[312] The combination of the "Chinese dream" with the "Chinese rejuvenation" created a dyad that symbolizes the new assertiveness of Chinese policy.[313] The "Chinese dream" naturally relates to the "American dream", but its meaning is different. It is not about middle class prosperity, but about the rejuvenation of China as a great power. Under Chinese conditions this concept is entirely different than everything else since 1976: "compared with his predecessors' stodgy ideologies, it unashamedly appeals to the emotions, it makes no allusion to ideology or party policy. It chimes, quite possibly deliberately, with a foreign notion and seems designed to inspire rather than inform."[314] It is supposed to boost legitimization for the CCP in times of slower economic growth.

Xi included many of the "Chinese dream's" ideas in his new foreign policy strategy presented on 29 November 2014 during the party's cadres' conference. Xi called for a new development model and two centenary goals: completing the building of a moderately prosperous society by 2021 and – more importantly in the context of foreign policy: realizing the Chinese Dream of the rejuvenation of the Chinese nation.[315] Xi's plans were a clear sign of "intensification of Sinocentrism" in Chinese foreign policy as the Chinese Dream is a "forthright acknowledgment of the Sinocentrism at the core of Chinese identity;[316] and perhaps the first step to restore the old China-dominated order in Asia.[317] No matter what the main purpose may be, these goals, particularly the latter, challenge Deng's "*tao guang, yang hui*" concept (though without naming it). It remains to be seen whether Xi Jinping will be able to fulfil his ambitious plans.

15. Putin and Xi

Vladimir Putin's and Xi Jinping's personal ties are the last factor in this "personal" approach to Russia-China relations. It is particularly important given the importance of personality ties in both cultures and their own characters as well: "It is well-known that Putin, a former KGB operative, attaches great importance to individual diplomacy, preferring to rely on a friendly personal relationship with other leaders to build stronger country-to-country ties."[318]

---

312 *Xi highlights national goal of rejuvenation*, English.People.Com, 2012, 30 XI.

313 B. Góralczyk, *Chiński sen* [The Chinese Dream], "Komentarz Międzynarodowy Pułaskiego" 3/2013.

314 *Xi Jinping and the Chinese Dream…*; *Chasing the Chinese dream…*

315 Xi Jinping, *The governance of China*, Beijing, 2014, p. 38.

316 Gilbert Rozman, *The Sino-Russian Challenge…*, pp. 246 and 171.

317 T.Miller, *China's Asia Dream. Empire Building along the New Silk Road*, Zed Books 2017.

318 A. Gabuev, *China's Pivot to Putin's Friends*, "Foreign Policy", 25.06.2016.

Putin and Xi are supposed to like one another, at least if one is to believe Putin (who said that that they have "trustful, good, even friendly relations")[319], and influential analysts ("those who have seen them at the closed talks, say there is liking between them, personal chemistry)."[320] This is different from the Putin's relations with the former Chinese leaders – Jiang Zemin and Hu Jintao.[321] Despite the language barrier, they were able to "develop deep personal ties."[322] Their friendship is supposed to have started during the APEC summit in Bali in 2013.[323] There must have been a cozy atmosphere there. Putin celebrated his birthday and during the meeting with Xi, apparently Putin pulled out a bottle of vodka for a toast after Xi gave him a cake; unsurprisingly the meeting took place in a "warm and friendly atmosphere."[324] A close relationship with Xi is now even more important since all the other "old Putin's friends", such as Gerhard Schröder and Silvio Berlusconi are already out of politics; that is why "Xi remains the only world leader of a major country that Putin can call a friend."[325]

Certainly, they have very much in common philosophically – in political philosophy they both refer to the 19th century political realism. They understand one another without words. According to the Russian press, Xi was supposed to tell Putin that they "share common characters."[326] Certainly they share dramatic experiences from the past: "both men went through the worst of their nations' times" (Cultural Revolution in China and the collapse of the Soviet Union); both men learned from their own experience the hard lesson that "they cannot have liberty without order."[327] That is why they detest Western interference in their domestic affairs so much: "Xi's remarks in Mexico in 2009 about 'some foreigners with full bellies and nothing better to do [than] engage in finger-pointing at us' did not go unnoticed in Moscow."[328] Putin and Xi are both realists, both dream of bringing back the lost glory and both want the end of the American hegemony. Xi Jinping's policy has been called "Bismarckian"[329], as was Putin's earlier. Although in many areas their interests contradict one another, this does not lead to serious conflicts: they do not burn the bridges,

319 *Ответы на вопросы журналистов* [Putin's Answers to Journalists' Questions], Kremlin.Ru, 05.09.2016.

320 *«Китайцы понимают, что Россия...*

321 D. Trenin, *From Greater Europe …*

322 A. Gabuev, *Friends with Benefits?…*

323 Ibid., *China's Pivot to Putin's Friends…*

324 *День рождения Путин отметил тортом и водкой* [Putin has celebrated his birthday with cake and vodka], "Эхо Сибири" 09.10.2013.

325 A.Gabuev, *China's Pivot to Putin's Friends…*

326 *Путин и Си Цзиньпин сошлись характерами* [Putin and Xi Jinping Share Characters], "Столетие" 24.03.2013.

327 Yu Bin, *Pivot to Eurasia and Africa: Xi Style*, "Comparative Connections" vol. 15, no 1

328 A.Gabuev, *Friends with Benefits?...*

329 F. Godement, *Xi Jinping's…*

they are predictable partners. Their good relations translated into concrete economic deals: USD 12 billion loan for Yamal LNG from the Chinese state bank's sale of a stake in Sibur to Sinopec, and the agreement to provide credit for the Moscow-Kazan high-speed railway without state guarantees.[330] More importantly, Putin-Xi personal relations strengthen Russia-China relations by providing it with a "new structural element", further strengthened by the fact that both are expected to stay in power into the 2020s, thus giving Russia-China relations "a welcome 'cadre stability.'"[331]

16. "Hot on top, cold at bottom"

Although Russian and Chinese leaders understood each other and display a considerable fondness for each other, the lower, the worse. Russian and Chinese elites struggle to find a common language, and the Russian and Chinese masses still keep reserved approach towards the other side. A decade or two ago this phenomenon was described as "hot at top, cold at bottom" and despite growing fondness, signs of rapprochement towards one another, this rule remains in place, though on a much lesser scale.

When Sino-Russian relations matured politically in 2000s (see further chapters), researchers started to mention "the missing link" in Russia-China relations: the society (or the masses, to use Marxist vocabulary). It was clearly seen that the social contacts between Russians and Chinese fall behind the political ones: "the lower the level, the weaker the sense of commonalities.[332] Yu Bin wrote in the mid 2000s that "despite unprecedented progress in the more tangible aspects of bilateral relations, the intangible mutual perceptions/misperceptions and understandings/misunderstandings, are still unstable, and even negative"[333]; and that ordinary Russians and Chinese do not have warm feelings towards one another: "the Russians and Chinese do not very much know, like, let alone love, one another."[334] Mikhail Titarenko, a very Soviet-style Russian sinologist summarized it in the best nomenclatura-style way: "there is a wide gap between deep understanding between Russian and Chinese elites and lack of information for mass circles of Russian society."[335] That is why political elites in Beijing and Moscow were faced with the challenging task of

330 A. Gabuev, *Putin-Xi Friendship Driving Russia-China Ties*, Carnegie Moscow 03.06. 2016; *Ради дружбы Путина и Си Цзиньпина* [Concerning the Friendship of Putin and Xi Jinping], Inosmi.Ru 17.03.2016.

331 D. Trenin, *From Greater Europe…*

332 G. Rozman, *The Sino-Russian Challenge…*, p. 268.

333 Yu Bin, *Pollution, Politics and Partnership*, "Comparative Connections" vol. 7, no 4

334 Idem, *China's Year of Russia and the Gathering Nuclear Storm*, "Comparative Connections" vol. 8, no 1.

335 М. Титаренко, *Геополитическое значение…*, с. 264.

bridging misperceptions and dislike between the ordinary Chinese and Russians that persist despite a decade of strategic partnership."[336] Surveys of public opinions showed that Russia's positive views of China are "a mile wide and an inch deep."[337]

Common stereotypes and anxieties do not help here. The traditional negative stereotypes presented the Russians in China as "barbarians from the North" (*lao maozi*, "hairy", or literally "old flurry") and Chinese in Russia as Asian "hordes" from the East (a reflection of Mongol invasion of Ruthenia and "yellow peril" syndrome from late 19th/early 20th century). Despite ceasing to exist in official discourse or even private talks, these stereotypes remain ingrained in both nations' psyches. Today they are complemented by contemporary ones ("Russians as culturally unable to accept the rise of China", "the Chinese as still culturally alien"), anxieties ("arrogant Chinese", wanting a "revival of charges of 'tsarist imperialism' and 'unequal treaties' once China is in commanding position") and a sense of economic superiority ("Russia's domestic disorder and chaos").[338] As one Russian analyst put in, "for the Chinese youths Russia is non interesting and non attractive, in general, Chinese understand that Russia used to be a great power that gave PRC much but due to corruption and ineffective management it is degradating and it has only resources, giant territory and nuclear weapons left."[339] Add Russia's lack of "Asianess" and remnants of a feeling of European superiority and deeply ingrained Chinese Sinocentricism (see earlier in this book) to see the complicated picture of Sino-Russian social relations. Naturally, it is not easily spotted – "the lack of respect for each other's social and political orders is tempered by mutual reserve in not openly raising criticism"[340] – but it exists beneath the surface all the same.

It is fair to admit that Russian and Chinese authorities have been trying to shape their respective societies in accordance with their political official optimism. Nonwithstanding such heavy-handed events as "Years" (of Russia in China and China in Russia) and other top-to-bottom activities[341], the general message from both Russia and China goverments to their societies can be described as "start to like one another". Russian state-controlled media have been portraying China in positive light since the early 2000s. It intensified after the Ukrainian crisis when the Russian elite suspended its suspicions about China (at least for a time being); since 2014 there has been an increasing number of TV programmes, documentaries, books as well as sponsored academic trips to China and exchanges with Chinese units (in some cases intensification of the

336 Yu Bin, *China's Year of Russia...*
337 A. Kuchins, op. cit., p. 47.
338 G. Rozman, *The Sino-Russian Challenge...*, pp. 251-269.
339 *«Китайцы понимают, что...* Lenta.Ru, 30.04.2015.
340 G. Rozman, *The Sino-Russian Challenge...*, p. 259.
341 А.В. Лукин, *От нормализации к стратегическому партнерству ...* p. 350.

existing programmes)[342]; all for the propagation of the "China chance" image in Russia. This, combined with the Russian sense of offense by the West, creates a good ground for social rapprochement. As for China, the official, Beijing controlled media usually back Russia in its struggles with the West (e.g. the Malaysian Airlines plane crash in eastern Ukraine) and present the bright picture of bilateral relations. It works to some extent: according to Zhao Huansheng, "Russia's image is improving in China, including among the younger generation – Russia is perceived as a country that resists 'international hegemony'"[343] and sometimes is even considered a most China-friendly country for significant part of China's population.[344] To some extent newly found fondness overlaps with post-communist nostalgia among the older generation of Chinese people who remember the "joint fight for socialism."[345] Moreover, the improved behaviour of Russian law-enforcement agents towards Chinese tourists helps here, too.[346] Yet this positive image is limited (as for most of the Chinese society Russia is irrelevant) and one-sided only (Chinese are more favourably inclined towards Russia than the other way round).[347]

Hence, despite all these top-down attempts to improve people-to-people Sino-Russian relations, it is easier said that done. Mutual anxieties and resentments went underground (like in the Russian Far East), but still exist. Personal conversation with ordinary Russians and Chinese are a good indicator, although they are naturally hard to measure. In-depth sociological research is much better – for example, it shows that despite intensified contacts between ordinary Russians and Chinese, mutual sympathy does not rise (especially on the Russian side).[348] Internet, the least censored medium in Russia and China alike, is another indicator, and good thermometer of social attitudes. Although usually irrelevant to bilateral issues, mutual resentments reappear in "moments of truth": controversial events, such as pollution in China that affects Russia, sinking a Chinese ship or closing the Chinese market in Moscow. Each time something happens in Sino-Russian relations, voices of discord appear loudly, "showing (…) weak cultural ties and popular distrust."[349] Even Russian analysts admit that "despite good Sino-Russian relations, population still holds a significant amount of stereotypes and out-of-date images (…) although both

---

342 Since mid-2000s there has been a growing interest in China among Russian scholars and students, Ibid., p. 401-405; only after Ukrainian crisis, however, this became really widespread.

343 Quoted in: M. Duchâtel, op. cit.

344 А.В. Лукин, *Россия и Китай*… p. 662.

345 Yu Bin, *China-Russia Relations. Trilateral Politics* … pp. 103-116.

346 Quoted in: M. Duchâtel, op. cit.

347 L.J.Goldstein, *A China-Russia Alliance?* "The National Interest", 25.04.2017.

348 *Прощание с «азиатскими Балканами» Восприятие китайской миграции на Дальнем Востоке России* [Farwell with Asian Balkans. The Perception of Chinese Migrantion to Russia Far East], 2014, SLON. Ru.

349 G. Rozman, *The Sino-Russian Challenge*…, p. 270.

sides' attempts give positive results, there is still not enough mutual understanding between both nations."[350] Thus, despite official propagation of a positive image by the other side by mass-media controlled by Kremlin and Zhongnanhai, Sino-Russian relations have still, though on a much lesser scale, been "hot at top and cold at bottom"[351], or "warm on the outside, tepid on the inside, and chilly underneath"; this, however, does not frighten Russian and Chinese elites, as "apathy (towards Russia) is better than antipathy directed elsewhere" (the West).[352] And after all, societies/masses are not so important in Russian and Chinese policy making.

III. "Democratization of International Relations": International Roles of Russia and China

Despite differences and sometimes contradictory interests, Russia and China agree on the philosophical level on how the world system of international relations should be built. Moscow and Beijing perceive the world through the prism of the 19th century power struggle, with the sole difference being that only a single hegemonic power – albeit weakening – exists now: the USA. Thus Moscow and Beijing reject, though softly, the current system which they consider unjust and want to modify it into a better one. Nothing better encapsulates these hopes as the somehow paradox, if not blatant phrase from their joint communiqués: the need for "democratization of international relations."[353] According to this rationale, US-dominated international relations are undemocratic and should be democratized by the inclusion of Russia and China (as well as other great powers) into collective decision-making on global matters. Further "democratization of international relations" (inclusion of more countries, particularly smaller, into decision making), is however neither needed nor wanted.[354]

350 А.В. Лукин, *Россия и Китай*… p. 687.

351 С. Тихвинский, *Воспиятие в Китае образа России* [The Perception of Russia's Image in China], Москва 2008, p. 219.

352 G. Rozman, *The Sino-Russian Challenge*…, pp. 57 and 267.

353 See for example: *Совместная декларация Российской Федерации и Китайской Народной Республики* [Joint Declaration of FR and PRC], Kremlin.ru, 02.12.2002.

354 B. Lo, *Russia and The New World Disorder*…, pp. xx and 42.

1. *"Soft Revisionists"*

Russia and China proclaim "strategic partnership"[355], "new model of international relations"[356] that supports Five Principles of Peaceful Coexistence, stands against hegemonism[357], the primacy of force over international law[358], and heralds the "democratization of international relations".[359] Moscow and Beijing portray their relations "as the very model of international cooperation – pragmatic, enterprising, and innovative", such is the "bombastic" language of their official communiqués."[360] It shows a mutual understanding on international relations – Russia and China have converged views "on the global strategic situation, the principles on which the international order should be based and the role of the US"; according to them, this US dominance is "a temporary aberration" of international politics, and rejections of the Western values and norms create a strong bond between them.[361] Hence, Russia and China "are united by a geopolitical worldview."[362] They are "the coalition of the unwilling"[363] or "conservative force"[364] – they hail multipolarity[365], object to the

355 *Совместная декларация Российской Федерации и Китайской Народной Республики* (Joint Declaration of FR and PRC) 25.04.1996 [in:] *Сборник российско-китайских договоров 1949-1999* [Collection of Russia-China Treaties], Москва 2000, pp. 333-337.

356 *Договор о добрососедстве, дружбе и сотрудничестве между Российской Федерацией и Китайской Народной Республикой* [The Treaty on Good Neighborhood, Friendship and Cooperation Between RF and PRC], Сайт Президента РФ; Михаил Титаренко, *Геополитическое* ..., pp. 269-271.

357 *Российско-Китайская совместная декларация о многополярном мире и формировании нового международного порядка* [Russian-Chinese Joint Declarion on Multipolar World and Forming of New International Order], [in:] *Сборник российско-китайских договоров 1949-1999*..., pp. 382-384.

358 *Российско-китайские отношения на пороге XXI века (Совместное заявление по итогам российско-китайской встречи на высшем уровне)* [Russian-Chinese Relations at the Turn of the 21the Century], [in:] Ibid., pp. 453-457.

359 *Совместная декларация Российской Федерации и Китайской Народной Республики* [Joint Declaration of FR and PRC], 26.03.1997, [in:] Ibid. pp. 491-501.

360 B. Lo, *The Axis of Convenience*..., p. 1.

361 M.Kaczmarski, *Russia-China Relations*..., p. 24; Idem, *Russia-China Relations and the West*, Working Paper Series Russia and the West: Reality Check, GDAP, March 2017.

362 M. Carlsson, S. Oxenstierna, M. Weissmann, *China and Russia – A Study on Cooperation, Competition and Distrust*, Report, Stockholm: Swedish Defence Research Agency, 2015, p.79.

363 D. Shambaugh, *Chinese thinking About World Order*," [in:] *China and the International System. Becoming a World Power*, eds. by Xiaoming Huang and Robert Patman, London-New York, Routledge 2013, p. 9.

364 А.В. Лукин, *Россия и Китай сегодня и завтра* (*Russia and China. Today and Tomorrow*), [in:] *Россия и Китай: четыре века*... p. 629

365 Although it was the Chinese who used this term first in 1997, multipolarity became a favorite Russian slogan. Although Russian authors love to emphasize that China "shares Russian

Western use of force (military interventions sanctioned by universal values), defend territorial integrity and state sovereignty form of external interference, and detest democratization attempts.[366] In Western media eyes, they are "partners in crime at the United Nations."[367] In general, their international agenda reflects the philosophy of the "Five Principles of Peaceful Coexistence" which is a clear sign of China-based inspiration.

A similar philosophical approach to politics made some authors describe Sino-Russian relations as a "strategic convergence"[368] or a "normative convergence"[369]; although it is not quite so (see the previous chapter); in the vision of the international relations, Moscow and Beijing agree: "China and Russia share elements of a common worldview. At the top of the list is the importance of a strong state that enjoys full freedom of action internationally."[370] "Russia and China see themselves as the co-architects of the international order on par with Western states (they) remain interested in the great-powers concert-type global politics".[371] Moscow and Beijing dream of the 21th century's equivalent of the 19th century "concert of powers", with its rough equivalence between major powers and strategic check and balances to restrain hegemonic influences. Thus, they propose "exclusive clubs" of great powers, where those powers would not be restrained by others' actions and would act in accordance with a concert of powers' logic.[372] In part this reflects their fears of "regime survival,"[373] but fear itself is insufficient to explain their mutual understanding, they have on a deeper, philosophical level: they agree that authoritarianism is a much better system to achieve stability than liberal democracy and that outsiders, particularly Westerners should not lecture any country on how to govern it, let alone conduct interventions based on high moral assumptions. Opposition to Western values and norms are "not occasional policies of misguided leaders but the fundamental orientation of the political elite, supported by population."[374] Finally, Russia and China consider the present unipolarity as an

---

perspective on multipolarity" (see, e.g. Ibid.), in reality China pays lip service to it and bandwagonds to this extensive usage of "multipolarity" rhetoric instrumentally only.

366 See for example: *Совместная Декларация Российской Федерации И Китайской Народной Республики О Международном Порядке В XXI Веке* [Joint RR PRC Declaration on International Order in 21th Century], Mid.ru, 27.02.2006; *Совместная декларация Российской Федерации и Китайской Народной Республики по основным международным вопросам* [Joint RR PRC Declaration on International Issues], 23.08.2008, Kremlin.Ru

367 I. Bond, op. cit.

368 K. E. Braekhus, I. Øverland, *A Match Made in Heaven? Strategic Convergence between China and Russia*, "China and Eurasia Quarterly" 2007, vol. 5, no. 2, p. 42.

369 R. Kagan, *The Return of History and the End of Dreams*, New York 2008, p. 59-80.

370 D. Trenin, *From Greater Europe …*

371 M. Kaczmarski, *Russia-China Relations…*, p. 134.

372 Ibid., p. 135.

373 Idem, *Russia-China Relations and the West…*

374 G. Rozman, *The Sino-Russian Challenge…*, p. 21.

ending one: "Moscow and Beijing see the world going through an epochal change away from U.S. domination and toward a freer global order that would give China more prominence and Russia more freedom of action."[375] Moscow is much more vocal on the above mentioned claims, as it genuinely hopes for "retro constructs" such as "a new Westphalian order through a modern-day Concert of Great Powers" (in today's vocabulary: multipolarity/polycentrism), or "global oligarchy."[376] China still wants to use opportunities of the current system and knows it is too early to replace it: "China may be revisionist in the sense of wanting a stronger position on the global chess board; but it has shown less inclination than Russia to tip over the board entirely."[377]

The Russians and the Chinese behave as if they considered the international system in the best realist way as anarchic, based on power politics and, consequently, built on an "organized hypocrisy" rule, whereby the logic of expected consequences dominates over the logic of appropriateness, The reasons for the prevalence of the "organized hypocrisy" in international politics are power asymmetries and the absence of any universally recognized legitimate authority. Stronger states can pick and choose from among those norms that best suit their material interests or ignore norms altogether, because they can impose their choices on weaker states in the absence of any legitimate institution that could constrain their coercion and take action against them[378]. Moscow and Beijing agree that the logic of consequences prevails – in their worldview, power relations dominate at the expense of allegedly universal values. They reject the Western idea of progress (e.g. in the Iranian and North Korean crisis they were unconcerned about non-proliferation) and consider the "US primacy and unipolarity as a temporary aberration of international politics".[379] Thus, their political behaviour is "based on traditional, 19th century *Realpolitik* imperatives: national security, power projection, management of the strategic balance and emphasis on the primacy of state sovereignty"; the only difference is the discourse: they have learned to use more modern and inclusive language.[380] All of this is, however, merely a smoke screen: ideology plays an instrumental role for the two nations[381] (for them democratic ideology is only a new tool of influence; the Chinese opposition to democracy is, however, visibly stronger –

375 D. Trenin, *From Greater Europe…*

376 B. Lo, *Russia and The New World Disorder …*, pp. xviii-xx and 56. More about multipolarity: p. 42-47. Bobo Lo writes about "a retro vision of Russian national values", too, p. 32. "global oligarchy" is taken from Dmitri Trenin, quoted in: Ibid., p. 76.

377 I. Bond, op. cit.

378 S. D. Krasner, *Sovereignty: Organized Hypocrisy*, New Jersey, Princeton 1999, pp. 1-9.

379 M. Kaczmarski, *Russia-China Relations…*, pp. 138 and 147.

380 B. Lo, *The Axis of Convenience…*, pp. 3-174; A. Petersen, K. Barysch, *Russia, China and the geopolitics of energy in Central Asia*, CRR Report 2011,16 XI.

381 The removal of ideology from Moscow-Beijing ties has been the most important stabilizing factor in their bilateral relations since the end of the Cold War, Yu Bin, *China-Russia Relations: Trilateral Politics…*

Russia, with its self-perception as a European country, cannot allow itself to reject this ideology completely, although it considers it as "window-dressing")."[382].

Therefore, Russian and Chinese perceptions are based on a common vision of the international system, based on combating American hegemony in international relations and axiological cohesion (shared approach to the UN role, sovereignty, international law or human rights) – "Moscow and Beijing" overlap in cultural pride in opposition to the threat of Western culture": they insist "on distinct values" and share the conviction that these values are endangered by the West, which serves as "a unifying force in bilateral relations."[383] As Radosław Pyffel, the current Alternate Director of AIIB wrote (before becoming director of this China-dominated global bank): "China and Russia share common values which Westerners do not want or are unable to understand, intrusively demanding introduction of democracy in these countries"[384]. They agree that the Western democratic agenda "breeds chaos"[385], serves as "the leading edge of neoimperialism"[386] and reject the notion of global governance, claiming that this is a Western idea that reflects "Western norms and rules and was shaped by unequal power relations, i.e. Western primacy";[387] Russian and Chinese leaders "resent Western government criticisms and denounce what they see as biased Western media coverage, foreign funding for nongovernmental organizations, and the use of Internet mobilization techniques to foment revolution."[388] Democracy, human rights, "humanitarian intervention", "responsibility to protect" or "limited sovereignty" etc., are thus understood as Western instruments of enlarging the zone of influence and interfering in domestic affairs of other countries. Therefore, the opposition against this entire Western, normative, liberal, democratic and supranational superstructure is a well-conceived defence of national interests – it is a form of "soft balancing" against US hegemony.[389] Thus, Russia and China may be called "soft revisionist" – they revise the current international system, but softly, without creating blocks or military alliances.[390] They avoid any precipitous moves, are unwilling to form an alliance and consequently face "entrapment", as they do not see

---

382 G. Rozman, *The Sino-Russian Challenge…*, p. 110.

383 Ibid., pp. 182-194.

384 R. Pyffel, *Chiny-Rosja: Kto kogo?...*

385 D. Trenin, *From Greater Europe...*

386 G. Rozman, *The Sino-Russian Challenge…*, p. 141.

387 M. Kaczmarski, *Russia-China Relations…*, p. 135.

388 D. Trenin, *From Greater Europe…*

389 Ch. Ferguson, *The Strategic Use of Soft Balancing: The Normative Dimensions of the Chinese-Russian 'Strategic Partnership'*, "Journal of Strategic Studies" 35, no. 2 (2012).

390 Fu Ying, *How China Sees Russia: Beijing and Moscow Are Close, but Not Allies*, "Foreign Policy", 14.12.2015; in the Chinese version of her article, Fu Ying explained that the reason for China's unwillingness to become Russia'a formal ally is history and its "bitter lessons", quoted in: Idem, *Zhong'e guanxi, shi mengyou haishi huoban* [China-Russia relations, are

a great advantage to formalizing the partnership.[391] They themselves prefer to call relations "strategic alignment,"[392], "flexible partnership" or "friendly neutrality"[393], carefully avoiding words like alliance or axis. They are stronger in words than in actions and – as long as their core interests are not touched (Taiwan for China, post-Soviet area for Russia), they usually restrain themselves to rhetoric condemnation of Western actions and quietly acquiesce to the new situation. With rising tensions on the South China Sea (as well as between NATO and Russia), however, this may change in the future.

2. *"Strategic Screen"*

Despite the common philosophical approach to international system, however, there are important differences. These are differences in style and philosophy, but also in roles, expectations and visions. The most clearly visible difference is the style of policymaking. Russia "tends to favour strong, active, and often surprising diplomatic maneuvers", whereas China "is more reactive and cautious"[394]: "Russia is mastered in boxing, while China is skilled in tai chi"[395]; "whereas the Russians do not shy away from confrontation and brusque in-your-face methods, the Chinese prefer Tai Chi gymnastics, with its many feints. Russian tactics can scare the Chinese; Chinese moves can confuse the Russians".[396] As Chong-Pin Lin underlines, "China prefers to play *go* rather than chess; in chess one side is often alarmed by the opponent's moves and incoming danger, while in *go* one may lose without knowing it to the last moment, when the game is over."[397] More deeply, there is difference in the philosophy, where "the cold pragmatism preferred by Chinese political elites remains in blunt contradiction with messianic motives present in Russian policies"[398]; although, naturally, Russia has a lot of pragmatism too, but its sober *Realpolitik* is mixed with its great power syndrome (see the previous chapter). The difference in philosophy is reflected in the understanding of the win-win situation, too: "The Chinese understand a win-win idea differently from the Russians. For them, it's not a roughly 50/50 deal; it's any deal ranging from

---

we allies or partners?], 2016, quoted in: M. Duchâtel, op.cit. In China's academic circles the biggest propagator of the idea of an alliance with Russia is Yan Xuetong.

391 L.J.Goldstein, op. cit.

392 Yu Bin, *Politics of "Reluctant Allies"*... pp.129-144.

393 Words of Zhao Huasheng, Quoted in: M. Duchâtel, op. cit.

394 Fu Ying, *How China Sees Russia*...

395 A. Gabuev, *Friends with Benefits?*...

396 D. Trenin, *From Greater Europe*...

397 Chong-Pin Lin, *Formująca się wielka strategia Chin: ku dominacji, ale bez walki* [The Formulating China's Grand Strategy: to dominate, but without fight], "Azja-Pacyfik" 9/2006, p. 83.

398 K K. Kozłowski, *Państwo Środka a Nowy*..., p. 198.

99/1 to 1/99, where the specific ratio depends on the negotiations. The only alternative is not to make a deal and make no money at all"; this difference is to blame for the fact that unless anything changes, "that ratio will be shifting closer to 1/99 in China's favour."[399] As one Chinese diplomat put it, "win-win just means you haven't negotiated hard enough."[400]

These cultural patterns translate into policy making style. Both Russia and China are rising powers, but they act differently. Contrary to Russia's megalomania, the Chinese attitude differs significantly: whereas Russia raises its global status, China lowers it. Beijing has few illusions about its weakness and limitations – China has come a long way, but there is still a lot ahead. Although the Chinese assume their innate superiority, they remember the "hundred years of humiliation" very well. That is why, although the "fifth generation" of Chinese leaders started to "raise their head", it is still very modest in comparison with Russia. The reason comes directly from Chinese political culture, according to which a state should rather hide its capabilities than proclaim and announce its might.

Until late 2009, there was an "informal division of labour" between Russia and China. Russia upgraded its position by positioning itself as a great power and thus dominated the global dimension of their relations. China, on the other hand, behaved passively and kept a low profile in order not to be entangled in global politics. This reflected the nature of policy-making in both Russia and China: "the Russian elite felt an inherent need to be involved in every major international issue, even if it did not have to offer in terms of potential solutions to international problems (…) from Russia's perspective, participation in global decision-making became yet another way for it to increase its prestige and to retain its voice"; China on the other hand "took the reverse approach, adapting to those norms and rules of the Western liberal order that it regarded as conductive to its own goals and focusing its attention specially on economic issues."[401]

China acts differently. Although it shares with Moscow a deep dislike for American hegemonism[402], it does not challenge the liberal world system directly (Beijing was even able to develop its own positive discourse on international relations, equally hypocritical to the Western one, expressed in phrases like "fairness and objectivity serve as guiding principles for Beijing when addressing international affairs.")[403] China simply knows it is too early – the time for challenging the system has not yet come. Moreover, it prefers to challenge the international system (U.S. hegemony) using others' hands so that they do

399 A.Gabuev, *Russia and China: Little Brother or Big Sister?*, Moscow Carnegie 05.07.2016.

400 Quoted in: B. Lo, *Russia and The New World Disorder*…, p. 310.

401 M. Kaczmarski, *Russia-China Relations*…, pp. 135-136.

402 А.В. Лукин, *От нормализации к стратегическому партнерству*…, p. 326.

403 Fu Ying, op cit.

not suffer setbacks such as lack of Western investments.[404] Thus, China "has not attempted to use its friendship with Moscow [as] a bargaining counter in dealings with the West (…) Russia is too weak to perform such a role" for China "strategic partnership" is "a supplement, not an alternative, to its burgeoning ties with the United States and Europe."[405] Beijing would not allow that the relations with Russia damaged the most important policy goal: foster conditions to facilitate the country's modernization. China understands perfectly well that its key partner is the United States, not Russia. Beijing "does not consider the international situation as a zero-sum game; its policy is more sophisticated. China strives not so much to limit Russia's or the US's actions in general, but to limit the possibilities of limitation of the actions by the USA or Russia. On the one hand Beijing strives to maximize its own freedom of action, on the other, it still hopes that the US and Russia would be able to conduct activities that guarantee stability, thus removing responsibility from Beijing's back."[406] That is why for Beijing the relations with Moscow are of first and foremost strategic importance – to secure its "strategic rear" in order to concentrate on domestic modernization and the South China Sea, to ensure the continued flow of energy and other commodity imports (advanced arms); beside these, Russia is a useful ally to limit the Western ideological pressure.[407]

These differences show the very different nature of policymaking in both countries. Russia loves "high politics" and disregards "low politics", which is best visible in the history of its membership in G-8. There it "abstained from issues it considered to belong to the sphere of low politics" – it was "a testament to Moscow's attachment to a high-profile political presence rather than a substantial belief in the effectiveness and indispensability of multilateral frameworks". The same can be said about crisis management; Moscow's guiding principle in the international sphere has been "to [be] involved, an aspect Moscow used instrumentally for prestige purposes (…) the general objective was to appear powerful."[408] This resulted in never-ending rhetoric wars on words with the Western world that continue until now and are likely to do so in the future. This tendency, combined with incurable Russian megalomania, causes triumphalism in time of success and tendency to rush, audacious actions in policy making. For example, the success in Syria in 2013 strengthened Putin's confidence to such an extent that he started to take action to establish an alternative global political-ideological centre. Since then, he has been striving to become the leader of the anti-Western block, challenging the USA po-

404 А.В. Лукин, *От нормализации к стратегическому партнерству*…, p. 326.
405 B. Lo, *The Axis of Convenience*…, p. 45.
406 K. Kozłowski, op. cit., p. 314.
407 B. Lo, *The Axis of Convenience*…, pp. 3-44.
408 M. Kaczmarski, *Russia-China Relations*…, pp. 135-136.

litically and axiologically (defence of "traditional values" against widely understood political and social liberalism).[409] In doing so, "Moscow is inclined to overestimate the extent of Western weakness."[410]

China, on the other hand, although it welcomes the idea of a concert of powers, does not feel the need to be present at every forum or organization – Beijing has been doing so only when important Chinese interests are at stake. Besides, before the 2010s it tried to find ways that could testify its declared non-confrontational stance: "Moscow punched above its weight while Beijing continued to hide its increasing capabilities; with the potential of regional power, Russia acted like a global superpower, China for its part, was transforming into a serious global actor and yet tended to act as a regional one."[411]

That is why Russia plays a very specific role for China: it is its "strategic screen". China simply loves to "hide behind Russia's back". In crisis situations, Beijing prefers to move into the shade; it calculates that it is better not to lean out, not to face criticism and negative consequences and quietly do its things. Russia functions here as China's "strategic screen". It was clearly seen during the Ukrainian crisis: "Putin, who has been building his position on anti-Americanism and demonstrational challenging the West in many aspects, suits China ideally; thanks to him China 'hides in the shade', it discretely supports him and thus gets needed time."[412] This strategy works because – what is important – it suites both sides. Moscow, contrary to Beijing, likes to be in the spotlight, to play above its position and potential – this is how it builds its position of an influential player, whose presence is necessary in solving global problems.

Although from the economic crisis of 2008, China has been steadily more and more active on the international stage (believing that being and becoming a global great power means global interests and responsibilities), overtaking Russia in many aspects, nevertheless, in the style of policymaking China still prefers to rather downplay than upgrade its international position. Although since 2013 Beijing remains quite assertive in its "Chinese dream" style, this assertiveness cannot be matched with Russian bravado[413]; and Beijing is still aware that China cannot afford a confrontation with the US yet.[414] The West

---

409 E.g. V. Putin, *A Plea for Caution From Russia*, "The New York Times" 11.09.2013.

410 B. Lo, *Russia and The New World Disorder…*, p. xxii.

411 M. Kaczmarski, *Russia-China Relations…*, pp. 135-137.

412 R. Pyffel, *Siedem powodów dla których Chiny nie włączą się w wydarzenia na Ukrainie i pozostaną w ukryciu* [Seven Reasons Why China Will Not Join The Events In Ukraine And Will Stay In The Shadow], polska-azja.pl 04.03.2014.

413 B. Lo, *Russia and The New World Disorder…*, p. 216.

414 As Liu Fenghua put it, at present China needs to complete modernisation, not transform the existing international order.", Liu Fenghua, *Zhong'e zhanlüe xiezuo moshi : xingcheng, tedian yu tisheng* [The pattern of China-Russia strategic coordination: formation, features, and prospects], 2016, quoted in: M. Duchâtel, op.cit.

remains the key partner in ending the grand modernization, and this has been Beijing's top priority.

3. *The USA and beyond the USA in Russia-China Relations*

The US role in Russia-China relations is crucial, yet challenging to elaborate. Some researchers overestimate it[415], other underestimate it.[416] Certainly Washington had been the central point of reference for Russia and China alike in the 1990s and the 2000s. With time, however, the US factor decreased in its overarching importance, though naturally it remains significant.

It was an "ideological-axiological" opposition against the West and the common displeasure of the US-dominated international relations that became the engine of the Russia-China relations in the 1990s.[417] After initial anxiety about the other side joining the Western camp, in the mid 1990s, Russia and China "agreed to join together as a minority in the contemporary world" and agreed on the message that "the post-Cold War era is best characterized as a struggle between two civilizations: theirs and the West."[418] Moscow and Beijing shared a similar perception of global affairs: both opposed the American unilateralism and disliked the Western values. For Russian and Chinese advocates of strong state such ideas as "check and balances, and democracy were being directed against unity and power", represent "a smokescreen" for US "hegemonic ambitions" and "cultural imperialism."[419] The NATO's intervention in Kosovo, in particular, had farfetched consequences. It strengthened the belief of the two countries in the US hegemonistic attitude. Their opposition against the West united them and made their rapprochement in the 90s possible. It was not, however, an alliance or a bloc. Russia and China simply strengthened their own positions against the West. Thus, the dynamics of their bilateral relations waxed and waned in accordance with Moscow-Washington and Beijing-Washington dynamics.

Vladimir Putin's first term of office at first repeated the former decade's scheme. Initial rapprochement with China was soon overshadowed by Putin's

---

415 Ch. Grant, *Russia, China and Global Governance*, London CER 2012, p. viii; Linda Jakobsen Paul Holtom, Dean Knox, and Jingchao Peng, *China's Energy and Security Relations with Russia. Hopes, Frustrations and Uncertainties*, SIPRI policy paper 29, Stockholm 2011, p. 41.

416 Fu Ying, op. cit.; naturally the semiofficial voices in Russia and China underestimate it, too: *Sino-Russian bond more than expediency*, "Global Times", 14.10.2014; Dmitri Trenin, *From Cooperation to Competition. Russia and the West*, Carnegie, 21.01.2015.

417 М. Л. Титаренко, *Россия и Восточная Азия: Вопросы международных и межцивилизационных отношении* [Russia and East Asia. The Issues of International and Intercivilizational Relations], Москва 1994, pp. 29, 99 and 154.

418 G. Rozman, *The Sino-Russian Challenge…*, pp. 20-21.

419 Ibid., pp. 120 and 195.

pro-western turn after 11 September 2001. This rapprochement, however, ended up in bitter disappointment. Moscow strengthened its position thanks to rising oil and gas prices – and turned to Beijing again to balance Washington. This time the Sino-Russian rapprochement had stronger fundaments. Their partnership became more multidimensional, substantial. Since the late 2000s, Russia-China relations stopped only being "the hostage" to US-Russia and US-China relations: "Russia-China relations has gained enough autonomy and maturity not to be dependent on the evolution of US policies and both states' relations with Washington (…) one cannot reduce Russia-China collaboration to strategic interaction with the US"; Sino-Russian relations "are not a mere reaction to the United States power and policies."[420]

Nevertheless, the influence of Washington still should not be underestimated. It remained an important factor, if not directly, then relation-wise (the Western opposition to Russian reintegration actions push Moscow into the hands of China, whereas the US pivot to Asia pushes China into the hands of Russia).[421] Domestic Chinese debates follow this logic by saying that "U.S. containment invites China-Russia counter-containment."[422] This line of thinking is reflected in Beijing's international mouthpiece Global Times blalant declaration, "Beijing and Moscow are fed up with Washington's pursuit of hegemony" and "the US is unable to beat down the Chinese dragon and the Russian bear at the same time."[423] Thus, although this "US factor" is less visible than during the 1990s and the 2000s, it did not disappeared either. Both countries still perceive the West as more important than each other. Geopolitically the relations in the US-China-Russia triangle are still working within the following, structural rule: the "USA with its policy push or pull Moscow and Beijing to one another."[424] Particularly Russia is still prone to use its relations with China as "geopolitically driven anti-agenda"[425] to which Beijing adhers, albeit with reservations and without burning bridges with Washington. "The USA factor" forces Moscow and Beijing to curb their mutual resentments, keep calm whatever happens and be tolerant to the irritating actions of the 'strategic partner'.

Approaches to the USA, however, differ between Russia and China. The United States remain the key point of reference for Russian political thinking. After 1991, Russia understood that its global position and the revival of the Russian economy and its integration with global financial structures controlled

---

420 M. Kaczmarski, *Russia-China Relations…*, pp. 120-129, 195; Idem, *Russia-China and the West…*

421 F.Lukyanov, personal conversation, Moscow 2013, 28 IX.

422 Quoted in: L.J.Goldstein, op. cit.

423 *US pressure spurs closer Sino-Russian ties*, "Global Times", 27.06.2016.

424 Yan Jiann-Fa, *Vladimir Putin's Deepening Rapprochement with China in the Tangled China-Russia-US Triangle*, NCCU, 20.05.2012.

425 B. Lo, *Russia and The New World Disorder…*, p. 227.

by the USA, depended on its relations with the West. Initial enthusiasm and acceptance of the Western development model ("shocking therapy") quickly gave way to a deep disappointment and resentment over the Western exploitation of Russian weakness. After 1991, there have been two basic Russian approaches to the United States. First is *bandwagoning*, used three times (in 1991-1996 and 2001-2003), and 2009-2012 ("reset" times). In all cases it ended up with deeper disappointment and resentments against the West – this in turn influenced relations with China. The alternative approach has been the balancing policy based on an attempt to limit US influence (in this policy, China has always been the key) – first during Primakov's Eurasian concept (1996-1999), then Putin's "Bismarckian" manoeuvering (2003-2008), and finally with the speed up of the reintegration of the post-Soviet era (after 2009), and growing contestation of the US global leadership. Having failed in rapprochement with the USA, Russia set itself on a rhetorical-ideological collision course with the West, portraying itself as the anti-US global leader: the US became "Russia's 'other.'"[426] Moscow still has an "old Americacentric obsession": asserts that the era of American dominance is over, but continues to take the United States as the prime reference point not just for Russian foreign policy, but for international politics more generally."[427] That is why for Russia its relations with China are serving as "an important psychological crutch" – it was the "most compelling explanation for the confident face Russia presents to the world."[428] That is why each time Russia-US relations deteriorates, Putin moves to China to show that he had other option to chose from. Ukrainian crisis was illustrative of that.

China is much different here. Although Sino-American relations are experiencing considerable tension (see below), they are, too, "characterized by a high degree of interdependence and cooperation" and are far more important for China and that with Russia, "Beijing has few illusions that Russia is a capable or even willing counterweight to the United States.And it scarcely believes in a tripolar world; Xi's 'new pattern of great power relations' is an openly bipolar concept."[429] For Beijing, Russia in China's relation with the USA is not a counterweight, but serves as the "peace from the North" – its strategic backyard that makes it impossible to encircle China by the USA. As for the challenging US-dominated system, China for long has not been interested in changing the global order – it has wanted "restraining the US primacy", but has not been "eager to bear the cost of such a policy" – it has tried to "keep a low profile and avoid unnecessary bargaining."[430] As Clinton Dines has commented China's position: "the Chinese want to sit in the front seat of

426 M. Kaczmarski, *Russia-China Relations*..., p. 119.
427 B. Lo, *Russia and The New World Disorder*..., p. 98.
428 Idem, *The Axis of Convenience*..., pp. 3-44.
429 Idem, *Russia and The New World Disorder*..., p. 148.
430 M. Kaczmarski, *Russia-China Relations*..., p. 118.

the car, but they don't want to drive."[431] Beijing has "envisioned bringing about a long period of close cooperation and peaceful competition with Washington, hoping to eventually achieve equality with it"[432] (and to overtake it later on). China still only wants to use the current international system to its own purposes – "today it is 'the sole 'revolutionary' or 'revisionist' power in East Asia (…) it is most committed to challenging the existing American-led order, even though it recognizes that it will be a long time before it is able to contest this directly."[433] Although China's policy is motivated by domestic needs (development leads to political stability), it contains tacit (since Xi Jinping less tacit) claim that the pro-American order must be changed (with time) and that China will return to its "natural" position as an Asia-Pacific, or perhaps global, leader; China has already changed the strategic picture of Asia-Pacific region and this will only deepen in the future. Beijing in its "Grand strategy" strives for dominance in East Asia, though without fight.[434] Its rise in the Western-dominated international system is an interesting phenomenon. Contrary to Japan, which rose within the system and the USSR, which did it against the system, China is both part of the system and wants to overthrow it.[435] It wants to exploit it to the maximum and then replace it – thus it is China that in the long term constitutes the biggest threat to *Pax Americana*.

Beijing has been able to hide it for some time; however, in 2011, Washington realized the danger and responded with "pivot to Asia."[436] The United States, so far focused mostly on the Middle East, came to understand that the Chinese were beginning to dominate in the key global region of Asia-Pacific. This was a possible threat to the US: if the US was pushed out of the region and lost its control over maritime routes in Southeast Asia, then the US global hegemony would end.[437] Thus, after a failed attempt to come to terms with China on American terms (G2), Washington decided to block Beijing's further development. The "Pivot to Asia" policy was nothing more than a new containment policy, targeted this time not at Moscow, but at Beijing and not openly, but with all diplomatic pleasantries. To put it in a metaphoric way, the Americans wanted to put a "necklace on a Chinese string of pearls"[438], but after Trump's withdrawal from the TPP the fate of the pivot remains uncertain.

---

431 Quoted in: B. Lo, *Russia and The New World Disorder…*, p. 262.

432 D. Trenin, *From Greater Europe…*

433 B. Lo, *The Axis of Convenience…*, p. 117.

434 Chong-Pin Lin, op. cit., pp. 78-97.

435 Xiaomin Huang and R.Patman, *Introduction. China and International System – Structure, Society, and Context*, [in:] *China and the International System…* pp. 2-3.

436 H. Clinton, *America's Pacific Century*, "Foreign Policy" 11.10.2011.

437 J.Bartosiak, *Pacyfik i Eurazja. O wojnie* [Pacific and Eurasia. On War], Warszawa 2016, pp. 450-630.

438 B.Góralczyk, *Amerykański „naszyjnik" wokół Chin – USA zwiększają obecność w Azji* [American necklet on China. The Americans increase their presence in Asia], WP.PL, 2014, 7 V.

To conclude, since 2011, Sino-American relations have been complicated and a clash of interests, if not a conflict, looms in the horizon. Russia, meanwhile, anticipates (if not waits for) a Sino-American conflict, as it, Moscow hopes, would give it much more room to maneuver (as a "geopolitical balancer") and a chance to regain its great power status: "concern about the asymmetry of the economic relationship with Beijing is outweighed by America's visible discomfiture with China's rise, satisfaction with Sino-Russian cooperation, and faith that China will need Russia for a long time to come— as a supplier of vital natural resources and as a good neighbor."[439]

4. *Russia's Foreign Policy Goals*

Another important issue that must be described here, are the foreign policy goals of Russia and China. The importance of foreign policy in both countries is different – in China domestic policy considerations prevail over foreign policy (the latter fulfils the overarching goal of economic development, a fundamental source of legitimization for the party); in Russia the opposite is true, as foreign policy is a source of legitimacy for the current regime. In a way Russian foreign policy is reactive: "it has a better idea of what it does not want than of what it does" – "it opposes a unipolar world dominated by a hegemonic power; dislikes Western-led moral interventionism; and is hostile to the 'encroachment' of the United States and Europe in the post-Soviet space", but that means it wants simply "to facilitate an external environment that supports the legitimacy and stability of the Putin system."[440]

Russia's two most important foreign policy goals are based on two elements: regaining the status of a global great power and maintaining the primacy on post-Soviet area.[441] The "near abroad" (or the post-Soviet area, though "near abroad" is a wider, yet more vague term) is considered the top priority (it has become most visible after 2009). Russia uses various instruments – from bilateral to multilateral (CIS) – and wide array of means (from diplomatic to military) to control the "near abroad". This area is considered the key one: realistic considerations (an influence zone, the buffer that surrounds the Russian core), as well as Russia's autotelic striving for the great power status, making it Russia's key foreign policy dimension. When researching the political thinking of the Russian political elites, it is very difficult to tell where rational, realistic thinking ends (that forces Russia to be a great power – Russia needs it to feel secure) and when autothelic mania to be a superpower, the need to be great, begins. This striving to dominate is based on considering the "near abroad" as the Monroe doctrine's Russian equivalent: no other great power is

439 B. Lo, *Russia and The New World Disorder*..., p. 53.
440 Ibid., p. 52.
441 M.Kaczmarski, *Russia-China Relations*... pp. 38-44.

allowed to interfere in "near abroad countries'" domestic issues without Russia's consent.[442] It is based on common history and on a claim of alleged superior rights over all former Ruthenian lands. Russia's great power ambitions in the "near abroad" also compensate Russia's failures in domestic affairs.[443]

Western Europe and the United States (see: above) are other important dimensions for Russia. Although politically less relevant than the USA, Western Europe – out of strategic, economic and cultural reasons – has been almost equally important to Russia. A strong position in Europe strengthens Russia's global position; trade with the EU makes up almost 50% of all Russia's foreign trade and it is where Russia makes the best deals on resources (although recently these deals are not as good as they used to be – due to UE Third Energy Package and other European measures to promote competition[444] – they are still very profitable). Finally, Russians, even those living in the Russian Far East, consider themselves culturally Europeans and demand to be recognized as such.[445] It is Western European countries, such as Germany, France or Italy that enjoy best relations with Russia (Moscow prefers bilateral relations rather than having to deal with the entire EU).[446]. Europe, or the West in general, remains the benchmark, despite all criticism directed towards it from Moscow. Although Russians "are cynical about the morality and intentions of Western policymakers, they remain susceptible to Western influence writ large"; it happens because "Westerncentrism" does not equate to "proWesternism", exhibited by members of Kremlin elite who operate on 'a barely concealed double standard': they excoriate the West (…) Yet they send their children to be educated at European and American universities; buy property in London; invest their money in Western banks and hedge funds; and pursue legal redress in British courts. In doing so, they act on the tacit— but unmistakable— assumption that 'the West is best.'"[447] As one Polish diplomat methaphorically put Kremlin's elite attachment to the West: "you do not buy Bentleys not to have spare parts for them and you do not send your lovers to Cannes not to visit them."[448] As for China, a typical Russian high-ranking official "has weak knowledge of China", "sometimes still thinks of it as poor and backwards country"[449], "goes there once a year, signs some documents, but those he deals with on the Chinese side seems absolutely strange for him and their country

---

442 N. Gvosdev, *Rival views of the thaw provoke another chill*, "The New York Times" 25.01.2006.

443 B. Lo, L. Shevtsova, op. cit., pp. 47-48.

444 B. Lo, *Russia and The New World Disorder*…, p. 183.

445 А.В. Лукин, *Медведь наблюдает за драконом. Образ Китая в России в XVII-XXI веках*, Москва 2007, pp. 312–322; the Russian elites have succeeded in personally integrating into (and with) Western society, B. Lo, L. Shevtsova, op. cit. p. 19.

446 Ibid.

447 B. Lo, *Russia and The New World Disorder*…, pp. 198 and 225.

448 *Wojny (chyba)nie będzie*[There won't be, probably, war],"Krytyka Polityczna", 30.11.2016.

449 А.В. Лукин, *Россия и Китай* …, p. 668.

remains unnoticeable"; even Putin's friendship with Xi is not necessarily good news for this proverbial Russian bureaucrat: "if our top leader is friends with the Chinese, then the whole elite need to become champions in friendship with China and that is hard to do."[450] The continued dominance of the West is not limited to the elites: "Russian scientists work in Western universities and research institutes; IT specialists and programmers go to Silicon Valley; Russian companies have sought Western technology and know-how; and middle-class Russians see themselves as part of a superior European civilization (…) despite the rise of Asia, the brain drain of young, ambitious Russians is to the United States and Europe, not to China and India."[451] And what is perhaps the most important difference with China is that the Russian brain drain – contrary to the Chinese one – does not come back from the West.

As for China, since 1991, it has been fulfilling an important dual role for Russia – psycho-political and real. First and foremost has been the psycho-political function as the equalizer for the West – a strategic alternative, no matter if real or virtual (see: the 2014 crisis in Ukraine): having an alternative to the West in case the relations deteriorated, China has been Russia's favorite bugbear – in both political and economic spheres (diversification of energy supplies). Finally, cultivating good relations with Beijing strengthened the self-perception of Russia as a global superpower. Since Beijing respects Russia's aspirations (although China's plans in Central Asia are being watched with suspicion by Moscow, the fact that Beijing is careful to not challenge Moscow's special privileges in the post-Soviet area makes it a bearable partner and "lesser evil" for Moscow than the West), relations with China reinforce the aspiration to great power status – thus "China's rise is not seen as threatening to Russia's status."[452]

The geopolitical perspective must be considered here, too: Russia, whilst trying to rebuild a position in the former Soviet area, needs to be secure from the east as well, it needs "peace from the East" and China secures it. In other words, the success of Putin's reintegration policy also depends on forging relations with China. The reality of growing confrontation with the West over Ukraine since 2014 has meant that Moscow feels that it is the Western, not the Chinese, attitude that challenges its interests: it is a mortal threat to the Russian integration project. Therefore, Russia chooses to oppose the West and needs the help from China[453]. To sum it up, in the present day Russia needs China, is perhaps, sometimes, dependent on it.

---

450 *«Китайцы понимают, что…* Lenta.Ru, 30.04.2015.

451 B. Lo *Russia and The New World Disorder* …, pp. 140 and 198.

452 M. Kaczmarski, *Russia-China Relations…* p. 46.

453 D. Trenin, *China's Victory in Ukraine*, Project Syndicate, 2014, 31 VII.

5. *China's Foreign Policy Goals*

As for China's foreign policy goals, the "*tifa*" play an important role. *Tifa*, or indicators for a country's strategy, are "meta-rules that cover a Middle Country's foreign policy goals", in accordance with "obedience to the party line but while maintaining essential flexibility."[454] The most important tifa are: "the multi-vector policy" *(quanfang wei waijiao)*, based on multilateral fulfillment of Chinese interests, not on ideology; "peace, development and cooperation" that should establish a peaceful environment for China; "the harmonious world" (respect for sovereignty and territorial integrity), combined with domestic "harmonious society" (Hu Jintao's leadership slogan) – the latter illustrates well the correlation between domestic and foreign policies of the PRC.[455] Since Xi Jinping came to power, new "tifa" have come into existence – "the Chinese dream" and, recently, "the One Belt One Road". China's most important foreign policy goals are: promoting economic development, building strong, independent international politics, defence of sovereignty and territorial integrity (the last one is quite sensitive in China given its own domestic situation in Tibet and Xinjiang, thus Beijing "does not approve of secessionism, annexations, or foreign military interventions—unless, of course, Beijing feels the need to intervene itself)."[456]

Economic development remains the most important goal. China's foreign policy is based on economic logics; its aim is to establish a favourable international environment for China's unstoppable development and modernization (domestic development keeps the legitimization of the CCP). In accordance with these goals, China strives to minimize threats, particularly in its neighbourhood. Besides, its aim is to gain access to markets, obtain foreign investments (particularly advanced technologies), build connections within the international environment that secures permanent development.[457] Simply put: China must develop to survive (and to become a great power), and to develop it needs contact with the world. That is why China uses every opportunity to persuade others that the Chinese rise is more am opportunity than a threat to the international environment.

China's other foreign policy goal is to minimize the potential limitation of political actions. Here, "China's encirclement threat" plays the most important role: Beijing is constantly afraid of hostile alliances; recently these fears were awoken due to the "US pivot to Asia". China is trying to counter a possible situation where the present hegemon (the USA) would be able to limit China's growth – Beijing does it through multilateral policy. Another issue is the ne-

454 K. Kozłowski, *Państwo Środka…* p. 40.

455 Ibid., pp. 40-50.

456 D. Trenin, *From Greater Europe…*

457 K. Kozłowski, *Państwo Środka…*, pp. 40-50.

cessity of the diversification of resources and supplies – critical for maintaining China's growth and limiting autonomous actions of ethnic minorities in sensitive regions of Tibet and Xinjiang as well as international activity around Taiwan.

Beijing's international narrative or the emphasis on the uniqueness of China's development model is another important feature. China, contrary to other countries, and contrary to the Mao times – does not want to export its achievements: it claims that these are results of specific Chinese conditions and may be successful only in China.[458] It is here where the old Sinocentristic approach to the world is revealed. China is so much convinced of its own superiority and of the worth of its own values and achievements, that it does not feel the need to prove them.

To fulfill its foreign policy goals, China considers four pillars: relations with the great powers are the most important one; the relations with neighbours has a priority; the relations with developing countries are fundamental, whereas multilaterality is the scene.[459] In China's outlook, the USA, the EU, Russia and Japan are considered great powers. Economic cooperation (since 2001 fulfilled via the strategy of going out, or *zou chu qu*) is carried out by means of various instruments, such as free trade zones, multilateral organizations or groups such as the G20. Chinese foreign policy is based on attracting others and creating alliances rather than on open competition/rivalry – "China conducts its foreign policy in a much diversified way, with the use of a wide array of possibilities offered by the present international order (in general China does not question the present international order but tries to exploit it for its own needs)."[460] Additionally, China has worked out a formula of cooperation with priority states or groups of states – so called "strategic partners" (*zhanlue huoban guanxi*). Relations with Russia are, therefore, located in this dual theoretical spectrum of Chinese policy. Moscow is an exceptional partner for China: at the same time a great power and a "strategic partner", but far less important than Asian neighbours (Japan, India, the ASEAN), the USA or the West in general: China is "significantly more committed to engagement with the United States, East Asia, and the European Union than it is to Sino-Russian 'strategic partnership'—energy deals notwithstanding".[461] China's approach to Russia is, too, full of contradictions: "on the one hand, Russia is considered to be China's

458 B. Góralczyk, *Chiński feniks. Paradoksy wschodzącego mocarstwa* [The Chinese Phoenix. The Paradoxes of a Rising Power], Warszawa 2010.

459 Hu Jintao, *Hold High the Great Banner of Socialism with Chinese Characteristics and Strive for New Victories in Building a Moderately Prosperous Society in All*, Report to 17th Party Congress.

460 K. Kozłowski, *Państwo Środka*… p. 55.

461 B. Lo, *Russia and The New World Disorder*…, p. 207.

major neighbour, its most important partner; on the other hand Russia is declining and has little to offer to China."[462]

That is why Russia's position in China's foreign policy may be called: "the most important secondary partner". If properly treated, this partner may be quite useful in foreign policy (securing strategic back-up, assuring energy supplies, providing an ideological opposition against the West) and domestic matters (the necessity for completing modernization). Besides, Russia is an important example of proof that China indeed is "peaceful". Russia carries much less importance for China than the other way round: Moscow is a useful source of supplies deeply needed in the modernizing project, albeit not the only one nor the most reliable. It is not however an ally in confrontation with the West (it is a convenient smokescreen behind which China can hide and win the interests of the Chinese quietly). Russia is insignificant to the Chinese domestic policy and is not central in Beijing's foreign policy: it is only a complement to the general strategy of "returning to the right place."[463]

From the Chinese perspective, Russia is a partner of limited trust and limited usefulness. For Beijing, in relations with Russia "the main weakness is the absence of a substantial economic foundation; there is too much geopolitics and too little economy."[464] Nevertheless, geopolitics can be useful, too. Despite the limitations of the Russia-China relationship, it can be very useful to China in tactical games with the West and so Beijing will push Russia to keep doing so. Besides that, in the Chinese policy towards Russia, concrete things matter: securing the strategic rear and the stability of energy supplies from the Russian Far East that is important – the rest is of less significance. China needs "peace from the North" and Russia guarantees it.

The new leadership of Xi Jinping's foreign policy, including policy towards Russia, has been influenced by the "dreamers" school. Although Xi Jinping's foreign policy is still *in statu nascendi*[465], one may dare to indicate a few most important features. Jin Canrong from Renmin University distinguished 4 most important concepts of Xi's foreign policy: maintaining good relations with the USA, the EU and Russia and with regional powers; more active policy in resolving problems with neighbors, more international engagement (via special envoys, modelled on the USA policy).[466] To put it in a less diplomatic way: Xi's policy is based on hierarchical principles of building relations with great powers first, then with neighbors, then with leading developing countries and finally on using multilateral organization as a useful political instrument.[467] In

462 M. Kaczmarski, *Russia-China Relations*..., p. 49.

463 Personal conversations, Beijing and Shanghai 2009-2015.

464 M. Kaczmarski, *Russia-China Relations*..., p. 49.

465 Xi's policy strategy was presented on 29 November 2014 during party's cadres' conference and later included in his book, *The governance of China*, Beijing, 2014, p. 38.

466 Jin Canrong, *Chinese Foreign Policy. New Trends*, lecture, Warsaw 14.05.2014.

467 Yu Bin, *Pivot to Eurasia*...

practice this means an attempt to establish "the dialogue of equals" with the USA without giving ground (see: inclusion to the 18th party congress report such phrases as "neointerventionism" together with "hegemonism" and "power politics" for the first time)[468] and growing assertiveness, if not toughness towards neighbors and geopolitical competitors (Japan, India).

In these circumstances of new, growing assertiveness, Beijing's new policy towards Russia is being built. Officially China strives to build "a new model of major-country relationship"[469], based on the "respect for each side's "core interests"[470]: in this new approach Russia is being considered the "most important strategic partner"[471], while relations with Moscow are a "partner-but-not-alliance relationship".[472] This rhetoric, naturally, plays on Russian heartstrings, but it is not true. The United States remains the reference point for China[473] and these kind of communiqués of strengthening cooperation with Russia are being deliberately sent to Washington. As for current Sino-Russian relations, both sides do not respect their own "core interests" fully. Nevertheless, contradictions do not cross "thin red lines" which cannot be said about Russian-US relations (see: Ukraine) or Sino-US relations (see: the US pivot to Asia). Xi Jinping in his emerging foreign policy is striving to build: par relations with the USA; "great power" relations with other important players (the UE, India, Russia) based on the *Realpolitik* model (mutual respect for own zones of influence); relations with regional leaders (such as Indonesia in South East Asia) based on "big-small brother" model; and politics of subordination of smaller neighbors. How, in light of present economic problems, this ambitious policy will be fulfilled remains to be seen.

6. *Russia and China in International Organizations, Groups and Forums*

In international multilateral organizations (the UN), groups (the G8, the G20) and forums (the BRICS), the asymmetry in favour of China is very clearly seen. Only in the UN can Russia can claim a more or less equal position to China, though even there it is *de facto* weaker. In the G20 and the BRICS China's dominance is obvious.

---

468 M. Swaine, *The 18th Party Congress and Foreign Policy: The Dog that Did Not Bark?*, The Hoover Institution, 14.01.2014.

469 *Foreign Minister Wang Yi on Major-Country Diplomacy with Chinese Characteristics*, World Peace Forum 27.03.2013.

470 F. Godement, *Xi Jinping's…*

471 *Golden opportunity to hone world-defining China-Russia partnership*, "China Daily", 22.10.2013.

472 Yu Bin, *H-Bomb Plus THAAD Equals Sino-Russian Alliance?*, "Comparative Connections" vol. 18, No. 1.

473 B. Góralczyk, *Chińskie sny* [The Chinese Dreams], "Obserwator finansowy", 21.07.2013.

China and Russia since the 1990s have been calling for a strengthening of the UN role.[474] This may appear contradictory, given the UN post-national and multilateral agenda and Russia's and China's attachment to the 19th century diplomacy style. This has, however, nothing to do with the UN's political agenda, but with the very simple fact that Russia and China enjoy a privileged position within the UN Security Council and want to keep it. This position within the Council, where they can veto Western projects (they usually do it together to share the criticism), is much stronger than their international position. This particularly concerns Russia for which the UN Security Council is important due to image reasons: it is "the most visible symbol of Russia's formal equality with the United States" and it "represents the most effective means of limiting or counterbalancing American power: exercising the veto, or, better still, the implicit threat of its use, is seen as a key guarantee of Russia's continuing centrality in global affairs (…) a way of forcing the United States to take Russia seriously."[475] For China this is important mean of enhancing its global importance, yet not the only one. Thus, Moscow and Beijing have good reason to support the UNSC (and to block its enlargement). Within the organization, however, China's position is much stronger than Russia's one, particularly in the General Assembly.[476]

As for the G8, for long it represented the stronger international position of Russia over China despite its lesser economic potential. Despite not fitting economically with the rest of the group, Moscow treated the G8 as a good playground for its need for prestige and great power credentials. Certainly, it privileged Moscow over Beijing which was absent in this equation. After the global economic crisis, however, the G8 position was undermined and Russia lost this footing completely when it was removed from the group after the Ukrainian crisis. In the meantime, the importance of the G20 grew, with China as the central country there, second only to the USA. Thanks to a wise policy of mediating between the Western and the developing world (China still considers itself a part of it), "perhaps without intending to, China took over the role that Russia had aspired to fulfill"; this in turn led to a decreasing of Russia's role, which since the 2008 crisis has kept a low profile in the G20.[477] The G20 and Russia's weak position within it is the best illustration of the truth that "few countries see Russia as a serious contributor to international public goods; they are not so much concerned about the morality of Moscow's actions as dismissive of its ability to make a positive difference (…) there is widespread

474 For example, *Совместная декларация об основах взаимоотношений между Российской Федерации и Китайской Народной Республикой* [Joint Declaration on Principles of Interrelations Between RF and PRC], [in:] *Сборник российско-китайских договоров 1949-1999…*, p. 150.

475 B. Lo, *Russia and The New World Disorder …*, p. 75.

476 M. Kaczmarski, *Russia-China Relations…*, p. 139.

477 Ibid., pp. 135-136.

perception, in the non-West as well as the West, that Russia has little to offer beyond naysaying."[478]

The story with the BRIC(S) is a bit different. In the case of this forum, analyses that come from non-member-states often emphasize the limitations alongside the notion that the BRICS countries "focus on the negative: they agree on what they disagree" – on dislike of the Western values and the post-national world.[479] But this is more than enough. The BRICS is first and foremost a political forum. It is more important than the Western critics would like it to be and less important than the non-Western apologists would hope it could be. The BRICS is a useful formula for member-states, a tool to use when needed and to ignore when not.

The BRICS has been very useful for Russia and China alike. If one may describe the BRICS' usefulness for Russia in one sentence, it would be: "it enhances its global influence at very little cost."[480] It meets the global needs for having an alternative to the West, it places Russia alongside the "rising powers" (though this is quite unnatural, since Russia has little in common with developing states) and builds its ego. The BRICS is useful for Russia and Russia is useful for others in the BRICS, so despite the fact that the BRICS could exist without Russia, there is no need to remove Russia from this body. Just as Western powers accepted Russia in the G7 for a long time (although its presence there was even more bizarre), the BRICS member-states accept its presence there now. The BRICS has unequivocally supported Russia, which gave Moscow an ephemeral feeling of creating an alternative to the West.[481] However, even if such an alternative would ever materialize, it would be a long process. success is uncertain and depends mostly on China – the most important country of the BRICS that dominates the organization. China was able to shape the BRICS in accordance to Beijing's vision (a non-political bloc that functions in accordance with the economic logic)[482] rather than an anti-Western political institutional alternative in the global dimension (as Russia wanted); thus: "China shapes the overall agenda of the BRICS (…) [and] in its current form benefits first and foremost its strongest participant, i.e. China."[483] Russia may like India or Brazil more, but building any global alternative must be based on China. Consequently, the BRICS is yet another aspect of international politics where Moscow's dependence on China increases instead of decreasing.

---

478 B. Lo, *Russia and The New World Disorder*…, pp. 72 and 211.

479 *Why Russia needs the BRICS*, Global Public, 2013/09/03; R. Weitz, *Is BRICS a Real Bloc*…

480 Д. Тренин, *Верные друзья*…

481 Z. Keck, *Why Did BRICS Back Russia on Crimea?*, "The Diplomat" 31.03.2014.

482 А.В. Лукин, *От нормализации к стратегическому партнерству*… p. 369.

483 M. Kaczmarski, *Russia-China Relations*…, p. 144.

7. *The Alexander Nevsky Paradigm?*

The dramatic events in Ukraine made Russia turn to China in order to withstand subsequent Western pressure and sanctions. After policy consideration in Kremlin, it was decided that the only chance to withhold the sanctions was to ally with China. Thus "pivot to Asia" was resurrected, or rather "pivot to China" born. But the rationale for this policy was chosen very interestingly. Russian analysts and policy makers started to refer current policy to the 13th century Ruthenian prince Alexander Nevsky. Thus this policy name can informally be called "Alexander Nevsky paradigm".

Alexander Nevsky (1221-1263) ruled as Grand Prince of Vladimir (1252-1263), at that time the center of Ruthenian political life. He became famous because of his military victories over the Swedish at Neva in 1240 and the Livonian Brothers of the Sword (Germans) at the Battle on the Ice (on Peipus Lake) that saved Ruthenia from the danger from the West. At the same time he agreed to pay tribute to the Mongols (who invaded and subjugated Ruthenia just a few years earlier) in order to strengthen his personal power over the bojars (as the critics say) and/or to be able to defend Ruthenia from the West (as the followers say). Nevsky also rejected the offer of the Pope to convert to Catholicism, to became a king and to fight together against the Mongols. Instead, he remained a vassal to the Mongolian Empire and took part in the Mongolian punitive expedition to Novgorod the Great. Nevsky died on his way back from Sarai, the capital of the Golden Horde (according to some voices he was poisoned, though the strong evidence is lacking). Before death he took monastic vows, after death he became canonized by the Orthodox Church.

In 2011 Putin called Nevsky a "shining example of serving Fatherland", who "did everything to unite everyone who loves Russia around his ideas and to make it prosper"; "despite the very difficult situation of Ruthenia's division, he started the momevemt towards unification of Russia."[484] Since then by "appealing to the legacy of Nevsky (…) Putin links defense of Russia's distinctive civilization, including religion with today's struggle against multiple threats from the West, whether ideas of freedom or programs to develop missile defense (…) existential threat to Russia."[485] In July 2014, in the moment of intensification of the Ukrainian crisis, Dmitri Trenin compared the current attitude of Russia towards China to the policy of Alexander Nevsky, who "successfully fought Western invaders while remaining loyal to the Mongol

484 *Путин привел Александра Невского как пример патриота* [Putin Showed Alexander Nevsky as an example of patriot], Gazeta.Ru, 23.05.2011.

485 G. Rozman, *The Sino-Russian Challenge…*, p. 122.

khans.[486] This reflected the domestic debate in Russia on the changing paradigms of foreign policy.[487] More importantly, however, the person of Nevsky was invoked by Russian Foreign Ministry Sergei Lavrov in his article on historical perspective of Russian politics. He wrote that the "Mongolian period was extremely important for the assertion of the Russian State's independent role in Eurasia" and "History doesn't confirm the widespread belief that Russia has always camped in Europe's backyard and has been Europe's political outsider". According to him, Nevsky "opted to temporarily submit to [the] Golden Horde rulers, who were tolerant of Christianity, in order to uphold the Russians' right to have a faith of their own and to decide their fate, despite the European West's attempts to put Russian lands under full control and to deprive Russians of their identity". Thanks to Nevsky's policy, Ruthenia "bent under but was not broken by the heavy Mongolian yoke, and managed to emerge from this dire trial as a single state, which was later regarded by both the West and the East as the successor to the Byzantine Empire that ceased to exist in 1453". Lavrov concluded "I am confident that this wise and forward-looking policy is in our genes."[488]

The context of this article is very clear. Russia instead of being "an outsider" in the West chooses to temporarily accept the dominance of a stronger state in the East hoping that thanks to it, Moscow will be able to uphold the pressure and wait out better times. Thus this approach may be called "Alexander Nevsky's paradigm". It remains to be seen whether it will be a long-term political shift or a short-term political twist shrugged off once relations with the West improve again.

8. Summary: The Changing International Roles

The years 1991-2017 have seen China's continued rise and Russia's sinusoid decline, rise and again decline. Nevertheless, up to until the 2000s, Russia was considered a more important player on the global scene. Since then and despite China's (then) attempts to keep low profile, Beijing has been steadily becoming more important globally. After the economic crisis in 2008, the situation improved for China and deteriorated even further for Russia: "as China has been accumulating more political and economic power, its relevance for the

486 D.Trenin, *China's Victory in Ukraine…*

487 *Лекторий СВОП: Почему Россия никак не может попасть в Европу* [Why Russia Cannot Land in Europe], SVOP.Ru, 24.05.2016; Александр Разуваев: *У России есть два достойных союзника* [Russia Has Two Noble Allies], Vzglyad.Ru 10.07.2015.

488 *Статья Министра иностранных дел России С.В.Лаврова «Историческая перспектива внешней политики России», опубликованная в журнале «Россия в глобальной политике» 3 марта 2016 года* , MID.Ru, 03.03.2016; in English: *Sergey Lavrov's article "Russia's Foreign Policy: Historical Background" for "Russia in Global Affairs" magazine*, Mid.ru 03.03.2016,

international order has been increasing; in the case of Russia, the economic recession stopped its process of resurgence, limiting Russia's importance (...) China has been gradually, and often inadvertently, taking over Russia's role as the West's major counterpart."[489] At the same time Russia started being viewed "by many countries as little better than a spoiler, with neither the capacity nor the inclination to solve global problems".[490] Russia is losing to China also in another aspect – soft power. Economically and culturally (*soft power*) Russia has little to offer to the world – "Russia's soft power potential has not reached beyond the post-Soviet area and has been seriously tarnished by the Ukrainian crisis of 2014."[491] The fact that Russian popular culture is very popular in the post-Soviet area "does not mean that their peoples wish to join the Russian Federation or to be an appendage of a 'Russian world' as envisaged by the Kremlin."[492] Beyond the Russian-speaking area, Russia is simply not attractive. China, on the other hand, is a globally acknowledged actor with an important role in the world.

The growing importance of China in the late 2000s and the early 2010s made Beijing more assertive – it started engaging more internationally and – what is particularly important – it raised its profile. According to some, the 2008/9 crisis "turned confidence to arrogance in China" and made "Chinese leaders prone to triumphalism."[493] Certainly, the rising dispute with Japan over the Senkaku/Diaoyu Islands and the growing Chinese assertiveness in the disputed islands of the South China Sea are the best examples of this new approach. This all testifies that for Xi Jinping China is already a great power, not only a "partial power."[494]. To paraphrase a well-known Deng Xiaoping's quote, one may say that Xi's China raised its head.

Perhaps it did it prematurely – economic turbulences in 2015 made China "wake up from the Chinese dream" – "the dreamers" who advocated ambitious foreign policy are losing ground for reformers now.[495] It remains to be seen to what extent China's economic slowdown and growing USA-China competition will affect China's international position and consequently influence China-Russia relations.

489 M. Kaczmarski, *Russia-China Relations*..., p. 155.
490 Ibid., p. 88.
491 Ibid., p. 25.
492 B. Lo, *Russia and The New World Disorder*..., p. 60.
493 G. Rozman, *The Sino-Russian Challenge*..., pp. 147-178.
494 D. Shambaugh, *China Goes Global. The Partial Power*, Oxford University Press, 2013.
495 B. Góralczyk, *Twarda pobudka z chińskiego snu* [Tough Awakening from the Chinese Dream], "Obserwator Finansowy", 28.12.2015.

Part One: Geopolitics and Beyond: Bilateral Political Relations 1991-2017

This chapter shows the changing, sinusoidal dynamism of Russia-China bilateral political relations from 1991 utill early 2017. It concentrates on a chronological presentation of events in order to elaborate the growing asymmetry in favour of Beijing. It focuses mostly on bilateral relations; although other aspects (such as Central Asia or Asia-Pacific) are mentioned, they are described in detail in further chapters.

1. Before 1991: Overshadowed by Russia

In the mid 19th century Russia exploited China's weakness and enforced relinquishment of the Amur basin and the Ussiriyiski Krai. Thanks to the activities of two extraordinary individuals – commander Gennadi Nevelski and East Siberia governor count Nikolai Muravyov-Amurski – Russia was able to cut the biggest part of the "Chinese cake" without a fight. From a Russian perspective it was a historical justice. From a Chinese perspective the annexation treaties in Aigun (1858) and Beijing (1860) are considered "unequal" – enforced on China by colonial powers. Since the mid 19th century, the model of Sino-Russian relations radically changed in favour of Russia that dominated the relations.

This advantage was maintained during the subsequent Soviet period. Since the very beginning, the USSR controlled and dominated, even created in a way, the communist movement in China. The Soviet influences were halted by Chiang Kai-shek's repressions. Chinese communists withdrew to the countryside where Mao Zedong's nationalistic faction took lead. Mao, being more nationalist than communist, despite heavy material support from Moscow and formal subjectivity to Stalin, was nevertheless able to remain independent. Chinese communists took power with a little help from Stalin (until the end of the Chinese civil war Stalin played on both sides, by maintaining contacts with both communists and the KMT nationalists). That is why from the beginning of the foundation of the People's Republic of China (the PRC), Chinese communists, despite de facto submission, strived to achieve maximum autonomy – and succeeded after Stalin's death. China's position in the communist movement rose steadily to such extent that in the late 1950s Beijing was able to challenge the USSR as the communist movement's leader. Although China lost this competition, rivalry led to a Sino-Soviet split that ended with clashes over Damansky/Zhenbao Island (won by the USSR). After these events China made a spectacular U-turn and joined the West, while Sino-Soviet relations almost ceased to exist; their normalization happened no sooner than in 1989.

The "Soviet" era of Moscow-Beijing relations was characterized by dominant influence of the USSR that permanently interferred with Chinese affairs, and by the ambiguous attitude of the Chinese communists who saw the USSR as a model for social and political modernization, but at the same time considered it a threat to the Chinese sovereignty.

Normalization of Sino-Soviet relations was fulfilled during Mikhail Gorbachev's visit to Beijing in May 1989 (before, throughout the 1980s, the normalization process was slowly under way). Nevertheless, this was the USSR's last moment of existence: the process of its dissolution already started. The Chinese leadership watched it with horror, remembering Tiananmen and associated it with domestic chaos and dissolution threat. The Chinese blamed Gorbachev for this state of affairs but nonetheless supported him in public – they considered Yeltsin's alternative far worse. They were, however, able to keep their criticism to themselves which bore fruits later. This last period of Sino-Soviet relations (1989-1991), beside the normalization of the relations, was marked by the signing of the border agreement in May 1991: it normalized the border issue and gave China back most of the disputed islands on Amur and Ussuri (including the Damansky/Zhenbao Island) in accordance with international legal standards. Several places, however, were excluded from this agreement – their status was finally resolved only in 2008.

The fall of the USSR and the lowering of Russia's status on the one hand, and market reforms and impressive economic growth of China on the other hand, decisively changed the dynamics of the bilateral relations. In consequence, China steadily gained advantage over Russia in the bilateral relations. This tendency not only did not slow in time, but even increased and intensified.

2. *From Lack of Interest to Rapprochement*

The year 1991 must be considered the *limes* (latin: boundary) – the limit point in the newest history of Russia. The fall of the USSR and its consequences weakened Russia. It remained, however, an important international and regional power. China, on the other hand, was strengthened by successful reforms, but weakened by Tiananmen repercussions – Western embargo on sales of arms and ideological anathema. In 1991, "Russia was the superpower's successor while China was the emerging power".[496]

Initially, Sino-Russian relations were determined by reserve and caution, a political *désintéressement*, "as if both countries turned their back on each other,

496 J. L. Wilson, *Strategic Partners. Russian-Chinese Relations in the Post-Soviet Era*, London 2004, p. 143.

and concentrated their foreign policy activities on different dimensions."[497] For "Atlantists" that ruled Russia, only the West mattered – it was the political and economic pattern of the reforms; China was associated with the Tiananmen massacre and possible threats in the future. For them, China was low on the agenda even in Asia – it fell behind Japan, India or South Korea. That is why relations with China became of secondary importance for Russia in 1992.[498]

Obstructed by the West, China concentrated on its neighborhood by developing and normalizing relations with its neighbors. The Chinese were unsympathetic for Yeltsin and his group of reformers, considering them the culprit of the USSR's fall and – consequently a hypothetical domestic threat for China (Yeltsin, on the other hand, also remembered the Chinese affronts to him during the last years of the USSR). The Chinese leadership, however, did not depart from one of China's foreign policy priorities: to accept the neighbors as they are.[499] Beijing quickly understood the benefits of good neighborhood policy with the new Russia – such as tranquillity in Central Asia, regional balance and counterweight for the US and Japanese influences in the Asia-Pacific region. A perspective of Russia's inclusion into the Western world meant an unwanted pressure for China – the last socialist power; finally, the decline of the USSR cancelled any threat for China from the North.[500] That is why China quickly recognized the Russian Federation and first diplomatic encouters soon followed.[501] In this first, uneasy period of initialization of bilateral contacts, overshadowed by mutual suspicions and resentments, it was important that both states inherited from the Soviet-China relations the institutional framework that was now reconstructed without major substantial changes.[502]

The diplomatic ice on the highest level was broken during Yeltsin's visit to Beijing in 1992.[503] It was the first Russian Federation President's visit to the

497 B. Rychłowski, *Stosunki Chiny – Rosja w okresie transformacji (Russia-China relations in Transformation Era)*, [in]: *Rosja-Chiny. Dwa modele transformacji (Russia-China. Two models of Transformation)*, Toruń 2000, p. 22.

498 Ю. М. Галенович, *История взаимоотношений России и Китая, к. IV* [The History of Bilateral Relations of Russia and China], Москва 2011, с. 26; Бажанов Е.П. *Эволюция внешней…*, p. 486-490; J. L. Wilson, *Strategic Partners…*, p. 145; Y. V. Tsyganov, *Russia and China: What is in the Pipeline?*, [in:] *Russia and Asia: The Emerging Security Agenda*, ed. G. Chufrin, New York 1999, p. 302.

499 А.В. Лукин, *От нормализации к стратегическому партнерству…*, pp. 302-303.

500 E. Wishnick, *Mending Fences. The Evolution of Moscow's China Policy from Brezhnev to Yeltsin*, Seattle, University of Washington Press 2001, p. 122; Li Jingjie, op. cit., p. 74.

501 On 27 December 1991 China's foreign minister Qian Qichen has recognized Russian Federation in his telegram, *История отношений России и КНР* [The Historu of Russian-Chinese relations], РИА Новости, 03.26.2007.

502 Li Jingjie, op. cit., p. 75; Ю. М. Галенович, *История взаимоотношеий…*, p. 25-26; J. L. Wilson, *Strategic Partners…*, p. 25.

503 Thoroughout 1992 there were meetings on top level (Yeltsin-Li Peng in the UN), on the level of foreign ministers and visits of officials dealing with military relations (arms sales); this has built the ground for Yeltsin's visit in December 1992, А. Бородавкин, *Россия и*

People's Republic of China and the first meeting of Yeltsin with Jiang Zemin. Yeltsin came to China during a difficult domestic situation: he was under pressure from a part of his team that wanted to lead an alternative foreign policy and was criticized by the nationalistic opposition for leaning to the West.[504] This criticism was associated with more general disappointment with the "Atlantic" foreign policy of Russia: unrealistic expectations of help, investments and "equal treatment" from the West gave way to a bitter disappointment. The perceived failure of the Western economic model of "the Washington consensus" was "accentuated by conspiracy theories alleging that those were intended to weaken, not reform, Russia."[505] In this situation, Yeltsin used this visit to demonstrate that Russian politics are not concentrated entirely on the West. On the other side, the Chinese leadership, still isolated after Tiananmen and seeing itself as the target of the West[506], welcomed this visit as an opportunity to strengthen the cooperation. During a two-day visit (17-19 December 1992), Yeltsin met Jiang Zemin and Li Peng, but not Deng Xiaoping (although he wanted to meet him).[507] The Russian President initially frightened his hosts: "his behaviour was vintage Yeltsin, virtually a paragon of unprofessional and indiscrete behaviour": in a press conference he disclosed that he had previously considered China as a country 'very much in one mold, under the Party's heel' and that Deng Xiaoping was "not in good health"; subsequently he cut short his visit by a day in order to return to Moscow and deal with domestic political struggles.[508] Soon however, when Yeltsin started praising Chinese successes for avoiding revolutionary means and shock methods – he started to be liked very much by his Chinese hosts.[509] They realized that "Yeltsin's anticommunism is not anti-Chinese."[510] Two sides signed a bombastic "declaration on principles of bilateral relations between the RF and the PRC"[511] that filled the legal gap, existing from 1980 (when the Soviet-Chinese treaty expired) and started a tradition of Sino-Russian joint-communiqués full with "eye-catching

Китай: по пути добрососедства и сотрудничества [Russia and China: on the Way of Good Neighboring and Cooperarion], "Проблемы Дальнего Востока" 5/2009.

504 E. Wishnick, op. cit., p. 123.

505 B. Lo, *The Axis of Convenience*..., p. 29.

506 G. Rozman, *The Sino-Russian Challenge*..., p. 163.

507 Deng showed his dislake to the man whom he considered guilty of destroying USSR, Ю. М. Галенович, *История взаимоотношеий*..., p. 33.

508 J. L. Wilson, *Strategic Partners*..., p. 26.

509 А.В. Лукин, *От нормализации к стратегическому партнерству*..., p. 306.

510 Li Jingjie, op. cit., p. 75.

511 *Совместная декларация об основах взаимоотношений между Российской Федерации и Китайской Народной Республикой* [Join declaration on mutual relations between Russian Federation and China People's Republic], [in:] *Сборник российско-китайских договоров 1949-1999*..., p. 150.

sloganeering, symbolism and summitry."[512] This led to an adaptation of a "similar position on the guiding principles of international relations"[513] (see: introduction). Besides these declarations, the two sides signed a few other agreements and documents (most of these, however, remained on paper), the most important ones being the reduction of troops on border areas, reduction of offensive arms and creation of the security zone within 200 km from the border.[514] Yeltsin's visit was a success: he described it as "ushering a new era in Russia-China relations" and "for once the hyperbole was appropriate."[515] This visit is being considered as Russia's return to the multidimensional politics after the "Western leaning."[516] It was, too, a "triumph of pragmatism and common sense" for both sides.[517]

Following the visit, Russian-Chinese contacts intensified, particularly in the economic sphere – China already in 1992 became Russia's second trade partner (mostly because of the arms sales; soon, however, it fell to the fifth position), contacts between peoples of Russia and China intensified (although this was limited in 1994 by the introduction of visas to Russia).[518] There was a continuing sense of realism of both sides, too.[519] During Yeltsin's conflict with the parliament, the Chinese stood aside and remained neutral; after Yeltsin suppressed his opponents, the Chinese leadership "displayed a distinct respect for the survival skills of Yeltsin."[520] In the initial Russian-Chinese relations what was important was a specific trend – a top-down "management" of the process of development of these relations. Closer relations between Russia and China have been built from top to bottom. Since the mid 1990s, the highest officials were meeting regularly; ministers and deputy ministers were having regular contacts via different commissions and committees. This helped to maintain a good atmosphere and prepared ground for long-term development of the relations.[521]

---

512 G. Rozman, *Sino-Russian Relations: Mutual Assessments and Predictions*, [in:] *Rapprochement or Rivalry…*, p. 147.

513 B. Lo, *The Axis of Convenience…*, p. 30.

514 *Сборник российско-китайских договоров 1949-1999…*, p. 155-197; Т. А. Шаклеина, *Внешняя политика и безопасность современной России. 1991-2002 Хрестоматия в четырех томах* [Foreign policy and Security of the Russian Federation 1991-2002], Москва 2002, т. III, p. 491.

515 B. Lo, *The Axis of Convenience…*, p. 29.

516 М. Л. Титаренко, *Россия и Восточная Азия…*, p. 124.

517 Г.В. Зиновьев, *Китай и сверхдержавы. История внешней политики КНР (1949–1991)* [China and Superpowers. History of PRC Foreign Policy 1949-1991], СПб 2010, p. 312.

518 А.В. Лукин, *От нормализации к стратегическому партнерству…*, p. 310-312.

519 В.Л. Ларип, *В тени проснувшегося дракона* [In The Shadow of the Awekeing Dragon]. Владивосток, 2006, p. 45.

520 J. L. Wilson, *Strategic Partners…*, p. 27.

521 B. Rychłowski, op. cit., p. 26.

The best example of this dynamism was the "constructive partnership" formula, created in September 1994, during Jiang Zemin's trip to Moscow.[522] It has been the first trip of the Chairman of the PRC to the Russian capital since 1957 and the first visit of the head of the Chinese state in Russia. Russians celebrated Jiang in the best tzars' way: he was hosted in the Kremlin Palace and was privileged to have a few private meetings with Yeltsin, in an unofficial way. Since then the two leaders liked each other.[523] It was not the mutual likeness, however, that made rapprochement possible, but interests. Both were interested in a stable and secure international environment. For Yeltsin, China's policy was one of the few dimensions where he was wholly supported by the political class. Disappointment with "leaning to the West", the NATO's enlargement to the East, the Western infiltration in Central Asia was widespread. In these circumstances, rapprochement with China became the logical answer for domestic and external weakness of Russia. The Kremlin started treating its policy in Asia-Pacific as a counterweight to the potential marginalization of Moscow in European affairs as well as a response to the US global influence. China's approach has been similar on this geopolitical level: these two "non-Western countries with large and unsatisfied great-power egos" seek to "to accelerate the decline of the lone superpower's preeminence in favour of multipolarity, and to block the spread of the Western civilization."[524]

There has been, however, a substantional difference between the anti-Western approach of Russia and China. Although Beijing, since 1982, has proclaimed an "independent policy" and expressed worries about American unilaterism, has nevertheless been prone to reproaching Moscow only to an extent, so that it would not lose political space to maneuver. China was not meant to create another alliance, particularly one against the USA – it just wanted to strengthen its position. At the same time China agreed to the Russian proposal of a "constructive partnership" to secure its own interests in the Russian Far East, where strong anti-Chinese resentments appeared. That is why Jiang Zemin in Moscow emphasized the bilateral economic cooperation by stressing the complementarity of Russian and Chinese economies; he hoped to overcome existing problems, quoting a Chinese saying: "it is better than to stop eating out of fear of choking."[525]

522 *Совместная Российско-китайская декларация 1994 года* [Joint Russian-Chinese declaration of 1994], [in:] *Сборник российско-китайских договоров 1949-1999...*, pp. 271-273. Besides this declaration, two sides signed *Joint declaration of Russian Federation President and China People's Republic Chairman on not directing strategic rockets*, Ibid., p. 274.

523 B. Lo, *The Axis of Convenience...*, p. 30.

524 G. Rozman, *Sino-Russian Relations. Mutual...*, p. 154.

525 Ю. М. Галенович, *История взаимоотношений...*, p. 73.

The Russian intervention in Chechnya marks the appearance of a new important factor in Sino-Russian relations: joint backing on thorny domestic issues (or the ones considered domestic), such as Taiwan, Tibet and Xinjiang and Chechnya, against international criticism. That is why in the subsequent "joint declarations", Russia and China emphasized such value as "state sovereignty", "territorial integrity" or "non-interference in domestic affairs". Russia backed the Chinese position on Taiwan and China in return did not say a word about the Russian activities in Chechnya. Chechnya was "a turning point in Russian-Chinese relations: it put an end to Russia's tendency to moralize to the Chinese about human rights."[526] Chinese prime-minister Li Peng, who visited Moscow on 25-28 June 1995, said that "we should not allow foreigners to rule in our countries."[527] For China, Russia became "the Tiananmen-proof partner, not risking the political, diplomatic, security, or commercial benefits of the relationship by criticizing the internal failings of the Chinese regime."[528]

3. *"Strategic Partnership"*

The year 1996 was crucial for Russia due to presidential elections and real concern of Yeltsin's failure. For the policy makers in the Kremlin, his reelection became the most important domestic and foreign policy task. As it turned out, it also influenced relations with China, particularly on two aspects – substitution of Andrei Kozyrev by Yegveni Primakov as Russia's foreign minister and signing a "strategic partnership" with Beijing.

Primakov, who became foreign minister on 10 January 1996, represented an entirely different vision of Russia's foreign policy: the Euroasianist one. Although his nomination might be seen as the culmination of the growing influence of supporters of euroasianism's ideas, it was nevertheless Yeltsin's election motivation that played a decisive role: he wanted to gain voters from conservative-nationalistic part of the society. It worked well: Kozyrev was personally blamed for Russia's decrease of prestige, so his removal helped Yeltsin a lot.[529]

Primakov's foreign policy – called "Euroasianist", "pragmatic" or "realistic" – is considered a breakthrough, a *limes* (latin: boundary) in Russian foreign policy. Primakov decided that Russia's security depended on Moscow's influences and that even weakened Russia may have balanced the US power by

526 J. L. Wilson, *Strategic Partners…*, p. 29.These attempts, done in early 1990s (by, among others, Kozyrev in 1992),were "strange anyway given the fact that Russia is not a ideal in this regards",А.В. Лукин, *От нормализации к стратегическому партнерству…*, p. 332.

527 Ю. М. Галенович, *История взаимоотношений…*, pp. 92-105.

528 S. W. Garnett, *Limited Partnership*, [in:] *Rapprochement or Rivarly…*, p. 11.

529 Е. Бажанов, *Эволуция внешней политики…*, p. 16; S. Bieleń, op. cit., pp. 72-76.

using the UN and be able to force the West to recognize it as a parallel power, with special interests in the "near abroad."[530] Primakov's policy was considered a Gaullism-style policy, but the real inspiration for Primakov came from the 19th century Russia's prince Alexander Gorchakov who had orchestred Moscow's foreign policy for 26 years and rebuilt Russia's position after the defeat in the Crimea war.[531] Primakov himself "was thoroughly at home with *Realpolitik* calculations" and was, like his Chinese counterparts, a firm adherent of the efforts to develop a multipolar world."[532] Here China was the key – Primakov did not even tried to conceal it: "Russia's Kissinger and architect of the Primakov Doctrine espoused a Sino-Russian (…) alliance against Western unilaterism."[533] Primakov, too, was highly valued in Beijing, where his nomination, marking a turn in Russian foreign policy[534], was accepted with satisfaction: "the same qualities in Primakov that aroused suspicion and distrust in the West were welcomed by China's leaders, who looked upon Primakov's career in the Soviet and Russian intelligence services as proof of his competence and expertise. In the Chinese view, Primakov was a consummate professional."[535] Nevertheless, Primakov's influence was not exclusive: Yeltsin's second term saw "dual-track" leaderships: on the one side there were "pragmatists" around Primakov that strived for global balance; on the other side, there was economy apparatus, whether guided by Anatolyi Chubais, Boris Nemtsov, or Sergei Kiriyenko, that worked closely with international organizations and looked for Russia's financial support there.[536]

The other key event in 1996, or maybe even in the whole decade of the 1990s, for Russia and China, was the proclamation of the "strategic partnership". It happened during the third top-level Russian-Chinese meeting, during Yeltsin's trip to Beijing (24-26 April 1996). It took place during the Russian presidential campaign, a few weeks before the first round. Chinese leadership, although formally neutral, was anxious about the possible outcome and silently hoped for Yeltsin's victory. Beijing feared that the alternative of Gennady Ziuganov or Vladimir Zhirinovski might lead to an increase in Russian nationalism, particularly in the Russian Far East; the Chinese preferred Yeltsin who

---

530 *Выступление министра иностранных дел РФ Е.М. Примакова на 51-й сессии Генеральной Ассамблей ООН* [Foreign Ministry Y.M. Primakov's Speech at 51 Session of UN General Assembly], [in:] *Внешняя политика России 1996* [Foreign Policy of Russia in 1996], Москва 2001, p. 449.

531 G. Chufrin, *Asia as a factor in Russia's international posture*, [in:] *Russia and Asia…*, p. 493.

532 J. L. Wilson, *Strategic Partners…*, p. 149.

533 M. L. Levin, *The Next Great Clash. China and Russia vs. The United States*, Westport–London 2008, p. 130.

534 A.B. Лукин, *От нормализации к стратегическому партнерству…*, p. 322.

535 J. L. Wilson, *Strategic Partners…*, pp. 30 and 149.

536 G. Rozman, *Sino-Russian Relations. Mutual…*, p. 158.

guaranteed stability.[537] That is why "Jiang welcomed Yeltsin in an unusually personal manner in April 1996, helping him to defeat his opponent, Ziuganov."[538] The other important factor that influenced this meeting was the international situation – a political crisis in Taiwan strait was taking place and the USA has just signed a joint declaration on security with Japan.[539]

That is why Moscow and Beijing not only traditionally backed each other on their political positions, but they also wanted to send a clear signal to Washington that the USA should take their interests into account. They wanted to "make this relationship appear stronger than it is"[540] (particularly Russia). This is how the "Western factor" since the mid 1990s became "the immanent factor in Russian-Chinese rapprochement and deepening of cooperation."[541] Anti-Western resentments were "fueled by humiliation and redemption and expressed itself in strident nationalism."[542] All that contributed to the fact that during the Yeltsin's visit, both sides manifested their rapprochement and friendly relations and decided to include the term "strategic partnership" in their joint declaration in 1996.[543]

It was Yeltsin who proposed this term: he tried to present it as a much bigger rank that that it was in reality (his was a way to compensate the subsequent PR failures on the international scene)[544]; Yeltsin himself confirmed this almost literally by saying: "to be respected from the West, we must cooperate with China."[545] "Strategic partnership" was to play an important role in strengthening Russia's international position, particularly in light of a visible disappointment in Western policy. China was supposed to become Russia's "bargaining card."[546] This revealed a wishful thinking characteristic for the Russian elite – most of them wanted to see relations with China as more important than they actually were. This attitude was typical for Russian culture, with its proneness to the extremes: "if it is friendship, then it must be as close as in the 1950s; if

---

537 E. Wishnick, op. cit., pp. 129-130.

538 G. Rozman, *The Sino-Russian Challenge…*, p. 245.

539 *Japan-U.S. Joint Declaration On Security – Alliance For The 21st Century*, Japan MFA, 17.04.1996.

540 G. Rozman, *The Sino-Russian Challenge…*, p. 263.

541 Ю. М. Галенович, *История взаимоотношений…*, p. 114.

542 M. L. Levin, op. cit., p. 99.

543 *Совместная декларация Российской Федерации и Китайской Народной Республики 1996* [Joint Declaration of Russian Federation and China People's Republic], 25.04.1996, [in:] *Сборник российско-китайских договоров 1949-1999…*, pp. 333-337.

544 L. Buszynski, *Overshadowed by China: The Russia-China Strategic Partnership in the Asia-Pacific Region*, [in:] *The Future of China-Russia…*, p. 266; E.Wishnick, op. cit., p. 130; Ю. М. Галенович, *История взаимоотношений…*, p. 119.

545 Е. Бажанов, *Актуалные проблемы международных отношений* [The Present Problems of International Relations], Москва 2002, т. 2, p. 419.

546 А. Воскресенский, *Китай и Россия* [China and Russia] p. 494; idem, *Russia's Evolving Grand Strategy toward China*, [in:] *Rapprochement or Rivalry…*, p. 124; Y. V. Tsyganov, op. cit., p. 304.

it is hostility, then it must be as dangerous as the old armed conflicts between Soviet and Chinese border guards on the Island of Damansky."[547]

The Chinese were clearly and effectively blocking these attempts. The PRC's preferred policy was not to join any alliances or political-military blocs. Chinese leadership under Jiang Zemin clearly stated that relations with Russia were being built on the rule "neither alliance, nor confrontation" and never went beyond this slogan.[548] Chen Qimao commented that a strategic partnership "is characterized by three 'nons' – non-confrontation, non-alliance and non-aiming at any third country."[549] Xi Laiwan added: "being good neighbours, good partners and good friends."[550] Dmitri Trenin commented: "China feels no need for alliance, especially with a weak and unpredictable Russia, and will never agree to Moscow's leadership"; the essence of "strategic partnership" with Moscow is to strengthen the security interests of Beijing: the "partnership will guarantee that Russia will not participate in any potential anti-Chinese coalitions (…) the isolation of China will never be complete thanks to the Russian 'safety velvet.'"[551] The "strategic partnership" is the best example of Beijing's pragmatic and long-term approach to Moscow: China "reconciled itself to the Kremlin's Westerncentrism (…) what mattered more to Beijing was that the 'strategic partnership' should serve concrete priorities: backing for its position on Taiwan, Tibet and Xinjiang; security building on China's northern and western frontiers; ensuring a steady stream of advanced weaponry; and political support for China's efforts to play a more active role in the world; to achieve these aims, the Communist leadership could (and did) put up with a lot."[552] Finally, for the Chinese, "strategic partnership" "fits into key tenets of Chinese foreign policy."[553] This is simply a comfortable, very capacious formula thanks to which China may develop cooperation with its bigger neighbor while winning the Chinese interests abroad.

The signing of the "strategic partnership" is a symbolic moment in Sino-Russian relations in the 1990s. Although enthusiastic voices about the beginning of a "new era" and uplifting Moscow-Beijing relations into the level unseen from the 1950s were exaggerated (during the 1990s the "strategic partnership" functioned mainly in rhetoric)[554], nevertheless the "strategic partnership" symbolized a new period in Sino-Russian relationship: it became similar to typical bilateral relations with its dominant pragmatism and emphasis on

547 A.Voskressenski, *Russia's Evolving…*, p. 118.

548 *Chinese Rule Out Alliance*, "The Moscow Times", 1997, 25 IV.

549 Chen Qimao, *Sino-Russian relations after the break-up of the Soviet Union*,[in:] *Russia and Asia…*, p. 298.

550 Quoted in: А.В. Лукин, *От нормализации к стратегическому партнерству…*, p. 309.

551 D. Trenin, *The China Factor …*, pp. 46-53.

552 B. Lo, *The Axis of Convenience…*, p. 32.

553 E. Wishnick, *Why a 'Strategic Partnership'? The View from China*, [in:] *The Future of China-Russia…*, p. 56.

554 J. L.Wilson, *Strategic Partners…*, p. 148.

economic issues; Russia and China became “simply neighbours”, the normalization of relations fulfilled their most vital interests.[555] For Moscow “strategic partnership” became one of the very few diplomatic successes in Asia and a vital reminder of Russian potential in seeking non-Western partners: “improved relations with China was (…) a major achievement” – Moscow “managed to end its parallel Cold War in the East on what looked like honourable terms.”[556] For Beijing the “strategic partnership” was one of the very symbols of its growing global position, a part of the most important policy goal – to become a global power. A normalization of the relationship with Russia was an important part of this strategy, though not its core. Moscow was needed politically, economically and militarily – and from the Chinese point of view it fulfilled its role. However, despite noticeable success in the relations between the two countries, Russia still remained West-dependent. This turned out to be particularly true during Yeltsin’s second term.

In the second part of the 1990s both sides were hurrying up to use the good conjuncture for negotiating and signing the most important documents and address the unresolved matters that might have got complicated should the conjuncture change. Despite what Russian old China hand Igor Rogachev called mutual “anti-confrontational immunity” that apparently has been created among both elites[557], Kremlin and Zhongnanhai were unsure about the future. This explains the readiness to create structures to prevent a reversal of bilateral dynamics in the future. The Chinese were afraid of the domestic destabilization in Russia as the result of Yeltsin’s weakness; the Russians feared power-struggle in China after Deng Xiaoping’s death.[558] Examples of this attitude can be seen in signing the agreement on reduction of military forces in the border zone of post-Soviet republics and China[559] – the reduction of the army haa for a long time been a thorny issue in Soviet-Chinese relations. Its solution must be considered a turning point in the Russian-Chinese relations.[560]

---

555 В. Баранов, *Переход к партнёрским отношениям стратегического взаимодействия во взаимоотношениях россии и китая (вторая половина 1990-х гг.)* [Transition to Partnership Relationship of Strategic Interaction in Russia-China Relations], [in:] *Россия и Китай: аспекты взаимодействия и взаимовлияния материалы IV Международной заочной научно-практической конференции* [Russia and China: Aspects of Interactions i Inter-Influence, Conference Proceedings], Благовещенск 2013, pp. 14-32; Т. А. Шаклеина, *Внешняя политика и безопасность…*, т. IV, p. 538.

556 D. Trenin, The China Factor…, p. 39.

557 И.А. Рогачев, *Российско-китайские отношения в конце XX — начале XXI века* [Russia-China Relations in Late 20th and Early 21th century], Москва 2005, p. 47.

558 G. Rozman, *Sino-Russia Relations. Mutual…*, p. 155.

559 *Соглашение о взаимном сокращении вооруженных сил в районе границы между Россией, Казахстаном, Киргизией, Таджикистаном и Китаем* [Agreement on Joint Reduction of Military Forces Between Russian Federation, Kazakhstan, Kyrgyzstan, Tajikistan and China] [in:] *Сборник российско-китайских договоров 1949-1999…*, pp. 385-392.

560 E.Wishnick, *Mending fences…*, p. 131.

Despite the development of this relationship, the Russian-Chinese "strategic partnership" in 1997-1998 went through a test of reliability in the changing international arena. The improvement of Sino-American relations, Russian-Japanese relations, nuclear chases in South Asia, financial crisis in Asia – all these proved that the Sino-Russian relationship was quite narrow. Particularly against the background of the developing Sino-American relations, Beijing's cooperation with Moscow faded. It was best seen during Yeltsin's subsequent visit to Beijing (9-11 November 1997). Despite signing the demarcation of the eastern part of the border[561] – so controversial in Russia – the summit "made lowering of the so-far foregoing dynamics apparent": the documents signed avoided most important bilateral issues and "came across as filling up the diplomatic emptiness."[562] In order to conceal the substantial emptiness of this visit, the Chinese side wanted to welcome Yeltsin in the imperial style. This showed the difference in China's relations with the USA, where concrete issues mattered; as Chinese Ambassador to Moscow, Li Fenglin summarized: "between China and the USA there is cooperation without sentimentalism; between China and Russia there is sentimentalism without cooperation."[563]

The improvement of Sino-American relations showed that already then, in the late 1990s, China become the main partner of the USA. It happened mainly thanks to the different style of policy making after 1991. Russian reactions "appeared rooted in short-term calculations and a sense of humiliation (...) Russians were flailing after their palpable disappointment at the enormous loss in stature resulting from the collapse of the Soviet Union (...) they were displeased with the world order they saw emerging but reacted less with a strategy to transform that order over a long period than with sharp gestures to land some blows immediately."[564] Against this background China presented a stable and long-term policy calculated on gaining time to strengthen domestically. China needed Russia as a counterbalance to the growing Western pressure and for strengthening its army. Russia was, however, only a part of the bigger, long-term strategy of China's return to power status – here the West was the key aspect, not Russia. Cooling relations with Moscow turned out to be the unavoidable consequence of strengthening Sino-Western relations. It was not, however, the only reason. The others were: short Russian-Japanese *détente;* sudden nuclear race between India and Pakistan, and financial crisis that made

---

561 *Совместная российско-китайское заявление (о завершении демаркации восточного участка российско-китайской границы) от 10 ноября 1997 г.* [Joint Russian-Sino Announcement On Completion of Demarcation of the Eastern Part of the Border], [in:] *Сборник российско-китайских договоров 1949-1999...*, pp. 408-410.

562 B. Rychłowski, op. cit., p. 35; Among signed documents, there was an agrement on protecting tigers and on developing diamond trade, *Сборник российско-китайских договоров...* pp. 428-430.

563 Li Fenglin, *Chinese-Russian relations after the fifth summit in Beijing,* [in:] *Russia and Asia...*, p. 6.

564 G. Rozman, *Sino-Russian Relations. Mutual...*, p. 165.

the level of the economic cooperation between Russia and China was very low. Russian-Chinese relations in 1998 faced a stagnation.

All this aspects showed very well that Russia and China did not consider bilateral relations as the most important foreign policy vector. Although both sides emphasized their partnership playing a central role in their foreign policies, the facts contradicted this. The years 1997 and 1998 showed that "Russo-Chinese relations looked superficial" and were "basically limited to traditional geopolitical issues."[565] Consequently, the partnership depended "on aspects of worldview that are more changeable than national interest, such as the psychological underpinnings of national identity that guide policy."[566] Their economic interests were also located in the West. For China, the USA was much more important than Russia because in the 1998 alone trade with the USA reached 60 billion USD, whereas with Russia it was only 5.8 billion; that is why "Beijing would not risk any rapprochement with Russia that could cost it loss of dollars."[567] For Yeltsin's Russia the West remained the most important reference point, it was there where Moscow hoped to receive loans that could put Russian economy back on its feet again in 1998. This is how both China and Russia could manage to go on without each other, but could not do it without the cooperation with the USA. That is why criticism directed to the West and joint backing on international issues were only a way to strengthen their relations *vis-à-vis* the West. The domestic bond of cooperation was even weaker: irrelevant or skeptical public opinion, hesitation or resistance in the partner's most important issues, insignificance of group lobbying for cooperation and strong nationalistic factor hampering rapprochement.[568] Russia in their communication with the Chinese were "content to limit themselves to the symbols of 'high politics' and do not condescend to the 'low politics' of commercial contacts (...) economic ties were too dependent on individual shuttle traders and arms dealers."[569]

How Russia-China relations were made an appendix to their relations with the West was best indicated by the events in the fall of 1998 and spring of 1999, when US's showcase of force in Kosovo drew Russia and China closer again. Nevertheless, there was a specific difference in the attitudes: China's engagement in the Kosovo crisis was limited, whereas Russia tried to play leading role in solving the conflict. This explains difference in reactions. Russia reacted rapidly: it refused the NATO any rights to interfere in Yugoslavia's domestic affairs and Prime Minister Primakov cancelled a long-organized trip

565 D. Trenin, *The China Factor*..., pp. 40-53.
566 G. Rozman, *Sino-Russian Relations. Mutual*..., pp. 151-162.
567 A. Voskressenski, op. cit., p. 133.
568 А.В. Лукин, *От нормализации к стратегическому партнерству*..., pp. 325-326.
569 D. Trenin, *The China Factor* ..., pp. 40-54.

to Washington by ordering to turn back his flight over the Atlantic.[570] Moreover, Russia, by trying to prove that it would not allow being prevented from speaking in Balkan issues, attempted to form an anti-NATO block. China, on the other hand, kept the distance as long as its basic interests were not endangered. Prime-minister Zhu Rongji did not follow Primakov's example: he paid a visit to the USA a few days later and received the US backing for China's entry to the WTO.[571] Only when China's embassy became bombarded in Belgrade did China react harshly – but it did so to strengthen its global position and push the USA to the defence in terms of ideological issues (like human rights).[572]

The 1990s, the decade of Sino-Russian relations, were concluded by Yeltsin's farewell visit to Beijing on 9-10 December 1999 (and his last visit as the head of the Russian state). This visit had a lot of personal accounts – both Yeltsin and Jiang tried to emphasize the closeness of the relations. Yeltsin said that he had suddenly woken up at night without knowing where he was, but then he remembered "with friends, in China."[573] The extent that this "friendship" was associated with bad relations with the West[574] was revealed by Yeltsin when he launched his strongest rant against the USA: "Yesterday, Clinton permitted himself to put pressure on Russia. It seems he has for a minute, for a second, for half a minute, forgotten that Russia has a full arsenal of nuclear weapons. He has forgotten about that (…) it has never been the case, and will not be the case, that he alone dictates to the world how to live, how to work, how to rest and so on. No, and again no. Things will be as we have agreed with Jiang Zemin. We will be saying how to live, not he alone."[575] In the strained international situation this statement reverberated but – as before – turned out to be mere words from a helpless Yeltsin. This visit concluded the first part of Russia-China political relations. On 31 December 1999, Yeltsin resigned from the RF presidency. In Sino-Russian relations it equaled the end of an era. *

Sino-Russian relations in 1990s went a long way. From initial distance, if not dislike, through "constructive" and "strategic" partnership, to close ties in the end of the century. Russia and China shared a joint outlook on international affairs – a protest against political and ideological dominance of Western pow-

570 *Into the fire*, CNN, 29.03.1999.

571 *Chronology of China-US Relations*. China.Org.Cn

572 B. Rychłowski, op. cit., p. 39.

573 Ю. М. Галенович, *История взаимоотношений…*, pp. 219-223.

574 This summit concluded with signing "Joint announcement" with the stron gest critique on USA (without naming it), *Российско-Китайское совместное заявление* [Russian-Chinese Joint announcement], "Российская газета", 11.12.1999.

575 *Ельцин напомнил Клинтону и миру: Россия остается ядерной державой* [Yeltsin Reminded Clinton: Russia Remains a Nuclear Great Power], "Независимая газета", 10.12.1999; В.Суховерхов, *Дружили два товарища…* [Two Comrades Made Friends], "Московский комсомолец", 10.12.1999.

ers. This was more clearly seen in China – due to the consequences of Tiananmen, Beijing throughout the 1990s was in ideological opposition to the West. In Russia it had more to do with "wounded pride": the unfulfilled hopes of the first period of the Russian Federation. This opposition against the West united Moscow and Beijing and gave dynamics, or even essence, to their *détente* from the 1990s. It was not, however, any alliance nor bloc, but rather a reinforcement of their positions *vis-à-vis* the West. To Moscow and Beijing the West, particularly the United States, remained the fundamental reference point. One may even say that Sino-Russian relations in the 1990s were merely an appendix to their relations with the United States and other Western states.

Nonetheless, Russia and China were able to achieve several successes. The most important were the following: demilitarization and arms reduction; border demarcation; noninterference in domestic affairs; arms sales and establishment of the mechanism of cooperation (for a detailed description of these issues, see further part of this book). The reduction in military calmed down the general mood in both countries, first and foremost in China which is always vulnerable to threat from the North. Demarcation of the border, although stormy, particularly in the Russian Far East, was also in interests of both those countries. It was China again which strived for it to a greater extent: Chinese leadership followed Deng Xiaoping's maxim "peace on the border" and wanted to close this thorny chapter. For Russia, giving back a few thousand square kilometers was a difficult psycho-political task, but again – it was in the Russian long-term interest: it postponed the threat of more serious Chinese territorial claims, at least for the time being. Although the demarcation process was not finished in the 1990s, it was completed later on, which remains Yeltsin's big political win. Noninterference in domestic affairs may seem quite pale in comparison to the other achievements, but given 400-years of the history of Sino-Russian relations, it must be considered a remarkable success, particularly from Beijing's position (China hates to be advised and generously rewards those who do not do it). Arms sales – as some say the "glue" of their relations in the 1990s, was in their interest. Russia had to keep the military-industrial complex alive, while China needed to modernize the army, by-passing the Western embargo. Despite anxiety on the Russian side and mutual misunderstandings, arms sales were an important and definitely positive part of their cooperation in the 1990s. Finally, establishing the mechanism of cooperation played an important part in building the fundamentals of permanent development of the relations. Thanks to establishing institutional and structural base (such as regular meetings on top level), Russia and China created a solid ground for their future relations – this would bear fruits in the next decade. Finally, the 1990s was a difficult beginning, a lesson of avoiding mistakes which enabled a better cooperation in the next decade.

Remembering successes, one must equally strongly emphasize differences. Throughout the 1990s, the Sino-Russian partnership was not "strategic", but rather utilitarian. Where Moscow and Beijing's interests converged, there both countries supported each other (see: Central Asia). Where these interests were divergent or contradictory, Russia and China did not pay attention to one another and were ready to sacrifice the "strategic partnership" for better relations with the USA. It was particularly evident in East Asia, where China did not become Russia's "door keeper". The most important divergence, overshadowing most of the successes, or rather pushing them into background, was Russia and China's main orientation towards the West. It always had priority over the "strategic partner's" reaction: Washington was always most important for both Moscow and Beijing.

Thanks to bilateral relations, Russia and China in the 1990s were (re)building their power statuses. In 1991, both countries were more or less equal in their international status. The 1990s showed clearly how they used their time. Russia did not maintain its superpower status, badly experienced the transformation into a free market, and although it strived at all costs to maintain the prestige, it fell to secondary power status. China, with its pragmatism and lack of emotions in politics (with the exception of Taiwan issue) steadily and consequently were striving towards its fundamental goal – rebuilding its central role in East Asia and beyond. This is why in the late 1990s, China's position was already stronger than the Russia's one.

4. Changed Leadership, Continued Policy Agenda

In the first one and a half years after Putin became the president, Russia's foreign policy was a continuation of the policy from the last period of "Yeltsin's decade": with Yugoslavia and Kosovo as dominating benchmarks.[576] This way Putin's rise to power did not at the beginning have a remarkable influence on the Russian-Chinese relations. Only with time, the economic cooperation became more intense and the military cooperation developed to an even greater extent while Putin's policy became much wider in Asia than that of his predecessor.

The Chinese side reacted to the Russian top power change as usual: recognizing the Russian decision and building relations with new decision-makers. Putin, however, did not visit China for a very long time: despite the first declaration from Kremlin that the first visit of president-elect would take place in China, Putin visited the United Kingdom first, and Beijing only in July 2000. However, although he met the Chinese leaders quite late, he continued to work on bringing both countries closer. During the two days of Putin's visit (17-18 July 2000) several documents were signed, and above all the "Beijing declaration", which indicated that both countries would maintain their anti-Western

576 It was best exemplified by national security conception from 2000 г., *Концепция национальной безопасности Российской Федерации*, "Независимая газета", 14.01.2000.

course until the end of the decade.[577] The "Beijing declaration" was a typical example of the Russian-Chinese vision of the international order and highlighted the necessity to establish a multipolar order: "this rhetoric conceals the need to regain (Russia) or get (China) influences free from interference of other powers, particularly the USA."[578]

A novelty that drew attention was a reference to the willingness to sign a treaty. The initiative of signing the treaty should definitely be assigned to the Chinese side (which was unusual given China's unwillingness to bind itself to treaties)– the aim was to reinforce the international position of China and to neutralize the uncertainty with regards to Putin (his deferment to visit China and some of his statements; among other, Russia's consideration of the access to the NATO raised China's fears); they wished to "bind Putin with treaty obligations."[579] The Chinese initiative composed well with the first attempts made by Putin, who wanted to assign a higher meaning to the relations with China. The official signing of the Russian-Chinese "Treaty on good neighborliness, friendship and cooperation" took place on 16 July 2001 during Jiang Zemin's visit to Moscow (15-18 July 2001). The treaty, which was composed of 25 articles, was signed for 20 years with a possibility of an extension for the next 5 years. It emphasized the basic assumptions of Russian-Chinese relations, which had evolved during the previous decade (like the strategic partnership).[580] It was rather general, as Russia and China once again published an agreement on "everything and nothing": maximal cooperation in all possible spheres and minimal level of responsibility for the results of this cooperation.[581] It was perceived in its geopolitical dimension as closing ranks against the domination of the United States in the global order. However, this treaty was something more than just another element of the game of both countries with the United States. Its rhetoric in most important geopolitical matters was much milder than in shared communications, which indicated that it had been planned for a long time.[582] Above all, the treaty was important in bilateral issues: it was a culmination of the process of normalization within Russia-China relations[583], it was a lawful reinforcement of the "strategic partnership" and it created a legal basis for the development of relations (a mechanism of regular

---

577 *Пекинская декларация* [The Beijing Declaration], Kremlin.ru, 12.07.2000.

578 M. Kaczmarski, *Rosja na rozdrożu*..., pp. 43 and 112-113.

579 J. L. Wilson, *Strategic partners*..., p. 162; Ю. М. Галенович, *История взаимоотношений*..., pp. 342-360; Лю Гучан. *«Договор века» и создание новой реальности китайско-российских отношений*, [in:] А.В. Лукин, *От нормализации к стратегическому партнерству*..., p. 330-333.

580 *Договор о добрососедстве, дружбе и сотрудничестве*....

581 Huei-Ming Mao, *The U. S. – China – Russia Strategic Triangle Relationship-Since the Beginning of the Bush Adinistration*, "Tamkang Journal of International Affairs" 2003.

582 J. L. Wilson, *Strategic partners*..., pp. 36-164.

583 И.А. Рогачев op.cit., pp. 117-118.

meetings on the summit).[584] Although the treaty was a success for both sides, its signing was primarily China's success: Beijing was the main initiator of signing this document, Chinese leaders were the ones who prepared it, and moreover this treaty was the one that summed up achievements of the previous decade (such as non-interference in domestic issues) securing the continuation of this heritage.[585] On the other hand for Russia it was a possibility of comprehensive deepening of the cooperation with China and strengthening Russia's position in the region of Asia-Pacific.

The treaty was concluded with the motto "friends forever and enemies never again",[586] which at least in the first part of this sentence was true in 2001. However, it did not change the fact that, as the near future showed, these relations, despite "friendship", could not move out from their Western-centrism: they focused mainly on the West.

5. 11 September 2001

Anew international incident – the terrorist attack on WTC on 11 September 2001 in New York – resulted in a pro-Western turn in Moscow's politics. Using the opportunity given by this attack, Putin decided to make a crucial turn in foreign policy, acknowledging that joining the United States would be the most beneficial move for Russia: it would help regain at least a part of its superpower status, and internally it would give time for modernization and would enable it to connect the conflict in Chechnya with the war against terrorism. It was a "pragmatic calculation of Russian interests, in which revival of Russian economics was dependable on the integration with world's financial structures."[587] The new Kremlin leadership considered it a chance to renew their position in great powers club and external world recognition of the "Euroasian Monroe doctrine" – guaranteeing Russian influence in the countries of "near abroad."[588] The basic aim of this new strategy was the resignation from the competition with the United States regarding the form of the international order and from conducting global policy (apart from the rhetorics): "Putin, knowing that he cannot win with the United States, decided to bandwagon to it."[589] Russia reacted calmly on the American withdrawal from the ABM and agreed upon American conditions of the SORT treaty, moreover it agreed upon the Baltic countries' access to the NATO and redefinition of the relations with the

---

584 М. Титаренко, *Геополитическое…* pp. 269-271.

585 Ю. М. Галенович, *История взаимоотношений…*, pp. 350-364; А.В. Лукин, *От нормализации к стратегическому партнерству…*, p. 332.

586 *Россия и Китай «навеки друзья и никогда – Враги»* [Russia and China"Forever Friends Never Enemies"], Pravda.Ru 16.07.2001; И.А. Рогачев op.cit., pp. 117-118.

587 J. L. Wilson, *Strategic Partners…*, p. 165.

588 N. K. Gvosdev, *The Sources of Russian Conduct*, "The National Interest"01.04.2004, no 75.

589 M. Kaczmarski, *Rosja na rozdrożu…*, pp. 43-57.

Alliance (NATO-Russia Council, 2002). Odd words from George Bush about seeing Putin's soul became the symbol of this new American-Russian rapprochement.[590]

Russian *bandwagoning* must have had brought negative consequences for Russian-Chinese relations – one of the most important "glueing elements" collapsed: the anti-Americanism[591] – "almost overnight the pretence of geopolitic evenhandedness gave way to an overtly pro-Western line"[592]. The Chinese leadership at the beginning also supported the "war against terrorism" because of pragmatic reasons, though in a much more reserved manner.[593] Good relations with the West were necessary for the further modernization of the country, and above all Beijing was eager to use the occasion to interpret the fight against Uyghur separatists from Xinjiang as a part of the world antiterrorist campaign. However, Beijing did not support Washington to such an extent as Moscow did: "China remained more wary and suspicious of the United States and less willing to jettison its analysis, rooted in classic *Realpolitik* assumptions."[594] Particularly the US presence in Central Asia was worrisome to China as Beijing feared the US Army might stay longer in Aphganistan, coming closer to Chinese borders, "surround China" and threaten Xinjiang and Tibet.[595]

These facts resulted in a situation, in which China and Russia after "09/11 *de facto* found themselves in two different camps, although naturally nobody disclosed it in public."[596] For a moment the Chinese felt "betrayed", particularly when Putin withdrew his objection to the ABM treaty.[597] Chinese reactions to Russian politics were traditionally balanced, however they revealed an increasingly rising level of anxiety: "Russia has again forgotten to explain to Beijing the change in its strategic priorities while continuing to declare its unchangeability."[598] Officially Moscow moved on to higher diplomacy and rhetorical acrobatics, as it tried to prove to China that an rapprochement with the United States does not threaten their mutual relations.[599] China of course did not take in such remarks. The Russian pro-American turn was received in Beijing with a strong feeling of disappointment – especially because it hurt Chinese interests, and it lead to a necessity for a greater acquiescence of Beijing

590 C. Wyatt, *Bush and Putin: Best of friends*, BBC News 16.06.2001.
591 M. Kaczmarski, *Rosja na rozdrożu*… 45.
592 B. Lo, *The Axis of Convenience*…, p. 53.
593 А.В. Лукин, *От нормализации к стратегическому партнерству*…, p. 334.
594 J. L. Wilson, *Strategic Partners*…, p. 167.
595 А.В. Лукин, *От нормализации к стратегическому партнерству*…, p. 334.
596 M. Kaczmarski, *Rosja na rozdrożu*…p. 117.
597 B. Lo, *The Axis of Convenience*…, p. 51.
598 J. L. Wilson, *Strategic Partners*…, pp. 168-170.
599 *Владимир Путин: между Москвой и Вашингтоном нет конкуренции за влияние на страны СНГ* [Putin: There is No Rivarly Between Moscow and Washington On the Influence over CIS], Интервью газете «Жэньминь Жибао» 04.06.2002.

towards Washington. China feared Russia might revert to ill-remembered Kozyrev-style diplomacy ("Kozyrevshchina") and join the US "hegemonic" course.[600] The negative Chinese position was displayed in bitter comments in the Chinese press and in the Chinese leadership concerns over Putin (Jiang was to say "We don't know what kind of a person Putin is, or what he thinks" and he ordered a detailed analysis on Putin and his political agenda).[601]

Although Russian-Chinese relations after Putin's turn towards the USA weakened, it does not mean they disappeared. Still a mechanism of regular meetings on the highest level functioned and was additionally intensified with the founding of the SCO, which gave much more possibilities for meetings. Wherefore, although the pro-Western turn of Moscow complicated the international aspect of relations with Beijing, it did not shake the base of Russia-China relations. Above all, it didn't damage well developing economic relations, which were helped by methods and calm of Putin's administration, which was quite the opposite to Yeltsin's chaos: the new team in Kremlin was more pragmatic and found some understanding on the Chinese side.[602] For the first time the economy and politics started to be set free from the indirect interdependency: trade perpetually rose and embraced wider and wider areas.

6. *Putin's Policy of Balancing Powers*

Although it is easy to determine the beginning of the Moscow's pro-Western turn, it is more difficult to establish a definitive finishing date. Without doubt it was a gradual process and disillusionment over the West and unfulfilled expectations towards the USA (poor results of approach towards West and especially lack of American concession for the Russia in the "near abroad"[603], after 11th September resulted in "closely the same disillusionment" as it happened in the times of Yeltsin)[604], went hand in hand with the growth of possibilities and ambitions of the Russian state on the international scene as a result of the rise in oil price – Putin started "building diplomacy of raw materials, especially gas."[605] Thanks to high prices of raw materials, Putin made an ambitious attempt to lead out Moscow to the geopolitical chessboard of the world powers, in order to get the central position between the West and "the axis of evil" countries and between the USA and China. The most important element of this

600 А.В. Лукин, *От нормализации к стратегическому партнерству…*, p. 335.

601 Willy Wo-Lap Lam, *Moscow Tilts West, Beijing Worries*, "China Brief" 2, Issue 12, Jameston 6 June 2002, pp. 1-3.

602 Ibid..

603 А.В. Лукин, *От нормализации к стратегическому партнерству…*, p. 340.

604 M. Kaczmarski, *Rosja na rozdrożu…*, p. 49.

605 L. Szewcowa, *Rosja przed nowym cyklem politycznym: paradoksy stabilności i petro-state* [Russia Ahead of New Political Cycle; the Paradoxes of Stability and Petro-State], [in:] *Imperium Putina…*, p. 22.

vision was an essential reinforcement and intensification of the Asian vector in the foreign policy.[606]

The revival of relations with China was the key, so Putin chose to visit Beijing on 1-3 December 2002 in order to "revive the lost impetus of relations with China."[607] During his visit he met, among others, Jiang Zemin and Hu Jintao, the new leader of the Communist Party (Putin was the first politician in this rank who met with him after he took the office). Moreover, his performance at the Beijing University was great, he arose students' enthusiasm, which "clearly contrasted with the cold welcome, which was given to earlier speaking Bush Junior."[608] Putin's visit meant above all a beginning of the return towards a more balanced policy of Moscow, which was best proved by the phrase about multipolar world included in the "join announcement" after the summit[609], that lacked in the treaty from 2001. It openly showed the "beginning of an end" of the pro-Western Putin's turn and return towards traditional politics of balancing the West by ensuring good relations with China. At that time Russia was able to lead balanced politics, get closer to China, and did not go too far from the USA. Soon Russia took an evidently anti-American position, which once more pushed the country into the Beijing's arms – mainly because of the war in Iraq.

Since autumn 2002, the USA, supported by the United Kingdom, led a diplomatic offensive which aimed at gaining consent for using power against Saddam Hussein. Meanwhile, Russia and China continued a campaign for a peaceful resolution of the conflict. Russia's and China's behaviour in the case of Iraq were completely different, although they shared the same position. China, who was against the war, remained in the second place, often being silent and trying not to expose on a confrontation with the USA. Russia was doing quite the opposite: adopted a very active role and together with France and Germany led a great campaign against war which led to the open break-up with the USA.[610]

For Russia, Iraq meant the end of the *bandwagoning* strategy, as it did not bring any kind of practical value, and the disputes between the USA, Germany and France gave a possibility of a return to the old Soviet strategy of dividing the West and putting Western Europe and the USA in a dispute. Iraq revealed some truths: Russia-American cooperation has got its own limitations, but the Bush Jr team did not acknowledge any of the post-Soviet countries as the sole sphere of the Moscow's influence. Since 2003, an anti-Western turn in the Moscow's politics started; its roots came from both the internal situation (growing autocracy), and the external factors (promoting democracy in the

---

606 Yu Bin, *One Year Later…*

607 A. Kuchins, op. cit., p. 41.

608 R. Pyffel, *Chiny-Rosja: Kto kogo?...*

609 *Совместная декларация Российской Федерации и Китайской Народной Республики* [Joint Declaration of RF and PRC], Kremlin.ru, 02.12.2002.

610 J. L. Wilson, *Strategic Partners…*, p. 173.

post-Soviet area). Moreover, Iraq added a new impulse to the Russian-Chinese relations, took them out of the shadow, and brought back the basic link-protest against the global domination of the USA.

Geopolitical calculations won above Russia's fears and anxieties connected with the change of the Chinese leadership into the hands of the Hu Jintao group. Hu himself chose Moscow as a place of his first visit abroad on 26-28 May 2003, and in this way dispelled apprehension. The visit was very important, because it sealed the hitherto political line of Russia-Chinese relations. Putin as the host showed deep intuition by organizing for Hu – uncertain and not knowing the Russian language – an informal meeting 2+2 together with wives on 26 March in Putin's *dacha*. With time, the relations of Vladimir Putin with Hu Jintao started to be good. More importantly, an attitude towards politics brought them together. Both of them were realists in international relations and their aim was above all to strengthen the power of their countries and influences. Despite all changes in time, the "individual engagement" of Putin in building good relations with China did not change.[611] Moreover, in Putin's politics towards China more things were actually done than in the times of his predecessor – visits finished with signing up economic agreements, important businessmen took part in delegations to China – all that proved that Russia was very serious about this issue. Russian-Chinese relations, above all the economic ones, became "mechanized" – the regularity of meetings and institutionalized mechanization helped much in mutual relations. Institutional frames of bilateral relations built slowly over a decade, brought peace and further cooperation. During Putin's rule the "strategic partnership" became a fact – earlier it was mainly rhetoric. In this context, the border issue was solved, moreover, it was followed by subsequent actions: opening regions close to the border for development and cooperation, institutionalizing political dialogue of high and middle rank, developing multisided military cooperation and improvement of human to human relations.

The issue of regulating the borders had a special meaning. It occurred during the groundbreaking visit of Putin in Beijing on 14-16 October 2014. Its most important result and success was the final regulation of the Russian-Chinese border issue.[612] A compromise consisted in the division of three last debatable islands – forty years lasting negotiation battle, closing a very problematic for the last decade issue of the demarcation of the borders. Both sides decided to give in –after all Putin decided to negotiate giving back the islands (the very issue caused serious resentment in the Russia's Far East). The Chinese leadership hoped for a greater cooperation with China on the regional issues, and on

611 B. Lo, *The Axis of Convenience…*, p. 40.

612 *Дополнительное соглашение между Российской Федерацией и Китайской Народной Республикой о российско-китайской границе на ее Восточной части* [Complementary Agreement Betwenn RF and PRC on Russia-China Border in Its Eastern Part, [in:] *Сборник российско-китайских договоров 1949-1999…*, pp. 318-323.

a positive end of the battle for the pipeline from Angars- Daqing.[613] Closing up this issue must be considered the personal merit of the Russian President, who managed to finish a long and strenuous process. The border issue was a Pandora's Box in the Russian-Chinese relations that was closed by Putin[614], and by that he probably accomplished even the "biggest success in his foreign policy."[615] However, apart from this achievement, the summit was typical for Russian-Chinese relations: there was a lot of assurance and elevated words with little details.[616] Thanks to this visit, the last fundamental problem was eliminated, but the game on the Asian board was still going on and the closest events complicated the relations.

Soon after the visit, Russian-Chinese relations started to gather black clouds. The first one was sentencing physicist Valentine Danilov for spying for the Chinese side[617], the second was the visit of Dalai Lama in Russia, which was badly received in China[618], and the third was the decision of the Russian government from 31 December 2004 regarding the ESPO pipeline in favour of sale on the Japan route to Skorovodkino and at the expense of the Chinese branch to Daqing.[619] The chosen route, which was the exemplification of the Putin's geopolitical game in Asia, appeared to give to Russia bigger possibilities, and above all helped to free it from too strong dependence from China in Asia. That is why it appeared that this decision was taken against the hitherto reassurances of Moscow about realizing the section in Daqing, and it could have had very bad consequences for the Russian-Chinese relations. However, future showed that it did not happen.

7. *Towards Rapprochement with China*

Since 2005, one can notice the next change in the Russian politics: a renewed engagement with China, though a limited and half-hearted one. First reason for Moscow's turn were, traditionally, its relations with the United States and the vision of the international order related to them. Washington did not even want to think of awarding Russia with the status of a "regional superpower" and to give it a special part in the CIS and – to use the Russian-Chinese terminology –

---

613 Yu Bin, *End of History. End of History, What Next?*, "Comperative Connections" vol. 6, no 4.

614 М. Титаренко, *Геополитическое значение…*, p. 277.

615 Д. Тренин, *Верные друзья?...*

616 Yu Bin, *End of History…*

617 *Физик Данилов сел на 14 лет* [Physicist Danilov Landed in Prison for 14 years], Polit.Ru 24.11.2004.

618 The Chinese interpreted Dalajlama's visit as the volating of the article 8 of the 2001 Treaty, Ю. М. Галенович, *История взаимоотношений...*, p. 346; А.В. Лукин, *От нормализации к стратегическому партнерству…*, p. 333.

619 *Russia approves Pacific pipeline*, BBC News, 31.12.2004.

it was consequently building hegemonic order in the world, breaching the most vivid interests of Russia through the activity of the Western institutions in the post-Soviet area, which was shown by supporting "colourful revolutions", treated in the Kremlin as a strategic element to encircle Russia.[620] The seemingly everlasting wave of colourful revolutions pushed Putin's Moscow once more to China. Beijing was also more and more worried about the "colourful revolutions", especially the one in Kyrgyzstan which could have caused the destabilization of the region and of Xinjiang.

The next factor resulting in the Russian-Chinese rapprochement was the fact that Russia started to pay more attention to China. It suppressed anti-Chinese behaviour on the political level, as well as on the psychological level, and started to cooperate more with China (on common challenges like war with terrorism or international criminality) rather than treat China as a threat (migration, illegal activity of the Chinese in Russia). In the 2000s decade it became possible to build a very important framework of Russian-Chinese political interaction: an institutional infrastructure was established, helping to transfer most problems regarding bilateral relations from the political level to the bureaucratic one.[621] Trade rose in an impressive way (only in 2005 it grew by 33%) and the "strategic partnership" was an "important psychological support" for Russia, especially taking into account the worsening relations with the West[622], for example on the occasion of the 60th anniversary of the end of the Second World War, the main guest was Hu Jintao. Several factors brought together the leaders of these countries: a more common outlook of Moscow and Beijing towards the world situation, which was not like before and not how they expected it to be, assertive politics of Bush, continuous military rise in Japan, nuclear issue in Korea, or the Taiwan issue.[623] A deepening convergence of the Russian and Chinese outlook resulted in Russia's greater engagement in Asia. The examples of the new Russian-Chinese assertiveness were visible, among others, in the following events: the first meeting of ministers of foreign affairs from Russia, China and India in Vladivostok[624]; the SCO summit in Astana, where a decision of accepting India, Pakistan and Iran as observers

620 Э. Качинс, В. Никонов, Д. Тренин, *Российско-американские отношения. Как добится лучшего?* [Russia-US Relations. How to Get it Better?], Москва, Карнеги 2005, p. 12.

621 *Китай. Угрозы, риски, вызовы развитию*, ред. В. Михаев, Москва Центр Карнеге 2005, p. 366.

622 B. Lo, *The Axis of Convenience*…, p. 44.

623 *Совместная декларация Российской Федерации и Китайской Народной Республики о международном порядке в XXI веке* [Joint Declaration of RF and PRC on International Order in 21th Century], [in:] *Сборник российско-китайских договоров 1949-1999*…, pp. 332-338.

624 *Совместное коммюнике неформальной встречи глав МИД КНР, РФ и Индии* [Joint Communique After Informal Meeting of Heads of MFA of PRC, RF and India], 03.06.2005, Генеральное Консульство Китайской Народной Республики в г.Хабаровске.

was taken[625]; in actions of president of Uzbekistan Islam Karimov (pacification of Andijan in May 2005) which resulted in the crucial change in Uzbekistan's foreign policy course (which was then Moscow's and Beijing's big success in the region). Precisely the maintenance of the current regimes in Central Asia, and the preclusion of Western interference in that region became another strong pillar of the Russian-Chinese growing rapprochement.[626] The best meaningful example was the part of declaration from this SCO summit where the organization called the USA to determine the date of troop retreat from Afghanistan.[627]

An even stronger signal of deepening cooperation between China and Russia was given by common military maneuvers – "Peace Mission 2005" in August 2005. These were first so important maneuvers of this kind in the history of both of them.[628] Officially these exercises were called "antiterrorist" maneuvers, but even the authors of these words probably did not believe in them. The kind of exercised actions – sea invasion, parachute invasion, sea blockades and shelling boats by submarines, precise bombardment from strategic bombers – clearly testified the main aim: to threaten Taiwan. Islanders and their alliances also acted: nearly at the same time maneuvers of the US Pacific Fleet, the Korean Fleet and "routine" Taiwanese exercises on resisting invasion from the continent were started, so that Russian-Chinese maneuvers were in the epicenter of the "war of words" in Eastern Asia.[629] However, in contrast to Beijing, which has an obsessive attitude towards Taiwan, Moscow wanted rather to make a power demonstration than to threaten somebody (that's why the exercises were taken from the primary localization *vis-à-vis* Taiwan to the province of Shandong) and to use this occasion to sell guns.[630]

However, despite the growing Sino-Russian cooperation, some cracks appeared. During Putin's meetings with the Chinese prime-minister Wen Jiabao in October and November 2005, the Russian leader "continued to stress that the two sides should optimize trade structures (meaning that China should purchase more Russian high-tech products)", while Wen "expressed the hope that existing agreements would be well implemented" (meaning: let Russia honour its obligations regarding the energy deliveries to China).[631] Worse still, on 13 November 2005 some 100 tons of benzene leaked into the Songhua River after an explosion at a chemical plant in China's Jilin Province, 600 km from the

625 *Декларация глав государств-членов Шанхайской организации сотрудничества* [Declaration of Heads of Member States of SCO], 05.07.2005, Sectsco.org.ru.

626 Д. Тренин, *Верные друзья*...

627 *Декларация глав государств-членов Шанхайской*...

628 *Мирная миссия-2005* [Peace Mission 2005], "Известия", 23.08.2005.

629 Yu Bin, *The New World Order According to Moscow and Beijing*, "Comparative Connections", vol. 7, no 3.

630 Ibid.

631 Yu Bin, *Pollution*...

Russian border. Water polluted by some 100 tons of benzene was drifting towards Russia which evoked panic and anti-Chinese campaign on the Russian side.[632] The Russians accused – correctly – the Chinese of providing not enough information and of a delayed reaction[633]; this gave way to accusations of the lack of good will and transparency in the trans- border relations. Although Chinese central authorities cooperated with their Russian counterparts to an unprecedented level to avoid the worst scenario (it was achieved)[634], the prime minister Wen wrote to Putin "pledging assistance in dealing with the aftermath of the toxic spill" and the local Chinese authorities were held responsible for these actions; this event showed the real face of Sino-Russian relations "at the bottom."[635] This ecologic catastrophe was a "a painful reminder that high-profile diplomacy is not the only priority between the two powers (…) it brought to surface the deeply held distrust and suspicions between the two sides, particularly among the Russians."[636] This unfortunate pollution event took place on the eve of the official opening of Russia's Year in China that was oficially intended to bring closer both nations but in reality remained "artificial steps to arouse interest in each other's culture."[637] This Russia Year was opened by Putin himself during his visit to China on 21-22 March 2006, well-known for his trip to Shaolin temple. Energy issues dominated the summit: Beijing, however, was not able to achieve what it wanted. Although two sides have signed an agreement on conducting feasibility study on the 70-km ESPO branch line to China, and Putin confirmed that the pipeline will be built, he did not mention any date.[638] This was a purposeful policy of slowing the pace of cooperation, keeping the agreements on paper only and moving back the deadlines: "Moscow used the very fact of signing initial agreements with China to incite competition among potential Asian customers and to threaten the EU member states with the redirection of resource flows to the East; Russia was in no hurry to conclude a final deal, being satisfied with endless negotiations."[639] For the Chinese leadership it "became painfully clear (…) that even the heartfelt sentiments behind China's Russian Year won't result in Siberian oil; (…)

632 *На Дальний Восток надвигается катастрофа* [A Catastrophe is Approaching Far East], Известия, 23.11.2005.

633 *На химической фабрике в Китае произошла серия взрывов* [A Chemical Plant in China Underwent a Series of Blows] , Lenta.Ru, 13.11.2005.

634 А.В. Лукин, *От нормализации к стратегическому партнерству…*, p. 345.

635 E. Wishnick, *Why A Strategic Partnership…*, p. 70.

636 Yu Bin, *Pollution…*

637 G. Rozman, *The Sino-Russian Challenge…*, p. 257.

638 *Протокол между ОАО «АК Транснефть» и Китайской национальной нефтегазовой корпорацией* [Protocol Between OAO Transneft and CNPC], [in:] *Список документов, подписанных в присутствии Президента России Владимира Путина и Председателя КНР Ху Цзиньтао* [The List of Documents Signed During Meeting Between President Putin and Chairman Hu], Kremlin.ru, 21.02.2006.

639 M. Kaczmarski, *Russia-China Relations…*, p. 55.

the Russian president only talked about Russia's oil, and did not allow it to flow to its energy-starved neighbour"; it was a "grand energy-Politicking."[640] As the frustrated Chinese National Development and Reform Commission Deputy Minister Zhang Guobao, stated: "one moment Russia is saying they have made a decision, the next saying that no decision has been made. To date, there has been no current information. This is regrettable. Currently, the Sino-Russian pipeline question is one step forward, two steps back. Today is cloudy with a chance for sun while tomorrow is sunny with a chance for clouds, just like a weather forecast."[641]

This "oil" coin had two sides, however. On one hand, it enabled Russia to maneuver, on the other it made China not interested in changing structure of trade. Putin himself complained about "trade irrationality", but the Chinese were unwilling to change it: "In the eyes of the Chinese, the Kremlin has overplayed energy politics, focusing on strategic and political calculation at the expense of economic rationality."[642] Besides, it was not so much of a political issue, but an economic one – Russian products have been uncompetitive on the Chinese market. Russians, being aware of that, pushed to obtain the contracts to construct more nuclear power generators in China – the nuclear area "means billions of dollars and years of employment for hundreds of workers."[643] That is why the issue of the ESPO started to look like a bargain – Moscow wanted to get the best possible deal for construction of this branch line.

The 6th SCO summit in Shanghai was the most important event of the summer of 2006. It took place on the fifth anniversary of this organization and showed its strength.[644] In that geopolitical situation, the presence of Iranian President Mahmud Ahmedinejad evoked many controversies, as Iran was, along with North Korea, a problematic ally for Russia and China. During Iranian and Korean crises, the Russian and Chinese diplomacies actively cooperated with one another, with slight difference in the fact that in Iran Russia was more active, whereas in Korea – it was China's role (this pattern changed only after 2009, when China became more active in the Iranian issue).[645] Aside of Korea and Iran, the most important political event of the summer of 2006 took place in St. Petersburg – it was the G8 summit on 15-17 July 2006. G8 had been becoming a more and more paradox formula for Russia: "Moscow failed in its attempt to be recognized by the West as a fellow democracy, which was

---

640 Yu Bin, *China's Year*... Even Russian authors admit that this situation deteriorated Chinese trust in Russia, А.В. Лукин, *От нормализации к стратегическому партнерству*..., p. 394.

641 *Frustrated China seen getting no promises off Putin*, "The Star", 20.03.2006.

642 Yu Bin, *China's Year*...

643 Ibid.

644 *Fireworks, cruise and handshakes precede SCO summit*, CCTV.Com, 14.06.2014.

645 Yu Bin, G-8, *Geoeconomics, and Growing "Talk" Fatigue*, "Comperative Connections", vol. 8, no 3.

supposed to be that club's common characteristic; nor was Russia recognized as a major economic power."[646] That is why it was the presence of "rising economies" of China, India, Brazil, Mexico and South Africa that saved the summit for – more and more criticized in the West – Putin[647]. A "constructive" role of China also helped here – Beijing has returned a favour to Russia which denied visa to Dalai Lama one month earlier.[648]

Mutual pleasantries did not impact the fundamental issue – economic interests. Two days after the G8 summit, the CNPC bought shares in Rosnieft worth USD 500 million (for the first time in history a Chinese company has bought shares in Russian oil sector)[649]; this price, however, was much lower than the speculated one (USDD 3 billion). China's "cautious and limited entrance into the Russian market reflected (…) strong sense of uncertainty about working with Russia on the energy issue."[650] Kremlin did not intend to lower Rosneft price for China, so Beijing – who still waited for the ESPO branch line – has bought much less than it could have. It was clearly visible, therefore, that where Russian and Chinese interests converged (geopolitics, military cooperation, regional issues) there they cooperated; where, however, these interests were divergent (energy and its price), there came words only, not actions.

For China, the ESPO's fate had remained unclear, while Beijing did not hide its displeasure on Russia's "contradictory attitude" on the energy issue"; for Hu Jintao's team the energy was a vital issue, and Russian energy had its own importance here – the Chinese leadership in 2003 has accepted the Northeast China programme of development basing on assumption of having the Russian energy.[651] Moscow's maneuvering, deference and delaying tactics on the ESPO proved particularly painful for Beijing – it all equaled to "breaking a promise."[652] Nevertheless, despite being frustrated, Beijing decided that it needs to accommodate to the existing conditions.

Lack of the Russian decision resulted not only from the strategic calculations, but also from the Russian dissatisfaction with the composition of Sino-Russian trade and its unsuccessful attempts for getting preferential treatment of Russian export of machineries (civilian aircraft, nuclear reactions, hydroelectric turbines)[653] – in a way Moscow tried to force China to accept a deal: in return for the ESPO branch line, it wanted to increase its machinery export to

646 Д. Тренин, *Верные друзья*….

647 Yu Bin, G-8, *Geoeconomics*…

648 *МИД России вновь отказал в выдаче въездной визы Далай-ламе* [Russia's MFA again denied Dalai Lama Entry Visa], ИА REGNUM, 08.06.2006.

649 *CNPC invests $500M in Rosneft's IPO*, China Daily, 19.07.2006.

650 Yu Bin, G-8, *Geoeconomics*…

651 В.Г. Дацышен, В.Л. Ларин, Г.Н. Романова, *Замок с границы снят. Приграничные регионы в российско-китайских отношениях* [The border has been unclocked. Border regions and Russian-Sino Relations], [In:] *Россия и Китай: четыре века*… op. cit., p. 471.

652 *Китай. Угрозы, риски, вызовы*… p. 366.

653 E. Wishnick, *Why A Strategic Partnership*…, p. 64.

China. Russians considered that good political relations should be transferred for economic preferences. This showed that Sino-Russian relations, contrary to US-Sino relations, did not depoliticize, the economy was not separated from politics.[654] China, however, had no intention to strike a deal with Moscow on the Russian terms because Russian products have been uncompetitive on the Chinese market. Despite growing volume of trade, there still existed an "imbalance between 'hot' political relations and 'cold' economic relations."[655] The reason was objective: Russian industrial products are "not the best in the world or the most attractive to partner country."[656] Even Russians themselves understood it: "If you do not count military equipment (...) and apart from civil aircraft (...) and power industry equipment it seems that Russia has nothing to boast of"; thus Russia hoped for contracts in civilian nuclear power construction[657]; but the Chinese once again have chosen the Western capital.[658]

The year 2007 was the "China's Year" in Russia. Politically, 2007 started on 12 January when Russia and China, in their first joint veto in the UN Security Council, blocked the resolution against the Burmese junta. Since then, they have worked together on many occasions to oppose or water down Security Council resolutions that included sanction provisions – "China does not like to stand alone to oppose a Security Council resolution."[659]

With 2007 Putin's Munich Speech, the "new assertiveness" of Russian foreign policy came to be visible; it illustrated the growing Russian elites conviction that Russia has regained the great power status.[660] China automatically became once more important: "growing irritation in U.S.-Russia and Europe-Russia relations has redounded to the benefit of China-Russia relations."[661] It was so despite the fact that China did not intend to back Russia on its protest against anti-missile shield (except, naturally, the moral and rhetoric support). Beijing let alone did not intend to follow Moscow's anti-Americanism.[662] This was visible during Hu Jintao's visit to Moscow (26-28 March 2007), a traditionally very grandiose one. In the "joint declaration" after the summit, two sides included specific dimensions of this partnership, such as "increasing

654 М. Титаренко, *Геополитическое значение...*, p. 330.
655 E. Wishnick, *Why A Strategic Partnership...*, p. 64.
656 Chen Qimao, op. cit., p. 294.
657 Yu Bin, *What Follows China „Russia's Year"?* "Comperative Connections", vol. 8, no 4.
658 *Westinghouse Wins $5.3 Billion China Nuclear Contract*, Bloomberg 16.12.2006.
659 Since 2007 China has not blocked any UN resolution without Russia's backing, D. J. Mitchell, *China and Russia*, CSIS, 2007.
660 *Выступление и дискуссия на Мюнхенской конференции по вопросам политики безопасности* [Speech and Discussion During Munich Conference on Security Policy], Kremlin.ru, 10.02.2007.
661 A. Kuchins, op. cit., p. 33.
662 B. Lo, *The Axis of Convenience...*, pp. 4-5.

trust" or "enhancing cooperation economic and security areas."[663] These dimensions, although proposed by Hu Jintao, showed the lack of trust on the side of the Chinese leadership.[664] It happened because of contradictory signals sent by Russia. On one hand Moscow has established "China's Year", but on the other on 15 January 2007 it introduced new migration law that aimed at elimination of foreign nationals as salespersons in Russia's retail market[665].That was "a serious blow to the businesses of Chinese in Russia" and "runs counter to the goal of (...) bringing ordinary Russians and Chinese closer."[666]

At the same time Beijing wasted no time to realize one of its most important goals – to diversify energy supplies and it was able to finalize the Central Asian gas pipeline in June 2007. China's Central Asian gas gambit fundamentally strengthened Beijing's position vis-à-vis Moscow. Since then, the Chinese were no longer resting on Russians' sufferance – they simply deprived Moscow of one of its most important arguments – monopoly on gas supplies. In return, the Chinese let Russia save face where it cost them little – on the propaganda level. They agreed to publicize the subsequent Sino-Russian joint military exercises (this time in Cheberkal) – it was important for Russia, given its strained relations with the West.

Year 2007 ended with announcement of transition of power in both countries. On 15 October 2007 Xi Jinping and Li Keqiang were included to the Standing Committee of the Central Committee of the Political Bureau of the CPC – this meant that they would be successors of Hu Jintao and Wen Jiabao. This was, however, overshadowed by Putin's announcement of 10 December 2007 of not biding for the third term and "proposing" the candidate: vice prime minister Dmitri Medvedev for the post of the president. Already then many commentators speculated that Putin would keep the real power and that he would be eligible to be "the successor" of Medvedev as the Russian President after Medvedev's term. The Chinese were as surprised as the Westerners, yet, "the Chinese analysis of Putin's plans to have his cake and eat it, too, were was far less cynical and/or sinister than that of the West (...) China seemed cautiously optimistic about future relations."[667]

Medvedev's failed attempt to modernize the country and his rather pro-Western approach are not part of this book. What is important in the context of Russia-China relations is that Medvedev has continued Putin's political line

---

663 *Совместная декларация Российской Федерации и Китайской Народной Республики* [Joint Declaration of RF and PRC], [in:] *Сборник российско-китайских договоров 1949-1999...* , pp. 491-501.

664 Yu Bin, *Russia Says "No" to the West and "Sort of" to China,* "Comparative Connections" vol. 9, no 1.

665 *Постановление Правительства Российской Федерации от 15 января 2007 г.* [Goverment of Russia Decision of 15.01.2007], "Российская газета", 27.01.2007.

666 Yu Bin, *Russia Says "No"...*

667 Idem, *Living with Putin...*

in dealing with Beijing. Despite being rather Western-oriented, Medvedev chose Beijing as the first place to visit after becoming the president: this was warmly welcomed in Beijing – the Chinese remembered well how Putin behaved in 2000. Medvedev's debut visit came in during a difficult moment – just after Sichuan earthquake (12 May). These unfortunate circumstances, however, played to his benefit – Russia helped China which contrasted with Western ambiguous stance.[668] Medvedev himself – showing a good knowledge of the Chinese culture and philosophy – impressed the hosts. Despite signing of a few agreements, the most important issues remained unchanged; nevertheless, "the Beijing summit did inject new energy to improve bilateral relations."[669]

Soon the good mood in Sino-Russian relations was tested by war in Georgia and the world crisis. The war annoyed the Chinese: they saw the conflict as "highly destabilising for the international system, and a threat to China's interests. Beijing's preference, as far as US-Russian relations are concerned, remains clear: no collusion and no collision between the two."[670] Beijing did not want to damage its relations with Russia, but did not want to jeopardize relations with the USA either. That is why China kept its traditional distanced[671] and ambiguous[672] profile and chose to remain neutral.[673] This was most clearly seen during the SCO summit in Dushanbe on 28 August 2008 when China, backed by Central Asian countries did not recognize South Ossetia and Abkhazia and blocked the Russian request to include a statement on the Dushanbe Declaration on joint action on security and conflict prevention issues. As a result, the SCO countries in the Dushanbe Declaration only "express[ed] their deep concern in connection with the recent tension around the issue of South Ossetia."[674] China's veto to change borders is completely understandable given China's domestic situation and the Taiwan issue. It is well-understandable for Central Asian republics with their artificial state borders, too. None of these countries had any interest in supporting Russia. China may understood Russia's intentions, but understanding is one thing, while supporting is another. If China had supported Russia on Georgia issue, it would have – domestically and internationally – too much to loose and too little to win. That is why it stayed neutral. This neutrality was not a sign of crisis in Sino-Russian relations, but showed its limitations.

668 А.В. Лукин, *От нормализации к стратегическому партнерству*..., p. 351.

669 Yu Bin, *Medvedev's Ostpolitik and Sino-Russian Relations*, "Comperative Connections", vol. 10, no 2.

670 Д. Тренин, *Верные друзья*....

671 *China calls for ceasefire in South Ossetia*, Xinhua.Com, 09.08.2008.

672 А.В. Лукин, *От нормализации к стратегическому партнерству*..., p. 352.

673 Yu Bin, *Guns and Games of August: Tales of Two Strategic Partners*, "Comperative Connections" vol. 10, no 3.

674 *Душанбинская Декларация* [SCO Dushanbe Declaration of Heads of State], 28.08.2008, Sectsco.org.ru.

In general, Sino-Russian relations at the eve of the economic crisis were good, yet limited. Slowdown in arms trade (arms sales to the PRC stagnated in contrary to the sales to India or Vietnam), barriers to more extensive energy ties (Moscow was determined to avoid falling into dependence from China, so it stalled joint projects and blocked Chinese investments in energy sector), and Russia's anxiety about cross-border co-operation in the Far East (Moscow sought there investments from the Asian states other than China); "taken together, these policies bore testimony to Moscow's uneasiness about China's rise and the Kremlin's hedging strategies against possible negative consequences of Beijing's increase in power."[675] This mood was best caught by the famous "axis of convenience" metaphor.[676]

8. *The Economic Crisis of 2008 and Its Consequences for Bilateral Relations*

The world financial crisis in 2008 influenced noticeably the Sino-Russian relations. The crisis hit Russia hard, lowering its GDP and forcing it to use almost a half of its reserve fund. China, on the other hand, managed the crisis well and strengthened. The crisis deepened the already existent imbalance between Beijing and Moscow: after that date nobody can doubt that China is "in the driver seat in this relationship."[677] Moreover, the crisis deprived Moscow of its best card: manipulation of the energy supplies. The autumn of 2008 ended the period of Putin's Bismarckian-style balancing policy, and began a clearly-seen process of the gradual asymmetry in favour of Beijing; the asymmetry that Moscow accepted and to which it adjusted accordingly. In the wake of 2008 crisis, Russia "substantially changed its approach to how it co-operated with China; contracts and agreements regarding oil, gas and electric energy exports were concluded and these were accompanied by the completion of the ESPO pipeline (…) arms trade revived; co-operation in the Russian Far East was reignited."[678]

The ESPO pipeline, the flagship Russian project in Asia, became the symbol of new realities. Due to the crisis, Rosnieft and Transnieft were unable to find sources to finance the project in Western banks – this made further investments almost impossible. This is when the Chinese came in with a "brotherly" help. They offered loans as pre-payment for further oil supplies transported through the Daqing branch line. This is how Russia agreed to build the energy supply infrastructure passing to China, and the initial plan of this pipeline was reactivated. It was a breakthrough: not only did the "the longest-running soap opera

675 M. Kaczmarski, *Russia-China Relations…*, p. 53.
676 B. Lo, *The Axis of Convenience…*, p. 1.
677 G. Rozman, *The Sino-Russian Challenge…*, p. 268.
678 M. Kaczmarski, *Russia-China Relations…*, p. 53.

in oil transportation history end"[679], but Russia did not receive any political concessions from China. This testified the "emergence of a new model of Sino-Russian relationship where Russia is the weaker state and China sets the agenda."[680] The crisis "altered the political logic underpinning Russia-China energy relations (...) the Kremlin could no longer afford to wait".[681] Thus, a new – this time real, rapprochement took place and Russia decided to bury its grievances and initiated a long-term co-operation with China in the energy sector (see: economic chapter of this book). Forced by crisis, Russia lost hopes of balancing the China's influence and instead decided to bandwagon to Beijing in this matter.

Despite this breakthrough of political rapprochement, Russia-China relations were in 2009 overshadowed by social incidents. The beginning of 2009 in Sino-Russian relations was impacted by the "New Star" ship issue. This Chinese cargo vessel (officially under the flag of Sierra Leone), due to misunderstandings with Russian trade partner left Nachodka port without permission from the Russian authorities and did not stop while being chased by the Russian Coast Guard; as the result they fired at the ship and damaged it – it started returning to Nachodka, but sunk during a storm – 7 staff members were missing, probably died.[682] As Yu Bin writes: "While Russian and Chinese diplomats were publicly trading remarks – a situation rarely seen since 1989 – Chinese media erupted with coverage of the incident (...) Although there were plenty of sober analyses, anger, disbelief, and criticism dominated the Chinese media (...) For many in China, there was too much unpleasant historical baggage regarding Russia's use of excessive force against an unarmed Chinese civilian ship."[683] The Chinese MFA demanded investigation from the Russian side[684]. Russia expressed "regret" over the incident, but insisted that it was the ship's captain fault.[685] A diplomatic stalemate followed – nobody wanted to make concession. Finally China did, sacrificing this case on altar of more important issues: Chinese diplomats stopped raising this issue while Beijing's

679 Yu Bin, *Embracing a Storm and Each Other?* "Comparative Connections" vol. 8, no 4.

680 M. Kaczmarski, W. Konończuk, *Rosja-Chiny: umowa o ropociągu do Daqingu jako przejaw nowego kształtu stosunków dwustronnych* [Russia-China. Daqing Agreement as an Example of New Model of Bilateral Relations], OSW, Warsaw, 30.10.2008.

681 M. Kaczmarski, *Russia-China Relations...*, p. 55.

682 *Ситуация вокруг судна «Нью Стар»* [Situation Around New Star Ship], РИА Новости 26.05.2009.

683 Yu Bin, *Between Crisis and Cooperation*, "Comparative Connections" vol. 11, no 1.

684 *Китай считает неприемлемым обстрел пограничниками судна «Нью Стар»* [China Considers Shooting the New Star Ship by Border Guard as Unfriendly], РИА Новости, 20.02.2009.

685 *Комментарий официального представителя МИД России А.А.Нестеренко в связи с инцидентом с судном «Нью Стар»* [Commantaries of Official Representative of RF MFA Nesterenko Concerning the Incident with New Star Ship], Mid.ru 20.02.2009.

police removed the family members of ship staff protesting in front of the Russian Embassy.[686] This incident showed very well that Sino-Russian relations have been "hot on top and cold at bottom".

The political summits dominated the "hot" political relations in the summer of 2009 – first came the SCO summit in Yekaterinburg (14-16 June) followed by the first, historical summit of the BRIC, again in Yekaterinburg (16-18 June) and Medvedev-Hu mini-summit (17 June) in Moscow. The choice of Yekaterinburg, situated on the geographic border of Europe and Asia, was hardly a coincidence. But it was the historical BRIC summit that drew most attention – because it proved that an academic concept became reality. The world economic crisis, however, effectively undermined plans for geopolitical ambitions. Faced by crisis, the BRIC took "within-the-system" approach" and multi-polar world slogans could not conceal the fact that "their economic well-being in the foreseeable future depends more upon their interactions with the developed West than with one another."[687] Moscow scored better with the Medvedev-Hu mini-summit that took place on on the eve of the 60th anniversary of the Sino-Russian diplomatic ties. Both presidents praised the history and overlooked the thorny late 1950s and 1960s. Hu Jintao, however, is his speech called for "trusting each other and treating each other in sincerity" which was a clear hint to Cherkizovsky market crisis (see: below.)[688] Despite its reservations, Beijing traditionally sacrificed this minor issue for the sake of more important ones. China backed Moscow on political issues. Both sides criticized the U.S. plans for an anti-missile shield, China supported Russian actions in Caucasus and announced plans for stronger presence of Russian companies on Chinese nuclear energy market; besides, China has granted Russia USD 700 million loan for Russian Vneshtorgbank.[689]

The summer of 2009 in Sino-Russian relations was marked by Moscow's city authorities' unexpected decision of shutting down Cherkizovsky market that was selling smuggled goods; this decision made 60 thousand Chinese working there redundant.[690] Corruption and lack of observation of the sanitary

686 *Пикетчики требовали от РФ компенсаций за гибель моряков с «Нью Стар»* [Protestors Demand RF Compansation For the Death of New Star Mariners], РИА Новости 18.03.2009.

687 Yu Bin, *Summitry: Between Symbolism and Substance*, "Comparative Connections", vol. 11, no 2.

688 *Выступление Ху Цзиньтао на торжественном вечере, посвященном 60-летию установления дипотношений между Китаем и Россией* [Hu Jintao's Speech on Celebrated Gala Dedicated to 6oth Anniversary of Relations Between China and Russia], Russian.Xinhua.Com, 18.06.2009.

689 *Совместное Российско-Китайское заявление об итогах встречи на высшем уровне в Москве* [Joint Declaration on the Results of Meeting on the Top Level], Kremlin.ru, 17.06.2009.

690 *Приостановлена работа крупнейшего вещевого рынка России* [The Suspention of Work in the Biggest Chinese Market in Russia], Радио Голос России, 29.06.2009.

norms were declared the official reasons, as certainly there was some ground for it, if according to approximate estimations, illegal Sino-Russian trade with fake Chinese goods was worth a few USD billions per year.[691] This, however, was only a pretext: Cherkizovski closure was "essentially a clash between rival Russian clans, with the Chinese caught in the crossfire."[692] This decision met with resonance from China – the Chinese MFA protested while Beijing sent a special commission to Moscow that secured Russian consent for returning part of the goods to the merchants and declaration for finding a new place for the market.[693] Although "the actual damage to bilateral economic relations may not be significant (…) the psychological and emotional damage and the credibility and reputation of the Russian economic climate, were enormous."[694] So, it was again "cold" at bottom in Sino-Russian relations. And "hot" on the top – at the same time another "Peace Mission" joint exercise took place. Both Moscow and Beijing simply stopped paying attention to Cherkizovsky market issue – they had more important matters, such as Putin's visit to Beijing (12-15 October 2009) during which two sides signed the interim agreement between Gazprom and the CNPC; signing this document without indicating gas price suggested Moscow's another round of strategic maneuvering to use its China policy as a leverage against Europe.[695]

2010 started with Kyrgyzstan crisis, affecting Sino-Russian relations. On 7 April, a revolt broke up against Kurmanbek Bakiyev. Russia quickly came to terms with the new Kyrgyz authorities by granting them loan and sending Russian troops to Kyrgyzstan; it demonstrated Russian dominant position in Kyrgyzstan.[696] Against this background, China's involvement was weak if none. Beijing adopted a "wait and see" approach born out of awareness of its limitations. This cost Kyrgyzstan-based Chinese loss of their goods (Chinese shops were looted) and Beijing – marginalization in Central Asian affairs.[697]

Kyrgyzstan, however, was soon overshadowed by US-Russia "reset", or softer approach to Moscow by Washington's new administration of Obama, in return for concessions on anti-missile shield and cooperation on Iran.[698] Russia accepted the reset hoping to strengthen its ties with the West in return for help in modernization and out of fears of China's permanent rise and Moscow's

---

691 А.В. Лукин, *От нормализации к стратегическому партнерству…*, p. 376.

692 Д.Тренин, *Верные друзья?…*

693 А.В. Лукин, *От нормализации к стратегическому партнерству…*, pp. 375-376.

694 Yu Bin, *Market Malaise and Mirnaya Missiya*, "Comparative Connections" vol. 11, no 3.

695 Idem, *Mr. Putin Goes to China. Ten Years After*, "Comparative Connections" vol. 11, no 4.

696 *Государственный переворот в Киргизии* [The State Coup in Kyrgyzstan], РИА Новости, 03.05.2010.

697 Yu Bin, *Reset under Medvedev: Zapad-Politik and Vostok 2010*, "Comparative Connections" vol. 11, no 2.

698 *Remarks by Vice President Biden at 45th Munich Conference on Security Policy*, Office of the Vice President 07.02.2010.

lowered status in the "strategic partnership."[699] Kremlin, too, wrongly assumed that Obama made the reset out of weakness; that backfired later on, when mutual misunderstanding caused "reset" to end with a bitterness on both sides.[700]

For a while, however, it seemed that US-Russia relations are going to change for good. Naturally, revival on Moscow-Washington line threatened to weaken Moscow-Beijing ties: "a cloud hung over Sino-Russian relations".[701] On 13 May 2010, Russia's Foreign Minister, Sergei Lavrov declared that "Russia is ready to assist in resolving the conflict between China and Dalai Lama and is interested in normalizing their ties."[702] Dalai Lama issue was symptomatic here. It showed Moscow's sense of strength – in normal circumstances the Kremlin is very cautious about not irritating China on Dalai Lama or human rights.[703] The impact of US-Russia relations was felt on "Yeonpyeong incident" as well (North Korean bombing of a South Korean island). Russia and China approaches were different. Beijing expressed "concern", but did not condemn North Korea[704], while Russia warned of "colossal danger" and said those behind the attack carried "a huge responsibility."[705] Different Russia's and China's approaches to the Korean crisis were logical given Korea's primary importance for China and only secondary for Russia[706]. Besides, Moscow under the "reset" with the USA softened its stance on anti-Iranian sanctions, too, "clearly squeezing China's strategic space."[707]

Nevertheless, despite its pro-Western leaning, Russia did not harm relations with China considerably, this time there was no return to the 2001 situation. Moscow did not play the US card in its relationship with China and avoided

---

699 D. Trenin, *Russia Hits the Reset Button*, Project Sindicate, 31.05.2010; *Is Russia Ready for Change?* Carnegie Moscow Center 06.02.2010.

700 B. Lo, *Russia and The New World Disorder*..., p. 172.

701 G. Rozman, *The Sino-Russian*..., p. 250.

702 *Фрагмент выступления С.В. Лаврова на Совете Федерации* [Part of S.V. Lavrov's Speech in the Federation Council], Geshe.Ru, 17.05.2010; interestingly, the part on Dalajlama was not included in the official stenograme of Lavrov's speech on Russian MFA site: *Стенограмма выступления Министра иностранных дел России (...) 13 мая 2010 года* [Stenogramme of the Speech of the Minister of Foreign Affairs], Mid.ru, Probably Moscow decided that China's patience has its limits.

703 Yu Bin, *Reset*...

704 *China expresses concern over alleged exchange of fire between DPRK, ROK*, Xinhua.Com, 23.11.2010.

705 *Северная Корея продолжает обстрел острова Ёнпхендо (North Korea Continues Firing the Yongpyong Island)*, BFM.RU, 23.11.2010; *США и Южная Корея в ответ на обстрел КДНР острова Ёнпхёндо проведут совместные военные учения* [USA and South Korea Conducted a Joint Drills in Return for Firing Yongpyong Island], News.Ru, 24.11.2014.

706 Yu Bin, *Coping with Korea*, "Comparative Connections" vol. 11, no 4.

707 Idem, *Mounting Challenges and Multilateralism*, "Comparative Connections", vol. 12, no 1.

making a choice in growing US-China competition in East Asia. The US-Russia reset did not become a "game changer" – "Moscow's closer relations with the US have not contributed to a slowdown in co-operation with China (…) the peak of the reset (2009-2011) was accompanied by Russia increasing its ties with China (it embraced new areas at the height of the reset), the importance of the US factor in Russia-China relations turned out to be decreasing."[708] Russia-China cooperation continued on a standard basis. In 2010, "Peace Mission" took place; Putin himself opened the ESPO branch to Daqing in August, Medvedev, while visiting China, supported Beijing in its anti-Japanese historical policy and opened the Russian pavilion on the Shanghai EXPO; finally, in 2010 China became Russia's largest trade partner in 2010.[709]

2011 started with the "Arab Spring" and its implications. Here, good Sino-Russian ties were overshadowed by Russia's turn on Libya. At the beginning of Libyan conflict both Moscow and Beijing had similar stance – they did not vetoed the UN resolution No. 1973.[710] What they differed in, were political goals: Moscow hoped to become an arbitrator in this conflict and could not allow itself to veto the resolution and antagonize Western countries.[711] Beijing since the very beginning was much more skeptical about Western plans; when it was abandoned by Russia, however, it chose the "lesser evil" scenario: to resign from vetoing and thanks to it not being criticized in the West (and in the Arab world). Russia's stance raised Chinese resentments: from Chinese elites' perspective "Moscow did not inform Beijing of its decision to change course" which, combined with Russia's mounting arms sales to Vietnam led to growing criticism of Russia by the Chinese in the internet under the label "Russia has never been reliable."[712] When it became clear that Western air-strikes are in fact a partial involvement in the crisis, and when Russian proposal for arbitrage was rejected (the West chose "regime change" instead of striking deals with Gaddafi), Moscow changed its position once again. Russia joined China, together opposing further air-strikes and accusing the West of manipulation and misinterpretation of the resolution No. 1973.[713] Naturally, Russian reaction had nothing to do with care for international community – it was simply a revenge for being put aside of designating Libya's future. Libyan conflict aftermath became clearly visible after two years, in 2013, when during Syrian conflict Moscow and Beijing, remembering bad experiences with Libya, presented a

708 M. Kaczmarski, *Russia-China Relations…*, p. 123.

709 Yu Bin, *Between Geo-Economics and Geo-politics*, "Comparative Connections", vol. 12, no 3.

710 *Security Council Resolution 1973*, UN Press Realese, 17.03.2011.

711 *Russia and China Team Up Against NATO Libya Campaign*, Forbes, 17.05.2011.

712 Yu Bin, *Politics of Two Anniversaries*, "Comparative Connections", vol. 12, no 2.

713 *Short War, Long Shadow.The Political and Military Legacies of the 2011 Libya Campaign*, Royal United Service Institute Report 2012.

much more firm stance in support for President Assad.[714] On more conceptual basis, after the Western intervention, "Russia and China embraced a consistent policy gearing towards preventing any form of Western interference in the Arab Revolutions; the international community, according to Russia and China, should offer 'constructive assistance' to states undergoing revolutionary turmoil."[715]

Russia could not agree with China on the gas issue – two sides were not able to fix the price during Hu Jintao's visit to Moscow in June 2011, nor during Putin's re-visit to Beijing in October 2011 (it was his only foreign visit during the election campaign). The price remained the most important obstacle. Gazprom demanded the EU-style price, Beijing wanted it much cheaper. China's position was hardened by opening of the Central Asian gas pipeline. Russia and China could not agree on Daqing branch line oil price, either. On the other hand, during Putin's visit the first ever memorandum of the "economic modernization" was signed.[716] Moscow indicated desire "to acquire technology from China in areas such as high-speed rail transport, the shipbuilding industry and alternative energy sources"; The question whether "Russia's efforts to involve China in its modernisation process" meant genuine recognition of Chinese success or whether it was "a signal to the West that Western countries need not be the sole source of technology and capital" remained open.[717] 2011 ended up with parliamentary elections to Russian Duma (4 December) and protests which did not threaten Putin's power (yet). Chinese reaction was traditionally a calm one: Beijing simply congratulated Putin upon his victory.[718]

9. The US Pivot to Asia and Its Impact on Sino-Russian Relations

China, threatened by the US pivot to Asia in 2011, vigorously started to prevent it – this is particularly true in case of the fifth generation of Chinese leaders.[719] For Sino-Russian the US pivot meant one important thing: it influenced, intensified and warmed political relations between Moscow and Beijing. This was possible thanks to cooling Russia-USA relations, too. For Russia "once the reset began to lose momentum from 2011, old habits of geopolitical balancing

714 *Opinion: Russia's attitude over Syria is significantly affected by West's deception over Libya*, Left Foot Forward 09.09.2013.

715 M. Kaczmarski, *Russia-China Relations…*, p. 148.

716 *Меморандум между Правительством Российской Федерации и Правительством Китайской Народной Республики о сотрудничестве в области модернизации экономики* [Memorandum between Goverments of RF and PRC on Cooperation in Modernization of Economy], Pravo.Ru.

717 *Russia/China Energy Cooperation Is the Biggest Challenge*, OSW, Warsaw, 12.10.2011

718 *China lauds Russian Duma elections – diplomats*, Ria Novosti, 09.12.2011.

719 Zhao Kejin, *China Turns to Southeast Asia*, Carnegie-Tsinghua 28.03.2014; M. Majid, *Southeas Asia Between China and the United States*, LSE.

returned; the traditional nexus of difficulties with Washington equating to enhanced engagement with Beijing reemerged."[720] Thus, "the inconspicuous fading away of the rest coincided with gradual deterioration of China-US relation (…) effectively Russia and China have found themselves on the same side vis-à-vis USA", thus China and Russia became "'united in assertiveness.'"[721]

This time it was China which initiated this rapprochement – endangered by Washington from the south and the east, China wanted to secure itself from the north. So, the American factor again influenced Sino-Russian relations. Moscow and Beijing united in opposition against Washington's policy: "they have been able to count on each other's 'positive neutrality'; Russia and China have refrained from criticizing each other in international forums and from supporting Washington's position."[722] What is important, however, is that political rapprochement did not translate into Chinese economic concessions. Finally, the results of this new rapprochement began to be clearly visible not at once. Before they materialized, two sides had to deal with domestic political problems.

2012 was a difficult year for Russian and Chinese leadership alike. Putin, victorious after the elections of 4 March 2012, had to deal with mass protests (under the leadership of Alexey Navalny who became popular after an anti-corruption campaign against the ESPO maladministration). Chinese leadership, on its turn, was shaken by the Bo Xilai case – a political and criminal scandal.

These political storms did not influence the bilateral relations. Year 2012 politically started for Russia and China on 4 February, when Moscow and Beijing jointly vetoed the UN Security Council resolution calling for Syrian President Bashar al-Assad to step down.[723] At the same time, Russia and China sent their special envoys to Syria breaking the diplomatic isolation of Damascus. Russian and Chinese stance on Syria showed how these countries learned the "Arab Spring" lesson: these policies by Moscow and Beijing "were directly shaped by the Libyan experience where Russia and China registered huge losses due to their too conciliatory approach toward the West."[724]

During Putin's reelection in March 2012, Beijing as usually accepted the reality: Hu Jintao congratulated Putin and emphasized that China "firmly supports Russia's choice of its own development path according to its national

720 B. Lo, *Russia and The New World Disorder…*, p. 142.

721 Marcin Kaczmarski, *Russia-China Relations…*, pp. 126-127.

722 Ibid., p. 128.

723 *Security Council Fails to Adopt Draft Resolution on Syria as Russian Federation, China Veto Text Supporting Arab League's Proposed Peace Plan*, UN Security Council 04.02.2012.

724 Yu Bin, *Succession, Syria and the Search for Putin's Soul*, "Comparative Connections" 2012, vol. 14, no. 1.

conditions"[725] which was a clear hint to the Western protests. Even a better proof of Chinese recognition came with deputy prime minister Li Keqiang's visit to Moscow (26-30 April 2012); Li was the first foreign dignitary to visit Putin after his re-election. This meeting must have been very interesting: "Putin was described as looking into Li's eyes and taking careful notes while listening to Li's remarks, something that Putin never did before in his meetings with other dignitaries. The Li-Putin talks were stretched from one hour to almost two hours; Li reportedly quoted Confucius words, 'Promises must be kept and actions must be executed.'"[726] Li Keqiang's visit took place during joint maritime exercises on the Yellow Sea (22-27 April 2012) – the largest bilateral exercises and – for China – the largest with any foreign navy.[727] The message they conveyed was strictly a political one, let alone that those were only Sino-Russian state exercises; these implications strengthened after Putin's visit to China in June 2012 (Putin in his third presidential term visited China quite late, as the forth country only) – in the joint declaration both sides emphasized the military cooperation.[728]

On 16 July 2012, an incident occurred on the Japan Sea – the Russian Border Guard vessel "Dzerzhinsky" has seized the Chinese ship under the accusation of poaching on Russian territorial waters. The Chinese MFA expressed "deep dissatisfaction" due to this fact[729], but two sides were able to cover this incident up so that it did not follow the 2009 New Star example and did not deteriorate the mood of Sino-Russian relations.

The summer of 2012 was marked by Sino-Japanese disputes over Senkaku/Diaoyu Islands that led to an outburst of nationalism and mass protests in China. Similar story, though on lesser scale, happened with Japan-South Korean disputes over Takeshima-Dokdo. The island issue – being number 1 in 2012 in Asia – did not influence Sino-Russian relations yet. However, another event impacted them, a bit overshadowed globally, but noticed in Russia – a Chinese vessel "Xuelong" (Snow Dragon) crossing the Arctic Ocean. "Xuelong" was the first Chinese ship that made it – it symbolized China's growing

---

725 *Председатель КНР поздравил Владимира Путина с победой на президентских выборах в России* [Chairman of PRC Congratulated Putin on Winning the Presidential Elections in Russia], Итар-Тасс, 05.03.2012.

726 Yu Bin, *Succession, Syria…*

727 *Совместные военно-морские учения Китая и России 2012 года* [China and Russia Joint Military Drills in 2012], Russian.People.Cn.

728 *Совместное заявление Российской Федерации и Китайской Народной Республики о дальнейшем углублении российско-китайских отношений всеобъемлющего равноправного доверительного партнерства и стратегического взаимодействия* [Joint Declaration of RF and PRC on Further Deepening Sino-Russian Relations to All Encompassing, Equal, Trustful Partnership and Strategic Colaboration], Kremlin.ru, 05.06.2012.

729 *Пекин требует от РФ тщательного расследования инцидента с обстрелом китайского судна* [Beijing Demands RF Detailed Investigation of the Incident with Firing Chinese Ship], РИА Новости, 20.07.2012.

interest in the Arctic (because of the need to exploit the natural resources and use the new transportation route – the Northern Sea Route)[730]; that is why China called itself a "near-Arctic state."[731] China's actions were quickly noted in Moscow for which the Arctic, with its resources and sea transport has been becoming one of the most important fields of political activity[732]. Russia did not like the Chinese attempts to enter the "great game on the Arctic."[733] When Xuelong crossed the Northern Sea Route, Russia started maritime exercises in this region. Quite coincidently, exactly when the Chinese icebreaker crossed the straits near Sakhalin, Russia decided to test whether its anti-ship missiles worked….[734]

The most publicized event in Sino-Russian relations in the second part of 2012 was the APEC summit in Vladivostok. Putin made Hu Jintao, who was about to leave the post of the PRC Chairman, the first speaker at the APEC summit and the first leader to meet Putin on a separate meeting. Hu in his turn has called Putin his "respected old friend"[735] and summarized Sino-Russian relations by outlining such tasks as "deepen strategic mutual trust", or "cooperate in investment to elevate both the quantity and quality of bilateral economic relations" which may be interpreted as a lack of satisfaction from Sino-Russian relations and a call for its improvement.[736] Also prime minister Wen Jiabao said goodbye to Russia with his last trip to Moscow (6-7 December 2012). Again, he stressed the need to develop economic relations which meant that the Chinese side was not fully satisfied with them.[737]

10. Xi Jinping and the Intensification of Sino-Russian Relations

Changes in the Chinese leadership did not lead to a substantial evolution of Chinese policy towards Russia. Xi Jinping with his assertive foreign policy

---

730 A. Gushin, *Understanding China's Arctic Policies*, "The Diplomat", 14.11.2013.

731 *What Is China's Arctic Game Plan?*, "The Atlantic", 16.05.2013.

732 *Основы государственной политики Российской Федерации в Арктике на период до 2020 года и дальнейшую перспективу* [The Principles of RF Govermental Policy in Arctica in Period from 2020 Onwards] Совет Безопасности Российской Федерации. Официальный сайт, 18.09.2008.

733 *Где-то в Китарктике. Пекин подбирается к полярным богатствам* [Somewhere in Chinoartika. China Attempts to Take Polar Riches], Lenta.Ru, 14.06.2013.

734 F. Hill, *Gang of Two. Russia and Japan Make a Play for the Pacific*, "Foreign Affairs" 27.11.2013.

735 *Встреча с Председателем Китайской Народной Республики Ху Цзиньтао* [Meeting with PRC Chairman Hu Jintao], Kremlin.ru, 07.09.2012.

736 Yu Bin, *Tales of Different 'Pivots'* "Comparative Connections", vol.14, no 3.

737 *Встреча Вэнь Цзябао и Дмитрия Медведева* [Meeting of Wen Jiabao and Dmitri Medvedev], Russian People. Com, 07.12.2014.

under the banner of the "Chinese dream" *de facto* continued the previous policy towards Moscow, though he intensified the political relations and was more eager to "grant Moscow face" in public. This, however, did not transfer to economic concessions.

During Xi' first foreign visit to Moscow (made on the way to Africa) on 22 March 2013 both sides emphasized their close ties. The Russians appreciated this gesture: there were a lot of fanfares and solemn voices emphasizing Russia's great power status.[738] All this served to cover up the basic fact that Xi's trip was nothing but the Chinese protocol's response to Putin's last year trip. More importantly, Xi went to Russia on the way to Africa – his most important destination.[739] This is how the Chinese showed the skill of their diplomacy – they covered up Xi's visit to Africa by his trip to Russia; they *gei mianzi* – "granted face" – to Moscow and sent signal to the West.

Nevertheless, of course, the visit was very important. His visit was packed with 20 meetings covering a wide range of topics, mostly on political and economic issues – the parties were debating on how to develop economic sphere; this was reflected in the "joint statement" which strikingly stated "a strategic task of translating high level political relationship into more tangible benefits for both sides."[740] Russia, who has long "been seeking to create a more solid economic foundation for its relationship with Beijing" still could not find "any real cause for satisfaction in this area" – "although the volume of trade has increased (…) its structure is still unfavorable to Russia, which exports almost exclusively raw materials to China, and in return imports manufactured goods."[741] The summit saw signing of 35 agreements and memoranda – some important (on banking and energy, including the documents that would smooth the supplies of energy to Russia; most of the memoranda were financed by Chinese banks which meant that China agreed for prepayment of Russian oil and gas); some less important, if not almost humoristic (on protecting migrating birds or cooperation in rabbit breading).[742] Despite impressive number of

738 *Заявления для прессы по итогам российско-китайских переговоров* [Declarations for Press after the Russian-Sino Talks], Kremlin.ru, 22.03.2013.

739 *China's Leader Tries to Calm African Fears of His Country's Economic Power*, "The New York Times", 25.02.2013.

740 *Совместное заявление Российской Федерации и Китайской Народной Республики о взаимовыгодном сотрудничестве и углублении отношений всеобъемлющего партнёрства и стратегического взаимодействия* [Joint Declaration of RF and PRC on Mutually Comfortable Cooperation and Deepening of All-Encompassing Partnership and Strategic Colaboration], Kremlin.ru, 22.03.2013.

741 *The Chinese leader in Moscow: geopolitical harmony, moderate progress on energy cooperation*, OSW, Warsaw, 27.03.2013.

742 *Документы, подписанные по итогам российско-китайских переговоров* [Documents Signed after Russian-Sino Talks], Kremlin.ru, 22.03.2013.

agreements, "most of them were just framework agreements or non-binding memoranda of cooperation."[743]

Another focus of the Sino-Russian summit were global affairs. For China, the "world order is marked by interdependence and instability (...) many alarming signs: the US pivot to Asia, crises in Korea, tensions in the East and South China Seas, uncertainties surrounding the situation in Afghanistan, and disagreement over the Iranian nuclear program, as well as the deepening civil war in Syria (...) Normalcy in relations with Russia is an island of stability in an increasingly chaotic situation."[744] That is why in the joint-statement both sides emphasized a "new type of great-power relationship" based on "principles of equality" or "mutual trust."[745] The goal of phrases like this was quite clear: "to demonstrate complete political harmony on global and regional issues between Russia and China, in order to strengthen the two countries' position towards the United States, and in the case of Russia, towards Europe also."[746]

The return of this kind of assertive rhetoric, so characteristic for Sino-Russian relations in the 1990s and the early 2000s was associated with the US pivot to Asia. Faced by this challenge, China arranged a public rapprochement with Russia which Xi' visit best demonstrated: "China feels that a clash with the United States in inevitable, so through rapprochement with Russia they formalize an ally."[747] Russian and Chinese commentators emphasized the personal relations factor – Xi and Putin were supposed to find a common language, while Putin made some remarkable gestures towards Xi (Putin was said to accompany Xi for eight consecutive hours in Moscow, which was unprecedented in Russian protocol, and invited Xi, as the first foreign head of state to visit the Russian Ministry of Defence and the Command Center of the Russian Armed Forces). Xi knew how to win Russian hearts – before the visit he organized leaks to the press that he has been brushing up on his Russian and even has been practising a recital of Russian poetry in front of confidantes while during the visit he quoted 19th century Russian philosopher and revolutionary Nikolay Chernyshevsky.[748]

The summit was quickly covered up by information about another North Korean crisis – Pyongyang again made nuclear test. During the summit, Russia and China have condemned the test and supported the UN resolution of 7

743 *The Chinese leader in Moscow...*

744 Yu Bin, *Pivot to Eurasia...*

745 *Совместное заявление Российской Федерации и Китайской Народной Республики о взаимовыгодном сотрудничестве...*

746 *The Chinese leader in...*

747 Personal conversation with Fiodor Lukyanov, Moscow 27.09.2013.

748 Yu Bin, *Pivot to Eurasia...*; *Путин и Си Цзиньпин сошлись характерами* [Putin and Xi Jinping Share Characters], "Столетие" 24.03.2013; *Китайско-кремлевская церемония* [China-Russia Ceremony], "Коммерсантъ" 23.03.2013; *China at crossroads as Xi takes wheel,*"The Sydney Morning Herald", 14.03.2014.

March, condemning this move.[749] Nevertheles, they both protested against further sanctions on Pyongyang. North Korean actions put Russia and China in "a diplomatic and strategic dilemma"; they had to admit that "nobody can influence the North Korean, not even China (it is a) brave new game of 21st century geopolitics, in which the 'shrimp' teases the 'whales'"; from Moscow and especially Beijing's perspective the worst was that "Korean crisis is being exploited by Japan to shake off the decades - long constitutional constraints imposed by the US."[750]

In the summer 2013, Sino-Russian relations were unexpectedly tested by the Edward Snowden story. China must have consulted Russia before agreeing for Snowden's flight from Hong Kong to Moscow[751]. The Russians played this game brilliantly. In public they showed how dissatisfied they were with having this problem (Putin called him in public "an unwanted Christmas present"[752]), in private they must have been delighted for getting such an useful idiot that was a PR catastrophe for the United States. The Chinese appreciated Russian skillfulness: they "seemed thrilled and amused at Russia's handling of the difficult, outsourced issue (…) described Russia's handling of the Snowden case (…) as highly skillful, extremely graceful and sophisticated (…) almost flawless allowing Putin to turn this troublesome issue into a bargaining chip with the US – a burden into an opportunity for strengthening Russian national interests (…) For all of this (…) Russia is China's strategic partner and deserves China's respect, and that China had a lot more to learn from Russia."[753]

The Chinese were certainly learning from Russians in what the latter are the best – fighting.Two mass joint exercises took place in the summer of 2013: "Joint Sea" drills and another "Peace Mission". These exercises were understood in the context of growing tensions between China and its neighbours on disputed island and Sino-Japanese rivalry: as one Chinese commentator put it: "it would help China break through the encirclement by Japan and the United States in the region."[754] The Chinese even heated up the atmosphere when their five ships, after returning from joint drill with Russians, sailed through Soya (La Perouse) Strait, east of Sakhalin and west of Japan Japan and the USA responded by conducting joint maritime exercises on Hokkaido, on a much bigger scale (the US and Japanese capabilities are far ahead of the Chinese ones).[755] As for Russia, these exercises were seen "as a stabilizing influence in

749 *Resolution 2094 (2013)*, United Nations Security Council.

750 Yu Bin, *Pivot to Eurasia…*

751 *A New Anti-American Axis?*, "The New York Times", 06.07.2013.

752 *Путин: США, по сути, заблокировали Сноудена на территории России* [Putin: USA in Fact has Blocked Snowden on Russia's Territory], РИА Новости 15.07.2013.

753 Yu Bin, *Summer Heat and Sino-Russian Strategizing*, "Comparative Connections", vol. 15, no 2.

754 Ibid.

755 *US, Japan launch drill to monitor China-Russia exercise*, Want China Times, 10.07.2013.

addition to strengthening the relationship; Moscow was (…) essentially taking a time-out when problems are more prevalent in Russian-American relations than their isolated points of cooperation in different regions of the world."[756]

Public attention concentrated on the joint exercises, was supposed to turn attention from another important fact – the unexpected and last-minute Russian own exercises in the Eastern Military District on the borderline with China (12-20 July); the largest drills after the USSR's fall.[757] This unexpected event must have had something to do with the Chinese demonstration on La Perouse Strait – although the Chinese ships were sailing on international waters, this Chinese show of strength for the Russians was like a red rag to a bull.[758] They immediately started exercises, probably to show the Chinese their place. Beijing was informed about the drills only hours before it started and through normal channels, although "according to an agreement with China of 1996 (Shanghai Agreement on Confidence-Building Measures in the Border Region), Russia is obliged to notify China prior (in certain instances, 30 days) to the start of exercises within the 100-km zone of the Russian-Chinese border"; although Beijing was irritated, it swallowed this bitter pill, hoping for arms contracts to be finalized.[759]

The second half of 2013 was dominated by the Syrian issue. Bashar al-Assad regime has used chemical weapons on 21 August, while Obama, unwilling to make an intervention, tried to secure international backing first and – when it failed – used a trick: although he did not have to, he asked the Congress to authorize an attack on Syria; Congress on its turn did not put this issue on agenda. Throughout the crisis, the United States and other Western states found themselves on the other side of the barricade than Russia and China. Moscow and Beijing have many times blocked anti-Assad resolutions in the UN, while Xi Jinping supported Putin during the G20 summit in Petersburg. It was Moscow, however, which took the lead as the global protector of Assad regime – it was Putin who prevented the American intervention and overthrow of Assad. China appreciated again Putin's actions by calling them an "outstanding performance" and saying that Syrian crises show than Russia is "an important balancer for the world today."[760] It's hard to be surprised by Chinese enthusiasm: using another country to question American global leadership remains the dreamed scenario for Beijing. But the Chinese elites were delighted by something more: "Putin's Russia did not exercise its power but simply reacted to a grave situation with its geostrategic instinct when facing a brief window

756 Yu Bin, *Summer Heat and Sino-Russian Strategizing…*
757 *Главное — маневры*, Газета.Ру.
758 F. Hill, *Gang of Two…*
759 Yu Bin, *Summer Heat…*
760 Idem, *Putin's Glory and Xi's Dream*, "Comparative Connections", vol. 15, no 3.

of opportunity"[761]. This appraisal was unsurprising, given the fact that the Chinese always admired professionalism, efficiency and mastery.

Putin celebrated his successes on his sixtieth birthday (7 October) on the APEC summit in Bali. The host, Indonesian President Yudhoyono played a guitar while signing Happy Birthday to Putin[762]. The atmosphere must have been even more cozy during celebration with Chairman Xi – this is where their amity is supposed to have started. The leaders discussed military-technical cooperation, arms sales and joint exercises, while President Xi called 2013 "a year of a rich harvest in our relations."[763]

Rich harvest did not mean that Russians lost their hopes for intensifying their activity in Asia. Moscow, knowing that the ultimate fate of the "Russian pivot" depends on making Russia independent from China in Asian policy, put on three cards: Japan, Vietnam and South Korea. With Japan, everything seemed to be going into the direction of a political thaw, but the Ukrainian crisis made it impossible. With Vietnam it ended as always – arms sales only (Hanoi still objects returning of the Russian navy). As for South Korea, its President Park Guen-Hye (now impeached) did not accept Russian proposals for trans-Korean investments.[764] Although Russia tried to distance itself from China, so far it failed. Russia's position is Asia remains weak. Even such beneficial opportunity as the US pivot to Asia did not help Moscow – it even decreased its place for maneuver: "So far, Moscow has not built lasting political or economic ties with any other countries in the region, and so its plans to redress the current imbalance have been little more than a series of empty political declarations (…) Russia's economic ties with China are not balanced by similar trade deals with other regional partners"; moreover "Moscow's ambitions to take on a more significant international role in the region are being hampered by the country's internal problems, particularly the economic underdevelopment which is endemic across Russia's Far East" – this all lead to a conclusion that "Russia remains a minor actor in the region's political and economic order, and the likelihood of significant changes in Moscow's favour remains low."[765] Therefore, it is rather China which uses Russia in Chinese games with the USA rather than Moscow playing the US pivot off against China.

A hidden competition with China was emerging in a much more important region for Russia – in Central Asia. Moscow was initially skeptical about Xi

761 Ibid..

762 *SBY sings 'Happy birthday' to Putin*, "The Jakarta Post", 08.10.2013.

763 *Chinese and Russian presidents meet for fifth time this year*, "China Daily" 08.10.2013.

764 *Seoul Cautious on Putin's Far East Development Push*, "The Wall Street Journal Asia" 13.11.2013.

765 M. Kaczmarski, *Russia's turn towards Asia: more words than actions*, OSW, Warsaw, 09.10.2012.

Jinping's New Silk Road Economic Belt, announced during his visit to Kazakhstan.[766] Although China has proclaimed "rejecting imperialist mentality", regarding its Central Asia policy and "seeking normal, win-win exchange" with others", it wasn't convincing, let alone for Moscow. Its reaction came at once: Deputy Foreign Minister Igor Morgulov said that "Russia and China are not competing for influence in Central Asia" and added that "our Chinese friends recognize the traditional role our country continues to play in this region, so we do not see any regional rivalry problems."[767] This announcement must be interpreted by the classical Soviet way – *a rebours* – the more official statement rejects rivalry, the more it proves that this rivalry is well and alive. Actions followed words: after Russian pressure, Kyrgyzstan rejected the idea of Chinese railway which meant that "having lost its monopoly over Central Asia's gas export, Moscow apparently drew the red line in Central Asia to avert China's railroad projects."[768]

Hidden competition in Central Asia did not influence the bilateral relations – the beginning of 2014 was very good for Sino-Russian relations. It started from announcement that Xi Jinping – as the first ever Chinese president – would take part in the Sochi Olympics opening ceremony. His presence, along with Japanese prime minister Shinzo Abe, politically saved the summit for Russia – the absence of Western leaders made the Sochi Olympics "the more politicized than any other Games in recent history."[769]

From the Chinese perspective, Western criticism on Russia "when there had been no major problems" showed that "the West was selfish, narrow-minded, and with little tolerance of others" (...) Perhaps "this was the way the West has sought to settle the 'final account' with Putin for his unhelpful behaviour regarding Syria and the Snowden affair."[770] Western diplomatic "quasi-boycott" made Chinese and Japanese presence even more important.[771] Xi's visit to Sochi was his second after becoming president – this time Xi did this to "save Putin's face". During their meeting, the leaders agreed on joint celebration of the end of the WWII anniversary (a hint on Japan), while Xi "invited" Putin to join the "New Silk Road Economic Belt". This was a clear message: public support for Russia (Xi's arrival to Sochi) in return for accepting the Chinese policy in Central Asia and Beijing's anti-Japanese political history. It is hard to tell whether the offer was accepted, because it was soon overshadowed by the Ukrainian crisis.

---

766 *President Xi Jinping Delivers Important Speech and Proposes to Build a Silk Road Economic Belt with Central Asian Countries*, MFAPRC, 07.09.2013.

767 Yu Bin, *Putin's Glory and Xi's Dream* "Comparative Connections" vol. 15, no 3.

768 Ibid.

769 D. Trenin, *Sochi: The Game of Politics*, Carnegie Center Moscow, 27.01.2014.

770 Yu Bin, *"Western Civil War" Deja Vu?"*, "Comparative Connections", vol. 16, no.1.

771 D. Trenin, *Sochi...*

11. Ukrainian Crisis and China-Russia Relations

Dramatic events in Ukraine were another factor in the China-Russia Relations. In the crisis, the position of China was essential for Russia. China kept "kind (or benign, or sympathetic, or friendly) neutrality" towards Moscow. In order to maintain Beijing's favour and above all "secure strategic rear", Vladimir Putin concluded a huge gas contract with China in May 2014.

Since the beginning of the protests, China kept distance and even treated the whole situation as a potential opportunity for itself. However, the dramatic deterioration of the situation in February 2014 brought China into an uncomfortable situation – for Beijing both relations with the West and with Russia are very important. From the Chinese perspective, one should not stand for any side and remain neutral as long as possible. The Russian annexation of Crimea was to surprise Beijing – this Russian action resulted in Beijing falling into an "Ukrainian trap". The way in which Beijing got out of the trap once again proved Chinese diplomatic capabilities. In the surrounding conflict, Beijing decided to maneuver, not to take a stand and hide behind Russia. From the Chinese point of view, the best solution from the "Ukrainian dilemma" was a "studied ambivalence", or even "strategic ambivalence."[772]

A tangible proof for Chinese neutrality was that Beijing abstained from voting during the ballot on condemnation of Crimea referendum at the Security Council of the United Nations (it was blocked by Russia). According to its strategy, China in the beginning phase of the crisis assumed a position of a player standing on the side and observing the ongoing conflict – as the Chinese rule tells: *zuo shan guan hu dou*, which means "Sitting on a hill watching two tigers fight". It was possible because of an impression of chaos: the following Chinese communicates instead of clarifying, brought less light to the Chinese position, which was consentient with the Beijing's intention.[773] However, along with the development of the Ukrainian crisis, and above all with the imposition of Western sanctions, the Chinese neutrality changed into a "kind neutrality" towards Russia.

It happened because of a couple of reasons. First of all, the Chinese implemented their other maxim, which is a Chinese equivalent to ours "divide and rule"- *yi yi zhi yi* which roughly means: "fight off one barbarian by another". In this specific case it meant to support the weaker – thus Russia, but not as much as to antagonize the West. From the Beijing's perspective, the Russian action was not praiseworthy, but less damaging than the American backup for Maidan (considered as a a Western-led conspiracy which overthrew the legal

772 D. Cohen, *China Maintains Studied Ambiguity On Ukraine As Russia Claims 'Concordance Of Views'*, "China Brief", Volume XIV, Issue 5, March 7, 2014; Yu Bin, *"Western Civil War"...*

773 R. Pyffel, *Siedem powodów....*

government, similarly to "color revolutions.")[774] The Russian annexation of Crimea, thus a violation of the territorial inviolability, was after all the lesser evil than the seizure of power by Maidan, as a result of overthrow of a legal government. China supported Russia, but in a way noticeable to win Russia's "gratitude" (and to empower itself vis-à-vis Moscow) and not significantly, as not to spoil the relations with the West. China called for "Ukraine's stability, economic development, and social harmony"; a key missing word in this statement was "sovereignty."[775] It was characteristic, because China usually stands its ground in the terms of sovereignty defence, however at that moment persisting in "sovereignty" would place China on the Western side of the barricade, and as a matter of fact on the side against Russia, which stocked to the "law of nation self-determination". Next reason for this slight lean towards Russia was of an internal nature. The situation in Ukraine influenced the Chinese imagination: vision of chaos, irrationality and extreme emotions leading to downfall and break-up[776] inscribed perfectly into the most negative archetype of chaos (*luan*) in the Chinese political culture – the absolute worst possible scenario, which can only be withheld by a strong power. When they observed Ukraine, the Chinese political elites saw in their mind's eye this scenario in their own country, if the power of the CPC fell. In such a situation, a natural reaction of the Chinese elites was to support the party who offered a hope for calming the situation down and bringing peace with arbitrary methods (in such situation everything is allowed). For the Chinese elites this was mainly Russia.

The "kind neutrality" of Beijing met with Russian gratitude, if not to say with enthusiasm. Putin thanked China for support in an emotional way.[777] It seems that Russian reaction was on one hand a political calculation (showing the Chinese support as something more important than it was in the reality), and on the other hand a proof of the importance of psychological factor in the Russian politics: Russians, who often operate with the extremes, felt that in the groundbreaking moment the Chinese supported them. However, the Chinese position primary resulted from reserved calculation of its own interest. Limited conflict between the West and Russia was and still is beneficial for Beijing. Crisis tied the USA to Europe, and at the same time diverted (at least partially) their attention from the Asia-Pacific region. Moreover, according to reasoning in Taoism, in which even in the worst possible situation one can find positive accents, China saw advantage in the Russian annexation of Crimea. Smart seizure of the peninsula created an interesting, and possible *casus* for the future

774 M. Kaczmarski, *Russia-China and the West*...

775 Yu Bin, *"Western Civil War"*...

776 Liu Zoukai, *Ostrożne zaangażowanie* [A Caution Engagement]; un unpublished article prepared for the Polish media.

777 *Обращение Президента Российской Федерации*[FR President's Adress], Kremlin.ru, 18.03.2014.

game for Taiwan and in disputes on the South China Sea.[778] Above all, the crisis strengthened the Chinese position, quite the opposite as happened in case of Russia – it narrowed down strategic field of Russia ("it guaranteed, that for a long time Russia will be China's safe and strategic backside").[779] Moreover, the Western sanctions led to a situation in which from the Russian perspective, China's relevance rose, as it is the only one important world's economy, that did not join sanctions. That caused a greater dependence of Russia from China as a source of independent funding: "A Chinese phrase for this is *xingzai lehuo*, or to take delight in other's misfortunes (sometimes translated into German as *Schadenfreude*). Despite the sympathies it has expressed, it is likely China feels itself better off for the suffering in Ukraine."[780].

Certainly the repercussions of crisis strengthened China *vis-à-vis* Russia, which became perfectly apparent during the visit of Vladimir Putin between 19-20th of May in 2014 in Shanghai. Although the visit was prepared earlier, its time coincided with the Ukrainian crisis, which resulted in the fact that geopolitics casted a complete shadow over this meeting – for Moscow it was important to display this meeting as a turning point in the relations, and as a true beginning of "Russian turn towards Asia". A symbol of this turn and the most important moment of the visit was of course signing up of the gas contract.

Putin arrived to the summit politically weakened due to a couple of reasons. Mainly, it was because of Ukraine – after the Western sanctions Putin wanted to demonstrate that "Russia is not alone" and that it has a couple of important partners somewhere else: "what mattered most to Putin was signaling to the United States and Europe that Russia was strategically independent, would not be intimidated by the imposition of sanctions, and possessed powerful friends."[781] Thus, Russia wanted this deal much more than China did. However, Russian position was also weaker due to long-term economic causes – shale gas revolution, increasing significance of the LNG in the world, as well as vivification of the European plans on lowering the dependence from Russia. All these features changed the balance of power in energy suppliers (Russia) and consumers to the benefit of the latter.[782]

Beijing made use of their supremacy. First it "waited out" Putin: first day it did not agree upon Russia's conditions and send controlled leaks to newspapers, that the contract will not be concluded. Putin was so desperate he was even going to ask Jiang Zemin for support. The Chinese side laid down hard bargain and held on to it: low price (around 350-380 USD for 1000m3 vis-à-

---

778 D. H. Paal, How *Does the Ukraine Crisis Impact China*, Carnegie Center Moscow, 24.03.2014.

779 D. Trenin, *Russia-China. The Russian Liberals Revenge*, Carnegie Center, 19.05.2014.

780 D. H. Paal, *How Does the Ukraine Crisis Impact China*, Carnegie Center Moscow, 24.03.2014; E. Rumer, *China the Winner*, Carnegie Center Moscow, 16.06.2014.

781 B. Lo, *Russia and The New World Disorder…*, p. 142.

782 E. Rumer, *China the Winner…*

vis Russian proposition 400 USD), and above all, the energetic investments on Siberia and the Russian Far East[783]. Gas pipeline is to be built on the Chinese debt – the price and fee mechanism is constructed in such a way that the Chinese *de facto* pay for the infrastructure – and will be responsible for it. This gives China huge possibilities of influence on Siberia – a transformation it into raw material base for China's development.

The summit full of fanfares lasted two days and was a huge political demonstration. It was connected with the Chinese-Russian maneuvers ongoing nearby. The summit finished with signing up forty-six agreements and memoranda[784]. However, "most of them are non-binding memoranda, letters of intent, or framework contracts"[785]: "In normal circumstances these documents wouldn't have reached the leaders' desks. This stack may have been meant to impress others."[786] That is why, gas contract aside, "economic results of the summit are at best modest". The summit's economic results well reflect "the structural problems in the economic relations between China and Russia (…) the two states' economic cooperation is based on a 'semi-colonial' model of simple trade exchange, under which Russia nearly exclusively sells China raw materials and imports mainly industrial products from China."[787] Signing up a contract had above all a political meaning. Political facade of the summit was also emphasized by the "joint statement", which was similar to the summit – only a relative Russia's success and an evident success of China.[788]

Russia obtained only a partial support from China (in the case of sanctions and the Russian critique of the Western actions in Ukraine), but not in the key issues for Russia, like federalization of Ukraine and neutrality, or condemnation of the Kiev government. "Putin did not obtain a full and explicit support from the side of «strategic partner»"; in the case of central Asia declaration was a compromise – Moscow managed to get Beijing's support for the idea of the Eurasian Union and assurance of respectfulness towards Russian business, but it had to acknowledge the Chinese "Silk Road."[789] To sum up these con-

783 W. Rodkiewicz, *Putin in Shanghai: a strategic partnership on Chinese terms*, OSW, Warsaw, 21.05.2014.

784 *Документы, подписанные в рамках официального визита Президента Российской Федерации В. В. Путина в Китайскую Народную Республику* [Documents Signet During President Putin visit to PRC], Kremlin.ru, 20.05.2014.

785 W. Rodkiewicz, *Putin in Shanghai…*

786 A. Gabuev, *Misreading Asia*, Carnegie Center Moscow, 03.06.2014.

787 W. Rodkiewicz, *Putin in Shanghai…*

788 *Совместное заявление Российской Федерации и Китайской Народной Республики о новом этапе отношений всеобъемлющего партнерства и стратегического взаимодействия* [Joint Declaration of RF and PRC on New Stage of All-Encompassing Partnership and Strategic Colaboration], Kremlin.ru, 20.05.2014.

789 W. Rodkiewicz, *Putin in Shanghai….*

siderations, one can add that China supported Russia there, where it was comfortable and beneficial from the perspective of their own business, and there, where it cost little – and nowhere else.

Generally the summit finished with the real success of China and relative, above all image-building success of Russia. This success was absolutely necessary for Russia, which was ready to pay a high price for signing up the gas deal. This is indicated by the words of Putin himself, who told that "Chinese are very serious negotiators", who "drank quite a bit of our blood during the negotiations."[790] On the other hand, the fact that gas prices soon fall down might indicate that it wasn't completely a bad deal for Russia.

Although Russian commentators announced programmatic optimism and highlighted the summit success and "equal conditions"[791], some of them like Dmitri Trenin admitted that China was the one who benefited mostly: "it will reshape and rebalance Eurasia, whose center of gravity will now move from Moscow to Beijing (…) such an outcome would certainly benefit China, but it will give Russia a chance to withstand U.S. geopolitical pressure, compensate for the EU's coming energy re-orientation, develop Siberia and the Far East, and link itself to the Asia-Pacific region."[792] Thus, its importance can only be compared to "Moscow's opening to Western Europe in the late 1960s."[793] One does not need to add that China is the biggest winner of this situation: "Putin, like a gambler, leaves his ancestral silver in a Chinese pawnshop to play for higher stakes with the West."[794]

12. Embracing One Belt One Road: The Recent Sino-Russian Relations

Events that took part after mid 2014, strengthened Russia's isolation in the West and enhanced Russia's turn to the East or to be precise to China. The shooting down of the Malaysian plane, the intensification of Russian activity in Ukraine and the following Western sanctions (which strongly hit the Russian financial sector, which soughed help in China or Singapore) hindered or even deprived for some time Moscow of the pro-Western option. This resulted in further weakening of Russia *vis-à-vis* China – Moscow "had fallen into the

---

790 Yu Bin, *Navigating Through the Ukraine Storm*, "Comparative Connections", 15 IX, Vol. 16, no 2.

791 Ф. Лукьянов, *Логичное партнерство* [Logical Partnership], "Российская газета" 21.05.2014.

792 D. Trenin, *Russia and China. The Russian Liberals…*

793 Idem, *From Greater Europe….*

794 J. Korejba, *Putin wali głową w mur (chiński)* [Putin bangs his head against (Chinese) Wall], "Nowa Europa Wschodnia" 11.06.2014.

arms of Beijing" and starting becoming a raw material addition for China.[795] Nevertheless, Russia decided to bandwagon to China and embrace its flagship project: One Belt One Road.

Russian analysts see Sino-Russian asymmetry similarly, yet in a different light. Although they acknowledge limited place of maneuver and feel the rapprochement with China forced by the Western actions, they put it in the longer perspective. According to Dmitri Trenin, "the epoch of post-communist Russia's integration with the West is over (…) Putin's vision of a 'greater Europe' from Lisbon to Vladivostok, made up of the European Union and the Russian-led Eurasian Economic Union, is being replaced by a 'greater Asia' from Shanghai to St. Petersburg". Therefore, the relations with China are something closer than the strategic partnership and "Russia's foreign policy has begun to prioritize China more than it did in the last half century", thus the relations between Russia and China can be called a new "entente."[796] Alexander Gabuev wrote that Moscow "turned fears into hopes" in its relations with Beijing: Russia has "reoriented its economy toward China" and eased informal barriers to Chinese investment in selling advanced weaponry and in Chinese participation in large infrastructure (roads, railways) and natural-resource projects: "it was hoped that China would become a major buyer of Siberian hydrocarbons, Shanghai and Hong Kong would become the new London and New York for Russian companies seeking capital, and Chinese investors would flock to buy Russian assets, providing badly needed cash, upgrading the country's aging infrastructure, and sharing technology."[797]

Therefore, the Western sanction played decisive role in Moscow's political choices in 2014. Western sanctions against Russia were naturally beneficial for China, but Beijing restrained from sanctioning Russia because of strategic, geopolitical and cultural reasons. Firstly, China interpreted pressure on Moscow as an attempt to "break Russia's will and make it obey U.S. rules" but also "as a warning to other non-Western competitors, above all China. Exemplary punishment of Russia, in that view, is to serve as a means to deter China."[798] Secondly, because the feeling of sympathy: the Chinese elites and the Chinese society which believe that the West is trying to curb China's further development feel that "for various reasons, China is still being sanctioned by the West" – thus, when the West did the same to Russia they reacted with sympathy.[799] The last reason why China did not bandwagon was the conviction that

795 R. Pyffel, *Po Boeingu w objęcia smoka* [After Boening into Dragon's Embrace], polska-azja.pl 31.07.2014; W. Rodkiewicz, *Turn to the East…*, p. 5.

796 D. Trenin, *From Greater Europe….*

797 A. Gabuev, *Friends with Benefits?….*

798 D. Trenin, *From Greater Europe…*

799 Yu Bin, *Russia's Pride and China's Power*, "Comparative Connections", vol. 16, no.3.

Russia can withhold the sanctions ("Russia has experienced many ups and downs, and it has the tenacity to withstand risks and dangers.")[800]

These two motives notwithstanding, China used its leverage over Russia during prime minister Li Keqiang's visit to Moscow in October 2014. During the meeting nearly 40 documents were signed– thus the unholy tradition of signing the bunch of papers during each top-level meeting was kept (this time, however, contrary to Putin's visit to Shanghai, there was no breakthrough).[801] As many times before, "the plethora of framework agreements and memorandums of understanding (MOUs)" acted as "a placebo, masking the inability— and sometimes lack of commitment— to achieve substantive deal".[802] And these MoUs usually take years to realize, if ever.[803]

The main aim of this meeting from the Russian perspective was to build closer ties with China "in order to reduce the Russian economy's financial and technological dependence on the West, and of diversifying Russia's energy markets."[804] The good example of that was signing the memorandum on the Chinese construction of a high-speed railway line from Moscow to Kazan which main intention was to undermine the position of the Western businesses interested in investing in the project, such as Siemens and Alstom (which would then lobby against the sanctions in Germany and France). This memorandum, however, has remained since then unfulfilled. This is due to the fact that Beijing demands "that the lion's share of equipment be produced in China."[805]

This meeting showed that China, by taking advantage of the weakness of Russian banks and companies (denied access to Western capital markets by sanctions), was interested in further access to Russian energy, in constructing infrastructure that helps to fulfill this purpose and in selling machines and technology; the Kremlin which was determined to reduce Russia's dependence on economic ties with the West, was "willing to pay a high economic price by accepting cooperation with China on conditions which are being increasingly dictated by Beijing."[806]

Internationally, the APEC summit in Beijing on 10-12 November 2014, saw Putin committing a *faux pas* by putting a coat on Xi Jinping's wife Peng Liyuan

---

800 *How long can Russia withstand the crisis?*, "Global Times", 22.12.2014.

801 *Визит Ли Кэцяна успешен, но новые соглашения предстоит реализовать* [Li Keqiang's visit is successful but new agreements should be implemented], Ria Novosti, 15.10.2014.

802 B. Lo, *Russia and The World Disorder*..., p. 210.

803 А. Габуев, *Вернуть нельзя сотрудничать: чем важны новые договоренности России и Японии* [Cooperate, Cannot Give Back; why New Russia and Japan Agreements are important], Carnegie Moscow, 19.12.2016.

804 E.Fischer, S. Kardaś, W. Rodkiewicz, *The rising cost of getting closer to Beijing: New Russian-Chinese economic agreements*, OSW, Warsaw, 15.10.2014.

805 Alexander Gabuev, *Friends with Benefits?*...

806 E.Fischer, Sz. Kardaś, W. Rodkiewicz, op. cit.

during outdoor meeting of the leaders that took place in the very cold November night in Beijing (this Putin's gesture might have been considered a tender one by the traditional Eastern European etiquette, though certainly unacceptable by the Western standards, let alone Chinese ones). Chinese media censored this scene, while Western ones had a lot of joy with producing with comments as "Russia's Don Juan-in-chief just got a little too friendly with Xi Jinping's wife" or "the first unspoken rule of diplomacy might be 'Don't hit on the president's wife.'"[807] Despite becoming a global viral scene, this incident neither influenced the Xi-Putin relations nor was particularly important politically. During the event, China-US deal on climate was much more important, as well as the fact that Xi Jinping put himself in a central position between the USA and Russia – it was "a visual coup" to the US hegemony.[808]

The beginning of 2015 was quite uneventful for Russia-China relations. Russia was concentrated on Ukraine and Iran, while China on its AIIB bank that challenges the Western financial-institutional underpinning of the global order. What was surprising in relation to the AIIB was that Russia joined this bank on the last moment, on 28 March 2015 (the deadline was 31 March) which unpleasantly surprised China. The same can be said about slow (or lack of) implementation of bilateral agreements and memoranda. The mood in Beijing, however, must have changed in April, when China became the first country to purchase Russia's S-400 anti-aircraft missile system (about $3 billion for at least 6 battalions of S-400 which China will likely receive in 2017.)[809] Russia, formerly unwilling to sell most advanced weapons, was forced to modify its stance due to dire economic situation.

In spring of 2015, Russia and China have traditionally staged another political show – this time the 70th anniversary of the end of the WWII's on 9 May 2015. Russia tried to present itself as a country that cannot be isolated and a one that keeps the history of victory over fascism. China, on the other hand, joined these celebrations because it helped Beijing to indirectly weaken Japan (Putin in his speech mentioned both German Nazism and Japanese militarism which he did for the first time.)[810]

During the Sino-Russian summit again the tradition was kept: 32 agreements worth $25 billion were signed (mainly framework agreement or memoranda, including… a memorandum on the construction of a high-speed railway line from Moscow to Kazan again.)[811] These documents were "quite vague,

---

807 *Putin Hits on China's First Lady, Censors Go Wild*, "Foreign Policy", 10.11.2014.

808 D. Trenin, *From Greater Europe…*

809 Yu Bin, *China-Russia, All Still Quiet in the East*, "Comparative Connections" vol.17 no.1.

810 *Выступление Президента России на параде, посвящённом 70-летию Победы в Великой Отечественной войне* [President Putin's Speech During 70th Anniversary of Victory in the Great Patriotic War], Kremlin Ru. 09.05.2015.

811 *Документы, подписанные по итогам российско-китайских переговоров* [Documents Signed During Russian-Sino Talks], Kremlin Ru. 08.05.2015.

and suggest that Beijing is only interested in developing cooperation with Russia in selected areas, such as energy, infrastructure and high-speed railways, and on conditions laid down by China" and consequently did not produce a breakthrough (there was no progress on energy cooperation).[812] What was important in the summit was a joint declaration[813] (about 70% of which was about foreign policy)[814] and another one, where both sides pleaded to cooperate in the Eurasian Economic Union (EaEU) and the Chinese New Silk Road projects.[815] This signifies a strive to avoid a clash of interests in Central Asia and was one of the first moves of making Central Asia a Russian-Chinese "condominium" (see: chapter on Central Asia). In a way Moscow made a virtue out of necessity here: "Moscow's previous efforts to block Chinese initiatives in the region proved to be ineffective, which may have increased its readiness to take China into account, rather than shut Beijing out."[816] This document signified growing shift in Russian policy makers towards accepting, instead of rejecting the Chinese idea of the New Silk Road (One Belt One Road). The Western sanctions are probably to blame for that: "It was obvious that Moscow was in a much weaker position to resist China's westward move, let alone to keep its Central Asian partners in line; the best alternative was to work with Beijing and benefit from China's investment spree."[817]

Good atmosphere of relations was followed by joint military drills with geopolitical hints. The same geopolitical reasons stood behind the BRICS summit in Ufa (7 July 2015) with its grandiose 13,000-word, 77-clause Ufa Declaration[818] and behind the SCO summit (15 July 2015) that officially started the procedures for granting India and Pakistan full membership as well as granting Belarus the status of observer (improved from dialogue partner), and taking Azerbaijan, Armenia, Cambodia, and Nepal as new dialogue partners.

---

812 M. Kaczmarski, Szymon Kardaś, *Russia-China. Ritual Demonstration Against the West*, OSW, Warsaw, 13.05.2015.

813 *Совместное заявление Российской Федерации и Китайской Народной Республики об углублении всеобъемлющего партнерства и стратегического взаимодействия и о продвижении взаимовыгодного сотрудничества* [Joint Declaration of RF and PRC on Deepening of All-Encompassing Partnership and Strategic Colaboration and Moving Towards Mutually Beneficial Cooperation], Kremlin.Ru, 08.05.2016.

814 "The document was by far the most foreign policy-focused document by top leaders of the two countries", Yu Bin, *Tales of Two Parades, Two Drills, and Two Summits*, "Comparative Connections", vol. 17, no.2.

815 *Совместное заявление Российской Федерации и Китайской Народной Республики о сотрудничестве по сопряжению строительства Евразийского экономического союза и Экономического пояса Шелкового пути* ([oint Declaration of RF and PRC on Cooperation in Connecting Eurasian Union and Silk Road Economic Belt] , Kremlin.Ru, 08.05.2016.

816 M. Kaczmarski, S. Kardaś, *Russia-China. Ritual Demonstration…*

817 Yu Bin, *H-Bomb Plus THAAD…*.

818 *VII BRICS Summit: 2015 Ufa Declaration*, BRICS Information Center, Toronto, 09.07.2015.

Geopolitics followed on China's first Victory Parade for the 70th anniversary of Sino-Japanese War on 3 September. Putin was the most important foreign guest who appeared on this celebration (most of the Western leaders did not show up), while Russian military contingent took part in the parade – for the first time in the bilateral relations. Despite high symbolism, however, the economic momentum of Sino-Russian cooperation was weakening: in the first six months of 2015, the value of bilateral trade fell 31.4 percent compared to the previous year due to the fall of energy prices that hit Russia hard; out of structural reasons (Russia's heavy dependence on energy exports to China), Russia's imports also declined significantly due to the ruble's devaluation. To make matters worse, China experienced economic slowdown and stock market crash, which challenged the overarching optimism concerning China's further rise. For Russia-China relations it meant that China's energy demand would not be as strong as in the past decade and thus it is unlikely that China would pay an excessively high amount for the Russian gas.[819]

On the other hand, China could pay for something it had been wanting for long: Su-35. After 8 years of negotiations, in November 2015, a $2-billion sale of 24 Russian Sukhoi-35 fighter-bombers to China was sealed[820], signifying Moscow's major departure from its previous policy of not selling to China the most sophisticated weaponry.

Finally, internationally the last quarter of 2015 was marked by Russia's entry to war in Syria. China has remained on the sidelines of the Syrian drama – this was done for an obvious reason: "China does not have as strong an influence in the Middle East as the other UN Security Council permanent members", and thus opted for "caution and impartiality" in this conflict.[821] Nevertheless, Beijing's favour to Moscow was clearly seen – the Chinese commentators emphasized Russia's political gains (the end of Moscow's global isolation) and the failure of the Western policy in the Middle East. China reacted positively to the Russian intervention, because thanks to it Beijing could do what it loves best: fulfill its goals with somebody else's hands. Thus, Russia has diverted the US attention from competition with China in Asia-Pacific and yet again has "shouldered the burden of open rivalry with the United States" and allowed China to link cracking of Uyghur separatists group with global war on terror; finally it could present itself again as a peaceful and neutral power in the conflict.[822]

2016 started for Russia and China – as well as for other great powers – with a big beat. North Korea conducted its forth nuclear test on 6 January. The USA and South Korea reacted strongly by announcing a possibility of deploying the

819 Yu Bin, *H-Bomb Plus THAAD* ...

820 *Confirmed: China Buys 24 Advanced Fighter Jets From Russia*, "The Diplomat" 20.11.2015.

821 Yu Bin, *H-Bomb Plus THAAD* ...

822 M. Kaczmarski, Jakub Jakóbowski, *China on Russia's intervention in Syria*, OSW, Warsaw, 19.01.2016.

THAAD missile defence system on the Peninsula (formerly Seoul disagreed to locate this system in the Peninsula, now for the first time it started reconsidering its position). This alarmed Moscow and Beijing, since the THAAD's radars could monitor any missile test and firing thousands of kilometers inside China and Russia – that is why Russia and China hardened their positions on both the North Korean nuclear test and the possibility of the deployment of the THAAD in Korea. For them both the Korean provocations and the Western reaction to it was bad news. But the latter was worse. Fyodor Lukyanov aptly summarized Russian and Chinese perception: "the North Korean threat is a wonderful pretext for strengthening the U.S. military and political presence on the Korean Peninsula in Japan and in the whole region. And it is undoubtedly projected on China."[823] Although eventually deployment of the THAAD did not materialize in the first half of 2016 (it did in early 2017, though its fate is uncertain given Trump's position on it), Russia and China announced its first-ever joint anti-missile drills in Russia. Moscow further supported Beijing by emphasizing the need to "stop internationalizing the dispute on South China Sea"[824] – so far Moscow has been trying to refrain from engaging in this issue and stay neutral.

While Korean Peninsula made Russia and China move closer, the Chinese activity in Central Asia distanced Moscow and Beijing for a while. China's close cooperation in security sphere with Pakistan and (particularly) Afghanistan that may include Tajikistan, also evoked alarm bells in Moscow. Moscow responded in its traditional way – by staging a show of force. Russia has conducted large-scale joint drill with Tajikistan in 15-20 March 2016 and announced in April that it will not deliver rocket engines to China.[825] These petty disagreements were not, however, particularly important. In late May two sides had their first joint headquarters missile defense exercise in Moscow while on 9th June during they joint naval excersises both countries' navies entered the waters "in a contiguous zone" near the Senkaku/Diaoyu Islands which showed Russia's first real step in siding with China over South China Sea's dispute.[826]

Very good mood continued during Putin's quick (24 hours) visit to China on 23 June 2016. The meeting traditionally ended with signing a bunch o papers – 37 agreements; most important included sale of stakes in a number of Russian projects to Chinese firms, an oil supply contract, joint investments in petrochemical projects in Russia, purchase of heavy helicopters, and the sale of Russia's advanced space rocket (RD-180) engine to China; there were, traditionally, almost humoresque aspects, too – two documents signed by those

823 Qouted in: Yu Bin, *H-Bomb Plus THAAD …*

824 *Интервью Министра иностранных дел России С.В.Лаврова СМИ Монголии, Японии и КНР в преддверии визитов в эти страны* [Foreign minister Lavrov's interview to Mongolian, Japanese and Chinese media], Москва, 12 апреля 2016 года, 12.04.2016, mid.ru.

825 Yu Bin, *H-Bomb Plus THAAD …*

826 Idem, *Politics of "Reluctant Allies"*, "Comparative Connections", Vol. 18, No. 2.

leaders of great powers mentioned cooperation in… hockey.[827] What was not signed, however, was the long awaited contract on financing the high-speed Moscow-Kazan railway. At the time of writing, this project still remains aspirational; only small part of the route is being developed and participation of Chinese companies, although probable, is still uncertain[828] (Moscow asks China for more money while at the same time luring Western companies to get involved despite sanctions.)[829] The signed contracts were clearly advantageous to China.[830] Even more so was the very long joint *communiqué* on the global strategic stability, where Russia and China expressed concerns over THAAD and where Putin moved closer to Beijing's stance in the dispute on South China Sea.[831]

This visit, as many other facts, has proved that despite all these traditional, grandiose words, after two years of Russia's "turn to China" the results were still poor. Russian hopes "are going through a painful reality check."[832] Russia's pivot has "stalled": given the fall in commodity prices in 2015 (and its consequences: decline of Russian economy and devaluation of the ruble) and China's economic problems, the Chinese companies are reluctant to invest in Russia – this in turn "has led to growing disillusionment among the Russian elite who had hoped that China might replace Europe as its top energy customer, leaving the Kremlin's turn to Asia hanging in the balance."[833] Economic data support this claim. Russian-Chinese bilateral trade fell from $95.3 billion in 2014 by 28.6 percent to $63.6 billion in 2015 (it makes just 1.5 percent of China's international trade that year) and despite that volumes of crude oil deliveries from Russia to China increased by 33.7 percent, Russia has only managed to attract $560 million in foreign direct investment from China (that is less than 0.5 percent of China's total outbound direct investment in 2015 and much less than the $4 billion in Chinese investment that Russia received in 2013, before the Ukraine crisis) and $18 billion of Chinese loans in 2015 (that made China the largest source of the external financing that year) – to put that

---

827 *Совместные документы, подписанные в ходе официального визита Президента Российской Федерации В.В.Путина в Китай* [Documents Signed During President Putin's trip to China], Kremlin Ru, 26.06.2016.

828 M. Makocki, T*he Silk Road goes north: Sino-Russian economic cooperation and competition,* [in]: *China and Russia. Gaming…*

829 *Russia asks China to boost Moscow-Kazan fast-speed rail project financing*, Tass, 18.05.2017.

830 Minxin Pei, *Vladimir Putin's China Visit Put His Weakness on Full Display*, "Fortune" 29.06.2016.

831 *Совместное заявление Президента Российской Федерации и Председателя Китайской Народной Республики об укреплении глобальной стратегической стабильности* [Joint Declaration of RF President and PRC Chairmant on Deepening Global Strategic Stability], Kremlin Ru, 26.06.2016.

832 A.Gabuev, *Friends with Benefits?….*

833 Idem, *China's Pivot to Putin's Friends….*

number in perspective, in 2013 Russia was able to attract $261 billion from the European Union and the United States.[834]

In late 2015 Russian elite seemed to be deeply disappointed with the lack of results of its turn to the East. Putin rejected meeting with major Asian businessmen during Vladivostok's first Eastern summit preferring instead to have a good time with American actor Steven Segal. Moreover, in November 2015 he skipped the East Asian Summit and the APEC Summit, for the first time since 2002 – "probably he yielded to a general atmosphere among the elites that in autumn 2015 stopped considering the 'turn to the East' as something important to prioritize" (deputy prime minister Shuvalev said "there is no turn to the East") consequently "Russia turned its backs on Asia and its face to Syria."[835]

Since mid 2016, however, despite Russian "frustration" with the result of its "turn to the East", Moscow out of political reasons (prolonged stalemate with the West) decided to continue going down this path. This has created the basic trend of "a deeper asymmetrical interdependence" that Moscow "without viable alternatives" may be "willing to accept the imbalance"; therefore "Moscow may end up providing crucial resources that Beijing needs to boost the latter's ambition to be the next global superpower in exchange for an economic and financial lifeline (…) The bitter pill of Russia's continued decline will be less painful amid Beijing's efforts to show symbolic deference to Russia's status as a great power."[836]

Thoroughout 2016 Russia has followed the way of moving closer to China. This has been evident in abandoning former Moscow's balanced position on South China Sea and embracing the China's view. It started from Foreign Minister Lavrov's remarks to East Asian press in April[837], and was followed by Putin adherence to China's stance during June 2016 summit in Beijing[838], the SCO 15th anniversary declaration in Tashkent,[839] Putin's remarks during the G20 summit in Hangzhou[840] and joint Russian-Chinese drills at South China Sea.[841] The Chinese side was visibly pleased by this Russian move (Chinese

834 Ibid.

835 Idem, *Поворот в никуда: итоги азиатской политики России в 2015 году* [A Turn to Nowhere. The Results of Russia's Asia Policy in 2015], Carnegie.Ru, 29.12.2015.

836 Idem, *Friends with Benefits?*….

837 *Интервью Министра иностранных дел России С.В.Лаврова*….

838 *Совместное заявление Президента Российской Федерации и Председателя Китайской Народной Республики об укреплении глобальной стратегической стабильности*…

839 *Ташкентская декларация пятнадцатилетия Шанхайской организации сотрудничества* [Tashkent Declaration of the 15th Anniversary of SCO], Infor SCO, 24.06.2016.

840 *Ответы на вопросы журналистов*, 5.09.2016, Kremlin.Ru.

841 *China-Russia naval drill to begin in S.China Sea*, "Global Times", 12.09.2016.

MFA Spokesman called it “the voice of justice from the international community”)[842]; Moscow’s turn on South China Sea’s issue has been interpreted as a returning favor for China’s “sympathetic neutrality” regarding Ukraine and Crimea.[843] Nothing testifies better to growing Sinocentrism in Russia’s Asian policy than Kremlin’s bandwagoning to China’s position on South China Sea: “Moscow has become more pro-Chinese on important regional issues (…) whereas it was once content to do the bare minimum— subscribing to the ‘one China’ policy vis-à-vis Taiwan and Tibet— it now leans toward Beijing in areas where it was previously neutral, such as maritime sovereignty in the South China Sea.”[844]

Despite very good state of Sino-Russian relations seen at the 2016 G20 Hangzhou summit (China’s red carpet treatment of Putin helped him partially escape Western ostracism), late 2016 brought unexpected clouds over Sino-Russian relations. A small cloud was China’s abstention from joining Russia to veto another Western resolution on Syria at the UN on 8th October 2016[845]; while a big cloud was the victory of the US presidential race by Donald Trump. The Republican candidate opposed the mainstream of his party (and almost all American establishment) in his approach to Russia. His warm words about Moscow in general and Putin in particular, combined with unclear “Russian connections” within Trump’s team and visible support of this candidate by Russia by its “cyber warfare” (internet trolls, leaks, attacks on Democrats’ sites and computer systems of electoral commissions)[846] as well as anti-Chinese rhetoric by Trump: this all created a new background for USA-Russia-China triangle.

Trump’s victory was welcomed with hope in Moscow. Russians dreamed of a new “reset” that would herald the dawn of the “concert of powers” logic, where Russia would be given free hand in the post-Soviet area. At the same time Trump’s victory evoked anxiety in Beijing. First actions of the president elect, such as telephone call to Taiwan’s president and his comments on China seemed to challenge the very foundations of Sino-US relations laid in the 1970s. The possibility of US-Russia rapprochement made Chinese, remembering Putin’s past actions, uneasy.[847] International speculations about Trump and

842 *China appreciates Putin's position on South China Sea Issue*, Xinhuanet, 08.09.2016.

843 Yu Bin, *China-Russia Relations: The Dawn of a Brave Trump World*, “Comparative Connections”, vol. 18, No. 3.

844 B. Lo, *Russia and the New World Disorder…*, p. 144.

845 F. Godement, *Introduction….*

846 *Moscow chooses Trump. Russia on the US presidential elections*, OSW, Warsaw, 09.11.2016.

847 Yu Bin, *China-Russia Relations. The Dawn* … pp. 103-116.

Putin "reversing Nixon's strategy"[848] raised the level of anxiety among Chinese elites even further.

However, nothing spectacular materialized. Geopolitics proved to be insufficient in explaining US-Sino-Russian dynamics. Judging by the perspective of May 2017, the new US president is losing his battle with US establishment that successfully blocks his revolutionary ideas and cuts Trump's people such as Michael Flynn. Politically speaking, Donald Trump may be the USA's equivalent of… Mao Zedong[849], but Trump's chances to stage another Cultural Revolution to get rid of his opponents within the party and beyond are much more slim. So far, the environment does not help Trump and makes it very difficult, if not impossible (for now) to seek rapprochement with Russia. Widespread accusations for Russian involvement in the US elections, general anti-Russian mood in the USA (perhaps historically a third "red scare") and Trump's understanding that he has too many fronts open, led the new US president to bury hopes for new deal with Russia, which means that perspectives for new US-Russia reset have moved away, at least for the time being.

What was important in case of Sino-Russian relations, was the fact that this time Russians learned the mistakes from the past and did not sacrifice their relations just for Western promises. In October 2016, during Valdai Internation Club, Putin has spoken highly of Sino-Russian relations.[850] This pattern repeated on other occasions: Russian president "had been extraordinarily careful and cautious not to undermine the bilateral relationship with China."[851] To put it simply, Russia waited and waited for Trump to make another reset without doing any sudden moves, so when it never materialized, Moscow lost little.

The same applies to China. In on April 6-7 in Mar-a-Lago, Florida Trump met with Xi Jinping in what was a (at least temporarily) breakthrough in cooling US-China relations. Trump, who ordered bombardment of Syria while enjoying a chocolate cake with his guest, clearly managed to find a common language with Chinese leader. After the summit Sino-American relations improved: American president ceased to criticise China (Beijing breathed a sigh of relief), while the latter in return abstained from the UN Security Council draft resoulation condemning Assad regime on April 12 (Russia blocked it.)[852] US-China normalization didn't come at the expense of Sino-Russian relations.

---

848 *Donald Trump attempting to play Nixon's 'China card' in reverse*, The Guardian, 12.12.2016: for criticism of this approach, see: *Russia and China's Enduring Alliance*, "Foreign Affairs", 22.02.2017.

849 *Trump: The True New Maoist*, "The Diplomat", 19.01.2017; *America's Mao Zedong*, Foreign Policy 01.02.2017.

850 *Заседание Международного дискуссионного клуба «Валдай»* [Meeting of the Valdai International Discussion Club], Kremlin.Ru, 27.10.2016.

851 Yu Bin, *China-Russia Relations. The Dawn* … pp. 103-116.

852 *Security Council Fails to Adopt Resolution Condemning Chemical Weapons Use in Syria, Following Veto by Russian Federation*, UNSC, SC/12791, 12.04.2017.

Although Beijing abstained in the UNSC, it signed BRICS's anti-Western declaration on Syria at the same time.[853] And after the Mar-a-Lago 2017 summit with Trump, Beijing was very careful not to upset Russia. April 2017 saw "a flurry of China's diplomatic overtures to Russia": three top Chinese officials visited Russia, all of them met President Putin and all emphesized importance of Sino-Russian relations; thanks to it, despite (alleged) Washington's hidden agenda of Trump-Xi meeting ("creating distrust between China and Russia"), this summit has not challenged "normal procedures of Sino-Russian interactions (…) two bureaucracies that have been in place for the past three decades."[854] Thus, despite Mar-a-Lago summit, Russia and China continued moving closer to one another. This has been best seen at the even that concludes the scope of this book: Silk Road Forum in Beijing.

Belt and Road Forum in Beijing (14-16th May 2017) was a showcase of China's power, ambitions and a new (vague) vision for international order. Xi Jinping gathered leaders from 28 countries, with Vladimir Putin being the most important guest (no. two in forum's hierarchy, after Xi but before Turkish President Erdogan). Russian president emphasized it by catching world's attention thanks to playing piano while waiting for bilateral meeting with Xi on the first day and by coming late for the official inauguration of the Forum on the second. Putin was also the most vocal enthusiast of the OBOR project after Xi, surpassing even his host in details disclosed to the public (contrary to Xi, Putin announced the route of the "new Silk Road" – via Kazakhstan and Russia – most probably against the wishes of the Chinese who prefer to keep the route, or routes, undecided to have more political options open).

Although there are voices in Russia which reveal uneasy facts about Moscow undergoing "severe reality check" about "deliberately vague" OBOR initiative (so far only two companies owned by Timchenko benefited from projects, with little else for Russia) which leads "to nowhere"[855], the official Moscow keeps the line by praising and embrasing Belt and Road. Nothing illustrates better Russia's change of mind about China than this: Moscow was initially reserved about OBOR project, but later, given geopolitical environment, decided to bandwagon to it by hoping to achieve as much as possible from cooperation with China on Chinese terms.

***

853 *Joint Communiqué on the Meeting of BRICS Special Envoys on Middle East*, 12.04.2017, www.brics.utoronto.ca.

854 Yu Bin, *China-Russia Relations: Trilateral Politics…*, pp. 113-122.

855 А. Габуев, *Шелковый путь в никуда* [Silk Road to Nowhere], Ведомости, 14.05.2017; *Behind China's $1 Trillion Plan to Shake Up the Economic Order*, "New York Times" 13.05.2017.

China-Russia relations in the first decade of the 21st century are characterized by impressive changeability, a real sinusoid. At the beginning, these relations were an extension of the model from the late 1990s, and as a matter of fact a supplement to relation of Russia and China with the West. Putin's political about-turn after 11 September 2011 testified to that, as well as later Russian disillusionment and renewed approach to China. The rise of raw material prices allowed Russia to play a more ambitious role in the world, which in the case of China-Russian relations had consequences on the politics of Putin with balancing in Asia. Its aim was to play off China, Japan and Korea against each other. Nonetheless, in the late 2000s, Moscow understood that it was impossible to do this, and decided to deepen the relation with China, making "a virtue out of necessity". From that moment China became the most important partner of Russia in Asia and the second most important in the world after the United States – the buildup of China's significance in Moscow was treated more as a "chance" rather than as a "threat". On the other hand, the "growing asymmetry" of mutual relations was treated as a necessity with which one needs to agree, albeit unwillingly. The reason for that was on one side the suppressed position of Russia – especially after the economic crisis in 2008, and on the other hand, psychopolitical matters: directing attention on different vectors of foreign policy ("close abroad", the West). Russia decided that in the Asian, secondary field of its foreign policy, if it does not have what it likes, it will like what it has – and it will benefit from the cooperation with China, whatever it will be. This resulted in the fact that the biggest winner of the mutual relations was Beijing. China-Russia relations can be described by paraphrasing a known Chinese diplomacy phrase – the "asymmetric win-win" for the Chinese benefit.

China-Russia relations regained intensification after Xi Jinping took office in 2013. Answering the threat from the United States and its "Pivot to Asia" in 2011, China stepped up to political relations with Moscow – once more the American factor influenced the Moscow-Beijing relations, though rather intensifying the existing cooperation than turning its direction. This political bringing together, however, did not mean Chinese economic concession – quite the opposite: Beijing maintains asymmetrical model of these relations. The Russian elites, who were conscious of the consequences of Russia's marginalization in Asia (which in the long term means global marginalization), announced an ambitious motto of the Russian "turn towards Asia". They know that the future of Russia as a world power depends on the position in the Asia-Pacific region, which slowly becomes the political and economic center of the globe. The "Russian turn" was to free Russia from overabundant domination of China, which caused the marginalization of Russia in the region, making it a raw material base for China. Despite resounding declarations, the "Asian turn" ended in the middle of 2016 as a "Chinese turn": with the signing up of the gas contract in May 2014, Russia – busy with the Ukrainian case – yet again put "close abroad" ahead of the Asian politics. Consequently, instead of diminishing dependence from China, it increased it. Thanks to the gas contract China made its first step to make Siberia a shelter for its own economy. This contract, as well as Moscow's recent embrace of OBOR initiative, means deepening asymmetrical model of Russia-China relation and everything indicates that this trend will remain – Russia is concentrated on the most important vector of its foreign policy, which is consolidation and reintegration of Post-Soviet territory and withstanding of Western pressure, it needs "peace for the East". It buys China's support, which brings deepening the asymmetrical model.

Part Two: Pipelines and Arms: Economic and Military Relations

Economic and military cooperation between Russia and China in the period of 1991-2017 has gone two different ways. Economic relations since the beginning were the "weakest point", a major obstacle that was overcome only in the late 2000s with cooperation in the energy sector (though the structure of trade remains structurally unfavourable for Russia). The military relations, on the other hand, experienced a sinusoid. They were very much intensified in the 1990s, then weakened in the mid 2000s and finally reappeared as one of the pillars of Russia-China relations in the 2010s.

I. Economic Relations

1. Economic Cooperation in the 1990s

Economic relations in the 1990s "developed slowly and chaotically"[856] and "remained largely stagnant"[857] (with the exception of arms sales that are described here separately). The reasons for this state of affairs lay mostly on the Russian side. Unsuccessful economic transformation, incompatibility of the economy with the free market needs, remnants of Soviet-style economic thinking and an out of date perception of China as a backward, developing country – these were the most important reasons. Moreover, geography also played against success. China is remote from most important Russian economic and political centers and weakly communicated with the Russian Far East. Finally, in economic relations, as in political ones, both countries are orientated to the West mostly. This all contributed to the fact that the volume of trade between Russia and China in 1999 was lower than that in 1992. It has remained quite low throughout the 1990s. Russia ranked 8th among China's trade partners, with volume of trade USD 11,927 billion, which paled into insignificance when compared to China's two other trade partners: Japan (USD 101,905 billion) and the USA (USD 97,181 billion.)[858] Nevertheless, the actual level of trade, for several reasons, was higher than the one indicated in the statistics. Most of the statistics did not cover the petty, "unorganized" shuttle/border trade (done by shuttle traders), barter exchange and illegal contraband (mostly

856 Y.V. Tsyganov, op. cit., p. 308.
857 J. L. Wilson, *Strategic Partners…*, p. 61.
858 Ibid., p. 65.

timber from Russia and consumption goods from China.)[859] According to cautious estimation, in 1997-1998 alone the volume of illegal trade from China reached at least USD 3.6 billion per year.[860] According to some opinions, "Russian trade imbalance with China would virtually disappear if the shuttle trade was included."[861] Moreover, part of the trade volume (in such areas as aviation and space industry) was not covered, or was lowered in statistics. Finally, both sides purposely did not include arms sales which constituted the basis of bilateral economic relations in the 1990s.

The volume of trade between Russia and China in the 1990s remained a sinusoid. The time from 1991 to 1995 may be divided into 3 periods: 1) fast growth (1991-1993), 2) slowing down (1994), 3) regulation and return to growth (1995). The years 1995-1996 indicated another growth, while the years 1997-1998 – another decline. Finally, since 1999, a new upward tendency started. One must, however, divide between the two aspects of Russian trade with China: the central planned exchange (such as arms sales) and the decentralized (barter) one. Although the latter one consisted of only 17% of all trade, it initially contributed to the growth and later fall of trade.[862] The noticeable growth of trade at the beginning of the 1990s happened thanks to the opening of the borders, uncontrolled border trade and Chinese arms purchases. The following slowing down in 1994 was connected with the wider "China disappointment" in the Russian Far East (anti-Chinese resentments), introduction of import customs and visas as well as an entrance of Western companies to the Russian market. Another growth in volume of trade was possible thanks to "top to down" support from both governments.[863] The years 1995-1996 saw frequent visits of decision-makers from economic resorts that led to many agreements (in such spheres as atomic energy, chemical industry, heavy industry but first and foremost arms sales) – this centralistic aspect contributed to growth of the volume of trade. The Subsequent fall (1997-1998) and later growth (1999) are connected with the "politicization of economic relations". In 1997-1998, both countries politically averted from each other, so there was not any backing of the economic projects by the state (see: Three Gorges), volume of trade slowed again (there were also strict economic reasons: economic crisis, incompatibility of Russian products in China etc.). The impulse towards another growth was given by Chinese Prime Minister Zhu Rongji, during his visit

---

859 L. Popova, *Recent Trends in Russian-Chinese Economic Cooperation*, "World Economic Papers" (special issue), 7/2006, pp. 37-46.

860 I.Topolski, op. cit., p. 146.

861 J. L. Wilson, *Strategic Partners...*, p. 65.

862 J.Thornton, *Reform in the Russian Far East: Implications for Economic Cooperation*, [in:] *Rapprochement or Rivalry...*, pp. 262-293.

863 This is the permanent factor in Sino-Russian relations, where political relations influence, or stimulate economic relations, not the other way round, А.В. Лукин, *Россия и Китай...* p. 669.

to Moscow in February 1999. Finally, in the late 1990s trade grew thanks to the cooperation in the energy sector. This would become the leitmotiv of Sino-Russian economic cooperation in the 2000s.

The decade of the 1990s, from the economic point of view was characterized by an export of Russian resources and semi-finished product (fertilizers, iron, timber) and by an import of Chinese textiles, cloths, shoes and leather products. Russian consumer was not able to buy more technologically advanced Chinese products (TV sets, electronics, video equipment) or – more often – was not willing to and chose to buy products made in other countries. Russian economic strategy towards China in the 1990s focused on promotion of the export of high tech products (the export of much of the Russian industries remained the only option to survive). Although this was based on reasonable grounds (both economies were complementary), it did not end up as a success – Russian products were simply uncompetitive on the Chinese market. Without considering military cooperation, they were able to succeed in two sectors only – the atomic sector and space industry.[864]

Except for arms, Russia in the 1990s was selling mostly products connected to transport, metals (iron and steel), chemicals, paper products and resources to China. The only consumer goods that Russians delivered to China were fish.[865] Finally, Russia provided China with atomic technology and technical assistance with building an atomic power plant – in return it received consumer goods, which were not listed in the statistics[866]. As for resources, its share in Russian-Chinese trade in the 1990s was low. Russia certainly succeeded in providing China machines and equipment, mostly in atomic, aviation and space sectors.[867]

During this decade, China exported mainly consumer goods: clothes, textiles, groceries, tools. Throughout the 1990s, Russia remained a sales market for China's consumption goods' surplus. Chinese products solved problems of the lack of everyday products, so severe in the first years of the Russian transformation.[868] In the mid 1990s, China imported mainly metals and chemicals (including fertilizers) that valued more than 50% of all import; export consisted of leather, wool products, animals and animal products, huts, umbrellas and shoes.[869] To sum it up, Chinese export to Russia concentrated on everyday items and lacked technologically advanced products sold to the West.

---

864 J. L. Wilson, *Strategic Partners...*, p. 79; Jing-dong Yuan, *Sino-Russian Defense Ties*, [in:] *The Future of China-Russia...*, p. 215.

865 R. Lotspeich, *Economic Integration of China and Russia in the Post-Soviet Era*, [in:] Ibid., p. 98.

866 I. Topolski, op. cit., p. 147.

867 J. L. Wilson, *Strategic Partners...*, p. 66; R. Lotspeich, op. cit., p. 98.

868 E. Bazhanov, *Russian Policy toward China*, [in:] *Russian Foreign Policy Since 1990*, ed. P. Shearman, San Francisco 1995, pp. 165-168.

869 I. Topolski, op. cit., p. 147.

Russian-Chinese economic relations were the continuation of the Soviet period and initially functioned within structures and mechanisms created during the last years of the USSR.[870] Despite that both sides recognized one another as a "most favoured nation" in March 1992[871], Russian activities in China were weak, chaotic and often characterized by underestimation of the neighbor.[872] The Russian minister of foreign trade Piotr Aven, for example, offered the Chinese Russian electronics which – due to their bad quality – were not being bought even in Russia.[873] Later on, institutional initiatives ceased to exist at all. Russian domestic situation was to blame: the Kremlin was paralyzed by decision-making chaos and a lack of agreement on the direction of investments.[874] Consequently, most of the economic projects formalized during Yeltsin's 1992 visit remained unfulfilled.[875] Li Peng's visit to Moscow in December 1996 and his meeting with Russian prime minister Victor Chernomyrdin raised hopes of stimulating the economic cooperation – Moscow and Beijing pushed to achieve a trade volume of USD 20 billion by the year 2000.[876] It turned out to be only a dream. It took Yeltsin four months to appoint a chair for the Russian side of the Commission to Prepare Regular Meetings of the Russian and Chinese Prime Ministers; its work was further impeded by economic crisis and never-ending replacements of Russian prime ministers (five between 1998 and 1999.)[877] As for the volume of trade, out of the declared USD 20 billion by 2001, Russia and China were able to achieve only half.[878]

Several factors contributed to the relative low volume of trade and backwardness of economic relations in the 1990s. Most of them had something to do with communist heritage.[879] First, the negative outcomes of Sino-Soviet split not only had negative consequences for the economic relations between the USSR and the PRC; . it, furthermore, led to shaping the Russian Far East

---

870 *Указ президента РСФСРО либерализации внешнеэкономической деятельности на территории РСФСР* [FR SSR President's Decree on Liberaliztion of Foreign Economic Activity on the Territory of FR SSR), Consultant.ru, 17.11.1991.

871 *Соглашение между Правительством Российской Федерации и Правительством Китайской Народной республики «О торгово-экономических отношениях»* [The Intergovermental Agreement between Russian Federation and China People's Republic on Trade-Economic Relations], [in:] *Сборник российско-китайских договоров 1949-1999*...pp. 109-116.

872 А.В. Лукин, *От нормализации к стратегическому партнерству*..., p. 372.

873 Ю. Б. Савенков, *Китай и Россия создают новый механизм торговых отношений* [China and Russia Create New Mechanism of Trade Relations], "Известия", 07.031992.

874 А.В. Лукин, *От нормализации к стратегическому партнерству*..., p. 324.

875 J. L. Wilson, *Strategic Partners*..., p. 68.

876 G. Rozman, *Sino-Russian Relations. Mutual*..., p. 156.

877 J. L. Wilson, *Strategic Partners*..., p. 68.

878 I.Topolski, op. cit., p. 147.

879 J. L. Wilson, *Strategic Partners*..., p. 71-72.

into "besieged fortress"[880], which effectively cancelled possibility of normal economic transactions for decades (for instance, the only telephone line from Vladivostok to China went via Moscow). Add objective factors: transportation infrastructure was completely unprepared to the new situation (no border crossings, bad roads, only two railways, bad communications between the Russian Far East and the distorted structure of costs, production and transportation).[881] Even 25-30% of all signed contracts between Russian and Chinese participants went unfulfilled because of transportation problems.[882] On the Chinese side, the consequences of the split were basically structural. In the 1950s, all industry and technology was modelled on Soviet patterns, with commercial, cultural and personal contacts that supplemented it. After the split, China turned its back on Russia by preferring Western goods and services; Beijing simply re-orientated its economy towards the West.[883] That is why for China Russia in the 1990s became a secondary direction, important only for border provinces. The second most negative factor was the influence of former communist policy on Russian-Chinese trade. During Soviet times trade was executed mostly in products exchange, or barter. Attempts to reform this system in the RF in the 1990s failed – barter remained the main form of trade exchange of Russia: in 1997 alone 73% of all Russian trade transactions were made in barter and other non-currency way.[884] When the USSR fell, Russian-Chinese trade became chaotic and uncontrollably symbolized by petty shuttle traders. Exchange remained, in the old Soviet way, by barter mostly. Theoretically, from 1995 Russian-Chinese trade was supposed to be made in hard currency only (initially in Swiss franc, then in USD), however, the absence of an institutionalized banking reform, the inconvertibility of Chinese yuan, the volatility of the ruble, and the lack of regularized settlement agreements between banks of the two states "all served to restrict the use of cash transactions as well as to impede the overall growth of trade volume."[885] Barter remained predominant in border trade as well as in contraband: Chinese consumption foods were exchanged for Russian resources (timber) and arms – it was the exchange of "rockets for coats."[886] Barter, except for its obvious disadvantages, had, however, some positive aspects – thanks to it Russia was being competitive on Chinese market.[887] Nevertheless, the economic crisis in 1998 was a severe hit on attempts to replace barter – it remained until the next decade. Finally, the

880 G. Rozman, *Turning Fortress into Free Trade Zone*, [in:] *Rapprochement or Rivalry…*, p. 177.
881 J. Thornton, op. cit., p. 265.
882 J. L. Wilson, *Strategic Partners…*, pp. 71-72.
883 В. П. Федотов, *Полвека вместе с Китаем. Воспоминания, записы, розмышления* [Half Century with China. Memories, Nortes, Thoughts], Москва 2005, p. 31.
884 C. Gaddy, B. Ickes, *Russia's Virtual Economy*, "Foreign Affairs", no 77, 5/1998, p. 56.
885 J. L. Wilson, *Strategic Partners…*, p. 73.
886 Alexei Voskressenski, op. cit., p. 134.
887 Y. Borisova, *Report: Ministry Cost Russia Billions*, "Moscow Times", 16.03.2001.

third negative factor was the remnants of communist thinking on economy. Russian elites still tended to perceive Russia as a technologically advanced industrial economy, while China as a backward rural and assistance-needing country. That is why they believed economic relations could be built on providing Russian technology, products and services in return for Chinese consumer goods. China, however, did not need Russian technology, because it had a better one – the Western one. Beijing was buying from Moscow what it wanted – limited amounts of high tech arms and military technology, skilled labor for development of the Chinese technological base (particularly military potential), resources – and nothing more.[888] The other remnant of Soviet-style thinking on the Russian side was emphasis on establishing cooperative economic arrangements based on large-scale bilateral government-supervised contracts and unease, if not holstility towards shuttle trade: many in ghd Russian leadership viewed the extensive shuttle trade as "anarchic, uncivilized, and reflective of the worst aspects of petty bourgeois commodity exchange"; consequently they did a lot to limit this.[889] Development of trade was thus hampered by suspicions or open hostility manifested in believing that China constituted a threat to Russian economic sovereignty: "economic negotiations between the two states were infused with a considerable irony in that the Chinese side, ostensibly still socialist, was an unapologetic defender of market norms and values; over time, the Chinese leadership became outspoken in its support of the shuttle trade and other forms of small-scale commercial activity that were often the object of derision in Russia."[890] The Chinese market-oriented approach had one significant implication for bilateral relations: China was unwilling to grant Russia a special status – "strategic partnership" did not cover economic issues. The 1990s decade of Sino-Russian economic relations stands clear as an example of unfulfilled agreements and unfinished projects[891]. The clearest example of Russian failure in China in the economic sphere turned out to be its lost bid for the construction of turbines to the Three Gorges Dam in 1997.[892] The Chinese subordination of politics to economics "came as a shock to a Russian leadership that bore the ideological heritage of a system in which profit was largely a meaningless category in the courting of friendship."[893] The Chinese saw it differently: one of the PRC's ministries of trade summarized it as follow: "between Chinese and Americans there is cooperation without friendship while between Russian and Chinese there is friendship without cooperation."[894]

888 Alexei Voskressenski, op. cit., p. 133.
889 J. L. Wilson, *Strategic Partners...*, pp. 75-76.
890 Ibid., p. 76.
891 E. Wishnick, *Mending fences...*, p. 135.
892 А.В. Лукин, *От нормализации к стратегическому партнерству...*, p. 372.
893 J. L. Wilson, *Strategic Partners...*, p. 77.
894 Chen Qimao, op. cit., p. 294.

With the (significant) exception of the military industry, where Russia was privileged, due to a Western embargo on China, Russian companies were having serious difficulties while entering the Chinese market – against Western competition they were almost helpless. China chose the West, not Russia, for its modernization: "China wants airplanes from Boeing or Airbus, not Tupolev; it has sought joint ventures with Audi and General Motors, not Lada."[895] Russian attempts to sell planes ended up in failure due to the reasons promptly summarized by the Chinese Ambassador to Russia, Li Fenglin: "The Russians want to sell us civilian airlines like the Ilyushin-96 and the Tupolev-204; but even Aeroflot doesn't want them, so there must be something wrong."[896]

This example illustrates a wider tendency: that of Western dominance in economic relations with both China and Russia. As in politics, also in economic relations, Beijing and Moscow orientated first and foremost to the West. Bilateral investments took place mostly there, where Western companies did not compete (arms sales to China or Chinese consumer goods to Russia) – "financially, economically, and technologically, both countries still depend more on the West than on each other."[897] Contrary to the USA, Russia did not have such investment possibilities to ensure the pace of Chinese modernization – it desperately needed investments for itself. China, on the other hand, was unwilling to invest in Russia – Beijing exported only cheap consumer goods, food and unqualified labor there, it reserved export of more sophisticated goods to the West. China was Russia's third trade partner in 1992, but only the fifth in 2000 (much more important was Germany, then the USA); for China, mostly the USA and Asian partners (Japan, South Korea) mattered. Moreover, in a sense, China was more important to Russia than the other way round. Since 1992, China has always been in the first five of the most important Russian export destinations, but for China Russia in the 1990s mattered only for three *Dongbei* (Northeastern) provinces and its heavy industry (in 1995 alone *Dongbei*'s share in all Chinese to Russia export was 71%).[898]

2. *Economic Cooperation in 2000-2017: The Geopolitics of Energy and Beyond*

In the 2000s and the 2010s, the Sino-Russian volume of trade has increased, but it has mostly happened thanks to energy cooperation. What characterized it was the emphasis on resources and "the geopolitics of energy" as well as an unbalanced trade. The character of the emerged economic relations started to

895 S. W. Garnett, op. cit., p. 10.

896 Quoted in: J. L. Wilson, *Strategic Partners...*, p. 77.

897 Alexei Voskressenski, op. cit., p. 132.

898 D. Kerr, *Problems in Sino-Russian Economic Relations*, "Europe-Asia Studies", 7/1998, pp. 113-56.

benefit China mostly – Beijing is gradually turning Russia into a "resource appendix" to the Chinese economy. Consequently, the disproportion deepens: China is Russia's second trade partner (after the EU), while Russia is China's sixteenth partner (it was the ninth before 2015).

Russia and China seem to be perfect energy partners that should share common interests. Russia is one of world's biggest exporters of energy, whereas China is the second biggest receiver. Add to this the public image of Sino-Russian friendship, "the strategic partnership" and joint statements about the will to cooperate on energy. This all should make the cooperation smooth. This was not so, however, due to geopolitical factors.

In the world of shrinking resources, "energy has come to symbolize the new geopolitics of the twenty-first century"; therefore, energy is essential for both re-emerging powers of Russia and China, but in very different ways: for Russia it is "the power-equivalent of nuclear weapons in the Soviet era."[899] A *boom* on oil prices after 1999 enabled Russia to come back as a global power. Russia, then, used energy as a power-projection in both Europe and Asia. In reaching towards Asia, Moscow "was striving to avoid dependence on any single customer who would be able to dictate the terms of cooperation."[900]

Using energy as a power-projection, however, cuts two ways. The more Russia wants to present itself as a reliable partner, the more it must strengthen its relations with Beijing and present it as problem-free (so it is vulnerable to the Chinese pressure). Russia conducts a policy of "creative doubt" to "foster in customers a measure of 'controllable uncertainty' of neither complacency nor panic (…) the China card is useful in neutralizing the pressure of Brussels (…)for Russian policymakers do not wish to 'abandon' the West so much as to modify its behavior in line with Russian interests."[901] Therefore, Beijing plays a critical role in Moscow's mood: it enables Russia to have the illusion of conducting independent policy from the West.

Energy is no less important to China than to Russia, but for different reasons: "China is growing like America was growing in the last century, but without the indigenous [oil and gas] reserves."[902] Without energy, China's rise as an emerging power would be stopped and the legitimization of the CPP would be severely undermined. China responded to these challenges by making the search for energy its top foreign policy priority and creating "resource diplomacy". These domestic imperatives underline the most important difference on approach to energy between Russia and China: "energy and geopolitics are as closely intertwined in China's case as they are for Russia – with one notable difference (…) Comparing with the complex motivations shaping Rus-

899 B. Lo, *The Axis of Convenience…*, p. 132.
900 Marcin Kaczmarski, *Russia-China Relations…*, p. 55.
901 B. Lo, *The Axis of Convenience…*, p. 140.
902 A. Petersen, K. Barysch, op. cit., p. 11.

sian energy policy, China's aims are straightforward. It seeks to maximize imports in order to sustain the process of domestic transformation"[903]. This difference is decisive. Without it, the energy cooperation would be complementary, with one of biggest world's exporter of oil and gas on one side and the globe's second larger consumer of energy on the other. It was, however, for long considered as the "unfulfilled partnership."[904]

Energy started to play an important role in Sino-Russian relations in the mid 1990s. Then, however, it ended on official declarations only: Russian oligarchs and state-owned Gazprom instead of focusing on Asia, were more interested in making quick money elsewhere. Because of China's "energy hunger" this began to change in 1999 and was intensified when Putin took office. Although in joint statements the importance of energy cooperation was regularly emphasized, the cooperation was overshadowed by problems, the main one being a different understanding of energy security. For Moscow, it means security of demand (oil and gas accounts for 60% of Russia exports and over a half of its budget revenue) – a loss of overseas markets would be catastrophic for prosperity and political stability; for China, on the other hand, it means security of supply – "reliable, long-term access is indispensable to its ability to meet the enormous challenges of (…) modernization."[905] Add to it objective reasons, such as lack of infrastructure of pipelines and the costly necessity of building it and subjective ones: mismanagement, corruption and "the Byzantine nature of business interactions within Russian energy sector."[906] Finally, Moscow was more interested in selling gas, whereas Beijing was much keener on buying Russian oil. That is why China wanted to build the ESPO pipeline, but the serious complications with it made Beijing understand that business contracts, governmental agreements and public statements mean next to nothing if they are not supported by political will. Beijing started viewing Russia as "a 'limited-use' partner, of far less importance than its main sources on the Persian Gulf and Africa."[907]

3. *The ESPO Oil Pipeline and the "Power of Siberia" Gas Pipeline*

The ESPO pipeline symbolizes the sinusoid nature of Sino-Russian relations. Although the first plans were made in Soviet times, it was only when Mikhail Khodorkovsky decided to build a pipeline to China (Angarsk-Daqing), that this project started to become real. In December 1999, Khodorkovsky came to

903 B. Lo, *The Axis of Convenience…*, pp. 133 and 141.
904 L. Jakobsen, P. Holtom, D. Knox, and Jingchao Peng, op. cit. pp. 20-31.
905 B. Lo, *The Axis of Convenience…*, p. 133-134.
906 J. L. Wilson, *Strategic partners…*, p. 84.
907 B. Lo, *The Axis of Convenience…*, pp. 133-141.

terms with the Chinese, who backed his project.[908] In 2002, however, a longer alternative appeared, proposed by Yukos' rival – Transneft and backed by Japan: to build a pipeline from Angarsk to Nakhodka in the Pacific Ocean. After Khodorkovsky's arrest in 2003 and Japan's financial package to build the longer pipeline[909], Moscow – hoping to play Tokyo and Beijing off one another (if the ESPO was built to Nakhodka Russia could export the oil to all regions; if to Daqing only, China would become the monopolist that could exhort pressure) – started to play for time. Russia's strategic plan was based on a hope of attracting not only Chinese, but also Japanese and Korean investments to the Russian Far East, so that they would balance one another and allow the Russian Far East to advance economically, which in turn would strengthen Russia's position in Asia. The ESPO was the key in this play: thanks to its longer route, the oil could be exported to many Asian markets. That would give Russia leverage over price (impossible if the route was made to China only). Moscow would probably skillfully use the price of energy as well as other non-business tools to conduct its Asian policy along the lines of its European policy. That is why the Kremlin on 31 December 2004 announced that Russia had chosen the longer option – now leading to Skorovodino and called the WSTO (*Wostochniy Sibir, Tikhiy Okiean*) or the ESPO (East Siberia Pacific Ocean) pipeline. That was China's failure in the first round of the struggle for the pipeline. To console China, Moscow agreed to build a separate ESPO branch line to China[910] – this was intended to neutralize the negative consequences of China ESPO's failure and Japan's victory. The details were, however, "deliberately left unresolved" and the construction was regularly postponed; this left China with only an export of 48 million tons of oil to China by rail from a 2004 contract.[911]

With time, however, the situation with the ESPO turned to China's favour. The construction of this pipeline became associated with the private interests of the Kremlin's key figures. For them, the project to Daqing was shorter, cheaper and easier to build.[912] In the meantime, relations with Japan deteriorated – Tokyo pulled back on several aspects of its financial package and insisted on ruling out the construction of the Daqing route: "against this backdrop strategic diversity as a core principle of Russia's Asian policy was founded on the reality that China was far better disposed towards Russia than a disgruntled

908 W. Konończuk, *Ropociąg Wschodnia Syberia – Ocean Spokojny (WSTO): strategiczny projekt – organizacyjna porażka?* [ESPO Pipeline: Strategic Project or Organizational Failure], OSW, Warsaw, 12.10.2008

909 *Japan-Russia Action Plan*, Ministry of Foreign Affairs of Japan.

910 *Список документов, подписанных в присутствии Президента России Владимира Путина и Председателя КНР Ху Цзиньтао* [Collection of Documents Signed During RF President Putin and PRC Chairman Hu Jintao Presence], Kremlin.ru, 1.05.2014.

911 M.Kaczmarski, *Russia-China Relations*..., p. 56.

912 B. Lo, *The Axis of Convenience*..., p. 145.

Japan."[913] In these circumstances, the best option available for Russia started to be to get as good a Chinese offer to finance Daqing route as possible. To make matters worse, in 2008 Russia was severely hit by economic crisis. The crisis "triggered a shift in Russia's policy in the oil sector (…) [and] modified the calculations on both the Kremlin and the key energy companies."[914] China used Russia's dire situation to fulfill the pipeline agreement. Chinese loans and credit (10 billion USD and 15 bln USD), given as a prepayment for future deliveries of oil (15 billion tons of oil per year for 20 years, total 300 million tons of oil)[915] enabled the completion of the Daqing branch construction (the oil started to flow to China in January 2011). This meant the return to the initial ESPO project (to Daqing) –one that goes directly to China (although Russia has since built the second branch, the ESPO transports resources to China mostly). The pipeline to Daqing "constituted a breakthrough in Russia-China energy cooperation, binding both states to a long-term commitment; Moscow agreed to supply Beijing with oil in return for loans, enduring security of demand and the prospect of entering a promising downstream market."[916] Economically, China benefited from this pipeline: the price was preferential (low compared to market prices; the Russian government forced Transneft to apply lower transportation tariffs and lifted the export duty on oil), Beijing achieved diversification of oil imports, provided a secure overland route and bound Russian energy state-owned companies to China (this has converted them to supporters of the collaboration with China) – in short, "the 20-year contract offered Beijing long-term security of supply at a highly advantageous price."[917]

Moreover, once China secured the pipeline, it started pushing for more favourable conditions. In turned out that "signing the contract is only the first stage in an often protracted and difficult process."[918] The CNPC wanted much more oil – increasing the volume of the planned import - in return for the construction the Tianjin refinery by the Russians. Faced by this precondition, a kind of blackmail, the Russians finally, in September 2010, gave in and agreed to send an additional 9 million tons of oil per year. Once they did this, the Chinese, in late 2010, demanded the price be lowered and, when deliveries started, refused to pay the price earlier agreed. This time the Russians were more firm (they made it public, threatened to sue the CNPC in the international court and started negotiating with Japanese companies on the exploitation of

913 Ibid., pp. 136-146.

914 M.Kaczmarski, *Russia-China Relations…*, p. 56.

915 *Соглашение о принципах строительства и эксплуатации нефтепровода «Сковородино – граница с КНР» между Китайской национальной нефтегазовой корпорацией и ОАО АК «Транснефть»* [Agreement of Principles of Building and Exploatation of Skorovodion-PRC border pipeline between CNPC and Transneft], Russian.China.Org.Cn, 29.10.2008.

916 M. Kaczmarski, *Russia-China Relations…*, p. 56.

917 Ibid.

918 B. Lo, *Russia and the New World Disorder…*, p. 146.

oil and gas). Finally, the Chinese paid the money, though they received a discount – "Beijing turned out to be a difficult negotiating partner, Russia received practically no concessions and had to give in to China's vision of cooperation."[919]

Russia yielded to these conditions due to the difficult economic situation and out of geopolitical considerations (even Putin himself has admitted that the ESPO is "not just a pipeline", but also "a geopolitical project").[920] Moscow's chosen strategy has been "to keep its share of the very profitable European market, while using its contacts with the Chinese as a tool to pressure the Europeans."[921] Moscow followed this logic and in 2013 concluded further agreements with Beijing. In 2013, Russia and China signed a series of new giant contracts on oil deliveries to China (to send 10 millions tons of oil via the Kazakhstani pipeline; to double the amount of oil sent to China via the ESPO – 15 million tons for 25 years, worth USD270 billion; to deliver another 10 million of tons for ten years), "taken together the series of contracts to which the Russian company agreed tripled the amount of oil to be sent to China (…) by 2020 Russia maybe expected to supply 56 million tons of oil", which would be around 20% of the total Russian oil exports and Russia would become the largest supplier of China, providing "up to one fifth of imports" – this all equals to the "second breakthrough in oil trade."[922]

So, China benefited most from the ESPO pipeline and its aftermath; Russia ended up "as the victim of the China card rather than its master."[923] It was supposed to be completely different: "when constructing the ESPO pipeline as the cornerstone of its energy policy in Asia, the Kremlin avoided favoring China and maintained room for maneuver, without falling into dependency on a single customer; later practice (…) [has] undermined the feasibility of such an approach, effectively contradicting Moscow's strategy (…) the pattern Moscow rejected in its policy towards the West was, in a modified version, accepted in relations with China."[924] Now, in 2017, Russia became China's biggest oil supplier, overtaking Saudi Arabia (Russia delivers 50 million tons of crude oil, or 1.05 million barrels per day), in addition to the oil sent via ESPO, China purchased 70 percent from the ESPO Pacific coast terminal, "effectively dominating Russian oil sales to the Asian market"; the existing infrastructure is mostly bound for China, too.[925] Therefore, the ambitious plans of the Russian great play on the Asian chessboard ended up with dependency on

919 M. Kaczmarski, *Russia-China Relations…*, p. 59.

920 *Владимир Путин выпустил восточносибирскую нефть в море* [Vladimir Putin Released Eastern Siberian Oil into Sea], "Ведомости", 29.12.2009.

921 Д. Тренин, *Верные друзья?…*

922 M. Kaczmarski, *Russia-China Relations…*, p. 59.

923 B. Lo, *The Axis of Convenience…*, p. 140.

924 M. Kaczmarski, *Russia-China Relations…*, p. 61.

925 Idem, *Russia-China and the West…*

China. The situation with the ESPO repeated itself in a paradoxical way with another Russian project in Asia – the Power of Siberia gas pipeline.

On 21 March 2014, the second after the epic ESPO pipelineproject in Sino-Russian relations was concluded – the two sides signed a gas contract for the pipeline "the Power of Siberia".[926] According to some, this contract, that had been negotiated for more than tens years, symbolizes the "Russian turn to the East"; others say it is a political consequence of the Ukrainian crisis and that it is China that benefits most from it.

The first talks about gas contracts started already in the 1990s, but nothing materialized. The idea reappeared during Putin's first years of reign. Despite signing a few memoranda and framework agreements (the first one in October 2004, the second in 2006, which planned 68 billion cubic metres per year)[927], the two sides were unable to come to a conclusion on the most important issue: the price of the gas. That is why "many of the documents signed later reiterated provisions which had already been agreed upon, and thus created the pretence of progress in negotiations that was necessary for image-building purposes."[928] This was due to two facts. First – the economic factor: the gas sector, unlike oil, was a place where Russia and China's interests diverged, because their needs were not complementary (since gas is more dependent of infrastructure, and Russia lacked an eastern gas infrastructure, this hinted at Russia's possible role as a gas provider to China); second – the political factor: Gazprom wanted to put pressure on Europe to renew long-term contracts (Moscow planned to supply gas to China from Western Siberian gas fields, the source of deliveries to Europe, and it conducted negotiations with China "in bad faith" – "the talks were only a façade that was supposed to help Gazprom gain concessions in the European market"), China on the other hand was in no hurry to strike a deal either – especially once Beijing constructed a gas pipeline to Turkmenistan in 2006.[929]

It was the economic crisis, again, that altered Moscow's calculations: "Gazprom, faced with waning European demand and the disadvantageous EU law, appeared to be much more interested in striking a deal with China"; at first Russia still hoped to convince China to use Western Siberian fields (a series of agreements between 2009 and 2011), but Beijing, already having a pipeline to Turkmenistan (as well as another one to Burma/Myanmar and LNG), wanted to get access to Eastern, not Western Siberian fields, as this would not require

926 *Газпром и CNPC подписали контракт на поставку газа в Китай* [Gazprom in CNPC Signed Gas Deliveries to China Contract], РИА Новости 21.05.2014.

927 Keun-Wook Paik, *Sino-Russian Oil and Gas Cooperation: The Reality and Implications*, Oxford University Press 2014, pp. 350-51.

928 S. Kardaś, *The eastern 'partnership' of gas. Gazprom and CNPC strike a deal on gas supplies to China*, OSW, Warsaw, 16.04.2014.

929 M. Kaczmarski, *Russia-China Relations…*, p. 62.

additional investments in China's domestic gas infrastructure.[930] That is why China was in no hurry to conclude the agreement.

Finally Moscow yielded and gave in to the idea of using Western Siberian fields. This led to reopening the negotiations, that were, however, uneasy. In May 2014, during Putin's visit to Shanghai, Gazprom and the CNPC signed a 30-year contract on 38 billion m³ of gas annually – Gazprom was supposed to be obliged to supply a total of around 82 billion m³ of gas during the first five years, i.e. around 16.4 billion m³ annually.[931] It is less than it was earlier considered– it is a modification of the original plan of using the Kovyktinskoe gas field; instead of the Western Siberia Chayandinskoe field in Yakutia as was originally indicated.[932] To fulfill this goal, a new pipeline – the Power of Siberia – will be built, approximately 4000 km long with a planned capacity of 61 billion m³ annually;[933] the beginning of exploitation was planned for 2019/2020 (it is already now delayed) and should achieve full capacity 2-3 years later.[934] According to the initial estimates, the pipeline's construction cost will reach USD25 billion, i.e. almost half of the expenses planned as part of the Eastern Gas Programme (USD60 billion).[935] Finding funds may be an additional challenge, like exploitation of Chayandinskoe; according to some rumours, the cost may be financed by a Chinese loan.[936] China agreed to make a USD25 billion prepayment accompanied by direct investments that may amount to USD20 billion (nevertheless, the final scope of China's financial participation remains unknown).[937] This all means that "Given the unknown—and therefore questionable—rate of return on these investments, the gas monopoly will remain a big spender rather than earner for at least a couple of decades."[938] Building the pipeline, exploiting gas fields and other expenses mean significant costs for Gazprom which – even if the Chinese loan is a possible option – may not bring payback if the oil prices remain low.

930 Ibid., pp. 62-63.

931 S. Kardaś, *The eastern 'partnership' of gas…*

932 *«Газпром» и Китай подписали Меморандум о взаимопонимании по поставкам газа по «восточному» маршруту* [Gasprom and China Signed MoU on Deliveries of Gas by Eastern Route], Газпром.Официальный сайт 22.03.2013.

933 *«Сила Сибири» Якутский и Иркутский центры газодобычи* [Power of Siberia, Yakutsk and Irkutsk Centers of Gas Extraction], Oil Capital.Ru.

934 M. Kaczmarski, *Russia-China and the West…*

935 S. Kardaś, *The eastern 'partnership' of gas…*; *Восточная газовая программа* [Eastern Gas Programme], Газпром.Официальный сайт.

936 *Пекин профинансирует* [Beijing Will Finance], "Взгляд" 18.06.2014.

937 M. Kaczmarski, *Russia-China Relations…*, p. 64; Until mid-2017 Gazprom was still not able to receive the USD25 billion Chinese prepayment; it received only Euro 2 billion credit from Bank of China.

938 M. Krutikhin, *A Mystery, Wrapped in Puzzle*, Carnegie Center Moscow 23.05.2014.

The price issue made this epic project last only so long. China, having painfully learned how Russia uses energy in politics, was aware that it cannot afford to be dependent on Russia – Moscow would mercilessly use it. That is why China pursued a dual strategy: it used imported LNG gas and broke the Russian pipeline monopoly in Central Asia. China benefitted from another unexpected factor: the "shale gas revolution" that led to a lowering of global gas prices. That is why Beijing wanted the contract price to be based on the price applicable at the US Henry Hub (in 2013 it was USD135 per 1000 m³ as compared to USD390 per 1000 m³ on European spot markets); the Russians, in turn insisted on adopting a formula based on the JCC (Japanese Crude Cocktail) index, where the average gas price in 2013 ranged between USD524 and USD582 per 1000 m³; finally the two sides announced that they would adopt an 'innovative' formula based on LNG prices, which are linked to oil prices, and in effect a final gas price has been set at around USD346 per 1000 m³.[939] The "secretive nature of the gas agreement" may show that "the contract contains something the Russian negotiators could not be proud of in the limelight of Russian public opinion."[940]

Considering the available information and the context of the negotiation process, it can be concluded that "the price formula adopted will bring more economic benefits to the Chinese side": prices ranging between USD350 and USD390 per 1000 m³ "would be, given the present situation on the Asian gas market, nearly 50% lower than the price of gas imported by China from Qatar (around USD680 per 1000 m3 in 2013)" but would be similar to the prices set in Gazprom's contracts with European customers (the average price in 2013 was USD380 per 1000 m³) and in the CNPC's contracts with Turkmenistan (around USD360 per 1000 m³) – "a gas price at this level could mean that Gazprom would have to carry out supplies to China below the break-even point"; moreover, "considering the expected fiscal preferences promised by the Russian side the implementation of this project could be barely profitable to Gazprom (…) "the cost-effectiveness of this project became even more dubious" after Putin's statement that Gazprom needs to be recapitalized.[941]

Another interesting aspect has been the fact revealed by Putin in his letter to European leaders that Russia, through lowering the gas price, had subsidized he Ukrainian economy for USD 35,4 billion.[942] So, considering USD350-390 for a similar volume of deliveries to Ukraine (the Ukrainian price was between USD410-430 for 1000m³), one may come to a conclusion that "Russia has decided to subsidize the Chinese economy for 100 billions of dollars."[943] On the

939 S. Kardaś, *The eastern 'partnership' of gas…*

940 M. Krutikhin, op. cit.

941 S. Kardaś, *The eastern 'partnership' of gas…*Krutikhin, op. cit.

942 *Письмо Путина европейским лидерам об урегулировании долга Украины за газ* [Putin's Letter to European Leaders on Ukrainian Dept on Gas], "Российская газета", 10.04.2014.

943 J. Korejba, op. cit.

other hand, within a few months following signing the deal, the global gas prices, tied to oil prices, collapsed. Thus, this price perhaps was not as bad for Russia as many tend to think.[944]

What is certain, rather, is that Gazprom's investments would not be compensated by a mirage of entering the Chinese gas market[945], a part of the "Russian pivot to Asia". Data and facts contradict these claims. China has enough gas – its own (shale gas), Central Asian (Turkmenistani), Burmese and LNG, so that Russia cannot dream of making it a second Europe. Besides, the volume of contract is much lower than that with Europe.[946] And Chinese interests are contradictory with Russia's: "the Chinese have no interest in assisting Russia to become a primary supplier across the Asia-Pacific; they do not just want the gas but also to control the regional gas market."[947] Moreover, in exporting gas to China alone, Russia "will have to fight for its expected status and face bitter competition with such major liquefied gas exporters as Qatar, Australia, Malaysia and Indonesia, and probably also with the USA in the next few years."[948] Russia is disadvantaged here by the heritage of previous political-business deals from the last two decades. All these factors show that signing the contract has first and foremost a political importance.[949] A diversification threat is intended to strengthen the Russian political position: "its aim is to suggest to Europe a possibility of reorienting gas deliveries to Asia; this in turn should make the European countries, already dependent on Russian gas, more prone to overlook Russian expansionism."[950] Nevertheless, the data once more proves to go against Moscow's plans: in 2015 Russia sold as much as four times the oil to EU than to China; and about 800 times as much gas and that in 2015 China "imported more natural gas from America than it did from Russia."[951] The low price of the gas and the impossibility of redirecting gas supplies from Europe to Asia (lack of pipelines) make the Russian threats hollow – or rather a PR tool only.

To conclude this agreement, this contract "is another breakthrough in Russia-China energy co-operation, but makes it more asymmetrical" for China "the deal with Russia broadens its import portfolio", "provides additional safe overland route" and is cheaper (it also diminished potential tensions over

---

944 D. Trenin, *From Greater Europe….*

945 *Россия прорубила "газовое окно" в Азию – благодаря, но не назло Европе* [Russia has broke open a gas window into Asia, thanks to, not against Europe], РИА Новости, 21.05.2014.

946 Akio Kawato, *Much Ado About Sino-Russian Axis*, Carnegie Center Moscow 10.06.2014.

947 B. Lo, *Russia and the New World Disorder…*, p. 147.

948 S. Kardaś, *The eastern 'partnership' of gas…*

949 *Путин о газовом контракте с КНР: китайцы – надежные партнеры* [Putin on Gas Contract with PRC – Hopeful Partners], РИА Новости, 21.05.2014.

950 J. Korejba, op. cit.

951 And Russia has sold almost three and a half times as much coal to the EU than to China, I. Bond, op. cit.

China's Central Asian gas deliveries); for Russia "the balance sheet is more mixed" – it is built exclusively for China and makes it more dependent on the Chinese market, especially now, when Gazprom abandoned plans of building a LNG terminal in Vladivostok, it has a high investing cost, therefore: "the profitability of the project is questioned, and is assessed as political rather than commercial".[952] That all makes the results of the gas contract "groundbreaking": it makes "China the only target for Russian gas in the East and binds Gazprom in the long term to the Chinese market; Gazprom will be developing new gas fields for the eastern pipeline which means that it cannot use the contract with China to divert gas supplies destined for Europe", moreover once "all gas-export projects are complete, in the early 2020s, Russia's exports to China may be expected to account for up to 25% of its total exports."[953] Therefore, this gas contract "does in practice accentuate the asymmetric nature of this co-operation, consistently turning the Russian 'partner' into an 'energy vassal' of China."[954]

Judging by the perspective of 2017, "the situation is still far from rosy" – the project is facing major challenges: "Beijing has refused to provide a planned $25 billion loan needed for pipeline construction, and Russian officials have complained that the conditions on offer from Beijing—requiring the participation of Chinese companies in the construction phase—are unacceptable"; to make matters worse, the gas pipeline "may remain unprofitable if the oil price does not increase significantly in the next fifteen years"; nevertheless, "officials on both sides remain confident that the pipeline will be built, though perhaps with delays."[955] In 2015 construction had begun on both Russian and Chinese territory.[956] However, the Chinese loan is still unknown while other prospects for other Gazprom projects (such as Western Route, or Power of Siberia II from Altai to Xinjiang) targeted at the Chinese market "remain bleak" due to disagreements over price: "the western route now appears to be a nonstarter, as do Gazprom's plans to build a third pipeline for Sakhalin gas to China via Vladivostok."[957]

The Russia-China energy cooperation, with its two symbols, oil and gas, thus witnessed a considerable transformation. From very promising, yet unfulfilled prospects in the 2000s to finalized, though asymmetric, ones in the 2010s. In the 2000s, Russia has tried to repeat its energy divide and conquer strategy in Asia, and avoid dependence on China. Kremlin had "pursued a de

952 M. Kaczmarski, *Russia-China Relations…*, p. 64.
953 Ibid., p. 67.
954 S. Kardaś, *The eastern 'partnership' of gas…*
955 A. Gabuev, *Friends with Benefits?…*
956 *Китай начал строить продолжение «Силы Сибири»* [China Started Construction Enlargment of Power of Siberia], Vedomosti.Ru, 02.06.2015.
957 Akio Kawato, op. cit.

facto policy of 'anyone but the Chinese' in energy exploration and development."[958] Despite its initial reservations, Russia after 2008 due to the economic realities of the crisis hS reversed its strategy and priotitised cooperation with China which strengthened their relations. Moscow became an important part of China's resource strategy, but at the same time the "energy realm has exposed Russia's increasing dependence on China", Moscow's policy "has been growing even more Sinocentric (…), while Russia's energy assumes that about one third of oil and gas will be directed to Asia, in fact it will be for China, not Asia."[959]

4. *Trade Volume*

Although Sino-Russian economic relations in the 2000s and 2010s intensified, this is nothing special: this example follows the global pattern of deepened integration in the global world. Sino-Russian economic relationship has also become much more unbalanced in comparison with the 1990s: resources started to dominate the picture.[960] Moscow, afraid that it would become China's "energy appendix" (almost 80% of the Russian export to China consists of energy and raw materials; machinery export is less than 5%); has been lobbying for increased export of machinery and technology, but Beijing has been unwilling to do so – China has mostly wanted to develop energy cooperation.[961] After the economic crisis, Moscow came to realize that besides resources, "it has nothing to sell to China."[962] In other words, the Kremlin decided to make a virtue out of necessity and intensified the economic relations with China, on Chinese terms. For these and other reasons, China remains the dominant Russian economic partner in Asia, with around $65 billion trade volume, whereas Russia's trade with Japan in 2015 was ($20 billion) while with South Korea $16 billion.[963]

Putin's approach to economy is in many ways similar to the Chinese one: strict political control combined with building on market mechanisms, as well as significant share of state in strategic sectors and regaining central control over Siberian natural resources. Nevertheless, despite a common approach to economy, "both governments generally treat each other in an objectively commercial fashion."[964] From an economical point of view, the Russians have for a long time viewed "China less as a primary market than a leverage against the

958 B. Lo, *Russia and the New World Disorder…*, p. 147.
959 M.Kaczmarski, *Russia-China Relations…*, p. 64.
960 А.В. Лукин, *От нормализации к стратегическому партнерству…*, p. 375.
961 E. S. Downs, op. cit., p. 164.
962 А.В. Лукин, *От нормализации к стратегическому партнерству…*, p. 375.
963 M. Kaczmarski, *Russia-China and the West…*
964 R. Lotspeich, op. cit., p. 89.

West"; there was little sense that "it represents 'one billion costumers' a potential El Dorado for the Russian corporate sector". [965] Only recently has it changed, as Russians are increasingly turning to China, hoping to secure deals in food and agriculture sector (resulting in "China's euphoria"), but the "going has been slow" due to the competition and barriers; Despite strategic partnership Bejing has been protecting its market by administration measures for two decades now.[966]

Although the volume of trade has increased eightfold during Putin's term, it started from a very low basis – it materialized thanks to political aspects: high oil prices, China's energy hunger, and intensified export of Chinese manufactured and commercial goods; one may compare Russia's volume of trade with China (around 10%) with the Russia-EU one (around 45%) to see the difference.[967] Thus, even from the perspective of the mid 2010s, the Sino-Russian trade volume "scarcely reflects the size and proximity of the two economies" and among China's trade partners Russia is ranked below such countries as South Korea, Malaysia, Australia, Brazil (not to mention the EU, the USA or Japan) and "resembles that of developing countries in Africa and Latin America with Beijing—export of natural resources in return for the import of manufactured goods".[968]

Despite official rhetoric of "economic complementarity", in Sino-Russian context "this means imbalance and inequality" – "while Moscow hopes that China will become an economic, as well as political and strategic counterweight to the West, Beijing (with the exception of a few niches, such as space and military design) sees Russia as little more than a resource-cow (…) a second-rate economy."[969] Patterns of trade confirm the Chinese outlook: Russia is not an important target for the Chinese export. For example, in 2011 China invested "US$300 million into the Russian economy— 0.5 percent of its total overseas amount that year (…)" and the investment was "focused mainly on natural resources extraction rather than value-added industries."[970] On the other hand, China is an important destination for Russian export: raw materials (energy, wood) and semi-finished industrial goods (chemicals and metals): energy compromises 68% of 2015 exports, while timber – another 13%.[971] Besides exporting resources, recent Russian exports to China of agriculture goods

965 Д. Тренин, *Верные друзья?*....

966 *Russia Seeks Food-Export Boom With China But Obstacles Abound*, "Bloomberg", 10.02.2017; А.В. Лукин, *От нормализации к стратегическому партнерству*…, p. 375.

967 B. Lo, *The Axis of Convenience*…, p. 84.

968 Idem, *Russia and the New World Disorder*…, p. 145. In late 2000s Russia was 7th-8th China's trade partner, but since then has been losing its position, to countries such as Malaysia, Brazil, South Korea or Taiwan, А.В. Лукин, *От нормализации к стратегическому партнерству*…, p. 384.

969 B. Lo, *The Axis of Convenience*…, p. 85.

970 Idem, *Russia and the New World Disorder*…, p. 145.

971 R. Lotspeich, op. cit., p. 115; *Russia Seeks Food-Export Boom*…

(fish, meat, chocolate, sunflower oil, beer, honey and ice cream), as well as amber, have intensified, comprising around 10% of all its export.[972] Russia invests in China mostly in the following sectors: chemicals, agricultural machinery, automobiles, construction, nuclear power and construction materials, river transportation, as well as primary sectors (agriculture, forestry and fishing).[973] Its biggest investement (beside energy) is joint construction of a titanium factory in Jiamusi in Heilongjiang; yet, Russian investements in China are very thin ("extremely insignificant" for the Chinese economy) and much smaller even than the Chinese investments in Russia.[974] Aside from energy, the Chinese are investing in the following sectors: wood processing, telecommunications equipment, textile industry, microelectronics, consumer appliances, services and agriculture.[975] The most important Chinese investments in Russia are the "Baltic Pearl" complex in Saint Petersburg, Park Huamin business-centre in Moscow (not finished yet) and the international trade centre "Greenwood" in Moscow capital district (Podmoskove); all of them have been constructed for more than a decade now (since the early 2000s) with much delays and problems on the way.[976] To make matters worse, in general Chinese investments in Russia are far behind in numbers than those to other destinations, such as Luxembourg, South Africa, Singapore, Thailand, Burma/Myanmar, Canada, Pakistan, Brasil, or Iran: "all those places seem to be more attractive for Chinese investors than Russia".[977]

In general, the trends of bilateral trade show a reversal of history. According to Dmitri Trenin, "In the past, much of this trade consisted of Russian machinery exports to, and raw material imports from China. Today, the roles have been reversed: Russia imports Chinese manufactured goods, including growing quantities of machinery, and exports raw materials – energy, metals and timber – alongside a few high-tech items."[978] Alexander Lukin echoes his words: "Russia and China exchanged their places: Russia became a provider of resources to Chinese industry, while China a supplier of ready-made production for Russian consumers (…) Russia is interested in China as a supplier of resources and in its market for its goods."[979] Bobo Lo has put it more drastically: "the economic relationship is so asymmetrical that it is beginning to acquire a neo-colonial tinge: a modernizing China exploiting a backward Russia for its energy and timber resources and as a market for low-grade foods

972 *Russia Seeks Food-Export Boom…* ; 30% according to Sofia Pale, *Russian Business Interests in China*, "New Eastern Outlook", 05.10.2016.
973 R. Lotspeich, op. cit., p. 122.
974 А.В. Лукин, *От нормализации к стратегическому партнерству…*, p. 385.
975 R. Lotspeich, op. cit., p. 122.
976 А.В. Лукин, *От нормализации к стратегическому партнерству…*, p. 389-391.
977 Ibid., p. 387.
978 Д. Тренин, *Верные друзья?…*
979 А.В. Лукин, *От нормализации к стратегическому партнерству…*, p. 382; Idem, *Россия и Китай…*, p. 651.

unsalable in the more discriminating West. Commercially, Beijing appears to rate Russia more or less on a par with countries such as Saudi Arabia, Angola or Sudan."[980]

Imbalance of bilateral trade relations started to worry the Kremlin around the mid 2000s. Even arms sales, so far the "pearl in the crown" of bilateral relations, consists only little more than 10% of all trade volume.[981] To make matters worse for Russia, the trade balance year by year has become more and more imbalanced. China's importance in Russian foreign trade annually increases: in 2010 China surpassed Germany and became Russia's first trade partner (the first partner if we exclude the EU and estimate the EU countries separately, if EU countries are considered combined, then the EU is the first partner); the Russia-China trade volume was USD 55 billion then (10% of all Russian trade).[982] To compare – in 2015 Russia was China's sixteenth trade partner[983]: "Russia is a less important trading partner to China than China is to Russia; Russian trade is a significant factor primarily for the northeast China, abutting Siberia. For the Chinese government officials dealing with economics, trade and finance, Russia is a non-factor."[984] This happens because of six reasons. First, China's imports are more strongly oriented to primary products; second, China relies much more on the EU and the USA than on Russia for imports that are technologically sophisticated; third, the composition of the Chinese exports to Russia follows the pattern in exports to other developed economies; the composition of China's trade with Russia is much more dynamic and prone to changes than the relatively stable compositions in China-EU or China-US trade relations.[985] Forth, geography restricts enhanced cooperation, as the most important Russian centres are located far away and those on the Russian Far East suffer from a lack of transport infrastructure; fifth, the size of the Russian market (a population of 146 million and the GDP per capita of $9,100) cannot consume as much of China's output as the West; sixth, the investment climate in Russia is bad (corruption, legal unpredictability, ineffectivness of governmental agencies) which makes investement risks too high for many (particularly for SME); all these contributed to the fact that Chinese investments in Russia were "anaemic: $3.8 billion from 2007 to 2016, compared with $24 billion from Germany."[986] In these circumstances, there is little beyond resources and cheap commercial goods to be traded.

---

980 B. Lo, *The Axis of Convenience…*, p. 85-86.

981 Yu Bin, *China-Russia Relations: Partying and Posturing for Power, Petro and Prestige*, "Comparative Connections", vol. 8, no. 2.

982 Д. Тренин, *Верные друзья?…*

983 *Russian Business Interests in China…*

984 Д. Тренин, *Верные друзья?…*

985 R. Lotspeich, op. cit., p. 106.

986 I. Bond, op. cit.; А.В. Лукин, *Россия и Китай…*, p. 669.

Russian attempts to deepen economic cooperation have been unsuccessful so far: "Russia's appeal for a balance in industrial development based on Chinese commitments to buying more than natural resources from Russia falls on deaf ears."[987] Russia has been losing its position even in its traditional areas to the Western competition (advantaged by the virtue of having better technology). In energy Russia hoped for much, but in the end the Chinese set the agenda. In arms sales and space technology, China has been pushing strongly – against Moscow's will – for license purchase and recently achieved it with Su-35. Growing Chinese export and decreasing import of Russian industrial goods contributed to the fact that Russia lost the positive trade balance.[988] Despite Russia and China's "proximity and complementary resource base, bilateral integration has not proceeded more rapidly or deeply than their separate integration with the rest of the world; the reasons for this are related to geography, social features and politics."[989]

It the last few years this gloomy picture has been changing a bit. Russia is striving to change the unbeneficial model of economic cooperation by trying to attract Chinese investments in return for sales of the most advanced technology. There is a potential in increasing Chinese direct foreign investments (but not the other way round) in the following areas: Far East/Siberia economic projects, cross-border transportation infrastructure, high–technology cooperation from commercialization to research and development, aerospace, environmental protection, agriculture, forestry, railways, ship-building, and alternative energy. In return Russia has been hoping for contracts in atomic energy, space industry (RD-18 rocket engines), aviation and helicopter building.[990] However, so far, these hopes ended up like the grandiose declarations on reaching 100 billion USD volume of trade until 2015[991] – on paper mostly. The same can be said about nuclear technology. Despite promising prospects in the mid 2000s, and Russian success in building two blocks of nuclear power plant Tianwan in Lianyungang (the contract was signed in 1997, but the power plan became full operational only in 2009)[992], the cooperation stalled: the implementation of several memoranda (including that of the construction of the third and forth block of the Tianwan nuclear power plant) have not followed, probably due to security issues after the Fukushima catastrophe in 2011.[993]

987 G. Rozman, *The Sino-Russian…*, p. 257.
988 Yu Bin, *China-Russia Relations: Partying…*, p. 161; B. Lo, *The Axis of Convenience…*, pp. 85-86.
989 R. Lotspeich, op. cit., p. 137.
990 Yu Bin, *Between Geo-Economics…*; *Russian Business Interests in China…*
991 *Пресс-конференция по итогам российско-китайских переговоров* [Press Conference after the Russian-Sino Talks], Kremlin.ru, 16.07.2011.
992 А.В. Лукин, *От нормализации к стратегическому партнерству…*, p. 396.
993 M. Kaczmarski, *Russia-China Relations…*, p. 69.

Cooperation in electric energy and coal works a bit better. Russia is already, since 2012, selling around 4 billion KWh of electric energy to China, and should this sector of cooperation grow, the Russian Far East may become "a powerhouse supplying northeastern China"; Russian export of coal to China intensified after 2009: after the contract of August 2010, Moscow agreed to export 15 million tons of coal annually, although it is only a small share in China's market (imports equate to 1% of China's consumption), even this is an opportunity given the size of this market.[994]

Potential Chinese investments in Russia are important for the Russian Far East mostly. Already in 2004, Chinese officials "promised $800 million worth of investments for Russia's far eastern territories"; however, "imports of Chinese capital have been slow to arrive – in 2008, the inflow was under $30 million, which rose to $45 million in 2009 – still a puny 0.5 per cent of all foreign direct investment in Russia's far eastern region."[995] According to the Russian TASS agency, recently (in 2017) Chinese investments in the Russian Far East are rising and account for about 22% of the total foreign investment volume[996], if it is indeed so, then perhaps this is the first good news for years for the Russian Far East.

In 2009, Moscow, finally liberating itself from anti-Chinese fear, accepted a plan of Chinese investments in the Russian Far East. This plan targets the following sectors: trade, forestry, energy, transportation, manufacture, and agriculture.[997] Needles to say, this program, if implemented, would make the Russian Far East even more dependent on China. The Russians "see the danger of becoming a simple 'raw materials appendix' to their neighbour but hope to be able to rebalance the relationship later, by producing semi-finished goods on their territory."[998] It remains to be seen whether they would be able to achieve it.

The 2015 fall of energy prices (particularly oil) and China's economic slowdown all seriously and negatively affected Russia-China economic relations. Russia dropped from being China's ninth partner to sixteenth place. In 2014, trade grew by 6.8 percent and reached a total of $95.3 billion; in 2015, however, it collapsed by 28.6 percent, to just total $68 billion ($64 billion by other estimations). It was not only because of the drop in commodity prices; Russian economic decline was more important: GDP decreased by 3.4 percent, and the

994 Ibid., pp. 68-69.

995 Д. Тренин, *Верные друзья?...*

996 *Moscow offers Beijing to set up center to support Chinese investors*, Tass, 09.01.2017.

997 *Программа сотрудничества между регионами Дальнего Востока и Восточной Сибири РФ и Северо-Востока КНР (2009 - 2018 годы)* [Programme of Cooperation between RF Far East and East Siberia regions and Northeast China regions, 2009-2018], Политическое образование.Ru, 18.07.2010.

998 Д. Тренин, *Верные друзья?...*

subsequent low purchasing power of Russian companies and households contributed to the sharp drop in Russian imports from China.[999] Nevertheless, both sides continued to cooperate, and – judging by early 2017 – trade is showing signs of increasing: it rose by 30% in April. By the end of 2016 Chinese companies had invested US$40 billion of cumulative investment in Russia, with about a quarter coming after the Ukrainian crisis; Chinese banks, despite being compliant with Western sanctions, have helped Putin's friend's companies, China offered Russia "critical technologies" such as an "electrical cable going from mainland Russia to Crimea, which helped Moscow withstand the Ukrainian economic blockade of the occupied peninsula"; on the other hand, Chinese companies are steadily taking over the Russian market from Western companies ("particularly in the IT and telecommunications sector where Russian SOEs and ministries are busy replacing Western equipment with products made by Chinese competitors").[1000] Russia still hopes to move beyond resources by selling machines, equipment and food to China; it remains to be seen whether Moscow will be able to achive that: "though there has been plenty of talk about Chinese investment in Russia and (to a lesser extent) Russian investment in China, the reality has yet to match up."[1001]

5. Summary

The growing asymmetry in favour of Beijing in Sino-Russian relations is best seen in their economic relations. Moscow and Beijing are still not the most important partners to one another. Moscow is China's sixteenth trade partner; whereas Beijing is Russia's second – but far behind the European Union. Despite decreasing it comprises almost 45% of Russian trade, compared to little more than 10% with China; over 90% of FDI to Russia comes from the West, which is also the biggest source of capital and advanced technologies; also 90% of all energy export goes westwards; "it will take two decades (at least) for Asia to become the primary destination of Russian oil and gas."[1002] Furthermore, the structure of trade shows China's advantage. China mostly buys resources and raw materials and sells consumption goods and food. The structure of trade follows almost a colonial pattern. Russia is aware of this fact and tries to change it; so far in vain. Two Russian attempts to engage actively with Asia through grand energy projects – the oil pipeline ESPO and gas pipeline The Power of Siberia – instead of decreasing Russia's dependence from China,

---

999 A. Gabuev, *Friends with Benefits?...*

1000 The official data for period 1991-2016 is $14.2 billion, but the number of $40 billion includes transactions through offshore jurisdictions and is more accurate, Alexander Gabuev, *Friends with Strategic...*

1001 I. Bond, op. cit.

1002 B. Lo, *Russia and the New World Disorder...*, p. 139.

increased it. Russia has no good idea of how to decrease its dependence on China and escape the fate of being a permanent "raw material appendix" to the Chinese economy. Moscow, however, after 2008 decided that "what is real is rational": instead of balancing China and trying to steer away from its dependence from China, Russia decided to bandwagon and get as much as possible from economic cooperation on Chinese terms.

II. Military Relations

Russian-Chinese military relations played a very special role. In the 1990s, the military cooperation was the most visible aspect of the "strategic partnership": "the glue of the bilateral relationship", "the hallmark of relationship", the key aspect of improving of relations and the only stable sector of trade and certainly an important reason for maintaining friendly relations between Moscow and Beijing.[1003] The level of Russia-China military cooperation decreased in the 2000s to increase again in the 2010s. However, researching this aspect is particularly hard, due to the inaccessibility of sources and difficulties with verification of data; this adds an aura of secrecy around this matter.[1004]

In the military sphere of Sino-Russian relations two questions are crucial. The first one: is the PLA, long considered technologically backward, overtaking its Russian counterpart? And the second: do China's enhanced military capabilities threaten Russia's security interests?[1005]

The People's Liberation Army has made remarkable progress in the last two decades, even more remarkable when compared to the demise of the Russian army. The difference in Chinese progress and Russian regress was so visible that some may come to the conclusion that Chinese military potential exceeds the Russian one – or will do shortly. It is a wrong conclusion: "despite the decline of the Russian army, they nevertheless still enjoy several critical advantages, including nuclear warheads and around a million of conventional forces."[1006] Moreover, modernization of the PLA is focused on navy and air force – this illustrates China's most important military and political goals – Taiwan and the South China Sea, not Russia.[1007] Finally, "the modernization of the Chinese military is far from complete – it still has a long way to go

1003 Jing-dong Yuan, op. cit., p. 203; S. W. Garnett, op. cit., p. 12; J. L. Wilson, *Strategic Partners...*, p. 112; Y. V. Tsyganov, op. cit., p. 302-310.

1004 К. Макиенко, *Опасно ли торговать оружием с Китаем?* [Is it Dangerous to Sell Arms to China?], Москва 1999, p. 1.

1005 B. Lo, *The Axis of Convenience...*, p. 75.

1006 Ibid., p. 76.

1007 D. Shambaugh, *Modernizing China's Military: Progress, Problems, and Prospects*, University of California Press 2004, pp. 1-13.

before it develops modern armed forces, let alone defeating such a strong adversary as Russia that enjoys the advantage of strategic depth"; nor is China planning to invade the Russian Far East in the predictable future: "compared to Chinese strategic objectives, the Russian Far East is a provincial side-show, hardly worth risking war with the world's second nuclear weapon state."[1008] The understanding of this fact led to growing cooperation, particularly in arms sales (from the 1990s) and in joint exercises (from the mid 2000s).

1. Arms Sales

Arms sales constituted the most important part of Russian-Chinese military cooperation in the 1990s. One may even say that it was the essence of this cooperation; beyond it not much happened. Here interests of China and Russia met perfectly. On the Russian side it was the military industrial sector that advocated intensification of contacts with China. The hard conditions of the Gaidar reforms, giant debts and a lack of new orders made acquiring financial means an absolute necessity. In these circumstances, "export became the only possible option of financing military sector", while trade with China was "manna from heaven for the Russian military-industrial complex."[1009] Between 1992 and 1999, defence enterprises produced 2 ships for domestic procurement and 11 for export sales, 31 tanks for domestic use and 433 for export, and 7 aircraft for the domestic sector and 278 for export; in 1996 military-technical cooperation with foreign countries provided work for over 400,000 employees of defence enterprises, while up to two-thirds of the working assets of enterprises of the military-industrial complex were produced by arms exports.[1010] Director of Rosvoomzheniye, the main export agency, A. I. Kotiolkin, admitted that 50% of factory units were financed by export; a significant part from selling to China alone (China was the most interested country in acquiring Russian arms).[1011] Reliance on export "gave rise to certain understandable but dysfunctional behavior (…) born out of financial desperation"; Chinese delegations to Russia reminded of shopping trips, while once symbols of Russian national pride such as Su-27, "representing the highest technological achievement of Soviet military prowess, became reduced to the status of a commodity

---

1008 B. Lo, *The Axis of Convenience…*, p. 79.

1009 А. В. Лукин, *Китай:медьведь наблюдает за драконом. Одраз Китая в России в XVII-XXI веках* [The Bear Watches Over the Dragon. The Image of China in Russia in 17-21th Centuries], Москва 2007, p. 472; Y. V. Tsyganov, op. cit., p. 311.

1010 J. L. Wilson, *Strategic Partners…*, p. 105.

1011 П. Е. Фельгенгауэр, *Оруже для Китая и национальная безопасность России* [Arms for China and Russia's National Security], [in:] *Россия в мировой таргoвле оружем: статегия, политика,экономика* [Russia in World Arms Sales: Strategy, Politics, Economy], Москва Карнеге 1996, p. 128.

on the marketplace."[1012] China became so attractive that the Russian military-industrial base developed its own "China policy": "to sell anything to anybody."[1013] The first years of Yeltsin's era favored uncontrollable trade. Although formally there were control of exports and Russia vowed to honor its international obligations to sell only defensive weapons, "neither the Foreign Ministry nor even the secret service were able to estimate exactly what was exported, particularly in 1992, popularly known as the year of no control."[1014] Enterprises had good reason to deal directly with the Chinese clients, bypassing official channels – it guaranteed that money actually ended up in their accounts, not in the "notoriously corrupted" state arms sales agency.[1015]

That is why the military-industrial complex remained the vocal and permanent lobbyist for cooperation with China, against the pro-Western policy of Kozyrev. With time their task got easier, for two reasons. Firstly, it was already the late Soviet times when the institutional framework for cooperation was created. Secondly, with time, the role of this complex in Russian policy making grew – since Gaidar's deposition, there was a military complex representative in every Russian government. The clear, visible sign of the complex's importance became the nomination of Arkadiy Volsky, a well-known lobbyist for cooperation with China, for the Russian-side chairmanship in Peace, Friendship and Development Committee, established in 1997.[1016] The lobbyists did not have to strive very hard to convince the political elites anyway – already in January 1992, Boris Yeltsin said that "arms sales are necessary for us to get foreign currency, urgently needed, as well as to keep the military-industrial complex alive."[1017] Arms sales, not included in Russian custom statistics, became niches in Russian export. Arms were one of the very few technologically advanced products which Russia was able to offer on the competitive global market. According to Pavel Felgenhauer, Russian policy towards China in arms sales was simple in its nature: "first, it's money; second, it's money; and third, it's also money."[1018]

For China, arms purchases from Russia became vital after the Western embargo on arms and military technology sales introduced on China after Tiananmen. The USSR's fall cancelled a military threat from the north, while change

---

1012 J. L. Wilson, *Strategic Partners...*, pp. 94-109.

1013 П. Е. Фельгенгауэр, op. cit., p. 136.

1014 Ibid., с. 136.

1015 A. Zhilin, *Generals Do Arms Business First*, Moscow News, 07.04.1995; А. В. Лукин, *Китай: медьведь наблюдает...*, pp. 470-473.

1016 А.В. Лукин, *От нормализации к стратегическому партнерству...*, pp. 316-317.

1017 A. A. Sergounin, S. V. Subbotin, *Sino-Russian Military-Technical Cooperation: a Russian View*, [in:] *Russia and the Arms Trade*, ed. I. Anthony, Oxford 1998, p. 196.

1018 P. Felgenhauer, *An Uneasy Partnership: Sino-Russian Defense Cooperation and Arms Sales*, [in:] *Russia in the World Arms Sales*, ed. A. J. Pierre, D. Trenin, Washington 1997, p. 87.

in military doctrine (to the so called "peripheral defence") as well as reorientation towards Taiwan and the South China Sea meant growing need for modern military equipment, particularly in aviation and fleet. Moreover, Beijing understood the need of acquiring advanced military technology. The Western embargo made it a necessity to find a place to get it. In the early 1990s it could only have been Russia. Moscow had other advantages – the Chinese military industry was built by Soviet specialists in the 1950s, while Chinese army was equipped with modified Russian arms along Soviet patterns. Moreover, Russia had no reservations about selling weapons and arms sales created no political problems in bilateral relations. Finally, Russian arms were relatively cheap and Moscow was prone to accept flexible prices, including barter. For example, 75% of the first contract to supply Su-27 and Kilo submarines was paid in barter.[1019] This provoked "considerable chagrin, if not outright despair, among Russian observers who were compelled to watch their sophisticated weaponry being exchanged for low-quality consumers items and foodstuffs from China."[1020] With time, however, Russia was able to increase cash transactions – in the late 1990s, all Russian-Chinese contracts on advanced military technology were signed in hard currency.

All these factors made Russia the most logical and most adequate arms supplier to China. Unsurprisingly, Russia became China's top arms supplier in the 1990s. Nevertheless, a proper estimation of volume of this trade remains difficult, because only a portion of information has been made accessible to the public. For sure, Russia remained China's unrivaled supplier of arms (around 90% of all arms delivered to China in the 1900s were made in Russia). As for Russia, China also remained critical, though for different reasons. After the USSR's fall, Russia lost some of its traditional markets in arms sales (Afghanistan, Syria), whereas others were limited by free market realities (Vietnam, Angola). Although in the early 1990s India was Russia's main receiver of arms, it changed quickly and China took the lead.[1021]

Signed in the late Soviet years, the contract for the delivery of the Su-27 became the historical first purchase of Russian arms by the Chinese (the Su arrived in China in 1992).[1022] Soon cooperation in arms sales developed so rapidly that it evoked neighbors' fears. It also contributed to a substantional increase in Russian-Chinese volume of trade to the level of 5.6 billion USD,

---

1019 Idem, Russia *Too Busy Arming China To Care About Consequences*, "St. Petersbourg Times", 17.07.1997.

1020 J. L. Wilson, *Strategic Partners*..., p. 104; see more: Jing-dong Yuan, op. cit., p. 219. On the other hand, the Chinese complained about the quality of Russian arms, R. Weitz, *China – Russia Security Relations. Strategic Parallelism Without Partnership or Passion?*, Washington 2012, p. 28.

1021 K. Ryan, *Russo-Chinese Defense Relations. The View from Moscow*, [in:] *The Future of China-Russia*..., p. 181.

1022 K. Makienko, *U. S. Congressional Research Service Report on Russia's Place in the Arms Market*, "Moscow Defence Brief" 5/2001, p.1.

that contrasted with its noticeable fall during last years of the USSR.[1023] During Yeltsin's trip to Beijing in December 1992, both sides signed a memorandum on the basis of military-technical cooperation (and confirmed sale of the Su-27 and an anti-aircraft S-300).[1024] Moreover, both sides set up a join governmental commission on cooperation in military technology. During his 1992 visit Yeltsin disclosed – "to the consternation of those who had labored to keep such figures secret" that Russian arms supplies to China had totalled 1.8 billion dollars for 1992.[1025] In 1992 alone, Russia and China signed many agreements on training, training programmes, Russian instructors and technician visits to China and of training Chinese military staff in Russian institutes. Soon this cooperation developed further. The importance of trade contacts and exports for Russia can be clearly seen in 1993 military doctrine, where military-technical goals and the key role of military cooperation in rebuilding military-industrial base is emphasized.[1026] During the trip to China of the RF minister of defence, Pavel Grachov, the two sides signed a memorandum on military-technical cooperation. The details remain undisclosed but clearly created ground for a series of transactions, technology transfers and technical courses for the Chinese (the license for the Su-27 was supposed to be the most important part of this deal).[1027] Moscow was less willing to admit cooperation in this area, but in February 1996 Russians revealed that Moscow sold the license for production of the Su-27 (the leaks revealed that it was the purchase of 48 Su-27s, including 6 already contracted; China was given the right to produce 200 Su-27s within 15 years without the possibility of reselling it to third countries; Beijing was supposed to pay 2.5 billion USD.[1028] The transfer of technology issue pushed by the Chinese since the mid 1990s split into two sides. The Russians "sought to preserve a 70 to 30 ratio of arms deliveries to technology transfers."[1029] From the geostrategic point of view, transfer of technology was

1023 B. Rychłowski, op. cit., p. 23.

1024 *Меморандум о понимании между Правительством Российской Федерации и Правительством Китайской Народной Республики о военно-техническом сотрудничестве от 18 декабря 1992 г.* [Memorandum of Understanding between Goverments of Russian Federation and China People's Republic on Military-Technical Cooperation], [in:] *Россия и Китай: сборник документов 1991-2006* [Russia-China: the Collection of Documents], сост. И. И. Климин, СПБ 2007, pp. 15-17.

1025 J. L. Wilson, *Strategic Partners...*, p. 95.

1026 *The Basic Provisions of the Military Doctrine of the Russian Federation*, "Federation of American Scientists", 02.11.1993.

1027 *Соглашение между Министерством обороны РФ и Министерством обороны Китая о военном сотрудничестве* 1993, 11 X, Bestpravo.Ru

1028 К. Макиенко, *Военно-технические сотрудничество России и КНР в 1992-2002 годах: достижения, тенденции, перспективы* [Russian-Chinese Military-Technical Cooperation in 1992-2002 Successes, Tendencies and Perspectives], документ 2, Москва 2002, pp. 41-42; Idem, *U. S. Congressional Research Service Report on Russia's Place in the Arms Market*, "Moscow Defence Brief" 5/2001.

1029 J. L. Wilson, *Strategic Partners...*, p. 97.

not the most rational behaviour – it could have meant arming a potential enemy in the future. High ranking Russian commanders raised this kind of concern with their "unordinary statements": Defence minister Pavel Grachov announced in 1995 that: "the Chinese want to peacefully conquer the Russian Far East", while his successor, Igor Rodionov included China in the "potentially main enemies of Russia."[1030] Rodionov's words "obviously recited the collective apprehensions of the General Staff (…) nothing illustrates the prevailing ambiguity among the Russian elites than the predicament of the military establishment: it has to approve massive Russian arms sales to China in order to salvage something from the crumbling national defence industrial base, while at the same time counting China among Russia's potential adversaries for the future."[1031] Besides, the elites themselves were divided over arms sales: military-industrial complex representatives lobbied for further sales, whereas security ministries blocked the transfer of the newest technology. Arms sales to China were also advocated by some specialists, who saw it "not only as a private interest of producers, but also rational calculations of strategic and national interests."[1032] In this approach arms sales were supposed to be the engine of long-term strategic partnership that would lead to new balance of power in East Asia. China, then, was not considered a rival, because Russia still had at least 15 years technological advantage. Except for this advantage, there was another reason why Russian experts did not consider China as a threat – Beijing's orientation towards Taiwan and the South China Sea. The most important reason, however, why Russia, despite reservations was selling weapons, was money. As Georgi Arbatov commented – "we made it easier for them because of the absolute failure of our economic reforms; for us the weakest point is the state of our economy"; "ultimately Russia, beset by increasingly severe economic problems with the August 1998 collapse of the ruble, yielded to China, jettisoning the 70 to 30 ratio."[1033]

To summarize: the most important Chinese achievement in arms sales in the 1990s must be the contract in 1992 for the delivery of the Su-27 multirole combat aircraft. This contract covered 26 Su-27s and Su-27 UBs with arms and the training of Chinese pilots. In 1995-1996 ota furtherher 22-42 planes were ordered and the license for production of 200 Su-27s in Shenyang was bought; besides this the PRC purchased air-to-air missiles, cargo aircrafts Il-27, Mi-17 and Ka-27 helicopters, aircraft engines RD-33 and potential rocket engines for Intercontinental Ballistic Missiles, radars for circular observation, fire control and warcraft radars, a rocket air-defence system – around one hundred strategic S-300 PMU-1s (SA-10) and Tor-M1s (SA-15), rocket anti-tank systems,

---

1030 А. В. Лукин, *Китай: медьведь наблюдает…* p. 480; Idem, *От нормализации к стратегическому партнерству…*, p. 325.
1031 D. Trenin, *The China Factor …*, pp. 41-53.
1032 S. Blank, *The Dynamics of Russian Weapon Sales to China*, Washington 1997, pp. 4-5.
1033 J. L. Wilson, *Strategic Partners…*, p. 97-99.

T-80U and T-72 tanks, infantry fighting vehicle MMP-3s, self-propelled artillery, multiple rocket launchers, 4 Kilo class submarines, 2 Sowriemiennyi type rocket destroyers with equipment and armament, system for aerial refueling, and special technologies to produce titanium used for building aircrafts.[1034]

Sino-Russian military relationship has been deepened during Vladimir Putin's first two presidential terms. Normalization and recentralization of trade and resigning from barter, marked the most important differences in comparison to the 1990s. The anxiety over selling modern weapons to China started eroding, with strategic calculations being replaced by commercial ones. Beijing remained the biggest receiver of Russian arms. In the early 2000s what differed from the 1990s was Russia's growing security and claim that China is not a threat. This led to increase in arms sales to China, even the most sophisticated ones. The fear over Chinese future aggressive moves disappeared: Russian generals mostly stopped being afraid of the Chinese military modernization.[1035] As a result, Moscow agreed on selling Beijing highly advanced military technology, such as: Kilo submarines, Sovremennyi-2 destroyers and SU-30MKK helicopters. During the 2000s and the 2010s, Russia has provided the majority of Chinese-bought weapons, and remains the leader of arms sales to the PRC.[1036]

While in the past arms sales was intended to save the military-industrial complex, now this complex is revived thanks to the enlarged spectrum of clients. Nevertheless, Beijing remained the main receiver of Russian arms (over 40%).[1037] Partly it was because of the size of the market, but more important was Moscow's conviction that selling weapons to China does not threaten national security: "Russian security elites might prefer today to be more cautious of Chinese military cooperation, but seeing few alternatives, they appear to have shelved their concerns."[1038] Naturally, the fact that such units as Kilo submarines or Sovremennyi destroyers cannot be used against Russia also played its role. Either way, "the traditional fear that Russian arms may be used one day against Russia's armed forces has become discredited."[1039]

That is why the beginning of the 2000s brought an increase of cooperation in arms sales. Putin's administration simply continued or even deepened the military cooperation with China. The new element was the fact that the state

---

1034 Data after: I.Topolski, op. cit., pp. 143-144.

1035 There are exceptions from this rule, in 2009, gen. Sergei Skokov, head of Russian land forces suggested that Russia may face "multimillion man army" from the East, while gen. Vladimir Chirkin commander of the Siberian Military District conducted exercises at the border with China in 2010, I. Bond, op. cit.

1036 *Annual Report to Congress. Military and Security Developments Involving the People's Republic of China 2013*, Office of the Secretary of Defence.

1037 *Conventional Arms Transfer to Developing Nations 1988-2005*, Congressional Research Service Report for Congress 23.10.2006.

1038 K. Ryan, op. cit., p. 196.

1039 B. Lo, *The Axis of Convenience...*, p 80.

regained control over arms sales. Since 2001, the Kremlin has started intensive "recentralization" of arms sales: since then, none of the "strategic materials" could have been sold without government knowledge and consent. This reinstated Moscow's control over its own military-industrial units. Putin's administration focused on the revival of the military-industrial complex considering it a means to bring Russia back to its great power status. This sector was heavily subsidized by central funds when the Kremlin decided that this would help to revive the Russian economy. China was very important here, because Beijing imported the biggest amount of arms. Unsurprisingly, cooperation has flourished. Beijing, among other weapons, has purchased thirty eight Su-27 MKK fighter jets, four S-300PMU-4 long-range anti-aircraft missile systems, eight Kilo-class (project 363) submarines and two 956EM destroyers; this was followed by twenty-four Su-30 MK2 fighter jets equipped with Kh-31 A antiwarship missiles for the Chinese navy.[1040] The level of Chinese purchases begun to drop at the end of the 2000s when further development was blocked by concerns over the transfer of the most advanced military technology.

In the 2000s, Russian concerns about selling China highly advanced weapons changed to a commercial, rather than security, nature. Beijing has since preferred purchasing technology instead of military equipment – theoretically good news for Moscow (Russia is an ideal provider, given the ties between the two countries in the defence industrial sector – China's defence industry was built in the 1950s with Soviet assistance) which reacted to it by selling more equipment, weapons system and licenses "that only a few years ago it would have declined even to discuss, let alone sell, including a Klub-S (SS-N 27) antiship and land-attack cruise missile, an improved version of the Moskit SS-N-22 antiship missile, and the Su-30MMK2 and Su-30MKK3 combat aircrafts that even Russian military is not equipped with."[1041] Nevertheless, Moscow was unwilling to sell high advanced technology due to one reason: Beijing purchases it and then resells it to third countries.[1042] In recent years China has become one of the most important exporters of arms. That is why Moscow preferred not to sell the newest licenses to China, choosing India and Vietnam instead[1043]. To make matters worse, Beijing attracted Russian military specialists – at least two thousand Russian technicians have been employed, legally or not, by China to work on laser technology, nuclear weapons miniaturization,

1040 J. L. Wilson, *Strategic Partners…*, p. 99.

1041 Jing-dong Yuan, op. cit., pp. 214-220.

1042 There is, however, an alternative view: "many of the systems that the Chinese had allegedly stolen were actually developed by Russian engineers in the 1990s through contracts with Chinese military SOEs. Military technology transfer was poorly regulated and lacked proper supervision at that time, and Beijing, like many others, was simply taking advantage of the chaotic environment", A. Gabuev, *Friends with Benefits?…*

1043 Jing-dong Yuan, op. cit., pp. 214-220.

cruise missiles, space-based weaponry and nuclear submarines.[1044] All this has continued to annoy Moscow: which is why obstacles on the development of trade in military relationship were of a commercial, rather than security, nature. The Chinese pace to modernize its military capabilities and purchase new technologies leads to the question as to how long Moscow will be competitive. So far Russian equipment has served to enhance the Chinese army's capabilities in the area of potential confrontation with Taiwan (navy, air force). Russian dominance, however, was also based on the fact that the other three most important world exporters – the USA, the United Kingdom and France kept the post-Tiananmen's arms sales embargo. Should it be lifted, Moscow would face strong competition and might even lose this attractive market. Fortunately for Moscow, this scenario seems unlikely.

Nevertheless, despite intensive cooperation in the early 2000s, this changed in the mid 2000s. Russia had problems with the fulfillment of existing arrangements, and clearly was losing heart for selling weapons to Beijing. China's share in Russia's arms trade fell from around 40% to a mere 10%.[1045] The reasons were that the Russian military-industrial complex revived and there was no longer a dire need to sell weapons to China – Moscow thus was no longer forced to sell the most sophisticated weapons to Beijing (they sold them instead to India and Vietnam), keeping in mind the fact of the Su-27 having been copied by China; add geopolitical considerations (fear that did not ceased to exist on the part of Russian military establishment) and the fact that the Chinese military industry believed it had achieved "saturation level" and was not forced to buy Russian arms any longer.[1046]

Nevertheless, in the late 2000s the trends reversed again. After 2009 active cooperation was restarted and – particularly after 2011 –intensified.[1047] Russia sold thirty-two Mi-171 transport helicopters (in 2009), 500 jet engines (in 2010), ten Il-76 transport aircraft (2011), fifty-five Mi-171 helicopters; together since the early 2010s, Russia's arms sales to China "have stabilized at a level of USD2 billion per annum, accounting for up to 15% of Russia's rising profits from arms exports."[1048] What differentiated these purchases from the earlier periods (the 1990s and the early 2000s), was that the structure of arms exports "changed significantly: deliveries of complete weapon system decreased, replaced by sales of high-tech components, training for the Chinese military and the servicing of equipment already in operation."[1049]

1044 Ibid.

1045 L. Jakobsen, P. Holtom, D. Knox, and Jingchao Peng, op. cit.

1046 M. Kaczmarski, *Russia-China Relations…*, p. 71.

1047 *Первый зарубежный визит Шойгу в качестве министра обороны совершает в Китай, выступая за тесное военное сотрудничество с Пекином* [Shoigu's First Foreign Visit as Minister of Defence Was to China], Business-Gazeta.Ru 21.11.2012.

1048 M.Kaczmarski, *Russia-China Relations…*, p. 72.

1049 Ibid., p. 72.

In accordance with the renewed trend, since the late 2009s new negotiations started on Chinese purchases of twenty-four Su-35 jet fighters, S-400 anti-aircraft missile system as well as USD2 billion contract on four Amur 1650 submarines.[1050] The Su case in particular is symptomatic here. So far Russia declined to sell the most advanced jet fighters to China (it did not want to see their copies being resold). Several reasons, however, made Moscow change its mind: diversification of supply sources by traditional Russian allies (India, Central Asian countries); the conviction that China was technologically developing so rapidly that it may soon not be interested in purchasing Russian equipment; the traditional argument – that is, financial benefits (contract worth around USD1.5 billion); and finally, the fact that Su-35 production is supposed to terminate soon (it will be replaced by a new model), which means that Russia would keep its technological advantage in jet-fighters.[1051] Moreover, Russian relations with India deteriorated with the delay of several contracts and Russia wanted to use China as leverage for India; as for Beijing's rationale for renewing interest in Russian weaponry, the reason was that the "technological gap on the Chinese side turned out to be a much more serious obstacle than had previously been thought".[1052] That is why China considered the Su as a way of fundamental strengthening its military position vis-à-vis Japan, Vietnam and other South China Sea partners as well as maintaining an advantage over India.

Since 2012, intensive negotiations over the Su-35 took place, but the final impetus to sign this deal was the Ukrainian crisis – the negotiations ended with the signing of the USD2 billion contract on twenty-four Su-35s in November 2015.[1053] Even earlier, in April 2015 Moscow sold 6 battalions of S-400 anti-missile systems to China[1054]; this transfer is "a game changer" in China-Taiwan relations "since the PLA would be able to shoot down Taiwanese fighter planes as soon as they take off."[1055]

This all means that Moscow has departed from its former policy of not selling the most advanced weaponry to Beijing. Most probably economic factors (low oil prices, Western sanctions) made the Kremlin modify its stance. This contract qualitatively transforms Russia-China military relations as Russia "reversed its usual pattern of arms sales in Asia, according to which India always obtained slightly better equipment than China. Now, Russia will provide the

1050 Yu Bin, *Tales of Different 'Pivots'*...

1051 Ibid.

1052 M. Kaczmarski, *Russia-China Relations*..., p. 72.

1053 Russia inks contract with China on Su-35 deliveries, Tass, 19.11.2015; Although Russians had been deliberately delaying deliverance of the Su-35 (as well as S400), aircrafts finally arrived in China in late 2016, Yu Bin, *Russia-China Relations. Trilateral*..., pp. 103-116.

1054 Idem, *China-Russia, All Still Quiet in the East*, "Comparative Connections" vol.17 no.1

1055 A. Gabuev, *Friends with Benefits?* ...

same class of arms to the two strategic rivals, as India became the second customer for the Su-35 and S-400"[1056]; selling of the Su-35 symbolically marks "the diminishing mistrust on the part of Russia towards China (...) and reaffirms the Sinocentric orientation of Russia's foreign policy in Asia".[1057]

2. Military Cooperation, Joint Exercises

In the 1990s formal contacts between the Russian and Chinese armies, except for the financial sphere, were quite limited.[1058] Although top level visits were carried out regularly, very rarely were they concerned about anything other than arms sales. Both sides have signed a few agreements not connected to arms sales, both armies started visiting each other, but there was no intensive cooperation. The reasons for this state of affairs can be best illustrated by an unsuccessful initiative of Pavel Grachov, Russian minister of defence. In 1995, without informing the Russian MFA and without an earlier consultation with the Chinese side, he proposed to China to establish a joint security system in East Asia, consisting of Russia, China, the USA, Japan and both Koreas.[1059] This utopian idea was bound to fail from the very beginning: China as a rule does not join any alliances. Unsurprisingly, Beijing politely rejected the suggestion. China, like Japan or South Korea, felt no need to tie its hand with joint security schemes in the region, preferring tried and tested channels of bilateral agreements with the United States. Russia was not needed here – thus in the 1990s there was no real cooperation. It started to change, however, in the late 1990s and the early 2000s. A high level of dialogue was established, with regular meetings of the ministers of defence and chiefs of general staff, and the joint commission on military-technical cooperation (the major forum for arms sales).[1060] In March 2008, Russia and China established a hotline between the ministers of defence.[1061]

In 2005, the then-Russian Minister of Defence, Sergei Ivanov, summarized Russia-China military relations as consisting of three aspects: "military-political consultations, and practical action of the troops during military exercises, as well as military-technical cooperation."[1062] So, in other words, the first aspect means the influence of military issues on politics (promoting multi-polar

1056 M. Kaczmarski, *Russia-China and the West…*

1057 Idem, *Russia-China Relations…*, p. 74.

1058 Д. Тренин, *Китайская проблема России* [Russia's China Problem], Москва 1998, p. 38.

1059 Г. И. Чуфрин, *Как перелезть через Великую китайскую стену?* [How to Climb Over the Chinese Wall], Московкое новости, 21-28.05.1995, № 36, p. 5.

1060 M. Kaczmarski, *Russia-China Relations…*, p. 70.

1061 Yu Bin, *From Election Politics to Economic Posturing*, "Comparative Connections", vol. 10, no 1.

1062 K. Ryan, op. cit., p. 192.

world) which was summarized in the "War Doctrine of the Russian Federation" from 2000 and remained a priority for a long time[1063]; the second aspect means joint drills, while the third one is arms sales. The first and third aspects have already been described here, so it is time to elaborate on the second one – joint drills. This became important in bilateral relations in the mid 2000s. Naturally, all three aspects were combined: arms and technology sales to China and joint drills served as geopolitical means of undermining American hegemony there, where American interests contradicted Russian and Chinese ones. The exercises that started as a political tool against the U.S. hegemony (for Russia) and a way to modernize the military (China) within a decade "symbolically marked a new stage of collaboration."[1064]

The first, historical, Russian-Chinese joint exercises called the "Peace Mission" took place between 18 and 25 August 2005 under the aegis of the SCO[1065]. These drills lasted eight days: 1800 Russian and 7200 Chinese soldiers participated in them.[1066] Although officially the drills were aimed at combating terrorism and the coordination of actions within the SCO, the weapons used and the scheme of exercises (amphibian landing, sea blockades and other operations unrelated to Central Asian deserts) – contradicted this claim.[1067] The "Peace Mission" of 2005 was therefore more a political declaration towards the West than real exercises.[1068] In the month prior to the exercises Russian and Chinese disagreed on several matters that showed the limitations of Sino-Russian cooperation. The Russians vetoed the idea of conducting a drill in the Zhejiang province (as a too obvious reference to Taiwan), whereas the Chinese changed the initial name for the drills – "Friendship Mission".[1069] However, there was no friendship there: the drills were joint only in name. During them there was practically no contact between the Russian and Chinese armies – they exercised separately. Besides, the Chinese soldiers apparently performed quite badly and the Russians could not refrain from showing them their superiority (the bad performance of the Chinese army reassured Russian generals that the hypothetical threat from China is out of question for the very

---

1063 *Военная доктрина Российской Федерации* [The War Doctrine of RF], Kremlin.ru, 21.04.2000.

1064 M. Kaczmarski, *Russia-China Relations…*, p. 70.

1065 *Начались российско-китайские учения "Мирная миссия – 2005"* [Russian-Sino Drills Peace Mission Started], "Российская газета", 19.08.2005.

1066 *Мирная миссия-2005* [Peace Mission 2005], "Известия" 23.08.2005.

1067 A. Cohen, *After the G-8 Summit: China and the Shanghai Cooperation Organization*, "China and Eurasia Quarterly", Volume 4, no. 3 – 2006), p. 56; K. Ryan, op. cit., p. 190-191.

1068 A. Frost, *The Collective Security Treaty Organization, the Shanghai Cooperation Organization, and Russia's Strategic Goals in Central Asia*, "China & Eurasia Forum Quarterly" 2009, Vol. 7 Issue 3, p. 99.

1069 Ю. М. Галенович, *История взаимоотношений...*, pp. 373-376.

near future).[1070] Geopolitical goals aside, the exercises served to foster trade – they were a kind of commercial show of Russian arms aimed at securing the Chinese contracts. During these drills, Russian presented Tu-95 and Tu-22M strategic bombers, Ilyushin-76 and Ilyushin-78 cargo aircraft (which the Chinese indeed bought later on).[1071] Nevertheless, political implications played the most important role: the drills were intended to demonstrate to the West that Russia and China consider themselves leading players in Asia-Pacific.[1072]

In August 2007, political considerations overshadowed other exercises –, though the reasons were different. On this occasion the "Peace Mission" was conducted on a more neutral ground – in Cheberkal.[1073] The drills did indeed looked like anti-terrorist exercises. Apparently, China in particular benefitted from the exercises as its army trained on international ground.[1074] The drills reverberated and took a traditional anti-American agenda – the U.S. military observers were not invited, journalists, however, were. Nevertheless, they could cover only the non-Chinese part of the drills – the Chinese army, remembering the poor performance in 2005, closed all exercises to the public.[1075]

After the "Peace Mission 2007" Moscow fundamentally changed its security policy in Central Asia. Since then, the emphasis has been put on the CSTO instead of the SCO – the marginalized joint Russian-Chinese exercises. For example, the "Peace Mission 2009" in Khabarovsk and in China's Dongbei was conducted on a much lesser scale – only 1300 soldiers from each side – and without an important politicized element[1076]. These exercises were indeed joint ones: soldiers were training together. But this came with a price – the Chinese had to pay for everything.[1077]

A subsequent "Peace Mission" was organized under the SCO banner on 9-25 September 2010 in Kazakhstan.[1078] During the drills, the Chinese for the first time used aircrafts outside their borders and tested the new equipment

---

1070 A. Frost, op. cit., p. 99.

1071 Jing-dong Yuan, op. cit., p. 220.

1072 M. de Haas, *The Shanghai Cooperation and the OSCE: Two of a kind*, Helsinki Monitor 18 p. 248.

1073 Again under the slogan of anti-terrorism and under the banner of the SCO, *Совместные а нтитеррористические военные учения "Мирная миссия 2007"* [Joint Antiterror War Drills Peace Mission 2007], Russian.China.Org.

1074 Jing-dong Yuan, op. cit., p. 221.

1075 A. Frost, op. cit., p. 99; K. Ryan, op. cit., p. 191; M. de Haas, *The Shanghai Cooperation Organization's Momentum Towards A Mature Security Alliance*, "Netherlands Institute of International Relations, 03.07.2007, p. 18; Idem, *The Shanghai Cooperation Organization...*, p. 243.

1076 *Начались российско-китайские учения "Мирная миссия – 2009"* [Russian-Sino Drills Peace Mission 2009 Started], Lenta.Ru, 22.07.2009.

1077 Yu Bin, *Market Malaise and Mirnaya Missiya...*

1078 *Совместные антитеррористические учения ШОС "Мирная миссия – 2010"* [Joint SCO Antiterror Drills Peace Mission 2010 Started]; РИА Новости, 24.09.2010; *Генштаб уехал на учения* [General Staff Went to Drills], "Российская газета" 10.09.2010.

(Russia did not send the newest one).[1079] On the other hand, Chinese performance this time "impressed and worried Russian experts (...) since the Chinese military demonstrated a capability to wage long-range land operations against Russia. This was not lost on the Russian high command (...) In 2010, Russia staged its biggest military exercise in two decades, Vostok-2010, in its far east."[1080] That is also why the Russian side lowered the agenda of another "Peace Mission": the 2012 one took place in a limited scope in Tajikistan.[1081] Since 2012, the agenda of the Peace Mission has started to transform from vaguely anti-terrorist goals to primacy of regional challenges, such as the potential instability of post-American Afghanistan.[1082]

Much more important were the first joint maritime drills, which, since 2012, have been staged yearly. The first took place in the Yellow Sea in 2012 on 22-27 April. Another in the Sea of Japan between 5 and 12 July 2013. These exercises showed that Russia and China decided to put stress on the navy cooperation – so far rather overshadowed – and again politics was the key. The area of exercises – the Japan Sea (the Chinese navy exercised here for the first time in history) and what was being exercised (resistance against unexpected assault from air and sea) proved that these drills were politically directed against Japan.[1083]

Soon another "Peace Mission" (2013) took place, this time bilateral, a Sino-Russian one. Differently from previous ones, these exercises "included a lot of socializing."[1084] This demonstrational rapprochement was intended to show deepened Sino-Russian cooperation. In 2014, military relations "Joint-Sea 2014" again became the most important one. These drills that involved twelve Russian and six Chinese vessels took place on 20-26 May and were opened by the PRC's Chairman Xi Jinping and Russian President Vladimir Putin[1085]. The area of the exercises – the South China Sea (first time in history) again indicated the political hidden agenda, clearly visible in the context of disputes over

---

1079 Yu Bin, *Peace Mission 2010 and Medvedev's Visit to China*, "Comparative Connections", vo.11, no.3.

1080 Д. Тренин, *Верные друзья?*....

1081 *Учения ШОС "Мирная миссия-2012" стартуют в Таджикистане* [SCO drills Peace Mission Start in Turkmenistan] РИА Новости 08.06.2012; *«Морское взаимодействие-2013»: Россия и Китай успешно одолели общего врага* [Joint Sea 2013 Russia and China Successfully beaten the common Enemy], Радио Голос России 11.07.2013. Other exercises worth mentioning took place on 22-27 April 2012 at the Yellow Sea, *Россия и Китай завершили военные учения в Желтом море* [Russia and China conducted maritime drills], "Российская газета", 27.04.2012.

1082 M. Kaczmarski, *Russia-China Relations*..., p. 70.

1083 *Главное — маневры* [The Drill are most important], Газета.Ру, 13.07.2013.

1084 Yu Bin, *Summer Heat*.... Another "Peace Mission" took place on 24-29 August 2014 in China (in Zhurihe in Inner Mongolia). These were the most numerous exercises in SCO's history, Idem, *Navigating*...

1085 *Открытие военно-морских учений «Морское взаимодействие – 2014»* [Opening of the Joint Sea 2014 drills], Kremlin.ru, 20.05.2014.

the South China Sea. By agreeing to place these exercises on the South China Sea, Russia sent a clear political message to Japan (which introduced sanctions on Russia); it may be also understood as Russia's repayment for China's neutrality in the Ukrainian crisis.[1086] Nevertheless, Russia's support was not full – it distanced itself from the most political part of the exercises that concerned directly the disputed islands.[1087] Earlier this year, in January 2014, China and Russia conducted the first exercises on the Mediterranean Sea, near Syria, that reflected China's growing ambitions there.

In mid-May both sides staged the Joint-Sea-2015 (I) drill in the Mediterranean (the drills followed the 2014 programme, but this time on larger scale) as well as Joint Sea-2015 (II) in the Sea of Japan in August. From a military point of view, despite impressive political scale, these "features were still far behind the scope and degree of interoperability of the US-led drills". But again it was politics that mattered here. Although "No one in either China or Russia has offered a convincing explanation for conducting two Joint Sea drills in 2015", the reason for that seemed to be political: "The choices of the exercise areas – the Mediterranean and the Sea of Japan – were widely perceived as sensitive to the West and Japan".[1088]

In general, the growing importance of maritime drills over the land ones "fitted first and foremost Beijing's strategic needs and reflected China's increased self-confidence in security and defence relations with Russia"; China "started playing the Russian 'military card'".[1089] These drills reflected the politicized nature of Russia-China defence relations: just as Russia played the Chinese card in the 2000s against the USA, so China played the Russian card against Washington and its East Asian allies in the 2010s.

In 2016, both sides announced the will to hold more drills[1090] and in May 2016 this materialized with the first-ever joint anti-missile drills in Russia ("Aerospace Security 2016") in Moscow[1091], which were a clear reaction to the US-announced will to place the THAAD system in the Korean Peninsula; and, even more remarkably, with Russia-China maritime drills near disputed Senkaku/Diaoyu Islands on the East China Sea: on June 9, 2016, one Chinese and three Russian warships entered the waters "in a contiguous zone" to the unpleasant surprise of Japan.[1092] Contrary to the non-controversial September 2016 SCO Peace Mission drills in Kyrgyzstan (first time in this country), other

1086 D. Trenin, *Russia Faces Tough Road to Success*, 19.05.2014, Carnegie Center Moscow.

1087 Akio Kawato, op. cit.

1088 Yu Bin, *Tales of Two Parades, Two Drills…*

1089 M. Kaczmarski, *Russia-China Relations…*, p. 76; Idem, *Russia-China and the West…*

1090 *China and Russia to Increase Number of Military Exercises in 2016*, "The Diplomat" 28.04.2016.

1091 *Russia-China Anti-Missile Drills*, Russia Today, 05.05.2016.

1092 Yu Bin, *Politics of "Reluctant Allies"…*, pp.129-144.

Joint Sea Russian-Chinese (12-19 September 2016) maritime drills were conducted in a "hot" place: on the South China Sea (first time ever); both sides, however, due to diplomatic dynamics (Philippines, Vietnam) lowered down the scale of drills by dispatching the smallest amount of combatants and placing the drills just off the Guangdong Province and far away from the disputed islands: they wanted "to speak softly while carrying a concealed, or semi-concealed, stick."[1093]

In general, the joint drills helped "to minimize and overcome" the differences between the two countries and, along with military-technical cooperation, they led to "arguably the highest period of cooperation" between Russia and China ever.[1094]

3. *Summary*

In the 2000s and the 2010s Sino-Russian military relations have intensified, which, since 200,5 was best exemplified by yearly or twice-yearly joint exercises (first on land then on land and on the sea). Although these drills, later supplemented by maritime drills, served political goals mainly, they nonetheless led to deepening of the relations. Trust between Russians and the Chinese in military relations improved a bit in the last years, too. Anxiety about China becoming a future aggressor, still present among some Russian generals, noticeably decreased. Russia knows that main vectors of China's foreign policy are directed to the east and southeast (Taiwan, South China Sea's islands) – this fact reassures Russia. Another factor that eases this anxiety is the awareness of the Russian army's fundamental advantage over the Chinese one. Although the PLA made remarkable progress lately, it is still far behind the Russian army. All those factors resulted in the intensification of arms sales in the early 2000s and again in the 2010s. Contrary to the 1990s, Russia stopped being afraid of selling China arms – strategic anxiety gave way to a commercial one (that China is copying and reselling these weapons further on). That is why Russia for a long time had optedto not sell the most advanced military technologies to China; this started to evolve in the late 2000s and culminated in 2015 when Moscow finally gave up by agreeing to sell the Su-35. The anxiety over copying Russian equipment probably must have been overshadowed by financial necessity resulting from Russia's difficult economic situation after the Ukrainian crisis.

1093 Idem, *China-Russia Relations*… pp. 103-116.

1094 E.Meick, *China-Russia Military-to-Military Relations: Moving Toward a Higher Level of Cooperation*, uscc.gov Report, 20.03.2017.

Part Three: China's Appendix? The Russian Far East

The Russian Far East plays a very specific role in Sino-Russian relations. In the 1990s, it was the main obstacle to Russia-China rapprochement, with economic backwardness and strong anti-Chinese resentments that culminated in the infamous and illegitimate accusation of a Chinese "demographic expansion". Since the early 2000s these voices started to tune down thanks to political pressure from Moscow and economic realities. Despite attempts, Russia, however, failed to develop this region and it remains quite stagnant. Since then, the Russian Far East has encapsulated "in the most direct sense the ambiguities of the Sino-Russian relations"; although the territorial question has been resolved, the regional future is unclear: the "Russian Far East has the potential to become the center of a new quality of bilateral and multilateral engagement in Northeast Asia, or a 'dead zone' fertile only in suspicion and recrimination."[1095] So far neither of these have materialized. In the late 2000s, Moscow decided to bandwagon to Chinese rise and to use it as an engine to the Russian Far East development; the results, however, are not impressive, at least not for now.

1. The Domestic Context

The Russian Far East is a unique place in Russia-China relations. Here these countries "met" for the first time in the 17th century. In the 19th century the land had seen the Russian Empire's most spectacular conquest. Here the two communist powers clashed over 1km of Damansky/Zhenbao Island in 1969. During Soviet times, Russian Far East had been heavily invested and supported by central authorities and – in almost the exact reversal – completely left alone after the USSR's fall. After 1991, the region became "the forgotten place" and voices about its "falling apart" from Moscow started to be heard. The Russian Far East has become the symbol of the negative consequences of the Russian transformation. The pioneer spirit, so present in the very first years of colonization, has given way to fatalism and demoralization.

The USSR's dissolution turned out to be a shocking experience for Far Eastern Russians. Liberalization of prices became a catastrophe for heavy-industry-based and central subsidies-based region. Poverty sunk in. Moreover, Moscow distanced from the Russian Far East even literally: the removal of subsidies on transportation cut inhabitants of the region off from the rest of the country. Moscow became an inaccessible place. Economic, financial, cultural and personal ties with the rest of the country were loosened, if sometimes not cut. Far

1095 B. Lo, *The Axis of Convenience...*, p. 56.

Eastern Russians found themselves at the rear of the country that had forgotten about them, in a place where the weakened central government could barely reach.[1096] Against this background, the first massive interaction with the Chinese took place. It was far from positive. After initial years, Soviet nostalgia soon set in, combined with anti-Chinese xenophobia and "siege mentality". The Russian Far East became the most vulnerable aspect of Sino-Russian relations, full of strains, mutual suspicions, distrusts and dislikes. It was there where the fear over "yellow peril" and "demographical expansion" – as well as local protests against demarcation of the border – came to haunt Sino-Russian relations and influence their economic relations.

2. *From Open to Closed Borders: The Russian Far East in Russia-China Relations in the 1990s*

The Russian Far East's influence on Sino-Russian relations in the 1990s was significant: it proved that these relations were very good only on a top level. The Russian Far East considered China a threat, or even an enemy, not a "strategic partner" and that is why the region became the biggest obstacle on the development of China-Russia relations.

Russia-China cooperation in the region in the 1990s had a very important influence on overall Sino-Russian relations. This influence can be divided into three periods: 1) in 1992-1993 when cross-border relations led the way to improved bilateral ties, 2) 1994-1995 when they spoiled the mood of the "constructive partnership", 3) 1996-1998 when they were unable to undergird "strategic partnership" with economic substance.[1097]

The first period was marked by a "euphoria of the lack of borders" from 1991-1993. It was influenced by factors from the 1980s: Chinese hopes for an economic connection of Northeastern China with the opening Russian market[1098]; Gorbachev's perestroika and liberalization in trade[1099] and growing importance of regionalism – regional authorities, such as Vladimir Kuznietsov,

1096 Л. Г. Ивашов, *Хоронить не спешите Россию* [Don't Hurry Up to Burry Russia], Москва 2003, p. 26; А. В. Лукин, *Китай: медьведь наблюдает…*, p. 324; J. Thornoton, op. cit., p. 265; T. Wites, *Wyludnianie Syberii i rosyjskiego Dalekiego Wschodu* [The Depopulation of Siberia and Russian Far East], Warszawa 2007, p. 9-164; Г. А. Агранат, *Возможности и реальности освоения Севера: глобальные уроки* [Possibilities and Realities of Colonizing Siberia: Global Lessons], Москва 1992, p. 145.

1097 G. Rozman, *Turning Fortress…*, p. 177.

1098 E. Wishnick, *Chinese Perspectives on Cross-Border Relations*, [in:] *Rapprochement or Rivalry…*, pp. 229-230; G. Rozman, *Turning Fortress…*, p. 232.

1099 The most important consequence for trade had this cooperation on joint-ventures from 8 June 1988, *Соглашение между правительством Союза Советских Социалистических Республик и правительством Китайской Народной Республики о принципах создания*

the first governor of Primorski Krai after 1991 and a big lobbyist for the cooperation with China, supported trade and hoped to integrate the region with the Asia-Pacific structures. On the other side of Amur, he found an even more enthusiastic supporter of border trade – Heilongjiang governor, Du Xianzong, who used to say "borders are limits, but there's no limit to border trade."[1100] These were there origins of "crazy trade" in the beginning of the 1990s.[1101]

When the USSR fell and the borders opened, the madness started: "border fever", "hot point", "euphoria of no borders" and many other euphemisms describe what happened in 1992 and 1993.[1102] All visas and Soviet bureaucratic obstacles for Chinese people were lifted so they very quickly found the loophole in the lack of foreign trade in the regions. Moreover, without having many requirements and without demanding hard currency, they were competitive. Given the fall of governmental subsidies and uncontrolled rise of prices, the Russian Far East's economy collapsed. Trade with China became the only way to survive: "the Chinese saved Far Eastern Russians from empty shelves."[1103] Most Far Eastern Russian politicians "favoured compensating for the central government's neglect with increased autonomy; they developed the slogan: 'there's no money, give us freedom' (*niet dienieg, daetie svobodu*)."[1104] As a result, the region was "invaded" by Chinese traders (in 1993 alone almost 2.5 million people crossed the border), while Russian border traders crossed the borders many times with cheap clothes, shoes, consumer goods, household articles. China imported construction materials, iron and other metals, fertilizers and fish. Russia has opened great trade opportunities for the Chinese; it was reflected in the saying: "if you want to make quick money, go to Russia."[1105] Russia in Chinese eyes became the symbol of a place for making quick money. Although both sides were eager to trade, the Chinese were more eager: they

---

и деятельности совместных предприятий (The agreement between USSR and PRC on terms of creation and action of joint-ventures), Пекин 08.06.1988.

1100 E. Wishnick, *Chinese Perspectives on Cross-Border Relations…*, pp. 230-235.

1101 M. McFaul, *The Far Eastern Challenge to Russian Federalism*, [in:] *Rapprochement or Rivalry…*, p. 320; P. Kirkow, *The Siberian and Far Eastern Challenge to Center-Periphery Relations in Russia: A Comparison between Altaiskii and Primorskiy Krai*, [in:] *Transformation from Below: Local Power and the Political Economy of Post-Communist Transitions*, ed. J. Gibson, P. Hansen, Cheltenham 1995, p. 233; J. L. Wilson, *Strategic Partners…*, p. 134.

1102 А. В. Лукин, *Китай: медьведь наблюдает…*, p. 291; G. Rozman, *Turning Fortress…*, p. 180; T. Troyakova, *A View from the Russian Far East*, [in:] *Rapprochement or Rivalry…*, p. 204; E. Wishnick, *Chinese perspectives…*, p. 236.

1103 В. Л. Ларин , *Россия и Китай на пороге третьего тысячелетия: кто же будет отстаивать наши национальные интересы?* [Russia and China at the Turn of Third Milleniu: Who Will Stand for our National Interets?], "Проблемы Дальнего Востока", 1997, № 1, p. 25.

1104 E. Wishnick, *Chinese Perspectives…*, p. 236.

1105 Li Jingjie, op. cit., p. 76.

did not mind barter and appeared to understand how to make a deal with minimum formality and paperwork; with a decrease of governmental contracts, the role of border traders increased, contributing to an unpredicted evolution of the model of trade between Russia and China.[1106] This first period "took a primitive form of barter mixed with direct administrative interference under weak market conditions and little institutionized oversight, which meant freewheeling disregard for contracts without corrective punishment (…) the notion that a 'time gap' (*shijian cha*) existed that allowed the Chinese only a brief window of opportunity spurred short-term behavior such as to make quick money instead of building long-term economic relations."[1107] It soon retaliated.

In the second period (1993-1995), trade almost collapsed. The decrease was equally spectacular as the former increase: its sharpness surprised both Russian and Chinese governments. There were several reasons: poor quality of Chinese goods, influx of the culturally alien Chinese that evoked the old fear of "migration expansion" and political usage of this anxiety by Far Eastern Russian politicians in their domestic power struggles.[1108] According to Far Eastern Russians, "Russia was selling its natural resources for peanuts (…) the RFE was in danger of slipping from an exploited outpost of central Russia to a true colonial-style supplier to China."[1109] For Far Eastern Russians, the "Chinese love affair ended" and gave turn to an "allergy" to anything Chinese.[1110] Here the media role was decisive. The press, freed from censorship, painted a dark picture of the Chinese minority. This combined with the policy of the new governor of Primorski Krai, Yevgeni Nazdratenko's, prepared ground for the peak of siege mentality in the region in 1994. Anti-Chinese resentments became an important social factor which led to the conviction that in the "good, old days" life was easier and less dangerous.[1111] This atmosphere, together with concrete political actions, such as introduction of visas, merciless chasing of Chinese immigrants, administrative repression on joint ventures with Chinese capital, restriction and tight control with travel documents, tightening of fiscal policy, introduction of new, higher customs and import and export tariffs as well as several other factors, directly contributed to the collapse of trade.[1112] The last factor was poor quality of Chinese goods. Out of all these reasons, uncontrolled trade from 1992-1993 led to a situation where economic contacts instead of building trust, created enmity: "the short-lived epoch of development of 'wild

---

1106 А. В. Лукин, *Китай: медьведь наблюдает…*, pp. 291-304; Chen Qimao, op. cit., p. 196; T. Troyakova, op. cit., p. 208; G. Rozman, *Turning Fortress…*, p. 182.

1107 G. Rozman, *Turning Fortress…*, pp. 184-185.

1108 А. В. Лукин, *Китай: медьведь наблюдает…*, pp. 290-294; В.Г. Дацышен, В.Л. Ларин, Г.Н. Романова, op. cit., p. 502.

1109 G. Rozman, *Turning Fortress…*, p. 187.

1110 А. В. Лукин, *Китай: медьведь наблюдает…*, p. 292.

1111 Ibid., c. 324; G. Rozman, *Turning Fortress…*, p. 189.

1112 T. Troyakova, op. cit., p. 209; Rozman, *Turning Fortress…*, p. 196.

barter' in Sino-Russian relations allowed many groups in the Russian Far East to survive the first period of transition reforms and handle the hunger for consumer goods (some individuals made good money as well) but generally left a permanent trace in the mentality of Far East Russians."[1113] Mutual trust between Russians and the Chinese fell very low.

Beijing, which wanted to maintain good relations with Moscow, accepted most of the Russian complaints and victimized regional authorities in Heilongjiang, in a way sacrificing them on the altar of good bilateral relations with Russia[1114]. This policy was repeated with anti-Chinese resentments on the Russian Far East. Beijing ignored the problem of local resentments and concentrated on developing relations with Moscow. Being sympathetic to the Russian fears over decentralization, China did not push for establishing special economic zones, did not complain about slow demarcation of the border, silenced domestic criticism and resorted to "quiet diplomacy" based on the principle "first become friends, later do business" (*xian jiao pengyou, hou zuo maimai*).[1115]

Making friends on the top level indeed succeeded. Making money was less successful. In the last period (1996-1999), both sides failed to transform the "strategic partnership" into real, economic achievements (though the trade increased slightly in the late 1990s). The Russian Far East's attitudes towards China remained the biggest obstacle to increase trade interaction: "in the regions, Russian-Chinese relations are not driven by geopolitical calculations and strategic considerations; people are preoccupied with pedestrian issues, such as emergency purchases of fuel, regular shipments of meat (…) or crime; as a result relations at the local level quite often contradicts the direction and tone set in Moscow and Beijing."[1116] The Russian Far East has perceived China as a revisionist power (border demarcation issue)[1117], as a state striving to achieve economic dominance (through migration and trade) and as an alien civilization that surrounds a European post. Given these perceptions, hypothetical integration with Northeast China was considered a threat that could lead to inequality and a loss of the power status. For the Russian Far East, China remained a strategic rival rather than a strategic partner. Japan, not China, was

---

1113 В. Л. Ларин, op. cit., p. 25.

1114 G. Rozman, *Turning Fortress…*, p. 191; E. Wishnick, *Chinese perspectives…*, p. 241.

1115 G. Rozman, *Turning Fortress…*, p. 193.

1116 T. Troyakova, op. cit., p. 219.

1117 Russian researchers like to point out that Chinese historians still claim that Russia had conquered these territories in 19th century and this is the official version in Chinese textbooks; this overlapps with opinions in Chinese internet that Russia took away these lands; thus there is anxiety that one day in the future China may demand "justice". А.В. Лукин, *Россия и Китай…*, pp. 664-665; Е.П. Бажанов: *Китай: От срединной империи до сверхдержавы XXI века* [China: from Middle Empire to Superpower of 21th Century], Москва 2007, pp. 305–306.

the partner of choice for Far Eastern Russians.[1118] They considered themselves a part of Europe, looked towards the West (Japan was considered as such), purposely turned their backs on China. Knowing that integration with Asia-Pacific is inevitable, they preferred economic contacts with Japan and South Korea. In 1997-1998, a Russian-Japanese political *détente* raised hopes for larger Japanese investments. Unfortunately, those did not materialize and Chinese border traders filled the loophole with barter. The Russian Far East had no choice but to accept the cooperation with China.

There was a slight improvement in economic cooperation between Russia and China in the late 1990s. Both sides signed a few agreements on regional cooperation to eliminate barter and to stimulate regional cooperation.[1119] Moreover, during this time Russian regional administration approach towards China changed –politicians such as Nazdratienko tempered their anti-Chinese rhetoric, which helped to foster Chinese investments.[1120] Thus, an increase in trade and development of regional cooperation followed. Nevertheless, this could not overshadow the generally negative outlook of all of this decade and the negative cultural and social consequences of the first mass Russian-Chinese contact in the borderlands.

Despite initial enthusiasm, the first Russian-Chinese mass contact proved to have damaging consequences for Sino-Russian relations. It took both sides a long time to recover from the negative consequences of this "cultural shock" in the 1990s. The uncontrolled flow of the Chinese evoked old Russian fear of losing land. This anxiety was skillfully used by local politicians in their power struggles with the centre. Sino-Russian relations became the hostage of Russian domestic politics – this in turn had damaging consequences for bilateral relations. Throughout the 1990s, the Russian Far East remained not only the wasted chance, but also the biggest obstacle to the development of Sino-Russian relations in this period.

3. The Final Demarcation of Russian-Chinese Border

The 4195.22 km long Russian-Chinese border has long been a thorny issue in Sino-Russian relations. Leaving aside its genesis and border controversies from the 1960s, it is worth pointing out that the USSR and the PRC in general solved this problem thanks to the May 1991 agreement on the Soviet-Chinese border. According to this document, the border was delimitated in accordance

1118 А. В. Лукин, *Китай: медьведь наблюдает…*, pp. 313-314; G. Rozman, *Turning Fortress…*, p. 196; J. L. Wilson, *Strategic Partners…*, p. 137.

1119 М. Л. Титаренко, *Россия. Безопасность через сотрудничество. Восточноазиатцкий вектор* [Russia: Security Via Cooperation; The East Asia Vector], Москва 2003, pp. 114-152.

1120 J. L. Wilson, *Strategic Partners…*, p. 139.

with international practice (the border line on rivers went along the main fair-water) – China received 1281 island, whereas 1163 remained in Russia; the USSR declared to transfer a part of Primorski Krai lands as well.[1121] This shift in the longtime *status quo* "indicated a sizable alteration of the balance of power – or more precisely, the imbalance of power – in the border area to the disadvantage of Russia."[1122] Although this agreement granted China 720 km², in light of (almost) complete demarcation of the border and to defuse potential territorial claims from China, it must be considered a big achievement of Russian (Soviet) diplomacy. That is why the Supreme Council of the RF almost unanimously (174 against 2 with 24 abstains) accepted this agreement in February 1992.[1123]

This was Moscow's perspective. The Russian Far East had another one. From the regional perspective this agreement was dishonest, inadequate and made by a distant and irrelevant government; secrecy of negotiations and not publishing the text of the agreement only increased this perception. News that Russia must give China back almost 1000 km² was shocking for local inhabitants. The ordeal started. Regional politicians quickly bandwagoned on these emotions by using demarcation as a tool to get support in their own games with central government.[1124] Such governors as Yevgeni Nazdratenko (Primorski Krai) and Victor Ishaev (Khabarovski Krai), not only "tried to conduct their own foreign policies"[1125], but also for of their own reasons, "having political goals in mind consciously provoked conflict over demarcation of borders" that significantly influenced Sino-Russian relations.[1126] Khabarovski Krai faced the most serious problem. Two out of three islands excluded from the agreement of 1991, were located nearby Khabarovsk city.[1127] Both governor and local Duma showed permanent enmity against any plans of giving China these islands; governor Ishaev himself was quoted as saying "mainly, these islands are

1121 *Соглашение между Союзом Советских Социалистических Республик и Китайской Народной Республикой о советско-китайской государственной границе на ее Восточной части* [Agreement Between USSR and PRC on Soviet-Sino State Border on its eastern part], [in:] *Сборник российско-китайских договоров 1949-1999…*, pp. 117-125.

1122 J. L. Wilson, *Strategic Partners…*, p. 116.

1123 *Верховный Совет Российской Федерации постановление от 13 февраля 1992 г. n 2348-1 о ратификации соглашения между ссср и кнр о советско-китайской государственной границе на ее восточной части* [The Supreme Counsil of USSR decision on 13.02.1992 on Ratification of Agreement Between USSR and PRC on Soviet-Chinese State Border on its eastern part].

1124 Акихиро Ивасита, *4000 километров проблем. Российско-китайская граница* [4000 kilometers of problems; Russian-Chinese border], Москва 2006, pp. 65-70.

1125 В.Г. Дацышен, В.Л. Ларин, Г.Н. Романова, op. cit., p. 478.

1126 А. В. Лукин, *Китай: медьведь наблюдает…*, p. 300; Akihiro Iwashita, *The Influence of Local Russian Initiatives on Relations with China: Border Demarcation and Regional Partnership*, "Acta Slavica Iaponica", 2002, vol. 19, pp. 10-13.

1127 Three Islands were excluded from the agreement and were left for "future generations": Bolshoi Ussuriski (Heixiazi), Tabarov (Yinlong) and Bolshoi (Abaigatu) near Manzhouli.

only sand" and that from Bolshoi Ussuriski island "one may bombard Khabarovsk."[1128] Equally sharp emotions were evoked around the idea of free passage for Chinese ships.[1129] Nevertheless, problems with Khabarovsk were finally solved thanks to postponing the demarcation of the two islands into the future and a compromise with Ishaev, who when the time came, decided to strike a deal with the Kremlin behind closed doors.

Nevertheless, the island issue and navigation on the Amur remained thorny even after the demarcation in 1997. Local press has created the most unbelievable stories about the Chinese conspiracy. According to these claims, Chinese diplomacy, "traditionally full of meanness", would demand in future to "not only have those two islands but Khabarovsk itself, the ancient Chinese city of Boli, as well" which would lead to crisis and consequently – war between two countries.[1130] As for giving back the island with graves of Soviet soldiers, it was considered a "national humiliation" whereas any concessions were "digging economic graves for Far Eastern Russians by our own hands."[1131] Even after 2000, when the temperature of disputes fell, Ishaev raised the island issue. He protested against any joint investments there and conducted several provocative actions such as planning to build a pontoon bridge linking the island to the mainland, thus preventing the Chinese from travelling along the waterway, building an Orthodox Church on Ussuriski Island and claiming that archeological research "had uncovered artifacts proving its indisputable native Russian origins."[1132]

All those disputes and protests were overshadowed by the reaction of the Primorski Krai' governed by Yevgeni Nazdratenko who accused central authorities of lack of patriotism and short-slightness.[1133] Nazdratenko, a former "Vostok" mining company director and a representative of industrial lobby with close ties to both military units and local mafia organizations, removed former governor Kuznetsov from power in 1993.[1134] Since then Nazdratenko has ruled in a style that combined features of a Russian medieval prince and communist apparatchik – he quickly concentrated power in his hand, took over the media and ruthlessly removed subsequent, democratically elected opponents. He based his popularity on a sharp protest against demarcation of border and on playing the "Chinese migration threat" card (see: below). In his supportive "Vladivostok" daily he published anti-Chinese pieces almost everyday.

1128 Акихиро Ивасита, op. cit., p. 77.

1129 G. Rozman, *Turning Fortress...*, p. 193; А. В. Лукин, *Китай: медьведь наблюдает...*, pp. 300-301.

1130 Ibid., p. 305.

1131 Ibid..

1132 J. L. Wilson, *Strategic Partners...*, p. 120.

1133 А. В. Лукин, *Китай: медьведь наблюдает...*, p. 305.

1134 M. McFaul, op. cit., p. 324; Kuznetsov, a democrat and reformer, opted for opening up the region to Asia Pacific, particularly China, В.Г. Дацышен, В.Л. Ларин, Г.Н. Романова, op. cit., p. 479.

He openly announced that he would sooner resign than agree on giving China back even a piece of Russian land. He found many supporters. Some considered China as an ecological threat; others protested against giving back land with soldiers' graves; the most controversial, however, have been the necessity of giving back the land in the Khasan lake. In 1995 Nazdratenko announced that he would demand cancellation of the 1991 agreement (the Chinese MFA commented on it as an "absolute lack of responsibility")[1135], soon however he minimisedhis position by demanding only changes, not cancellation of the entire agreement. Anyway, this did not lead to resolving the conflict: the local administration effectively blocked the conclusion of the demarcation[1136]. Moreover, Nazdratenko's tactics on making a big media fuss over the demarcation problem started to bear fruits – the governor gained some support in the Duma.[1137] Nevertheless, the Duma in 1995 confirmed Russia's position on the 1991 agreement while Yeltsin ordered to quickly finish the demarcation works.[1138] The president's administration was aware that time was running out – the final date of demarcation (1997) was within only two years. Nazdratenko did not even consider listening to the presidential order and was able to make a lot of problems for Yeltsin's administration. Despite requests and threats, the Kremlin was not able to silence him. As a result, in 1997 the demarcation became the most important issue in Sino-Russian relations: in 1997, chances of settlement were clouded and obscured by uncertainty.[1139]

What was important in all of this chaos was the Chinese position. Beijing kept calm and considered Nazdratenko and other regional politicians' behavior

1135 M. McFaul, op. cit., p. 322; Akihiro Iwasita, op. cit., p. 71.

1136 Б. И. Ткаченко, *Россия-Китай: восточная граница в документах и материалах* [Russia-China: the Eastern Border in Documents and Materials], Владивосток 1999, pp. 277-304.

1137 Акихиро Ивасита, op. cit., p. 72.

1138 *Распоряжение Президента Российской Федерации от 19 февраля 1996 г. № 77-рп «О мерах по завершению демаркационных работ на Восточной части российско-китайской государственной границы», Сборник законов законодательство Российской Федереаци* [Presidential Decree on Terms of Ending the Demarcation Work on the Eastern Part of Russian-Chinese state border], Sbornikzakonov.ru.

1139 Demarcation was difficult not only due to the obstruction from local administration. Yeltsin himself didn't want to conclude it before 1996 elections – he didn't want to lose voices and hence he slowed down its pace. Moreover, demarcation found objective problems – lack of sources, lack of benzene for ships, etc. Акихиро Ивасита, op. cit., p. 76; А. П. Деревяннко, *Российское Приморе на пороге третего тысячилетия* [Russian Primorie at the Turn of the Third Millennium], Владивосток 1999, p. 259; Б. И. Ткаченко, op. cit., p. 318; А. В. Лукин, *Китай: медьведь наблюдает…*, p. 304.

a result of the breakdown of the central authority in Russia rather than as Moscow's deliberate hidden agenda.[1140] The Chinese "proved willing to compromise" and they agreed to adjust the borderline in the Khasan region so that the graves of the Soviet soldiers would remain within the Russian territory; nonetheless "the Chinese also let it be known that there were limits to their patience."[1141] The threat of a split with China mobilized Moscow: "if the strategic partnership was not to sink into oblivion, Yeltsin had to stick to the 1991-1992 commitment and to his 1994 declaration that the demarcation agreement is sacred."[1142] Beijing's position helped: the Khasan compromise, reached in August 1997, moved the demarcation from deadlock[1143]. China yielded in the thorniest of issues: Soviet soldiers' graves remained in Russia and with this compromise even a hypothetical possibility of gaining access to the Japan Sea by China disappeared.[1144] At the same time, the Kremlin was finally able to silence Nazdratenko, probably as a part of a deal that Yeltsin would not try to remove him.[1145] Thanks to all these, Russia was able to sign the declaration of the end of demarcation during Yeltsin's visit to Beijing on 10 November 1997 (it was this visit's biggest achievement).[1146] On the territory of 4204 km (without three disputed islands), 1182 border posts and 24 buoys were posted (the last one three days before Yeltsin's visit).[1147] The border issue was almost completely closed (with the exception of three disputed islands, covering 408 km^2) on 8 April 1999, when the Joint Russian-Chinese Demarcation Commission finally decided about the island sharing (1163 islands to Russia, 1281 to China) and the length of borderline – altogether 4195 km (578.18 km on land, 3547.01 on rivers, 70.03 km on the Khanka lake).[1148]

The final demarcation of the border had to wait for another decade to materialize. When it finally did, it became one of the most important events in Russian-Chinese relations in the 2000s. With the signing of the additional protocol on agreement on the Eastern part of the Russian-Chinese border in October

1140 G. Rozman, *Troubled Choices for the Russian Far East: Decentralization, Open Regionalism and Internationalism*, "Journal of East Asian Affairs" 1997, no 2, p. 560; J. L. Wilson, *Strategic Partners…*, p. 121; Акихиро Ивасита, op. cit., p. 83.

1141 L. Wilson, *Strategic Partners…*, p. 121.

1142 G. Rozman, *Sino-Russian Relations. Mutual…*, p. 169.

1143 Акихиро Ивасита, op. cit., p. 83.

1144 Ibid., p. 83, Chen Qimao, op. cit., p. 295.

1145 J. L. Wilson, *Strategic Partners…*, p. 119.

1146 *Совместное российско-китайское заявление (о завершении демаркации восточного участка российско-китайской границы) от 10 ноября 1997 г.*,[The Joint Russia-China Announcement on Demarcation of the Eastern Part of the Border] [in:] *Сборник российско-китайских отношении 1949-1999…*, pp. 408-410.

1147 Акихиро Ивасита, op. cit., p. 85.

1148 *Заключительная сессия российско-китайской демаркационной комиссии* [Final Session of Russian-Sino Demarcation Comission], "Дипломатический вестник. Официальные материалы" 1999.

2004[1149] one of the longest and most complicated matters in Russian-Chinese relations has been resolved.

Although other thorny issues had already been settled in the previous decade, at the beginning of the 21st century, the belongingness of the three islands on Amur and Ussuri – Bolshoi Ussuriski/Heixiazi, Tabarow/Yinlong and Bolshoi/Abagaitsu remained unfinished. On October 14th 2004, foreign ministers of Russia and China signed the "additional agreement", while on 14 October 2008 the border posts were erected. This is how the "400 hundred years' border conflict" (and 40 years of difficult negotiations) ended.[1150] The three disputed islands were divided in a compromise: Tabarov (Yinlong) was given back to China, whereas Bolshoi Ussuriski/Heixiazi and the third island, Bolshoi/Abagaitu, were divided divided in half.[1151] Although in accordance with the previous principles (a borderline along the main fairway) it should have been returned entirely to China (it is located on the Chinese side of the Amur). It should have been entirely Chinese due to historical reasons, too – this island was captured by the USSR only in 1929. Nevertheless, its location (near Khabarovsk airport) and social sentiments made it impossible for Russia to accept its relinquishment.[1152] In return for a concession on Bolshoi Ussuriski/Heixiazi Beijing was granted a concord on sailing for Chinese war and trade ships on the Amur and Ussuri. This agreement had a symbolic and compromise nature also because 50% of Bolshoi Ussuriski/Heixiazi Island constitutes 350 m², or 500m² less than the area of Damansky/Zhenbao Island which was fought over between the USSR and the PRC in 1969.[1153] In general, China received 3575 km². The official ceremony of transfer of the islands took place on 14 October 2008 and was purposefully given a low rank.[1154] It was a dual compromise. The Kremlin was able to silence the Far Eastern critics of this agreement, while Beijing managed to pacify the nationalistic voices that demanded the transfer of all Bolshoi Ussuriski/Heixiazi Island. Prudence won on both sides – after 400 hundred years, Russia and China gained a mutually recognized border.

1149 *Дополнительное соглашение между Российской Федерацией и Китайской Народной Республикой о российско-китайской государственной границе на ее Восточной части (Пекин, 14 октября 2004 года* [The Additional Agreement between RF and PRC on Russian-Chinese State Border in its Eastern Part] [in:] *Сборник российско-китайских договоров 1999-2007…*, pp. 318-323.

1150 Yu Bin, *End of History…*

1151 *Дополнительное соглашение между Российской Федерацией и Китайской Народной Республикой….*; Bolshoi/Abagaitu island is not always considered a distinct island (but the part of the river), hence many researchers do not even mention it, saying that only one (Tabarov/Yinlong) and half island (Bolshoi Ussuriski/Heixiazi) was given back to China, e.g. Ian Jeffries, *Political Developments in Contemporary Russia*, Routledge 2011, p. 389

1152 А.В. Лукин, *От нормализации к стратегическому партнерству…*, p. 342.

1153 Ibid.. Zhenbao/Damansky Island was given back to China in 1991.

1154 *Россия торжественно передала Китаю 337 квадратных километров близ Хабаровска*, News.Ru, 14.10.2008; Ю. М. Галенович, *История взаимоотношений…*, p. 450.

4. *Chinese Migration to the Russian Far East*

The Chinese migration to the Russian Far East remains one of the most controversial issues in Sino-Russian relations. This topic was used ideologically in the 1990s and became a perfect pretext for Russian regional politicians in their struggle with the center. The "Chinese migration" issue was not associated with Sino-Russian relations sine qua non, but with the Russian domestic situation. It remains a great example of how the social ideological constructs influence, change and create the political reality.

The mass arrival of the Chinese migrants at the beginning of the 1990s created a great social change. Until then, a literally locked and militarized region all of the sudden became open and uncontrolled. The Chinese influx was clearly visible, the sketchy data, however, makes it difficult to estimate their proper amount (e.g. in 1988 in the Amur Oblast' 6,233 Chinese crossed the border; in 1992 – 287,215) and therefore it opens door for speculation.[1155] The sudden appearance of such a number of Chinese evoked old Russian anxieties about "Chinese demographical expansion" into the Russian Far Eastern regions. This fear has long history.[1156] In the late 19th century, the Chinese constituted 1/3 of the population of this region.[1157] However, the Stalinist purges and forceful repatriation of the Chinese in 1937 as well as tightened closure of the border practically eliminated their presence – in the next few decades in the Russian Far East "there were more Gypsies than Chinese."[1158] Now, after 1988, these anxieties resurrected: the Russian antipathy towards the Chinese entering their country was based on a fear that this might contribute to the Sinization of the Russian Far East and the ultimate loss of sovereignty over these lands. Furthermore, due to deteriorating economic situation and elimination of state surcharges, a mass outbound migration of the Russian-speaking population left the region: as a result of depopulation of the the 1990s, the Russian Far East lost 7% of its former population.[1159]

In 2000, the population of the Russian Far East consisted of 7.2 million people, whereas the three neighbouring Chinese provinces of the Chinese North-East had 105 million people. For some, these numbers spoke for them-

1155 G. Vitkovskaya, Z. Zayonchkovskaya, K. Newland, Chinese Migration into Russia, [in:] *Rapprochement or Rivalry…*, p. 347.

1156 С. Л. Тихвинский, op. cit, p. 215.

1157 Э. Паин, *Нелегалы на берегах Амура* [Illegal Migrants on the Banks of Amur], Российские вести, 1997, p. 3; J. L. Wilson, *Strategic Partners…*, p. 123; Г. Витковская, Ж. Зайончковская, *Новая Столупинская политика на Далнем Востоке* [New Stolypinian Policy in the Far East], [in:] *Перспективы Дальневосточного региона межстранное взаимодействия* [Perspectives of Far Eastern Region, Interstate Joint Cooperation], Москва 1999, p. 80-120.

1158 T. Trojanowa, op. cit., p. 215.

1159 T. Wites, op. cit., p. 7; G. Vitkovskaya, Z. Zayonchkovskaya, K. Newland, op. cit., p. 351.

selves. The message was clear: an uncontrolled Chinese migration into emptied spaces is inevitable. The mass arrival of Chinese merchants after the visa lifting in 1988 and the fall of the Soviet controlled economy, as well as the need for cheap Chinese labor, all contributed to the noticeable Chinese presence in this so far homogenous region. This evoked old fears: in the mid 1990s, there was a deluge of articles and books about "quiet expansion", "demographical incursion", the "yellow flood", the "go North movement", the "dangerous invasion" or even the "yellow plague".[1160] The Chinese were depicted in black colours as a gang of thieves, contrabandists, bandits, mafia-men, who exploit Russians, pollute domestic economy, take away money and natural resources and make the ordinary people poor.[1161] Governor of Primorski Kraj, Yevgenyi Nazdratenko personally said that "among the Chinese there is a bulk of criminals, sick and drug-addicted."[1162] The Chinese authorities were accused of all sins: from an attempt to get rid of the unneeded population and growing crime numbers, to charges that stimulating migration and creating Chinatowns is a purposely made policy to put forward territorial demands later on. Nevertheless, the reasons for the Chinese migration were of an objective nature: the Russian demand for consumption goods, need for cheap labor (in agriculture and construction sites), lack of control institutions on the border as well as lthe egal framework, growing economic integration of the neighboring regions, and a mass population gap between the two sides of the border. These objective reasons, however, did not matter – the phobias about "yellow peril" were soon exploited by local politicians, primarily governors Yevgeni Nazdratenko and Victor Ishaev who bandwagoned on to the anti-immigration wave.[1163]

1160 Press articles can be find in the following titles Л. Л. Рубаковский, *Маштабы проникнования иммигрантов на Далний Восток* [The Scale of Immigrants Arrivals to the Far East], [in:] *Современная социално-демографическая ситуация и запатность населения России* [Contemporary Sociodemographical Situation and Population of Russia], GKS.ru, p. 30-38; А. В. Лукин, *Китай: медьведь наблюдает…*, pp. 294-297.

1161 В. Ларин, *Китай и Дальний Восток России в первой половине 90-х: проблемы регионального взаимодействия* [China and Russian Far East in the first half of 1990s: problems of regional cooperation], Владивосток 1998, p. 72.

1162 М. Г. Носов, *Российский Далний Восток и Китай: проблемы сегодняшнего дня и перспективы сотрудничества* [Russian Far East and China: problems of today and perspectives of cooperation], [in:] *Миграционная ситуация на Дальнем Востоке России* [Migration Situation in Russian Far East], Москва Карнеге 1996, p. 33.

1163 Ishaev has popularized the name "quiet expansion", first in the press and then in his book, В. Ишаев, *Дальний Восток России: долговременные перспективы сотрудничества в Северо-Восточной Азии* [Russian Far East: long term perspectives of cooperation in Northeast Asia], Хабаровск 2000; В. И. Ишаев, *Китайские женихи оказываются фиктивными мужьями* [Chinese Men Turn Out to Be Fake Husbands], "Российская газета", 30.10.1999, p. 3; А. В. Лукин, *Китай: медьведь наблюдает…*, p. 296; Ishaev's stance was intriguing: he was anti-Chinese and, at the same time, happaned to propose… one economic zone between China and Russian Far East, В.Г. Дацышен, В.Л. Ларин, Г.Н. Романова, op. cit., p. 481.

These kinds of voices reached Moscow – it was not only the local press writing about "two millions" of illegal Chinese immigrants, it was also covered by Izvestiya (one of the main Russian newspapers) and later on, by other mainstream media and the state TV. They all published information such as "The Chinese already outnumber Russians in the Russian Far East by 1.5-2 times" or that "some cities already have a Chinese outlook."[1164] The scholars were next to follow: Alexander Yakovlev from the Institute of Far Eastern Studies of the Russian Academy of Science concluded that "the Chinese intensify their mass infiltration of the Far East – of the lands they consider theirs."[1165] Professor Yevgeni Gilbro from the Diplomatic Academy of Peace under the UNESCO estimated the number of Chinese to be… 8 millions![1166] So far this is the record that vastly exceeds the most populist estimations. Finally, there were artists: Alexander Solzhenitsyn and Nikita Mikhalkov cried out about "Moscow's indifference about the region and gradual, quiet Chinese occupation of the Russian Far East."[1167] But it was the politicians who exploited the "yellow peril" most – from nationalist Zhirinovski to liberal Yavlinski (the latter estimated the number of the Chinese to be 5 millions).[1168] Even government members, like Defence Minister Pavel Grachov (who said that "Chinese want to conquer the Russian Far East by peaceful means")[1169], the Minister of Construction Efim Basin (who wrote in an official article in 1995 that "the Chinese and Koreans are literally occupying our Far East")[1170] and Yelstin himself ("180 thousand Chinese live illegally in Khabarovsk oblast") joined in.[1171] This is how popular claims of "millions of immigrants" were followed by not only populists, politicians or journalists, but even high ranking governmental officials, such as the head of the Federal Migration Service, Oleg Romanovsky, who told the Russian state Duma that there were "between 400,000 and 700,000 illegal Chinese migrants in the Russian Far East"; which meant that Romanovsky "had little idea of the actual number of the Chinese; whether

---

1164 G. Vitkovskaya, Z. Zayonchkovskaya, K. Newland, op. cit., p. 356.

1165 A. Яковлев, *Международная политическая обстановка в СВА и положение России в регионе* [International political situation in East Asia and Russia's position in the region], "Проблемы Дальнего Востока" 1995, № 2, pp. 3-16.

1166 E. Гильбо, *Перспективы китаизации России* [Perspectives of Sinization of Russia], Русское Дело.

1167 V. Shlapentokh, *Russia, China and the Far East: Old Geopolitics Or a New Peaceful Cooperation?*, "Comunist and Post-Communist Studies", 1995, vol. 28, no 3, pp. 307-318.

1168 J. L. Wilson, *Strategic Partners…*, pp. 123-124.

1169 A.B. Лукин, *От нормализации к стратегическому партнерству…*, p. 325.

1170 A. Валентинов, *Единая Россия в пространстве и во времени (беседа с Е. Басиным)* [One Russia in Space and in Time. Discussion with E. Basin], "Российская газета", 01. 1995, p. 16; quoted in: A.B. Лукин, *От нормализации к стратегическому партнерству…*, p. 320.

1171 This speech was made during election campaign, quoted in: T. Troyakova, op. cit., p. 215.

these 'migrants' were long-term settlers, seasonal workers, or shuttle-traders; or whether they were legal or illegal."[1172]

In general, since the beginning of the 1990s, the Chinese migration scale was permanently present in the Russian media and the political discourse – and it was always exaggerated: the number of 2 million was widely quoted. Myths about millions of Chinese immigrants resulted from concrete political actions of local politicians and had nothing to do with reality. It, however, became a part of culture – a fear that the Chinese would arrive in millions ("if one million Chinese cross the Russian border every day, they will be marching on for three-and-a-half years") is common in Russia.[1173]

It was impossible to challenge these voices in the 1990s and only the following decade brought a change here. Reasonable commentaries, like the ones from the Foreign Ministry or the Presidential Administration (Emile Pain quoted Pavel Minakir's research of the Russian Academy of Science which estimated that the Chinese made up only about 3% of the Russian Far East's population, whereas at the beginning of the 20th century there were 1/3 of them) fell on deaf ears in the 1990s.[1174]

Migration became a political problem and an issue in bilateral relations. Officially Beijing condemned illegal migration, but it emphasized that numbers proclaimed by Russians are vastly overestimated – according to the Chinese, there were around 1,000-2,000 Chinese illegal migrants. In accordance with Chinese statistics, there were around 300,000 Chinese in all of the CIS area, the majority on a non-permanent basis.[1175] In general, the PRC government tried to ignore these aggressive statements; only the MFA limited itself to sending a few protest notes against mistreatment of the deported Chinese citizens. At the same time Beijing was symphathetic to Russian anxieties: it tried to limit the migrant's flow and was determined not to allow this issue to complicate bilateral relations.

The anti-Chinese campaign in the Russian Far East influenced Russian domestic policy action. In 1994, the Russian government re-introduced visas for the Chinese and tightened control on trade; the regional authorities in their turn initiated strict control and deportation of illegal immigrants – this led to the dramatic fall of bilateral trade. The number of Chinese, never high, fell even lower, while the anti-Chinese campaign slowed down… to burn again in 1996. This time it was directly linked with Moscow's attempt to remove

1172 B. Lo, *The Axis of Convenience…*, p. 60.

1173 Д. Тренин, *Верные друзья?…*

1174 Э. Паин, *Нелегалы на берегах…*; P. A. Minakir, *Chinese Immigration in the Russian Far East: Regional, National, and International Dimnsions*, [in:] *Cooperation and Conflict in the Former Soviet Union: Implications for Migrations*, ed. J. R. Azrael, E. A. Pain, Santa Monica 1996, p. 94.

1175 D. Kerr, *Opening and Closing the Sino-Russian Border: Trade, Regional Development and Political Interests in Northeast Asia*, "Europe-Asia Studies" 1996, vol. 48, no 6, p. 960.

Nazdratenko. The governor fired back with his favourite trump card: blaming Moscow for the region's financial problems and accusing it of dealing with China above Far Eastern Russian's head. This worked – he succeeded in uniting people behind him under the banners of xenophobia and anti-Chinese resentments.[1176]

This is why the mass campaign started. There was a flood of anti-Chinese articles showing unbelievable data about migration, threatening a conspiracy plot about the political background of this migration and Beijing's planned action, and lamenting about "treacherous Kremlin" who behind the Far Eastern Russian's backs gave away Russian lands to the Chinese. Moreover, the Chinese communities, homogenous and closed for others were supposed to be "spy-nests" or even "army back-up". The record goes to the Novosti tabloid, which in March 1997 published an edition with a cover entitled "Will there be war tomorrow?"[1177] In turn, monographs about "the yellow expansion" started to appear with press articles (such as a the 1996 book entitled "Yellow peril")[1178] as well as a series of documents about border issues. The Chinese were accused of all possible sins: from singular crimes, the PRC's policy of mobilizing the army on the borders, to condemnation of Russia-China cooperation even in such areas as drug-trafficking.[1179] All these factors contributed to one tendency in the 1990s: limited access into the region. The actions taken by local authorities directly contributed to the creation of a "siege mentality" – the region remained "the first line of defence against the outside world"[1180] and became "a zone of the political absurd."[1181] The Far East became the symbol of Russia's weakness in Asia, "the sick man of Asia."[1182]

The numbers show clearly that the so-called "yellow peril" was nothing more than a power struggle between the centre and regions in Russia (and, from a social point of view, a belated mirror of the old Western stereotypes about Asia from the late 19th – the early 20th century). In 1997, the Moscow Carnegie Center conducted a special project "Chinese migration in the Russian Far East and Siberia" and thoroughly counted the number of Chinese migrants. According to Pavel Minakir, the director of the Economic Research Institute of the Far Eastern Branch of Russian Academy of Science, there was no more than fifty to eighty thousand Chinese people during 1992-1993 period.[1183]

1176 Quoted in: M. McFaul, op. cit., p. 330.

1177 А. В. Лукин, *Китай: медьведь наблюдает…*, p. 298.

1178 *Желтая опасность* [Yellow Peril], ред. Б. Дяченко, Владивосток 1996.

1179 А. П. Деревянко, *Российское Приморе на пороге третьего тысячилетия (Russian Primore at the Turn of the Third Century)*, Владивосток 1999, p. 276.

1180 T. Troyakova, op. cit., p. 222.

1181 V. B. Amirov, op. cit., p. 277.

1182 R. Menon, *The Sick Man of Asia: Russia's Endangered Far East*, "The National Interest" 2003, no. 73, p. 99. See also: Parag Khanna, *The Second World. How Emerging Powers are Redefining Global Competition in the Twenty First Century*, New York 2008, pp. 71-78.

1183 P. A. Manakir, op. cit., p. 94.

Most of them were seasonal workers and students. The amount of illegal migrants was even smaller: during the "foreigner" campaign conducted by border guards in Primorski Krai, Khabarovski Krai and Amur Oblast' only… five to six thousand people were deported. During this campaign it turned out that the Chinese made up only a small percent of all the arrested – most were from the Caucasus.[1184] According to different estimates done by L.L. Rybakovski, a demographer and director of the Demographical Center in Moscow's Sociopolitical Research Institute of the Russian Academy of Science, the amount of immigrants was around hundred thousand.[1185] Galina Vitkovskaya, deputy director of Carnegie's project claimed that the most realistic estimates told about a few hundred thousand (between two hundred thousand and three hundred thousand, from Irkutsk to Primorski Krai); in October 1996 in Primorski Krai and Khabarovski Krai between thirty thousand to seventy thousand Chinese lived, including shuttle traders.[1186] Moreover, Vitkovskaya in 1999 said that "the bigger Chinese communities in the Russian Far East simply don't exist": according to her research the biggest group of Chinese lived in… Moscow (twenty to twenty five thousand people) and the majority of the Chinese migrants left Russia after the crisis in 1998.[1187]

Other research results match these data. Based on his thorough research, conducted with other experts, Aleksander Larin in 2009 has proved that "the most reliable number of the Chinese in Russia is between two hundred to four hundred thousand; maximum five hundred thousand, while in the Russian Far East – around two hundred thousand."[1188] Vilia Gelbras, who was the first one to conduct all-encompassing research on the Chinese presence, agrees with this estimation – according to this researcher, there are around two hundred thousand to four hundred and fifty thousand Chinese in Russia.[1189] Naturally, the data from various sources differ. According to the Russian Federation national

---

1184 T. Troyanova, op. cit., p. 216.

1185 Л. Л. Рыбаковский, О. Д. Захарова, В. В. Миндогулов, *Нелегалная миграция в приграничных районах Дальнего Востока: история, современность и последстия* [Illegal migration in the border regions of the Far East: History, Contempory and Consequences], Москва 1994, p. 19.

1186 Г. Витковская, Ж. Зайончковская, op. cit., p. 98; G. Vitkovskaya, Z. Zayonchkovskaya, K. Newland, op. cit., p. 357; Ж. Зайончковская, *Перед лицом иммиграции* [Facing Immigrantion], "Pro et Contra", 2005, no 3, p. 73.

1187 *Does Chinese Migration Endanger Russian. Security*? Moscow Carnegie Center Briefing Papers, 1999, VIII, vol. 1, no 8, p. 1.

1188 А. Г. Ларин, *Китайские мигранты в России. История и современность* [Chinese Migrants in Russia. History and Contemporary Times], Москва 2009, p. 149.

1189 В. Гельбрас, *Китайская реальность России* [Chinese Reality of Russia], Москва 2001, pp. 39-40.

census from 2010, there were twenty-eight thousand Chinese in Russia (the number is clearly lowered).[1190]

Larin himself quotes the research done by S.Y. Prichod'ko and K. Vnukova that claimed that there were one hundred and fifty thousand totwo hundred thousand Chinese; the immigration service data[1191] estimated the number to be around two hundred thousand; he writes also that within this range of two hundred to four or five hundred thousand, illegal immigrants are already listed (their number is decreasing year by year, though they still make up around half of all the Chinese in Russia).[1192] Another important piece of research on Chinese immigration is that of Anatoliy Vishnevskyi, Mikhail Alexeev and Vilia Gelbras. Vishnevski claims that there are between four hundred thousand to six hundred thousand Chinese in Russia (2009 data).[1193] He has also showed that only around 30% of all Chinese in Russia live in the Russian Far East (the others live in Siberia – 29% and Moscow – 28%; St. Petersburg has only around 3,5%."[1194]

Even a glimpse at that data shows a great chaos in this matter. Different state agencies have completely different data, no to mention data from Russian researchers. Nevertheless, one thing is clearly visible: there are hundreds of thousands Chinese in Russia, not millions.

Mikhail Alexeev noticed that the Russian Far East has "distinctly peripheral role in the global context of the Chinese migration", the number of settled migrants has been "statistically insignificant". Most of the migrants were short-term visitors: tourists, shuttle-traders, businessmen, employees, poachers, smugglers and students. The Chinese remained "a marginal ethnic segment in Primorski Krai and in the Russian Far East generally". His work ends up with a clear statement: "forecasts of hundreds of thousands, if not millions, of Chinese workers moving into the Russian Far East to develop its vast natural resources so far remain in the realm of fantasy."[1195]

1190 28943 to be exact, *Всеросийская перепись населения 2010, Национальный состав населения* (All Russia Census 2010), Федеральная служба государственной статистики. Interesingly, in the previous census, in 2002 г. The number of Chinese was estimated to be 34577, *Всеросийская перепись населения 2002 Том 4: Национальный состав и владение языками, гражданство* (All Russia Census, Nationalities, Languages and Citizenship, 2002).

1191 А. Г. Ларин, op. cit., p. 255.

1192 Ibid., pp. 148-152 and 255-257.

1193 *Население России 2009, Семнадцатый ежегодный демографический доклад* [Population of Russia. 17th Yearly Demographic Account], отв. ред. А. Г. Вишневский, Demoscope.ru.

1194 Ibid.

1195 M. Alexeev, *Chinese Migration into Primorskii Krai: Economic Effects and Interethnic Hostility*, [in:] *Slavic Eurasia's Integration into the World Economy and Community*, ed. Shinichiro Tabat, Akihiro Iwashita, Sapporo 2004, p. 336.

Vilia Gelbras' research was concentrated on the Russian Far East alone. Gelbras has noticed the increased number of Chinese arrivals, but commented that "most of the Chinese arrive to Russia legally", while "the scale of that migration is too insignificant to panic, let alone to speak about Chinese demographic expansion". Besides, "Chinese migration to Russia is not a spontaneous migration of people to a new place of residence, and not a search for a promised land. There has emerged a specific form of the movement of manpower that serves the flow of goods". Gelbras' data from Vladivostok and Khabarovsk prove that the number of immigrants who live with their families in the Russian Far East has stopped; the Chinese consider the Russian Far East a place where one can get rich quickly, but not as a place where they would like to live.[1196] Most of the Chinese who arrive to the Russian Far East are petty traders from markets or seasonal/short-term workers[1197]. In general, "the income of the majority of the Chinese immigrants is low; the idea that they take away Russians' jobs – a favourite slogan of xenophobes – is nothing more than a myth."[1198] Finally, the region itself (and the entireity of Russia) is not an attractive place to migrate: "few Chinese have decided to settle in Russia. They have been deterred by the cold climate, the lack of business opportunities and poor local hospitality."[1199]

The Russian Far East in not a popular destination for the Chinese because of the fact that – as Larin put it – "Russia is a factor that complicates one's life" due to several reasons: "low efficiency of state structures' work, widespread corruption of governmental officials and time-consuming bureaucracy."[1200] The militia, or now the police, remains the most important problem – "probably there isn't a single Chinese person in Russia who wouldn't be harmed by militia"; Larin concludes, "the main obstacles faced by immigrants are the same as for their Russian colleagues; they are all parts of the same business atmosphere in Russia."[1201]

Nevertheless, the Chinese presence has been a serious problem, but not due to immigration. This threat was misunderstood as a "flood", a "creeping immigration" that foresees annexation by China. This was a modern reconstruction of the "yellow peril" syndrome from the late 19th and the early 20th century.[1202] Gelbras is right when he says that "the real problem is not the number

1196 V. Gelbras, *Chinese Migration in Russia*, "Russia in Global Affairs", 2005, vol. 3, no 2 (April-June), p. 179; see also: Idem, *Китайская реальност…* Москва 2001.

1197 А. Г. Ларин, op. cit., pp. 174-179.

1198 Ibid., pp. 175-179 and 219.

1199 Д. Тренин, *Верные друзья?…*.

1200 А. Г. Ларин, op. cit., pp. 215.

1201 Ibid., pp. 186-187 and 192-273; It is fair to add, however, that recently Russia's police attitude towards the Chinese has improved.

1202 A. Łopińska, *The "Yellow Peril" syndrome in contemporary Russia*, "Sensus Historiae. Studia interdyscyplinarne", vol. VIII, no 2012/3, pp. 41 -58.

of Chinese immigrants but the fact of how they harm the economy."[1203].This is not a "criminalization" of social life, as anti-Chinese propaganda would like to see it. The most popular transgressions among the Chinese are of an economic nature. The Chinese know Russian law poorly but this is due to the fact that they deal with official matters via middle-men and if they face militia (police) "it rarely has anything to do with rule of law."[1204] Moreover, the majority of economic transgressions are jointly done by Russians and the Chinese: "Russian economic and administrative mechanisms often not only allow but even provoke an immigrant to act against the law (…) the Russian grey economy forces the Chinese businessman to bypass the law. And the Chinese businessman acts as the Russian does: he simply follows the rules of the game – 'when in Rome, do as the Romans do.'"[1205] As Larin rhetorically asks: "if we are unable to deal with our criminals who bring a lot of damage to the state, why should we demand from China to control their own citizens who do not harm their own country – they are just breaking foreign laws on foreign land?"[1206]

Thus, the real challenge for the Russian Far East is of an economic, not immigration nature. The bilateral trade is unbalanced – China exports cheap consumption goods and imports natural resources, like timber. Moreover, most of the trade is illegal and conducted by criminal groups from both sides of the border. Their activity "inflicts damage on Russia's economic security and checks the development of a civilized market economy"; furthermore, it "strengthens Russia's position as a raw-material appendage of China; this turns Russia, primarily, into a market for Chinese goods, thus preventing economic growth, especially in the Far East."[1207] As a result, the Russian Far East instead of pushing Russia into Asia, "may become part of East Asian rather than Russian periphery, and increasingly subservient to Chinese requirements."[1208] When one looks at Chinese policy toward the Russian Far East, one may find many similarities with the Chinese policy toward Laos; the same neocolonial mechanism functions here: China exploits the region for its resources and in return floods it with low quality goods.

Far Eastern Russians are aware of China's growing importance. The majority of them claim that only China benefits from the cooperation and that the Chinese influence on the economy is negative. The general perception is that the Chinese are much better employees – entrepreneurial, talented, hard-working and sober. On the other hand, they are considered canny, sly, mean and

1203 V. Gelbras, *Chinese Migration…*, pp. 183-186.
1204 А. Г. Ларин, op. cit., p. 185.
1205 Ibid., pp. 268, 418.
1206 Ibid., p. 271.
1207 V. Gelbras, *Chinese Migration…*, p. 183-186.
1208 B. Lo, *The Axis of Convenience…*, p. 62.

aggressive[1209]. An interesting recent phenomenon is the increase of mixed marriages between Chinese men and Russian women – and a corresponding rise in Sinophobia among Russian men.[1210] According to the latest data, only 8% of Russians support mixed marriages, whereas 40% are indifferent or against them: this result may be interpreted as "another example of chauvinism, or maybe chauvinism plus migrant-phobia."[1211]

Fears of "Sinization" are based on the hermetic closeness of the Chinese communities.[1212] Far Eastern Russians dislike the Chinese because they stick together, help one another and do not assimilate. Nevertheless, the Chinese in Russia are not a Diaspora. They are temporary guest workers (most do not live there longer than five years), not citizens nor permanent inhabitants. They do not grow their roots and do not invest their capital here. They establish their own hotels and restaurants, but these function to serve the Chinese niche only. The Chinese do not fight for their political rights and do not want to challenge the equilibrium with the locals. In sum: they form "a quasi-diaspora."[1213]

So, why does migration remains a thorny issue in Sino-Russian relations? This is due to deep Sinophobia of Far Eastern Russians whose chauvinism is targeted not only at Chinese immigrants, but claims Beijing has bad intentions as well. Far Eastern Russians blame not only migrants, but also China for many misdoings.[1214] In fact, the opposite is true. Although Beijing is unable to control many areas of economic and social life, the Chinese government tries to cooperate with Russia rather than leaving this issue alone – the Chinese officials are prone to accept subsequent Russian limitation of free movement.[1215] If China indeed has bad intentions for the regions, these are of an economic nature – to explore its natural resources instead of assimilating; this, however, falls far behind the top priority of China's Russia policy: the secure China's strategic back to have "peace from the North". In the 2000s and 2010s, anxieties over the "Chinese threat" significantly waned ("fear left everyday life; people care about practical cooperation with the Chinese neighbours"), though there are still such voices in Russia (such as a bizarre claim from Rodina party economist Mikhail Deliagin who said in 2006 that the Chinese "undertook military drills inside Russia" (sic!) and that Russia should arm itself in the Far East, or the equally intriguing statement from general Vladimir Ovchinski who

1209 В. Ларин, *В тени проснувшегося дракона* [In the Shadow of the Awakening Dragon], Владивосток 2006, pp. 274-275.

1210 Pharag Khanna op. cit., pp. 75-78.

1211 А. Г. Ларин, op. cit., p. 200.

1212 Ibid., p. 181.

1213 Ibid., p. 159-181.

1214 B. Lo, *The Axis of Convenience*..., pp. 63-64.

1215 А.В. Лукин, *Китай опасный сосед*..., p. 85.

claimed that the Chinese mafia is controlling Russia).[1216] According to the latest data (public opinion surveys from 2000-2013) Far Eastern Russian anxiety on losing land to China has recently waned (only 24% of respondents still fear that in comparison to 61% in 2000). At the same time, however, there is a paradox. Although the anxieties of losing land have waned, "geopolitical anxieties and xenophobia remained at the same level". There is still a common perception of "large migration", the level of xenophobia remains high (approx. 54% of all respondents called for the deportation of all immigrants, legal and illegal, including their children), while the perception that China gains more in bilateral trade strengthens. Besides, Far Eastern Russians often have contacts with the Chinese even less (a drop from 84% to 61%), have even more negative attitude towards mixed marriages (approx. 90% are against marriages of their relatives with immigrants) and more often (77% opposed to 65% in 2000) support the slogan "Russia for Russians", *Россия для русских*). This data can be interpreted via the prism of strengthening central authority and its efficiency, the increase of income of the inhabitants and their more frequent visits to China (though these trips do not lead to lowering the negative opinion towards the Chinese). At the same time the claim that the Chinese consider the Russian Far East theirs and that they would demand this land in the future, has remained high.[1217] This may be interpreted as follows: thanks to the consolidation of power by Putin, Far Eastern Russians stopped being afraid of losing their land to China today, but they still are afraid of that scenario tomorrow. The dislike toward the Chinese has not lowered either.

All these resentments are born out of the general anxiety about Russia's future (combined with China's rise). The general depopulation trend in Russia and growing population in China is a good example. Beijing's concrete actions mean little when compared to different demographical patterns of the neighborhood regions. Real actions cannot reduce the anxieties if Russians still believe in "territorial determinism" – if they are many and we are few, sooner or later they will come here. When a Russian "hears a Chinese partner's casual remark that Lake Baikal is the 'common heritage' of both countries, he shivers"[1218] (the same happens when the Chinese call for "one economic space" in the Russian Far East and Northeast China).[1219]

Sinophobia makes it impossible for Far Eastern Russians to see that, as a matter of fact, there are too few Chinese in the Russian Far East, not too many.

1216 Idem, *Россия и Китай сегодня и завтра* [Russia and China. Today and Tomorrow], [in:] *Россия и Китай: четыре века*..., pp. 632 and 688.

1217 *Прощание с «азиатскими Балканами»*..., ; see also similar data from 2008, Ларин В.Л., Ларина Л.Л. *Окружающий мир глазами дальневосточников (по итогам опроса населения 2008 г.)* [Surrounding World in Far Eastern Russian Eyes], [in:] *Россия и АТР*, Владивосток, 1/2009.

1218 Д. Тренин, *Верные друзья?*...

1219 G. Rozman, *The Sino-Russian*..., p. 257.

Economically speaking, only the Chinese are able to fill the gap created by depopulation; without it, the further development of the Russian Far East is impossible.[1220] Northeast Chinese are perfect immigrants here – they are accustomed to the Russian climate, many are peasants and have experience of working in Russia and dealing with Russians.[1221] Yet, firstly, Chinese workers prefer to go to work elsewhere (Western Russia, or better still, Western Europe)[1222] and secondly, Russia has no possibility to assimilate the Chinese, it is unable to make them useful citizens; Russia lacks the ability of being a "melting pot" like the USA; local intolerance, xenophobia and dislike mixed with growing nationalism, anxiety of territorial demands in the future – these all make a "Russian melting pot" rather impossible to materialize.[1223] As for the sources of the Far Eastern Russians' approach toward the Chinese, these are "Russia's weak economic, political and military position in Asia-Pacific."[1224]

5. *Big Plans, Little Results: Russia and the Russian Far East in the 2000s*

Vladimir Putin upon taking his office started dealing with the Russian Far East energetically: he dismissed governor Nazdratenko who symbolized the dark 1990s.[1225] Then, in Blagoveshchenks Putin made an important speech – he said that unless Russia immediately starts investing in the region, it would loose it, while the Far East's inhabitants would start speaking Chinese, Korean and Japanese.[1226] This was combined with Putin's general vision of strengthening the state and its central institutions. He was able to resolve the border issue. However, other major impediments, such as the dysfunctionality of the local economy, unprepared for market realities and dramatic depopulation, remained. The demographic issue, combined with political and security issues, presented Putin with a dilemma – he wanted to develop relations with China, which meant increasing trade and human contacts, including interregional links with Chinese provinces. On the other hand, he could not ignore economic and social tensions arising from local Sinophobia. There was also a strategic dilemma:

1220 В.Г. Дацышен, В.Л. Ларин, Г.Н. Романова, op. cit., p. 487.

1221 А. Г. Ларин, op. cit., p. 275.

1222 А.В. Лукин, *От нормализации к стратегическому партнерству…*, p. 391.

1223 А. Г. Ларин, op. cit., pp. 278-282.

1224 Ibid., pp. 340 and 422.

1225 He was replaced by governor Sergei Darkin, who intensified cooperation with China with such projects as Suifenhe-Prigranichnyi border complex, В.Г. Дацышен, В.Л. Ларин, Г.Н. Романова, op. cit., p. 481.

1226 *Вступительное слово на совещании «О перспективах развития Дальнего Востока и Забайкалья»* [Entry Word on Meeting 'Perspectives of Russian Far East and Zabaykale Development], Kremlin.ru, 21.06.2000.

"could Moscow use the injection of Chinese commerce to revive the RFR and satisfy consumer demand without risking a *de facto* Chinese take over?"[1227]. After sixteen years Putin in power, this dilemma is still present, though Moscow in the late 2000s and the early 2010s moved rather towards cooperation with China than balancing it.

Since the fall of the USSR, Moscow has been striving with a permanent failure to create a development strategy for the Russian Far East. Although there were strategies in the 2000s, they remained mostly on paper.[1228] As Russian researchers admit, the "distance between understanding the challenge and ways to react to it turned out to be impossible or irreducible" as "the gap between declarations and real actions by center became very wide."[1229] The Russian Far East continues to be one of the most backward regions in Russia; its economy is increasingly dependent on Chinese goods, services and labor, depopulation trends are not reversing, while Putin's policy is barely more effective than during Yeltsin's era.[1230] The Kremlin has no idea what to do with this region. It has been trying to stimulate domestic migration from Western Russia and that of Russians living outside Russia (in the former USSR) but this have been successful. Even if they arrived in vast numbers they would not fill the full need for labor; besides there is not a clear economic basis for this idea of resettling Russians from other regions.[1231] The idea to develop the region through grand energy investments so far has failed, too. Such projects are not labor-intensive, so its effect on unemployment is marginal; they are more often virtual than real and always combined with present geopolitics; if they are finally fulfilled, profits end up in Moscow or on private accounts.[1232] The idea to attract Japanese and South Korean investments (which could create jobs), in

1227 B. Lo, *The Axis of Convenience…*, p. 59.

1228 *Федеральная целевая программа «Экономическое и социальное развитие Дальнего Востока и Забайкалья на 1996-2005 и до 2010 года»* [Federal Programme of Economic Development of the Far East and Zabaikale 1996-2005 and to 2010], NCS.ru This programme was partially successful, as it led to the development of local transportation scheme; *Стратегия социально-экономического развития Дальнего Востока и Байкальского региона на период до 2025 года* [Strategy of Socioeconomic Development of the Far East and Zabaykale region until 2025], Распоряжение Правительства РФ от 28 XII 2009 N 2094-р, Закон-Прост.Ru; *Стратегия развития России в АТР в XXI веке* [Strategy of Russia's Development]. Аналитический доклад, Москва, Совет Федерации, 2000.

1229 В.Г. Дацышен, В.Л. Ларин, Г.Н. Романова, op. cit., p. 470.

1230 B. Lo, *The Axis of Convenience…*, p. 66-70. The Chinese who come there "are surprised by the poverty and mismanagment in Russian border regions", А.В. Лукин, *Россия и Китай…*, p. 668.

1231 В. Ларин, *В тени проснувшегося дракона…*, p. 121

1232 B. Lo, *The Axis of Convenience…*, p. 67.

opposition to resources-interested Chinese only – was dear to central and regional leaders alike, but never materialized.[1233] Political problems with Tokyo and Seoul, high level of corruption (even by Russian standards) and criminality discouraged investment there. As a result, the central authorities neglected the region, its main sources of income come from China; without Chinese goods and Chinese traders, Far Eastern Russian consumers would not be able to survive[1234]: The Far Eastern provinces' dependence on China on foodstuffs and consumers' goods is around 60-80%.[1235] This is unsurprising: without revenues from Moscow, Far Eastern regions turned toward China, but the intraregional cooperation between the Chinese and Russian provinces could be stronger, should the Russians not block such ideas as free trade zones.[1236] They are blocking them in classical bureaucractic manner: regional Russian officials formally support cooperation with China but informally they make its fulfilment difficult by introducing bureaucratic barriers.[1237] They have been doing this out of a "defensive mentality in which the fear of losing control outweighs the sense of opportunity"[1238]; this fear is present in the reluctance for an even stronger dependence on China and in the belief that trade benefits China mostly. The Russian Far East exports mainly timber (around 47%) and oil-products (19,5%), while importing machinery (44%) and textiles (30%).[1239] Until 2010 there were no bigger Chinese investments, while Russian companies did not venture to the Chinese market. To make things worst, most of the trade has been done illegally or semi-legally.[1240] This all results in Moscow's lack of an idea of what to do with the region: "the result is policy confusion, with the emphasis on half-backed schemes such as attracting labor from western Russia or prestige projects like APEC 2012 in Vladivostok"[1241] (the latter costed "50 percent more than the London Summer Olympics a month earlier").[1242] Since the USSR's fall Moscow has regularly proclaimed the need to revive the region and to create a development strategy; in 2012 the Kremlin even founded a separate ministry (Ministry of the Development of the Far

1233 For the Chinese the access to Far Eastern Russian resources is "a factor of strategic importance", В.Г. Дацышен, В.Л. Ларин, В.Г. Дацышен, В.Л. Ларин, Г.Н. Романова, op. cit., p. 483.

1234 А. Г. Ларин, op. cit. p. 416.

1235 В. Ларин, *Азиатско-тихоокеанский регион в начале XXI века: вызовы, угрозы, шансы Тихоокеанской России* [The region of AP in the beginning of 21th century: challenges, threats, chances of the Pacific Russia], Владивосток 2010, p. 146-147.

1236 M. Kaczmarski, W. Konończuk, *Po obu stronach Amuru* [On both banks of Amur], Nowa Europa Wschodnia 5/2012.

1237 В.Г. Дацышен, В.Л. Ларин, Г.Н. Романова, op. cit., p. 495.

1238 B. Lo, *Russia and the New World Disorder…*, p. 139.

1239 В. Ларин, *В тени проснувшегося дракона…*, p. 121

1240 M. Alexeev, op. cit., p. 341.

1241 B. Lo, *The Axis of Convenience…*, p. 67.

1242 Idem, *Russia and the New World Disorder…*, p. 161.

East), headed by Victor Ishaev, former governor of Khaborovsk.[1243] In reality, however, the region has been forgotten by central authorities, their ambitious programmes remain on paper, while bureaucratic structures, such as the already mentioned Far East Ministry do not fit the reality (the latter was implicitly confirmed by Putin by dismissing Ishaev in 2013).[1244] Hence, China remains the only real option for the region. Ambiguity has been the result. On the one hand the regional administration benefits from economic contacts with China; this keeps the region alive (socially and politically stable). On the other hand, "Russians loath to admit the extent of their dependence, both because they fear it and because it is humiliating"[1245]. They "see the danger of becoming a simple 'raw materials appendage' to their neighbor but hope to be able to rebalance the relationship later, by producing semi-finished goods on their territory."[1246] So far it has been only wishful thinking.

6. *Pivot to China: The Russian Far East in the 2010s*

On a political level, Moscow and Beijing have done a lot to minimize tensions that arise from the Chinese presence. Beijing has always been cooperative when Moscow wanted to strengthen the visa regime or regulate border trade; it has reiterated that it has no territorial claims and reacted with restraint to the accusations of Far Eastern Russians. Moscow in turn rejected the notion of the "Chinese threat" and allowed the border trade to grow. The dialogue on both sides improved remarkably, particularly on the thorny issues from the 1990s – the demarcation of the border and "illegal migration". The border trade grows, intraregional relations between local politicians are good, if not friendly – but "economic opportunities stemming from co-operation with China were balanced with security concerns."[1247] This was part of the problem: "the largely positive state of relations in the RFE" relied "disproportionately on the 'suspension of disbelief.'"[1248]

In the late 2000s and the early 2010s Russia understood the importance of Asia-Pacific in global politics and the role the Russian Far East plays in attempts to upgrade Russia's profile. As Fyodor Lukyanov wrote, "the main

1243 *Указ Президента Российской Федерации о структуре федеральных органов исполнительной власти* [RF President's Decree on structure of Federal Executive Organs] , "Российская газета", 22.05.2012.

1244 *Указ Президента Российской Федерации о Ишаеве В.И.* [RF President's Decree on Ishaev V.I.], Kremlin.Ru, 31.08.2013.

1245 B. Lo, *The Axis of Convenience*..., p. 67.

1246 Д. Тренин, *Верные друзья?*....

1247 M. Kaczmarski, *Russia-China Relations*..., p. 77.

1248 B. Lo, *The Axis of Convenience*..., p. 69.

challenges associated with Russia's Asia future are from inside, not outside."[1249] The Russian Far East is crucial here: the region is "at once Russia's shop-window in Asia, and a barometer of its turn to the East": so far it has been "one of the most backward regions in Northeast Asia, exceeded in this respect only by North Korea" which translated to regional recognition of Russia as "little more than a purveyor of natural resources and weapons"; but "if the Kremlin could transform it into a hub of intra-regional cooperation, then Russia would become an Asian-Pacific power."[1250] Hence, as Russia's most important regional goal has been to remain in the Asian game, Moscow needs to develop the Russian Far East – "Russia's future in the East depends on what it will do with Far Eastern provinces."[1251] Regional cooperation (with such initiatives as Great Tumen Initiative[1252] or Tumangan project[1253]) being far away from "big politics", plays a key role here. Domestically the basic challenge is the "new colonization" of Siberia and the Russian Far East, without doing so, "Russia will not be able to dream about playing a significant role in Asia."[1254] This is combined with the necessity of the development in Siberia and the Russian Far East through infrastructural projects.[1255] The Russian Far East needs "dual integration" (with Asia-Pacific and with the rest of Russia); or it will slip into being "double periphery."[1256] In short, Russia needs to use the dynamism of Asia to develop its Far Eastern part.

The most important rationale behind these plans is, obviously, the need to keep a great power status: "three hundred years ago the great power status was dependent on the position on the Baltic Sea and the Black Sea; now it depends on the position on the Pacific."[1257] Hence, from the Kremlin perspective, the Russian Far East matters "as a springboard for asserting Russia as a Eurasian empire and Pacific power", which in effect made the 21st century objective (upgrading economic conditions of the region), a mirror of 19th century mission "of asserting Russia's "great power-ness" in Asia; Regional development for

---

1249 Ф. Лукьянов, *Поворот на восток* [Pivot to the East], SVOP, 15.02.2010,

1250 B. Lo, *Russia and the New World Disorder…*, p. 160.

1251 Personal conversation with Fiodor Lukyanov, Moscow 28.09.2013

1252 For more, see: *Overview. Greater Tumen Inicjative.*

1253 *Проект «Туманган»* [Project Tumangan], Tumanga.ru

1254 *Фёдор Лукьянов: «Азия – это не периферия»* [Asia is not periphery], Городские новости 12.03.2014.

1255 А. Ларин, *Несколько замечании о возрождении Дальнего Востока России на фоне возрожденмия китайской нации* [A few remarks about the revival of Russian Far East against the background of Chinese nation's revival], [in:] *Азиатско-тихоокеанское сотрудничество и место России в региональном развитии* [AP cooperation and Russia's place in regional development], Москва 2014, p. 19.

1256 N. Kuhrt, *The Russian Far East in Russia's Asia Policy: Dual Integration or Double Periphery?*, "Europe-Asia Studies", vol. 64, no. 3, May 2012, pp. 478-483.

1257 *Ф. Лукьянов: Мы и новая Азия* [We and the new Asia], Совет по внешнй и оборонной политике, 11.11.2013.

its own sake holds little attraction for the Kremlin."[1258] Thus, making full use of the Pacific potential "is a passport to the future; failure to integrate the east would spell the demise of Russia as a major player."[1259] The latter would equal to "a cascade of domestic and external risks: further deindustrialization (and criminalization) of the local economy; social demoralization and unrest; and the steady erosion of Russian sovereignty."[1260]

In search for ways to develop the Far East, Russia has finally accepted the reality and turned to China. Moscow wanted – as Putin wrote it – to "catch the Chinese wind"[1261], to turn the "fortress into free trade zones."[1262] Thus, the idea of the Far East's development was based on external sources (capital), mostly Chinese ones.[1263] The pro-Chinese agenda of Moscow with regards to the Russian Far East was a substantial turn: it "implied a growing Russian openness and acquiescence to a Chinese presence in the Russian Far East", this "incremental shift has confirmed Russia's gradual accommodation to the new bilateral balance of power."[1264] Moscow again decided that it must accept the reality (of Chinese domination) and make the most of it. The programme of development of the Russian Far East with participation of the Chinese capital (around 250 joint ventures, such as new infrastructure, roads, railways, terminals, bridges, border crossings; investments in exploration of natural resources and manufacturing), accepted in 2009, was a clear sign of this new policy.[1265] In this "milestone programme" two key ideas seemed to exist: "attracting investment from China into Russia's Far East and coordinating the development of the two states' adjacent border regions."[1266] This was followed by opening special economic zones in Russia's Far East (comprising of Vladivostok and 15 other maritime administrative districts) in 2015.

Russia agreed to this programme because the perception of China in Russia, or at least among the Russian elite, had changed: "for the last 300 years Russians have been accustomed to seeing China as weak, backward, and inferior in virtually every respect"[1267]; even a few years ago "Russians were asking whether the Chinese have TV sets, now they see China's power."[1268] Now when they look at China today, "they see an economic giant; a financial power armed with the world's largest foreign exchange reserve, a new science power

1258 B. Lo, *Russia and the New World Disorder*..., p. 160.
1259 D. Trenin, *Moscow on the Pacific: the Missing Piece in the Pivot to Asia*, Carnegie Center Moscow, 30.10.2013.
1260 B. Lo, *Russia and the New World Disorder*..., p. 160.
1261 В. Путин, *Россия и меняющийся мир*....
1262 Yu Bin, *Tales of Different 'Pivots'*, ...; Gilbert Rozman, *Turning Fortress*...
1263 *Программа сотрудничества*....
1264 Ibid.
1265 Ibid.
1266 M. Kaczmarski, *Russia-China Relations*..., p. 77.
1267 B. Lo, *Russia and the New World Disorder*..., p. 143.
1268 А. Г. Ларин, op. cit., p. 237.

and technology producer; and an increasingly capable military force."[1269] But old habits die hard, and the Russians' approach to China combines fascination with anxiety: "Moscow is far from ready to accept China as the senior partner and more influential power. To admit this would be at odds with the message of a resurgent Russia second to none."[1270] Nevertheless, despite reservations, Russia decided to bandwagon and to attract Chinese investments to the region and develop it using them. On the other hand, Moscow "made a virtue of necessity" – nobody but China wants to invest there, while Russia is too poor to develop it by itself. In the deteriorating financial situation, "Russia may not allow to spend a billion investments in a region neglected for decades."[1271] That is why it considers Chinese shares better than nothing. The Russians simply came to terms with inevitable (for the Russian Far East there is no choice: China or nothing)[1272] and decided to gain as much as possible.

Unfortunately, from the perspective of 2017, the programme of Chinese investments and other incentives cannot be considered successful – only a couple of projects have been fulfilled; the rest remain on paper. This is due to the fact that "the mechanisms of fulfillment of the Programme have not been included"[1273], "one may come to a conclusion that the programme is not being fulfilled."[1274] Furthermore, the investment climate in Russia contributes to the fact that there are roughly two types of investments into the Russian Far East: "projects that consider Russia as an resource appendix to the Asian economy and semi-legal or illegal schemes to deliver Chinese production into Russian markets."[1275] Moreover, many profits from Chinese investments instead of supplying Russian economy are stolen by private individuals.[1276] Finally, contrary to what they proclaim, the Chinese are not rushing to invest in the region either. Firstly, they changed the concept of development of China's Northeast (*Dongbei*). In the 1980s and 1990s they sought to advance cooperation with Russia[1277]; now they have decided that concentration on deepened cooperation with Southern China is a better option instead; secondly, the Chinese are not keen to invest in the Russian Far East because "they simply want to take the

1269 Д. Тренин, *Верные друзья?*….

1270 B. Lo, *Russia and the New World Disorder*…, p. 143.

1271 *Rosyjski Daleki Wschód: zaplecze surowcowe Chin*….

1272 Personal conversation with Chen Yurong, CIIS, Beijing 01.06.2010.

1273 В. Кулешев [и другие], *О некоторых аспектах совершенствования российско-китайского межрегионального сотрудничества* [On several aspects on the existance of Russian-Sino interregional cooperation], "Проблемы Дальнего Востока" № 6/2010, p. 67.

1274 А. Ларин, *Несколько замечании*…, p. 19.

1275 *Ф. Лукьянов, Поворот на восток*….

1276 А.В. Лукин, *Россия и Китай*…, p. 668.

1277 Li Jingjie. *Sino-Russian Relations in Asia Pacific*, [in:] *Engaging Russia in Asia Pacific*, eds ву Watanabe Koji, Tokyo 1999, p. 63.

resources and nothing more."[1278] Currently, cooperation with the Russian Far East is of primary importance to only one Chinese province (Heilongjiang); even for other Dongbei's provinces (Jilin, Laoning) it is not so important now.[1279] This is why the "cooperation programme" that was intended to be the engine of regional development becomes another factor in the Russian Far East becoming a raw material appendage to China.

Facing the failure of this programme, Russia did not give up but decided in 2011 to re-engage China and renew the list of joint ventures – one of the major goals was to attract Chinese investments in manufacturing, processing and infrastructure construction; judging by the recent perspective, however, "China has been able to increasingly define the direction the Far East development takes, according to its own needs; the support it provided for the joint development of the region focused on creating transport infrastructure and the exploration of resources; Russian hopes (…) have not been fulfilled."[1280] Thus, from the perspective of 2017 not much has yet changed.[1281] The Russian President's Envoy to the Russian Far Eastern Federal District Yuri Trutnev in 2015 openly blamed the Chinese government for not encouraging Chinese investors to go to Russia, moreover, he must have been deeply frustrated, because he even compared Russia to… Angola and pointed out that unlike in Angola, China is not eager to invest in Russia: "Does Angola really have a more stable and favorable investment climate than Russia?" he asked rhetorically.[1282]

This scenario means increasing the dependence on China. In the long term, if not already, the cooperation with China becomes a vital necessity for Far Eastern Russians – something inevitable.[1283] If Russia fails to succeed in the challenging and "truly intimidating national task" of upgrading Asia-Pacific's backwater: the Russian Far East, "a byword for bad governance, corruption, and neglect"[1284], then the economic Sinicization of the Russian Far East, not its military annexation, seems to be the most probable scenario for the future: "Russia may not necessarily 'lose' those provinces in a formal way to China, but it will see them increasingly gravitate towards it. In another great reversal, the 21st century Khabarovsk, a Russian border city on the Amur, may look like the late 19th century Harbin, founded by Russian merchants and railwaymen

1278 Personal conversation with prof. Oleg Timofeyev, from Amur University in Blagoveshchensk, Łódź 07.06.2014.

1279 В.Г. Дацышен, В.Л. Ларин, Г.Н. Романова, op. cit., pp. 485-499.

1280 M. Kaczmarski, *Russia-China Relations…*, p. 78.

1281 However, if one is to believe Russian Tass agency, recently Chinese investments in the Russian Far East are rising and accounts for about 22% of the total foreign investment volume, *Moscow offers Beijing to set up center to support Chinese investors*, Tass, 09.01.2017.

1282 Yu Bin, *Into the Syrian Storm: Between Alliance and Alignment*, "Comparative Connections" vol. 17, no.3

1283 M. Kaczmarski, *Russia-China Relations…*, p. 78.

1284 B. Lo, *Russia and the New World Disorder…*, p. 224.

in the middle of Chinese Manchuria: a foreign outpost in a neighbouing country, and the centre of an expanding zone of influence."[1285]

The Kremlin policy makers are aware of this challenge. Therefore, while embracing China, they have tried simultaneously to balance its influence by other Asian states. Hence, the idea of the "Russian pivot to Asia" (or the Russian turn to the East – more in the last chapter). Its basic concept is the idea of a comprehensive Asian strategy that combines coordinated domestic development alongside positioning itself in the Asia-Pacific as well as enlarging and deepening ties with Japan, South Korea, India, Vietnam, Singapore, and Indonesia, so that cooperation with Asia-Pacific is not limited to China.[1286]

Nevertheless, the success of the Russian pivot remained doubtful from the beginning due to domestic reasons. Even supporters of the Russian pivot saw big obstacles that would hamper its fulfillment. The preferred development model (basing on energy super projects) "cannot be applied here – the economic and geographical realities do not favor it."[1287] To make matters worse, the Russian elites "are too busy worrying about day-to-day survival to draw up a consistent policy for relations with Asia"; that is why the "Kremlin's Asian policy will be for the most part an imitation (…) It is no surprise that journalists joked that the (APEC) summit looked just as absurd as a man in a bird suit flying with Siberian cranes (as Putin tried to do)."[1288] What was even more disturbing, was the traditional disjunction between rhetoric and substance, poor implementation of programs, no follow-up and lack of sustained interest in long-term development of the region; the current economic situation does not help, either: "at a time of recession and tight budgetary constraints, the prospects for the RFE look very bleak without massive foreign investment"; attracting non-Chinese Asian partners failed, too: "in the current environment China is not just the partner of choice, but sometimes the only partner."[1289] The Ukrainian crisis and its aftermath effectively stopped the dreams of a Russian pivot to Asia. Moscow, busy with confrontations with the West over Ukraine, despite all its grandiose declaration to the contrary, has turned its attention away from Asia: developments after the Ukrainian crisis "confirmed that what passes for an Asian strategy is often directed at fulfilling 'greater' goals: countering the United States in global geopolitics; establishing an alternative legitimacy to Western-led governance; reinforcing Russia as an independent center of power; and reaffirming its uniqueness and indispensability."[1290]

1285 Д. Тренин, *Верные друзья?…*.

1286 *Логичное партнерство* [Logical Partnership], "Российская газета", 2014, 21 V.

1287 А. Ларин, *Несколько…*, pp. 19-20.

1288 L. Shevtsova, *Russia's "Pivot" to China: Is It Real or Fake?* Carnegie Center Moscow, 28.03.2013.

1289 B. Lo, *Russia and the New World Disorder…*, pp. 160-161.

1290 Ibid., p. 163.

Judging by early-2017, Russia's pivot to China has not brought a substantial change and many deals have traditionally remained on paper due to several factors. The most important one was the fall of commodity prices, particularly oil, which hit Russian-Chinese trade hard. But there were Chinese domestic reasons, too. China's economic slowdown as well as Xi Jinping's anti-corruption policy made Chinese companies very cautious on investing in new projects, particularly in the energy sector. Moreover, contrary to Russian hopes, Chinese banks and financial institutions are as strict as Western ones about compliance with the sanctions regime (they feared Western contractions, since the West is much more important to China, Chinese banks decided not to take chances) and are not executing interbank transactions with Russian banks; to make matters worse, Russian companies are unable to issue debt or equity on Chinese stock exchanges (even in Hong Kong). Finally, Chinese banks are unwilling to provide loans in dollars or euros to Russians (with the exception of strictly political banks, such as the China Development Bank and the Export-Import Bank of China which gave loans to the Yamal LNG project following a personal order from Xi Jinping himself). Therefore, "on balance, Russian elites' hopes that Chinese financing would make up for the loss of Western capital markets appear exaggerated."[1291] Thus, the hope that Shanghai, Hong Kong and Singapore would replace London, New York or Frankfurt for Russian banks has failed.[1292]

Despite the lack of results, however, Russia continues its attempts to turn to the East, which strengthens the already deep asymmetry in favour of China. If Moscow follows this path, it will probably soon be forced to accept Chinese companies' ownership of substantial stakes (including joint control with Russian minority stakeholders) in strategic deposits of natural resources or/and joint ventures between Chinese companies and Russian businessmen with ties to the Kremlin, in those joint ventures Beijing would provide technology and financing while Russians would ensure the Kremlin's approval of projects and bids. In this new scheme, "the mutual benefits that both sides derive will compensate for the growing inequality between them. China will offer Moscow an economic lifeline, while Russia will provide vital resources (military and civilian technology, natural resources, and diplomatic support, including in the UN Security Council) to propel China's rise as a global powerhouse that can compete with the United States."[1293] The paradoxal social consequence of Kremlin's turn to China is that "one of Moscow's atavistic anxieties— Chinese domination of the RFE and Eastern Siberia— is closer to being realized."[1294] That is why, from the perspective of mid 2017, the Russian pivot to Asia may be metaphorically summarized by Deng Xiaoping's well-known words; Deng

1291 A.Gabuev, *Friends with Benefits?...*

1292 Idem, *Поворот в никуда....*

1293 Idem, *Friends with Benefits? ...*

1294 B. Lo, *Russia and the New World Disorder...*, p. 161.

said that different names given to Vladivostok by the Chinese and Russians have reflected different political goals: the original Chinese name, *Haishenwai,* meant "sea slug," whereas the Russian name means "the ruler of the East."[1295] Today, despite Russian plans and dreams about pivoting to Asia, Vladivostok in the political sphere is more a "sea slug" than "the ruler of the East".

***

Putin's governance of the Russian Far East meant a modernization and reform attempt. The finalizing of the demarcation of the border with China was undoubtedly a success, as was silencing voices that made claims of "immigration expansion" by China in the region. Reforming the Russian Far East was much less successful: it remains one of the most neglected regions of Russia. The ESPO-based development attempt has failed. Russia, therefore, turned to an idea of cooperation with China. Nevertheless, from the perspective of April 2017, this has not yet been fulfilled. Beijing is more interested in the import of the Russian Far East's natural resources than in participation in its development. Beijing's policy toward the Russian Far East is reminiscent of that taken toward Laos. On the one hand China exploits the region economically, taking resources and other raw materials, on the other hand it floods it with low quality goods. As a result of this neocolonial economic policy, the Russian Far East is beginning to become China's raw material appendix. This is a result of the Chinese monopoly in the region and Russia's weakness there. The Kremlin elites are aware of the consequences – thus they initiated the "Russian pivot to Asia" to get Russia out of isolation in Asia-Pacific. Unfortunately, from the perspective of early 2017, this "turn to the East" remains "wishful thinking" more than a reality, and if it is a pivot, then it is to China only, not Asia. It increases instead of decreases Russia's dependence on China. Therefore, the only reasonable thing Russia can do in this situation is to make best use of what is on the ground: to try to work out benefits in the game played by Chinese rules.

1295 Quoted in: H. Kissinger, *On China*, New York, Penguin Press 2011, footnote no. 14 to Chapter no. 3.

Part Four: Central Asia: Towards Sino-Russian Condominium

Central Asia has a special place on the geopolitical map of the world. This region has a unique geopolitical feature: it is landlocked and hardly accessible; it is removed from the global political and economic centers (which makes it difficult for Central Asian states to develop external relations); and finally it is handicapped hydrologically: the deficit of water remains the source of permanent tensions between Central Asian states (which are relatively weak politically and divided over many issues). Geographical location and vast natural resources are the main factors of great powers' interest in the region[1296]. Here interests of Russia and China became convergent right from the beginning.

1. Russia in Central Asia

Since the 19th century Russia has "enjoyed a hegemonic position in Central Asia", consequently "Moscow has invariably looked upon Central Asia with a patrimonial eye."[1297] For Russia, Central Asia is a part of the "near abroad", while its dominant position here has been based on economic and communication connections between the region and Moscow inherited after the USSR and on personal contacts with Central Asian elites whose security Moscow safeguarded (arms deliveries, garrisons) and on the universal fluency in Russian language in the region.[1298] This all gave Russia a giant advantage over other powers in the region. For years, the great powers respected Russia's position and have not interferred with the Central Asian affairs – Washington did not even do it during the Cold War. Even after 1991 it had "predisposition to look to Russia to guide these states into more stable and democratic futures and to play the role of policeman if good guidance failed."[1299]. Moscow, however, initially after 1991 was not eager to play this role. Russian reformers considered Central Asian republics an unnecessary burden for Russia, while Central Asian elites appeared to share this outlook.[1300] The Russian perspective was

1296 А. Малашенко, *Центральная Азия: на что рассчитывает Россия?* [Central Asia: What Russia is Counting On], Москва 2012, p. 16.

1297 B. Lo, *The Axis of Convenience…*, p. 91.

1298 W. Górecki, *Even Further from Moscow*, OSW, Warsaw 2014, p. 6.

1299 M. Brill Olcott, *Central Asia, Russia and the West*, [in:] *Russia and Asia…*, p. 137.

1300 А. А. Картков, *Россия и Централная Азия, (Russia and Central Asia)* [in:] *Россия в Азии: проблемы взаимодействия* [Russia and Asia: The Problems of Interaction], ред. К. А. Какарев, Москва 2006, p. 229; И. Звягельская, *Становление государств Центральной Азии. Политические процессы* [The Establishing of Central Asian States. Political Processes], Москва 2009, p. 41.

based on a "paternalistic assumption" that Central Asian republics are destined to be dominated by Russia.[1301] Consequently, "it was not that the republics seceded from the USSR, but that the USSR simply abandoned them to their fate."[1302] Russia had been steadily withdrawing from the region – its engagement to a bigger extent was based on inertia and mechanical use of all Soviet connections.[1303] This, combined with a more active policy of other actors (the USA, Turkey, Iran) and the de-sovietisation process, de-rusification in local conditions, led to Russia's decreased position in the region.[1304] Only Primakov's nomination in 1996 slowed this negative process down. He conducted his first foreign visit to Central Asia and emphasized that relations with the region would be "the highest priority of Russian foreign policy."[1305] Nevertheless, Moscow's deeper engagement materialized only in the next decade.

Russia's re-engagement with Central Asia in the 2000s was in a way provoked by the external development – the U.S. incursion into the region, which questioned Russia's hegemonic position in Central Asia. Initially the Russian Federation not only did not oppose the US intervention, but even supported it. Soon however, the Kremlin policy-makers realized that a long-term American presence threatenedRussian interests. Consequently, Moscow turned toward Beijing. Russia and China joined on mutual need to remove the USA from the region. That is why the mid 2000s saw intensified Sino-Russian cooperation in the region, best exemplified by the Shanghai Cooperation Organization (SCO). Nevertheless, cooperation started to coexist with competition when China started steadily challenging Russia, with its New Silk Road project – in competition with the Russian Eurasian Union. The result was an ambiguity in Russian and Chinese policy in Central Asia.

Despite Russia's re-engagement after 09/11, "Russia's influence has eroded significantly over the past two decades since the collapse of the USSR"; only after Russia declared reintegration of the post-Soviet area as one of its top priorities in 2012, the further erosion of Russian influence was halted.[1306] For Moscow, Central Asia is "often viewed as a 'soft underbelly', i.e. a buffer whose presence could improve the impermeability of the Russian borders", besides it matters as "a major source of raw materials (uranium and hydrocarbons that are re-exported to the West) and of a cheap workforce"; moreover, Central Asia is important as an area covered by Russian integration initiatives";

1301 W. Górecki, *Even Further from Moscow* ..., p. 15.

1302 Д. Тренин, *Post-Imperium: Евразийская история* [Post-Empire: Eurasian History], Москва 2012, p. 176.

1303 V. V. Naumkin, *The emerging political balance in Central Asia: a Russian view*, [in]:*Russia and Asia*...p. 85.

1304 W. Górecki, Even Further from Moscow..., p. 16.

1305 G. Chuffrin, op. cit., p. 477.

1306 W. Górecki, *Even Further from Moscow*..., pp. 18-26.

finally it "is the last part of the Soviet ecumen, apart from Belarus and Armenia, where the Kremlin can still feel like a political leader (...) For this reason, Moscow's presence and influence in Central Asia are essential for its prestige"; thus "Russia's basic and most important goals are to maintain its influence there (and expand it, in the optimal scenario) and to restrict the influence of other actors (...) The loss of this region, understood as the dominance of another external player being entrenched there (...) would also be painful for Russia in symbolic terms."[1307]

2. *China in Central Asia*

China for the first time appeared in the region as an important actor after the USSR's fall. For Beijing, Central Asia mattered mostly for its implications for Xinjiang. The declarations of independence of the new post-Soviet republics threatened transferring freedom tendencies from Central Asian nations inside China. The Xinjiang issue and its separatism became Beijing's main concerns.[1308] That is why "security issues are at the core of Chinese engagement in Central Asia – China wants to protect Xinjiang from possible destabilization, while the main field of play for China are economic issues"; China's relations with Central Asia "have been an effect of two parallel processes of fundamental significance for the global order: the disintegration of the Russian/Soviet empire in Asia, and the other – the sudden rise in China's position"; Xinjiang's relations with Central Asian countries and this province's growing rise have been the local equivalent of these processes – for China, Central Asia has functioned mainly as the way to make Xinjiang rich and stable.[1309] That is why after the USSR's fall China put emphasis on economic cooperation with the region, hoping that increased trade volume would lead to greater prosperity and consequently – stability of the difficult Xinjiang province.[1310] At the same time, China started advocating development of transport network which was supported by the UN and Asian Development Bank.[1311] Nevertheless, transportation lines with China in the 1990s remained sporadic and increased only in the 2000s and the 2010s. This was the exact opposite to the integration of Central Asian economies with Russia – a common heritage after the USSR's fall. Unsurprisingly then the region's volume of trade with China fell behind the one with Russia (trade with Russia was seven times larger in 1995 while in

1307 Ibid.; D. Trenin, *Russia and Central Asia: Interests, Policies and Prospects*, [in:] *Central Asia: Views...*, pp. 81-83.

1308 M. Brill Olcott, *Russian-Chinese...*, p. 385; R. Weitz, op. cit., p. 54.

1309 A. Jarosiewicz, K. Strachota, *China vs. Central Asia. The achievements of the past two decades*, OSW, Warsaw 2013, pp. 5-32.

1310 E. Wishnick, *Mending fences...*, p. 137.

1311 R. Weitz, op. cit., p. 53; M. Brill Olcott, *Russian-Chinese...*, p. 384.

2000 – six times). This is, however, only the official data. The real volume of trade between China and Central Asia, particularly Kazakhstan and Kyrgyzstan has been difficult to estimate – for example in the early 1990s it was mostly barter, which makes it impossible to show accurate data.[1312] Nevertheless, there is no doubt that Central Asia's cooperation with China in the 1990s had been much lower than with Russia – this changed only in the 2000s.

Having their policy goals of Xinjiang in mind, China since 1991 has done a lot to establish good relations with new the republics' leaders and persuade them that it is better to base their interests in Beijing rather than to care about their cousins the Uygurs in Xinjiang. Although Central Asian leaders initially had difficulties with understanding the Chinese specifics, they were quick to learn the realities. China was too big and too important to risk looking for trouble with it in the case of the Uyghurs. That is why since the 1990s Central Asian leaders have tried to intensify top-level relations with Beijing and they have not mentioned the Uygur issue. It came easier for them thanks to the fact that Uygur separatism was potentially dangerous for their regimes as well. Therefore, by supporting China's integrity, they cared for their own business, too.

The anxiety over spreading of disliked ideologies such as liberal democracy or Islamic fundamentalism to the Chinese territory was another factor in China's engagement with Central Asia. Here Beijing could count on leaders of Central Asian republics.[1313] In general, their cooperation with China was stable, though in regional capitals the anxiety over China's weight, its potential and possible imperial aims never ceased to exist. It was another reason to come closer to Russia, particularly after 1996: "given the choice between Russia and China, most in Central Asia would choose 'the devil' they know over the one they do not know."[1314]

Initially China respected traditional Russian dominance in the region. For China, Central Asia is "a region with a high potential for instability"; that is why Beijing "respected Russia's interests and initiatives regarding regional security issues."[1315] In the 1990s and the early to mid 2000s, Beijing considered this region as zone of exclusive Russian influences and interests which meant that China, contrary to other international actors "initially approached in caution and respectfully to Russian interests (…) which contributed to both countries' general rapprochement."[1316] China concluded "a tacit bargain with Moscow": in return for recognition of the status quo in Central Asia and deference of Russia's regional leadership, Moscow continued "to take care of business"; for China it meant one thing: "with its 'strategic rear' covered, China could

1312 M. Brill Olcott, *Russian-Chinese…*, pp. 388-390.

1313 C. E. Ziegler, *Russia and China in Central Asia*, [in:] *The Future of China-Russia…*, p. 235.

1314 M. Brill Olcott, *Russian-Chinese…*, p. 375.

1315 A. Jarosiewicz, K. Strachota, op. cit., pp. 5-32.

1316 K. Kozłowski, *Państwo Środka a Nowy…*, pp. 11, 120, 150.

then focus on domestic modernization and Taiwan."[1317] Central Asia throughout the 1990s and until the late 2000s remained the place where Russian and Chinese interests converged and overlapped, cooperation became "harmonious."[1318]

For the time being, Beijing had been able to "forge its weakness into a positive image of a country which does not interfere with the internal problems of its neighbours; this 'affirmative' policy was also based on discreet support for individual countries in case of tension in relations with Russia or the USA."[1319] At the same time, however, China since the 2000s had been preparing to enter the oil and gas market in the region to ensure steady supply of resources to Chinese economy. Energy aside, another dimension for China has been transportation – establishing the New Silk Road since the 2010s.[1320]

China's entry to Central Asia in the 2000s diametrically altered the strategic picture of the region and in the long-term it proved to be more important than American involvement (see: below). China's renewed interest has been consistent with "more permanent realities" not just "extraordinary concatenation of circumstances" like in the case of the USA.[1321] The United States is leaving Central Asia, whereas China is here to stay – for a long time. China wants to achieve a dominant position not out of historical or messianic reasons (like Russia), or ideological ones (like the USA), but because a stronger presence meets its interests – the Chinese are convinced that economic cooperation is linked with security issues: fighting poverty will remove the cause of "three evils" (terrorism, separatism and extremism), and would protect Xinjinag.[1322] So far it has proven to be true – "in the post-Soviet Central Asia time appears to be on the Middle Country's side."[1323]

Access to energy, the need to diversify deliveries and the creation of a web of oil and gas pipelines connected with domestic ones have been China's other key interests here.[1324] Moscow's unreliability as an energy provider made Beijing intensify its involvement in Kazakhstan, Turkmenistan and Uzbekistan – Central Asia is said to have the third biggest energy resources while geographic proximity plays to China's advantage. Contrary to Russia, whichstrived to

---

1317 B. Lo, *The Axis of Convenience*..., p. 92.

1318 R. Weitz, op. cit., p. 51.

1319 Ibid.

1320 A. Jarosiewicz, K. Strachota, op. cit. pp. 5-32.

1321 B. Lo, *The Axis of Convenience*..., p. 98.

1322 Zhao Huasheng, *China and Central Asia*, [in:] *Central Asia: Views from Washington, Moscow and Beijing*, ed. E. Rumer, D. Trenin, Zhao Huasheng, New York 2007, p. 157

1323 K. Kozłowski, *Państwo Środka a Nowy*..., pp. 120-150.

1324 Zhao Huasheng, *Security Building*..., p. 294-295; Shi Ze, *Relations Between China and Central Asian Countries Face Opportunity of All-Round Development*, "China International Studies" 2005 (Winter), p. 83.

keep its monopoly in the region, China wanted to eliminate Russia's intermediacy and establish direct contacts with Central Asian republics.[1325] Russia wanted to keep its position of the unquestionable leader, whereas China hoped for a "concert of Central Asia."[1326] At the same time, however, China in the long-term strives to establish the traditional Chinese vassal model of state-to-state relationship in Central Asia; Beijing wants to peacefully subordinate these countries without the need to establish direct control[1327]. Moscow, in its turn, was very cautious in masking its dissatisfaction with the growing Chinese involvement: the Kremlin decided to use the local anxieties of Chinese dominance – the Central Asians fear China more than Russia.[1328] For a long time the camouflaged competition with Beijing gave way to joint containment of the USA in Central Asia[1329], with Chinese growing involvement, however, this may change.

3. Border Issues: "The Shanghai Five"

The border issue was one of the most challenging problems inherited after the USSR. There is no natural border between China and Central Asia and there has never been one between Russian and Chinese territories. Soviet-Chinese conflicts from the 1960s and unregulated border issue did not help to stabilize and normalize the relations. China for its part strived not only to demarcate but also to demilitarize it and build confidence measures. Here Shanghai's agreement on strengthening mutual security and confidence-building measures – subsequently called the "Shanghai agreement"[1330]whereas its signatories, The Shanghai Five – proved to be the single most important step. The agreement itself meant that China dropped its earlier claims against the Russian Empire

1325 Selbi Hanova, *Perspectives on the SCO: Images and Discourses*, "China and Eurasia Quarterly" 2009, Vol. 7, no. 3, p. 79.

1326 F. Tolipov, *East vs. West? Some Geopolitical Questions and Observations for the SCO*, "China and Eurasia Quarterly" (July 2005), p. 22; E. B. Rumer, *China, Russia and the Balance of Power in Central Asia*, "Strategic Forum" 2006, No 223 (November), p. 5.

1327 N. Swanström, *China and Central Asia: A New Great Game Or Traditional Vassal Relations?*, "Journal of Contemporary China" 2005, vol. 45, no 14 (November), pp. 576-581.

1328 A. Frost, op. cit., p. 98.

1329 V. Paramonov, O. Stolpovski, *Russia and Central Asia: Multilateral Security Cooperation*, Advanced Research and Assessment Group, Defence Academy of the United Kingdom, 2008, III, p. 10; M. Troickiy et.all, *A Russian Perspective on the Shanghai Cooperation Organization*, [in:] *The Shanghai Cooperation Organization*, SIPRI, May 2007, p. 44.

1330 *Соглашение между Российской Федерацией, Республикой Казахстан, Кыргызской Республикой, Республикой Таджикистан и Китайской Народной Республикой об укреплении доверия в военной области в районе границы* [Russian Federation Kazakhstan, , Kyrgyzstan, Tajikiistan and China Intergovermental Agreement on Confidence Building in the Border Areas], [in:] *Сборник российско-китайских договоров 1949-1999...*, pp. 365-373.

and the USSR.[1331] That is why the Chinese concession must be understood as a compromise made to normalize relations with Central Asian republics; this compromise cost Beijing little, but enhanced Chinese possibilities of political influence as well as opportunities of economic benefits. Besides this, the mechanism applied during the Shanghai Five agreement proved to be "a textbook example of the general emphasis on agreements and multilateral negotiations as typical features of the Chinese diplomacy."[1332] Since then, the "Five" format has started being used as an effective platform of cooperation between China and the region and expanded impressively.[1333] Since the very beginning China became the leader of the "Five"; Russia largely neglected the formula. The "Five" achieved success because "the countries involved share similar international norms of behaviour they have taken a gradualist approach which allows time to build up trust and coordination among themselves."[1334]

4. *The USA Moves In*

11 September 2001 became the time *limes* (latin: boundary) for Central Asia. In Russia "Putin was said to have made a 'strategic choice' (…) Russia was powerless to stop the United States from entering the region" – Putin simply "made a virtue out of necessity."[1335] Besides, the US entry had its security advantages: it removed the Taliban, the "Sword of Damocles" that loomed over Central Asian countries.[1336] Putin aimed at making a breakthrough in Russian-American relations to get material profits necessary for rebuilding the Great Russia.[1337] This thinking was based on one crucial assumption: that the American presence would be temporary. This began to change when the Kremlin realized that the Americans were planning to stay for longer and intended to promote democracy ("colour revolutions"). This was too much for Moscow: the United States became "part of the problem", not the solution."[1338] This led to choosing option No. 2: cooperation with China to contain the Western intervention.

9/11 had a decisive importance for Chinese policy towards Central Asia, too. Putin's speedy endorsement of the American military cooperation "came

1331 M. Brill Olcott, *Russian-Chinese…*, p. 377.
1332 K. Kozłowski, *Chiny a Nowy Jedwabny Szlak…*, p. 125.
1333 A.B. Лукин, *От нормализации к стратегическому партнерству…*, p. 356.
1334 Qingguo Jia, *The Success of Shanghai Five: Interests, Norms and Pragmatism*, Commonwealth Institute.
1335 B. Lo, *The Axis of Convenience…*, p. 93.
1336 Zhao Huasheng, *Security Building in Central Asia and the Shanghai Cooperation Organization*. Slav.hokudai, p. 264.
1337 B. Nygren, *The Rebuilding of Greater Russia: Putin's Foreign Policy Towards the CIS Countries*, Routledge, Abingdon, New York 2008, p. 249.
1338 B. Lo, *The Axis of Convenience…*, p. 94.

as a shock to the Chinese leadership"; Beijing could not believe that Moscow would permit, let alone support deployment of the US troops in Russia's sphere of influence; to make matters worse, "relations with China were unceremoniously pushed into the background."[1339] That was a very bad news: "the Chinese leadership perceived a significant political discomfort due to the unexpected arrival of American troops in a region abundant with natural resources that lies at China's rears."[1340] The old Chinese fears of the Middle Kingdom's encirclement by hostile countries reappeared with new power. Putin's behavior made Beijing realize a number of truths – the first: for Russia, relations with the West "would always take precedence", the second: Sino-Russian axis is still a function of Russia's relations with the West; the third: "Russia would not support Chinese interests in Central Asia, except on a purely coincidental basis"; the forth: the United States was now a major power in the region, not Russia.[1341] Nevertheless, the Chinese leadership, in accordance with the tradition of Chinese strategic culture, has hidden the feelings. They kept calm and waited for the cooling of Russian-US relations and weakening of the US status in the region. This allowed China to gradually and quietly build its position in the region without alarming the other powers. Nevertheless, "the key lesson of the early post-9/11 period remained: in Chinese eyes Russia became both untrustworthy and weak"; thus, China started more active policy towards Central Asia, one that involved expansion of ties with Central Asian republics.[1342] The Shanghai Cooperation Organization became the tool for this policy.

5. *The Shanghai Cooperation Organization*

Not so long time ago the Shanghai Cooperation Organization (SCO) drew attention and caused considerable stir. To some it was a positive multilateral organization that addressed the "universal threats"; other saw it as "anti-NATO", a quasi-alliance directed against the Western model of democracy. The apologists claimed it successfully resolves practical issues, while critics argued that the organization is an empty shell.[1343] Recently the SCO has been losing its influence in the region.

1339 Ibid., p. 96.

1340 K. Kozłowski, *Państwo Środka a Nowy…*, p. 168.

1341 Akihiro Iwasita, *The Shanghai Cooperation Organization and Its Implications for Eurasian Security: A New Dimension of 'Partnership' after the Post-Cold War Period*, [in:] *Slavic Eurasia's Integration into the World Economy and Community*, eds. S. Tabata, A. Iwashita 2004.

1342 B. Lo, *The Axis of Convenience…*, p. 97.

1343 Ibid., p. 104; for more, see: Wu-ping Kwo, Ahiau-shyang Liou, *Competition and Cooperation Between Russia and China in Central Asia and 'Shanghai Cooperation Organization: Analytical View from International Regime*, National Chengchi University, 18.04.2005;

Officially, the SCO is built on the Shanghai Spirit[1344], but this concept is rather vague.[1345] The SCO's hallmark has been its fight with "three evils": terrorism, separatism and extremism[1346]. Compared with other organizations, the SCO language of statements and documents is rather defensive/conservative: member-states dislike the propagation of democratic values and emphasize non-interference in domestic affairs instead.[1347] Protest against "hegemonism" and "imposition" of the Western patterns was quite frequent in its announcements, particularly in the mid-2000s.[1348] The overall impression the SCO member-states tried to convey was that of "an organization that was growing dynamically, but from a modest base."[1349]

Initially nothing but geography united the member-states.[1350] The SCO was founded on 15 June 2001 in Shanghai by Shanghai Five countries and Uzbekistan (that was admitted a day earlier).[1351] During that summit the "Shanghai convention combating terrorism, separatism and extremism" (the "three evils") was adopted.[1352] In accordance with the SCO chapter, all member-states are equal and the decisions are taken without a vote (consensus) and without veto right.[1353] Mongolia was granted an observer status in 2004, followed by Iran, Pakistan and India in 2005 and Afghanistan in 2012 (India and Pakistan became members in 2017). With the exception of Mongolia, each time the observer status aroused controversies. Probably that is why the SCO stopped granting this title and replaced it with a more flexible formula – a "dialogue partner" (Belarus and Sri Lanka in 2010, Turkey 2012, Azerbaijan, Armenia, Cambodia, and Nepal in 2015). The declared main goals are security issues,

Yang Shu, *Reassessing the SCO's Internal Difficulties: A Chinese Point of View*, "China and Eurasia Quartely", Volume 7, no. 3/2009, p. 18; A. Cohen, op. cit., p. 58.

1344 *Mutual trust, mutual advantage, equality, mutual consultations, respect for cultural variety and aspiration for joint development, Декларация о создании Шанхайской Организации Сотрудничества* [The Declaration of Establishment of SCO], Sectsco.org.ru, 15.06.2001.

1345 *Декларация пятилетия Шанхайской организации сотрудничества* [SCO Fifth Anniversary Declaration], Sectsco.org.ru, 15.06.2006; *Хартия Шанхайской Организации Сотрудничества* [SCO Charter], Sectsco.org.ru,15.06.2002.

1346 *Шанхайская конвенция* [Shanghai Convention on Fight Against Terrorism, Separatism and Extremism], Sectsco.org.ru, 15.06.2001.

1347 T. Ambrosio, *Catching the 'Shanghai Spirit': How the Shanghai Cooperation Organization Promotes Authoritarian Norms in Central Asia*, "Europe-Asia Studies" 2008, Vol. 60, No. 8, p. 1332.

1348 Zhao Huasheng, *Security Building*…, p. 284.

1349 B. Lo, *The Axis of Convenience*…, p. 105.

1350 A. Cohen, op. cit., p. 53.

1351 *Декларация о создании*….

1352 *Шанхайская конвенция* ….

1353 *Хартия Шанхайской*….

economic, social and cultural cooperation.[1354] In reality, avoiding conflicts between member-states remains the most important goal[1355], while "maintaining border and regional security" remains the most fundamental function of the SCO.[1356]

The SCO official declarations are grandiose in form, but lacking in substance, without details of implementation and with a gap between declarations and the real actions; subsequent statements appear to conceal the lack of progress or ritual hollow preaching.[1357] Parallels with the NATO and the EU are "obviously absurd."[1358] More appropriate are the ones with the OSCE, but the latter has more members and more power.[1359] The SCO is first and foremost "a platform that potentially enables member-states to fulfill their specific goals."[1360] Somehow the SCO reminds the CIS – the rhetoric outweighs achievements – "there is no the SCO policy per se", much of its activity is "geopolitical bluff" intended to create "the perception (or at least the illusion) of there being a new and serious player on regional and international scene."[1361]

However, the SCO "amounts to more than just a mini-CIS plus China": the SCO has demonstrated "an impressive solidarity on occasions": the 2005 call for a final timeline for the removal of US soldiers from Afghanistan[1362] or a contribution to closure of the US air base in Khanabad in 2005.[1363] Besides, the SCO has some achievements in the security sphere, like combating terrorism. Finally, the SCO is "a genuinely multilateral organization, even if some member-states are more equal than others" (the weakest, Kyrgyzstan and Tajikistan, can make themselves heard).[1364] The Georgia crisis in 2008 and the SCO unwillingness to recognize South Ossetia and Abkhazia proved it well.[1365] For many, China is the real leader of the SCO, the Organization remains an important tool for Beijing's Central Asian policy.[1366]

In the mid-2000s it was very popular to perceive the SCO as an opposition to the West. There were voices about the SCO being "anti-NATO", "Eastern

---

1354 *Краткие сведения о ШОС*, SCO, www.sectsco.org.ru

1355 I.Oldberg, *The Shanghai Cooperation Organisation: Powerhouse or Paper Tiger?* FOI, Swedish Defence Research Academy 2007 p. 13.

1356 Zhao Huasheng, *Security Building…*, p. 294.

1357 M. Laumulin, *The Shanghai Cooperation Organization as 'Geopolitical Bluff'? A View From Astana*, "Russie.Nei.Visions" 12.06.2006, , p. 6.

1358 B. Lo, *The Axis of Convenience…*, p. 106.

1359 I. Oldberg, op. cit., pp. 10-44.

1360 K. Kozłowski, *Chiny a Nowy Jedwabny Szlak…* p. 191.

1361 M. Laumulin, op. cit., p. 6.

1362 *Декларация глав государств-членов Шанхайской организации сотрудничества* [SCO Heads of State Declaration] 05.07.2005, www.sectsco.org.ru.

1363 B. Lo, *The Axis of Convenience…*, p. 106.

1364 Ibid., p. 106; S. Hanova, op. cit., p. 74; I. Oldberg, op. cit., p. 25.

1365 N. Swanström, *Georgia: The Split that Split the SCO*, CACI Analyst, 03.09.2008.

1366 I. Oldberg, op. cit., p. 29.

NATO", "new Warsaw pact"[1367], or even "League of Dictators"[1368]. This perception was based on conviction that the prime reason to exist for the Organization is to undermine the American presence in Central Asia; the SCO itself gave some ground to this kind of assessment.[1369]

Although the SCO is neither a full security organization nor a trade block nor anything else, it would be wrong to consider the SCO as nothing more than simply a geopolitical bluff: Central Asian republics are concerned about security, Islamizm and only when the US started the export of democracy "they bought into Moscow's overtly anti-U.S. agenda"; similarly, China's top priority has been "the security of China's far west rather than strategic competition with Washington."[1370] To sum up: "ultimately the SCO is a modest organization of modest achievements, a reality implicitly recognized by its members, whose main foreign policy activity is either directed elsewhere (Russia, China) or channeled through bilateral relations (Central Asian states)."[1371] Membership in the SCO has paid off to every member-state: for Russia it has been a forum to maintain its position and to control the Chinese cooperation with the region; for China it has legitimized its ties with Central Asian republics and allowed to increase its status via growing economic advantage. For both Russia and China the SCO allowed keeping the foreign powers (the USA) away from the region, or limiting their influence. As such it indeed became "a significant development of Sino-Russian cooperation in Asia", as Mikhail Titarenko wanted to see it.[1372] For Central Asians the SCO have been helping to maintain independence and have at least pretended an equal voice with Russia and China. The mid-2000s concerns about the SCO were premature because the member-states, let alone observers, are much diverged, with contradictory interests that make it difficult to find a common language. This all highlights the internal limitations – the normative convergence is too narrow, integration remains scant and cooperation is hampered by cultural differences, mutual distrust and contradictory interests.[1373]

The SCO is a temporary solution – a tool for Russia and China to check one another and control ambitions.[1374] These have been different: Moscow wanted to use the SCO as a tool to keep its monopolistic position on energy and energy transit in the region, whereas China intended it to be the engine of trade and investments in the region. Thanks to the SCO formula, these interests have

---

1367 F. W. Stakelbeck Jr., *A New Bloc emerges?*, "The American Thinker" 05.08.2005.

1368 R. Kagan, *League of Dictators?*, "Washington Post", 30.04.2006.

1369 *Декларация глав…*

1370 B. Lo, *The Axis of Convenience…*, p. 108; See also: A. P.Sznajder, *China's Shanghai Cooperation Organization Strategy*, University of California Press, May 2006, p. 95.

1371 B. Lo, *The Axis of Convenience…*, p. 108.

1372 М.Л. Титаренко, *Геополитическое значение…*, p. 444.

1373 S. Hanova, op. cit., p. 72; Yang Shu, op. cit., pp. 17-21; Yu Bin, *Central Asia Between Competition and Cooperation…*

1374 A. Frost, op. cit., p. 105; B. Lo, *The Axis of Convenience…*, p. 110.

been meeting and balancing – the cooperation within the organization limits the possibility for a conflict.[1375] Nevertheless, cracks have already appeared and are likely to increase in the future. Currently the SCO has two wheels – security and economy, the former being more important.[1376] Beijing wanted to shift the SCO's agenda towards economic cooperation and integration, while Moscow underlined security issues and military and geopolitical aspects.[1377] This conflict of interests was clearly visible in the Russian veto for Chinese-backed idea of the SCO free trade zone. The member-states cooperate closely in trade, but not financially or in the banking sector – the Central Asians "do not want the Soviet-time hegemony to reappear, this time with Beijing as the decision-making center."[1378] As for Russia, its approach towards the SCO has been moderate – it supported the Organization politically but remained cautious in practical cooperation.

Moscow's organization of choice in Central Asia has not been the SCO, but the CSTO. Since the very beginning, Moscow has tried to foster a closer cooperation between the SCO and the CSTO – it wanted to become a "bridge" between those two organizations; such a "marriage of convenience" would strengthen Russia's position in Central Asia.[1379] Unfortunately for Moscow, this idea was first blocked by Uzbekistan, and then by China[1380]. Lack of any real achievements by the CSTO[1381] makes it difficult for it to camouflage its main geopolitical goal: fostering a Russia position in the region.[1382] That is why the most important difference between the SCO and the CSTO lies it the fact that the former is Beijing's multilateral instrument of influence, whereas the latter – is Moscow's one.

In the 2000s there were two most important approaches to Sino-Russian relations in Central Asia. According to the first one, those two countries effectively cooperated in combating terrorism and ideological and strategic threats from the West. The alternative one claimed that real cooperation is scant and possible only thanks to a common foe – the United States; without it Russia and China would compete (or already had started competing). Both approaches were correct to some extent.[1383] That is why the SCO served well within the concept of a "partnership" – non-enemy and non-friend, or in other words, a "peaceful buffer."[1384] With time, however, especially after 2013, the buffer is becoming less and less useful. Russian veto for a Chinese-backed SCO free

1375 A. Cohen, op. cit., p. 54; Zhao Huasheng, *Security Building*…, p. 296.
1376 Zhao Huasheng, *Security Building*…, p. 311.
1377 A. P. Sznajder, op. cit., p. 99.
1378 K. Kozłowski, *Państwo Środka a Nowy*…, p. 208-209.
1379 Yu Bin, *Between Cooperation and Competition*, "Comparative Connections", vol. 9, no 3.
1380 A. Frost, op. cit., p. 99.
1381 W. Górecki, *Even Further from Moscow*…, pp. 84-87.
1382 D. Trenin, *Russia and Central Asia*…, p. 100.
1383 B. Lo, *The Axis of Convenience*…, p. 113.
1384 Akihiro Iwasita, *The Shanghai Cooperation Organization*…, p. 275.

trade zone and/or bank and Chinese veto for Russian-backed SCO fund[1385] have *de facto* blocked the development of this organization. Russia prefers to work on financial mechanisms outside the SCO framework, such as BRICS.[1386] As for China, although it is visibly the dominant member of the SCO, Beijing is frustrated with current state of affairs within the SCO that does not allow for further economic development "and could not wait for Russia to start the economic cooperation within the SCO."[1387] Thus China has allowed Russia to symbolically dominate the SCO recent agenda and orientate it towards international and security issues instead of regional – "thus the the SCO is becoming a forum, symbolically dominated by Russia, for coordinating the members' positions on global issues" instead of being "an organization which actually influences the situation in the region."[1388] It remains to be seen whether the admittance to the organization of India and Pakistan as full members (accepted in 2015, confirmed in 2016 and included in 2017) will change these dynamics (or the opposite: strengthen the recent ineffectivness). According to some, like Li Jinfeng or Alexander Lukin, this will make the SCO a China-Russia-India-led organization and boost its importance.[1389] Others, like Yan Xuetong, say that this is the final nail in the Organization's coffin ("the SCO is in fact dead").[1390] Whatever the outcome turns out to be, China has accepted this enlargement, seen as benefitting Russia, but blocked further enlargement of Iran in order not to complicate its relations with the West.[1391] Beijing has been trying, too, to use the SCO institutional framework to enhance its One Belt One Road project, but the results are not yet satisfying. What is certain is that China, seeing structural obstacles within the organization, lost its primary interest in the SCO (at least for the time being), and turned toward bilateral diplomacy instead.

1385 А.В. Лукин, *От нормализации к стратегическому партнерству…*, p. 364.

1386 Yu Bin, *Russia-China*…pp. 103-116.

1387 А.В. Лукин, *Россия и Китай…*, [in:] *Россия и Китай: четыре века…*, p. 649.

1388 A. Jarosiewicz, *Chinese tour de force in Central Asia*, OSW, Warsaw 18.09.2013.

1389 Li Jinfeng, *Shanghai hezuo zuzhi kuo yuan: Tiaozhan yu jiyu* [SCO enlargement: opportunities and challenges], quoted in: M. Julienne, *Back to the basics: Counter-terrorism cooperation and the Shanghai Cooperation Organisation*, [in:] *China and Russia. Gaming…*; А.В. Лукин, *Россия и Китай сегодня и завтра* [in:] *Россия и Китай: четыре века…* , p. 649.

1390 *«Не понимаю, почему Россия не настаивает на формировании альянса с Китаем»* [I Don't understand why Russia is not pushing for forming an alliance with China],interview with Yan Xuetong, Kommiersant.Ru, 17.03.2017.

1391 Yu Bin, *Politics of…* pp.129-144.

All Central Asian republics enjoy strong political, social and cultural ties with Russia. Despite that, they all jealously guard their independence. Central Asian leaders entered international politics in 1991 having little experience in dealing with non-Soviet world. Former nomenclature members after the USSR fall found themselves nationalists and set a clear course for independence and sovereignty. This meant an attempt to liberalize from Moscow's zone of influence, or at least maneuvering much more space than during Soviet times. This forced them to conduct a balancing of powers policy that started in the early 1990s and continues until now. This differentiates the regional political landscape from the pre-1991 era: the Central Asian countries, particularly Kazakhstan, are no longer passive subjects in the great powers' games[1392]; they have an empowered position and they are able to play off one another's contradictions and maximize benefits for their own sake. Central Asian elites tried to counterbalance Russia's influence by the West first, but Washington's agenda and its support for colour revolutions led Central Asians to turn toward China, a more suitable model for them. Thanks to Beijing's engagement in the region, and its credits, the republics are now able to demand higher rates from Moscow for their natural resources. Chinese policy success in this regard is even more remarkable when the initial reserve, alienation and endangered, that characterized Central Asians' approach to China in the early 1990s, is taken into account[1393].

Uzbekistan, the most populous Central Asian country, stands as a good example of the balancing policy – it has been maneuvering most spectacularly with its "'sinusoidal' policy (involving longer periods of co-operation with the West, interspersed with periods of closer relations with Moscow)"; under Islam Karimov's leadership Tashkent set a clear course for independence, distanced itself from Moscow (Uzbekistan is the only country without Russian military bases in the region) and tried to achieve leadership in Central Asia in an assertive way (that quite often meets with neighbours' opposition)[1394]. Tashkent believed that the balancing policy, sometimes in an aggressive way, is the best way of preserving its independence and sovereignty.[1395] Independence in the Uzbek style meant a public fight with "postcolonial syndrome" – desovietisation and derusification.[1396] At the same time, however, Tashkent "developed

1392 Чжао Хаушэн (Zhao Huasheng), *Новая ситуация в Центральной Азии и Шанхайская организация сотрудничества*, quoted in: А.В. Лукин, *Россия и Китай сегодня и завтра* op. cit., p. 644.

1393 A. Jarosiewicz, K. Strachota, op. cit., pp. 20-30.

1394 W. Górecki, *Even Further…*, pp. 56-57.

1395 M. Kuryłowicz, *Polityka zagraniczna Uzbekistanu wobec Rosji* [Uzbekistan's Foreign Policy Towards Russia], Kraków 2014, p. 113.

1396 W. Górecki, *Even Further…*, pp. 56-57.

cordial, albeit quiet, military ties with the United States and NATO."[1397] The interest was mutual: the USA had chosen Uzbekistan as a buffer against both Islamism and Russian expansionism. In 1999, Uzbekistan joined the GUAM (Georgia, Ukraine, Azerbaijan, Moldova), now GUUAM, an ephemeral attempt to establish a pro-Western alternative to the CIS[1398]. Nevertheless, Uzbekistan did not break its relations with Moscow – the Collective Security Treaty was established at the Tashkent summit in 1992 (in 1999 Uzbekistan pulled back and did not join the CST successor – the Collective Security Treaty Organization created in 2002).[1399] Moreover, Karimov was the first one in region who showed in public China as an alternative development model, one worth implementing in Central Asia.[1400] At the beginning of the 2000s, Karimov was the West's biggest ally; against this background ties with Russia "remained anemic."[1401] Moreover, Uzbekistan has distanced itself from integration initiatives. This all changed after the Andijan events on 13 May 2005.[1402] Karimov feared losing his power while Moscow and Beijing were able to convince him that the Andijan protestors/rebels were supported by the USA. When the Western countries condemned bloody pacification of Andijan, Moscow and Beijing supported Karimov, who thanked them by making a spectacular political turn. He quit the GUUAM in May 2005, after the SCO summit in June 2005 he demanded the Americans to leave Khanabad air base[1403] and signed an ally treaty with Moscow in 2005 that made him return to the CSTO and agree to have Russian soldiers on Uzbekistan soil.[1404] Tashkent's turn has been so spectacular that Russian President Dmitri Medvedev has called this country their "key strategic partner in Central Asia."[1405] Despite all that, Karimov has not cut all his ties with the West: the reason was Uzbekistan's economy being in such a bad shape that it needed external sources. That is why although Karimov expelled the US airbases in Khanabad, he allowed the Germans to main-

1397 C. E. Ziegler, op. cit., p. 237.

1398 V. V. Naumkin, op. cit., p. 84.

1399 *Договор о коллективной безопасности* [Joint-Security Treaty], 15.05.1992, Организация договора о коллективной безопасности. Официальный сайт.

1400 M. Brill Olcott, *Russian-Chinese…*, p. 374.

1401 C. E. Ziegler, op. cit., p. 237.

1402 The goverment surpressed the Andijan protests then, *Preliminary findings on the events in Andijan*, Uzbekistan, 13 May 2005, Organization for Security and Cooperation in Europe, 20.06.2005.

1403 *В Узбекистане закрыта американская военная база* [American Base Closes in Uzbekistan], Lenta.Ru 21.09.2005.

1404 *Договор о союзнических отношениях между Российской Федерацией и Республикой Узбекистан* [Treaty on Relations of Alliance between FR and Republic of Uzbekistan], Mid.ru, 19.07.2006.

1405 *Начало встречи с Президентом Узбекистана Исламом Каримовым* [The Beginning of Meeting with President Islam Karimov of Uzbekistan], Kremlin.ru 06.06.2008.

tain a refuelling station in Termez for the US and European air military personnel.[1406] At the same time he has been cultivating close ties with Beijing that transcended the improvement of economic relations. Uzbekistan has been the key transit country on the Chinese gas pipeline from Turkmenistan that broke the Russian monopoly in the region. Moscow has tried to keep Uzbekistan within its orbit but Tashkent's suspension of membership in the CSTO on 20 June 2012 – that demonstrated Tashkent's ambition to conduct independent policy – worsened Russian-Uzbek relations. This suspension came only two weeks after Vladimir Putin's visit; this undermined the regional image of Russia and its president.[1407] This solidified Uzbekistan's image in the Kremlin as "a prickly partner", ready "at any moment to jump into bed with the United States or China", with whom relations "have gone through many ups and downs, and remain difficult" and whom Russia would like to ignore but cannot do so given geopolitical considerations.[1408] As a result, "political relations between Moscow and Tashkent are characterized by total distrust", but Russia remains the transit monopolist for Central Asian resources to Europe and is still a vital trade partner for Uzbekistan.[1409]

When summarizing Uzbek policy, one may clearly see a permanent – better or worse – attempt to balance Russia, China and the West and keep them at arm's length – Uzbekistan's "foreign policy can be compared to pendulum motion: every two to three years, Uzbekistan turned away from Russia and other CIS partners and moved closer to the West, and vice versa."[1410] This balancing has not been as skillful as Kazakhstani (see: below): Tashkent "has managed to alienate Moscow and Washington at different times, partly because of the crudeness of its balancing, and partly because President Islam Karimov has proved a capricious 'ally.'"[1411] It remains to be seen whether Uzbekistan will be able to maintain balancing policy after Karimov's death in September 2016 and Mirziyaev's ascendence to power (after all, Mirziyaev is from the same Samarkandian clan).

Kazakhstan remains Central Asia's most important country, its economic leader, "the bright point of Central Asia", with a prosperous economy, stable society, velvet authoritarianism and Nazarbaev's effective foreign policy of balancing foreign powers.[1412] It "has been the most successful of the ex-Soviet republics judged by the criteria of political stability, economic growth, and foreign policy management."[1413] As the result, Kazakhstan has won its regional

---

1406 C. E. Ziegler, op. cit., p. 239. West's share in Uzbekistan's economy remains limited.
1407 W. Górecki, *Even Further from Moscow…*, p. 59.
1408 B. Lo, *Russia and the New World Disorder…*, pp. 121-122
1409 Ibid.
1410 M.Laumulin, *Virtual Security of Central Asia*, "Russia in Global Affairs", 7.10.2012.
1411 B. Lo, *Russia and the New World Disorder…*, p. 121.
1412 C. E. Ziegler, op. cit., p. 242.
1413 B. Lo, *Russia and the New World Disorder…*, p. 112.

rivalry with Uzbekistan over Central Asia's leadership – its stable political system, and favorable economic development has become a pattern for the region.[1414]

From Kazakhstan's very beginning of independence, Nazarbaev has maneuvered brilliantly between Moscow, Beijing and Washington and he continues to conduct a multi-vector policy until now: he has "achieved all this without, for the most part, upsetting Russian sensitivities or provoking imperial envy in Moscow – Kazakhstan remains "Russia's most reliable and useful partner among the ex-Soviet republics.'"[1415] His "multisector" policy ended with good relations with all major players and even enabled the country to play beyond its real position. Favouring regional integration projects was part of this strategy (Nazarbaev was the first to propose the creation of the Eurasian Union in 1994) – it was considered a good way to balance Chinese influences, but mostly as a nation-building process which emphasized stability, international cooperation and being a sovereign subject with global ambitions.[1416]

Astana has strong ties with Moscow – economic (most of Kazakh's oil has been transported via Russian pipelines), political and military (membership in regional organizations, presence of Russian army and Baikonur enclave) and psycho-political (protesting against democratization and human rights).[1417] In the the 1990s there were also good personal relations between Yeltsin and Nazarbaev. Nevertheless, problems such as discrimination of the Russian minority and nation-building on rejection of Soviet heritage have continued to exist and made Nazarbaev distance himself from Moscow in the 1990s. Russia was not interested in closer ties either – Yeltsin even affronted Kazakhs by not attending the official inauguration of the new capital – Astana in 1998.[1418] Although Nazarbaev indeed distanced himself from Moscow, he did it without burning bridges.

As for relations with China in the 1990s, the Uygur issue played a decisive role. Kazakhstan has the biggest population of Uygurs outside China but Astana has supported Chinese position and kept its own Uyghurs with tight grip. Nevertheless, in the quasi-free Kazakh media, pro-Uygur voices did appear, but never to an extent where they could harm relations with Beijing. Kazakhstan did not have the slightest interest in supporting Xinjiang's Uygurs – such an action might have had negative domestic implications (the transfer of separatism to Kazakhstan). The politically troublesome border with Xinjiang had, however, its economic benefits. In the 1990s Kazakhstan became China's biggest regional trade partner. Development of trade has not been disturbed by

1414 A. Wołoska, *Kazakhstan: Regional Success Story*, OSW, Warsaw 15.10.2004.

1415 B. Lo, *Russia and the New World Disorder…*, p. 113.

1416 W. Górecki, *Even Further…*, p. 78.

1417 Д. Тренин, *Post-Imperium…*, p. 180.

1418 K. Syroezhkin, *Russian policy in Central Asia: a perspective from Kazakhstan*, [in:] *Russia and Asia…*, pp. 105-106; C. E. Ziegler, op. cit., p. 242.

frictions and anti-Chinese resentments (e.g. immigration threats and complaints over the low quality of Chinese goods).[1419]

Since the 2000s, Russian-Kazak political relations have been good[1420], but economic relations remain problematic. Moscow and Astana have been divided by contradictory interests: Moscow wants to maintain its dominant position in energy transit, while Kazakhstan tries to undermine it and lesser its dependence on the Russian transit routes. The two sides are, however, able to compromise, so that "Russian-Kazakh relations can nevertheless (with some reservations) be determined as partnership-based, which cannot be said about Russia's relations with Kyrgyzstan, Tajikistan, Uzbekistan and Turkmenistan."[1421] At the same time Kazakhstan actively cooperates with the United States and with China. The USA is one of the biggest investors in this country.[1422] Thanks to a skilful foreign policy, until recently Kazakhstan has been able to "play an international role beyond its size."[1423]

The 2000s saw an impressive development of Sino-Kazakh relations, particularly in the economic sphere (increase of trade volume, especially in energy). Kazakhstan is China's biggest Central Asian neighbor and the most important Central Asian country, and since until recently it was the only country in the region to have signed a strategic partnership agreement with China[1424]. As a result, it became China's most important trade partner in the region, in terms of both import and export.[1425] Kazakhstan benefited from the increased Chinese engagement in the region and Sino-Russian stalemate over the ESPO pipeline. In 2006, the Kazakhstan-Xinjiang three thousand kilometers' long oil pipeline started operating, diversifying the Chinese need for oil from Russia.[1426] Despite this pipeline and the fact that Chinese companies have dominated the Kazakhstani upstream oil sector, most of Kazakhstani (as well as all Central Asian) oil continues to be exported via Russia.[1427] In other words, Astana played the "Chinese card" without burning bridges with Moscow.

Astana continued successful "dual-track" tactics even after the conflict in Georgia in 2008. Nazarbaev decided not to irritate Moscow by withholding Georgian investments and rejecting taking part in the NATO drills in Georgia,

---

1419 M. Brill Olcott, Russian-Chinese…, p. 394.

1420 *Договор между Российской Федерацией и Республикой Казахстан о добрососедстве и союзничестве в XXI веке* [Treaty Between RF and Republic of Kazakhstan on Good Neighborhood and Alliance in 21th Century], Kremlin.ru, 11.11.2013.

1421 Wojciech Górecki, *Even Further*…p. 79.

1422 E. A. Feigenbaum, *The Shanghai Cooperation Organization and the Future of Central Asia*, Speech at Nixon Center, Washington D.C., 6.09.2007, p. 3

1423 C. E. Ziegler, op. cit., p. 243.

1424 A. Jarosiewicz, K. Strachota, op. cit., pp. 30-32.

1425 Ibid., pp. 58-60.

1426 *Kazakhstan-China oil pipeline opens to commercial operation*, "China Daily", 12.07.2006.

1427 Marcin Kaczmarski, *Russia-China Relations*…, p. 92.

but at the same time intensified actions aimed at diversification of deliveries.[1428] Kazakhstan has been promoting the Russian project of the Eurasian Union, but at the same time set the boundaries for this process and is distancing from Moscow.[1429] From the Astana perspective, the Eurasian Union is a security net against too much dependence from China.[1430] However, after Russian actions in Ukraine, Kazakh's anxieties over Russian dominance resurfaced[1431], despite the official backing of the Kremlin's policy.[1432]

To sum up, one may say that so far Kazakhstan has been the biggest beneficiary of Sino-Russian-US rivalry in Central Asia. Thanks to a wise balancing policy Astana has maintained good relations with all of them and thus gained a lot. In the changing circumstances of the intensified Russian integration policy, emergence of an alternative Chinese project and succession isuue combined with recent systemic changes in the Kazakhstani system of power, however, the question is whether Kazakhstan will be able to maintain its independent, successful policy.

Turkmenistan was self-isolated in the 1990s and became important in Central Asian policy in the 2000s. In the 1990s, Turkmenbashi-Niyazov's Turkmenistan had been another rhetorically anti-Russian state in Central Asia. Turkmenbashi, an unusual political figure, has tried to conduct an independent policy ("permanent neutrality").[1433] Anti-Russian rhetoric did not disturb him from selling gas to Moscow (Turkmenistan remains Central Asia's biggest reservoir of gas) for very little which allowed Gazprom to re-sell it to European markets for much more. It helped Turkmenbashi to isolate the country and proceed with more and more grotesque social engineering based on his personality cult. Until his death in 2006, relations with Moscow concentrated on gas, whereas relations with Beijing – although correct – did not reach noticeable dynamics. This changed after Turkmenbashi's death in 2006. His successor, Gurbanguli Berdimukhamedov changed the isolationist policy of his predecessor and dynamically started seeking new partners to make himself independent from Russia.[1434] Although Berdimukhamedov has not departed from neutralism and isolationism fully, he allowed foreign investment in the economy's most important sector: gas exploration. His goal was to internationalize cooperation to liberate Turkmenistan from Russian dominance in gas delivery. Berdimukhamedov still sells gas mostly to Russia, but the "gas conflict" in April

1428 K. Kozłowski, *Państwo Środka a Nowy Jedwabny…*, p. 253.

1429 W. Górnicki, *Even Further from Moscow…*, p. 79.

1430 A. Jarosiewicz, K. Strachota, op. cit., pp. 30-60.

1431 A. Jarosiewicz, *Kazakhstan's attitude towards integration with Russia: less love, more fear*, OSW, Warsaw 26.05.2014.

1432 B. Lo, *Russia and the New World Disorder…*, p. 113.

1433 *Permanent Neutrality of Turkmenistan*, United Nations. Resolutions Adopted by the General Assembly, A/RES/50/80.

1434 K. Kozłowski, *Państwo Środka a Nowy Jedwabny…*, p. 254.

2009 made him realize the necessity of diversification – Turkmenistan suffered from this conflict more than Russia did.[1435] Ashkhabad faced a dilemma: whether to subordinate to Russia or seek new sources of income. The Chinese extended a helping hand at the decisive point by offering a USD4 billion load for future gas deliveries. This was a breakthrough: the finalization of gas contract in 2009 (Central Asia-China gas pipeline that goes from Turkmenistan via Uzbekistan and Kazakhstan to China) that broke the Russian monopoly in the region.[1436] Since then, the ties between Ashkhabad and Beijing have been becoming more and more close – Turkmeni policymakers look toward China now.[1437] During Xi Jinping's September 2013 visit to Central Asia new gas agreements, that monopolized Turkmeni gas resources, have been signed which "have finalized the process whereby China has replaced Russia as Turkmenistan's patron and main sponsor."[1438]

Two remaining Central Asian countries – Tajikistan and Kyrgyzstan – clearly fall behind. **Tajikistan** is closely linked to Russia via historical, cultural and social ties and the Russian military presence (that will remain there for the next 20 years).[1439] This state has been the most vulnerable and unstable in the region, the least well governed, it has undertaken the most painful transformation and it has had the biggest number of islamic fundamentalists.[1440] Tajikistan's most traumatic experience was the civil war in 1992-1997.[1441] It ended with a compromise between the fighting sides: the opposition gained access to power (30%) whereas Russia remained the guarantor of the country's stability.[1442] Consequently, since then Tajikistan remains Moscow's closer ally and has been in a state of strong dependency from Russia.[1443] Like other countries of the region, Tajikistan used the US intervention in Afghanistan to strengthen its position: it allowed the USA to use Tajik airports and air zones. Moscow, however, backfired. Until now the Kremlin's favorite tactic has been a carrot and stick approach. Hydro energy and Tajik guest workers in Russia (the most important part of economy – their income covers 47% of Tajikistan's GDP and ranks it in the first place in the world in this category) are the effective instruments of Russian influence. Thanks to these factors, despite Tajik attempts to maneuver (such as rejection of Moscow's proposal to put Russian soldiers on

1435 W. Górecki, *Even Further from Moscow…*, pp. 60-64.

1436 A. Petersen, K. Barysch, op. cit., p. 3.

1437 Ibid.

1438 A. Jarosiewicz, *Chinese tour de force...*

1439 *Russians Continue to Guard the Tajik Border with Afghanistan*, Satrapia. The Gazette of Central Asia, 21.09.2012.

1440 K. Strachota, *Tadżykistan: czas próby* [Tajikistan: Test Time], Warsaw, OSW working paper no. 15, 10/2004.

1441 Ibid.

1442 M. Olimov, *The policy of Russia in Central Asia: a perspective from Tajikistan* [in:] *Russia and Asia*…p. 121.

1443 W. Górecki, *Even Further from Moscow…*, p. 46.

the Tajik-Afghan border), Russia maintains the dominant position in Tajikistan. Although the "Rakhmon regime's near-total dependence on Russian support undercut its leverage" in dealings with Russia, Dushanbe, however, is able to secure some benefits from the Kremlin by "threatening Russia with weakness, playing on fears about regime collapse and regional destabilization (...) in these circumstances, Moscow believes that it has no choice but to maintain substantial assistance to Tajikistan."[1444] China, which has been building roads and investing twice as much as Russia in Tajikistan, has been becoming Dushanbe's almost equally important partner. This came with a price, though: in 2002 Tajikistan ceded thousand kilometers in Pamir to China in return for dropping the claim for 28 thousands km².[1445] This decision evoked anti-Chinese resentments in Tajik society. Tajikistan, like Kyrgyzstan, maintains good relations with Russia and China alike to hamper the regional power ambitions of Uzbekistan and such Tashkent's belligerent moves as closing of the borders[1446]. Tajikistan remains an outlet for Chinese goods (consumers goods and machines; China exports mainly resources and scrap metal).[1447] How will Tajikistan use the competition between Russian and Chinese integration projects remains to been seen. Balancing may become beyond its capabilities.

Kyrgyzstan has remained another weak Central Asian country. It has been the most democratic country in the region and (perhaps because of it) one of poorest and most unstable countries of the region and at the same time a place where the interests of Russia, China and the USA cross. China is Bishkek's main trade partner (2/3 of all imports), while Russia remains the most important political partner. Kyrgyzstan's first president, Askar Akaev initially sought to turn to the West which enthusiastically supported his efforts to introduce democracy, liberalization and "transform his country into 'the Switzerland of Central Asia'"[1448]; he even called it, bafflingly, "the country of the human rights" (!)[1449]. Soon, however, he resigned from these, potentially dangerous for his regime, experiments and returned to his good, old authoritarian ways. He governed badly, though – the country sunk into corruption, nepotism and malaise. In his foreign policy, Akaev initially sought to balance Russia with the Western influence. With time, however, he became more and more compliant and did not question the pro-Moscow *status quo* in the region. As for China, Kyrgyzstan as a border country was naturally interested in develop-

---

1444 B. Lo, *Russia and the New World Disorder...*, p. 126.

1445 *Рахмон отдал Китаю тысячу квадратных километров Таджикской земли* [Rakhmon gave China back a thousand kilometers of Tajikistan's land], Tajik News 21.01.2011.

1446 E. Azarkan, op. cit., p. 414.

1447 A. Jarosiewicz, K. Strachota, China vs. Central Asia ..., pp. 32-43 and 61.

1448 C. E. Ziegler, op. cit., p. 241.

1449 *Аскар Акаев провозглашает Киргизию страной прав человека* [Akaev Announces Kyrgyzstan a country of human rights], Фергана.News, 22.10.2002.

ing relations, particularly the economic ones. The increase in the bilateral volume of trade in the 1990s was impressive: China became Bishkek's fourth trade partner; in 1997 alone the volume increased by 47% in comparison with the previous year; in the 1990s Kyrgyzstan – thanks to border trade – became China's second Central Asian partner (after Kazakhstan).[1450.]

In the 2000s, Kyrgyzstan went through two upheavals (the revolutions/*coups d'état* in 2005 and in 2010), two dictatorships (Akaev's and Bakiev's) and ethnic clashes (Uzbek pogroms). The Tulip Revolution from 2005 resulted in Kurmanbek Bakiev taking over power. Like his predecessor, he continued to give the green light for existing and stationing Russian and American bases alike (for a long time Kyrgyzstan had been the only country in the world to have them both) – for the USA Kyrgyzstan mattered because of the need to provide supplies to Afghanistan. Moscow has pushed Bakiev to close the American base in Manas and in January 2009 he announced this decision. However, already in June 2009, he changed his mind and enraged Moscow by allowing Americans to stay (he changed the name "air base" to a "transit point" and increased the lease three times, to 60 billion USD).[1451] Moscow revenged this by introducing a 100% export toll for oil[1452] and by endorsing the 2010 revolution that overthrew him. The current president of Kyrgyzstan is Almazbek Atambayev, who took the office on 1st December 2011. He tried to maneuver with the Manas base, too. Finally, however, he yielded in 2013; the base was closed in June 2014. Since Bakiev's removal Russia's influence has been increasing – Moscow is steadily making Kyrgyzstan more and more dependent, despite balancing attempts by the Kyrgyz elites.[1453] As for Kyrgyz-Chinese relations, trade naturally dominates – the Kyrgyzstan-China volume of trade surpasses that of Kyrgyzstan-Russia three times.[1454] Kyrgyzstan is an outlet for Chinese goods (consumption goods, equipment, machineries; all financed by Chinese loans) but has a negative trade balance.[1455] Should the New Silk Road materialize, it is likely to increase. Besides, anti-Chinese resentments are visible in Kyrgyzstan (social anti-Chinese anxieties hamper the economic relations between Beijing and Bishkek); that is why Bishkek tried to balance Chinese influence with good relations with Russia (see: joining the Eurasian Union). Moscow agreed on this, due to being "anxious about China's expanding footprint", although subsiding Kyrgyzstan "does

1450 M. Brill Olcott, *Russian-Chinese…*, pp. 392-400.

1451 *In Reversal, Kyrgyzstan Won't Close a U.S. Base*, "The New York Times", 23.06.2009.

1452 *Путин: Бакиев наступает на те же самые грабли* [Putin: Bakiev stand on the same rakes], Вести.Ru, 07.04.2010.

1453 W. Górecki, *Even Further from Moscow…*, pp. 26-40.

1454 C. E. Ziegler, op. cit., p. 242.

1455 A. Jarosiewicz, K. Strachota, op. cit., pp. 60-61.

not come cheap, the anticipated strategic dividends and psychological comfort make the expense worthwhile for the Kremlin."[1456]

Finally, there is also **Mongolia.** Although it is not a Central Asian country by the region's narrowr definition, it can be understood to be so in the wider form. This is a country with probably the most difficult geopolitical location in the world.[1457] Mongols have learned to play Moscow and Beijing off one another, to win contradictions between them and to keep an equal distance. Most importantly, they've tried to find "a third neighbour"[1458], which unfortunately did not work out. Mongolia therefore needs to balance Russia and China, and so far it has done it successfully.[1459] For Ulan Bator in the 1990s, distancing from Moscow (with the withdrawal of 100,000 Russian troops in 1992) did not mean intensifications of relations with Beijing (the ethnic friction in Inner Mongolia as well as mutual prejudice made any real normalization impossible). As for China, it considers Mongolia "a country only temporarily independent which should return to their supervision"[1460] and given the size of China there are "strict limits to Mongolia's ability to alter the rules of the game that China has set."[1461] Xi Jinping's 2014 visit to Mongolia (the first one in eleven years), officially called by China "visiting relatives", may be understood this way.[1462] Fortunately for Ulan Bator, so far the Chinese tactics in Mongolia has been patient: "China has had the luxury of just waiting for the ripe fruit to fall into its hands."[1463] Given the decreasing geopolitical options for Ulan Bator, Mongolia realistically has no choice – the most natural option seems to be leaning to Russia, considered a lesser evil.[1464] Mongolia has tried this by its "skip China" strategy of building a railway to Russian seaports instead of the Chinese ones (much shorter and cheaper).[1465] But relying on Russia is very controversial in Mongolia –Mongolians are unwilling to agree with the Russian saying that "one old friend is better than two new ones."[1466] Russia itself does not make this decision easier. Russia's "bulldozer tactics certainly hampered its image as a self-proclaimed friend of the Mongolian people" –

1456 B. Lo, *Russia and the New World Disorder*..., p. 126.

1457 B. Niedziński, *Czy Mongolia powinna odejść od balansowania między Rosją a Chinami?* [Should Mongolia leave its balancing policy between Russia and China], polska-azja.pl 27.06.2014.

1458 *Mongolia's 'Third Neighbour' Foreign Policy*, Asia Society, 23.06.2013.

1459 B. Niedziński, *Czy Mongolia powinna odejść*...

1460 Ibid.

1461 S. Radchenko, *Sino-Russian Competition Competition in Mongolia*, "The Asian Forum" 22.11.2013.

1462 *Visiting Relatives and Friends to Discuss Cooperation Joining Hands to Develop a Better Future*, MFAPRC, 22.08.2014.

1463 S. Radchenko, op. cit.

1464 B. Niedziński, *Czy Mongolia powinna odejść*....

1465 Yu Bin, *Russia's Pride and China's Power*, "Comparative Connections" vol. 16, no.3.

1466 S. Radchenko, *Sino-Russian Competition*...

Moscow has supported the pro-Russian candidate for presidency Nambaryn Enkhbayar in the 2009 elections; not only did he lose, but ended up in prison for corruption.[1467]

So far Moscow and Beijing have been happy to maintain a balance in Mongolia: "they have been very careful with respect to each other's positions in Mongolia; neither is openly calling the other a 'competitor'. (…) instead, the Sino-Russian competition is more like shadow boxing, with each trying to undercut the other's interests but only indirectly. Unfortunately for Russia, it is almost certain to lose this match, simply because it is in the wrong weight category. The Sino-Russian relationship today is a throwback to Nerchinsk and Kyakhta, and will certainly not change in Russia's favour."[1468]

To summarize these descriptions with the post-crisis landscape, the years after the economic crisis of 2008 have intensified Russian and Chinese actions in the region and weakened Central Asian republics' position *vis-à-vis* Russia and China respectively. That meant Kyrgyzstan and Tajikistan are *de facto* dependent on Russian help. Moscow has also retained significant influence over Kyrgyzstani and Tajikistani energy sectors.[1469] Thus, the weaker Central Asian states, Kyrgyzstan and Tajikistan were subordinated politically by Russia. Central Asia's strongest countries Kazakhstan, Uzbekistan and Turkmenistan, however, have been able to secure to bigger or lesser extent a great dose of their independence by maneuvering between Moscow and Beijing. Mongolia still balances China and Russia's influences but is likely to be dominated by China.

7. *Between New Great Game and Sino-Russian Condominium*

Since 2008, China has been engaging with Central Asia more and more boldly. It has "secured access to the bulk of natural resources and managed to significantly increase its economic profile", Russia in turn has "lost its pre-eminence, but held on to its dominant position in the areas of politics and security".[1470] These new political realities of a more assertive China and uncompromising Russia have been best symbolized by their integration projects: China's 2013 the "Silk Road Economic Belt", or the "New Silk Road" and Russia's Eurasian Union. Thus, two contradictory integration concepts emerged that best illustrate the growing competition between Russia and China in Central Asia, called by a catchy phrase "new Great Game". So far Moscow and Beijing were

1467 Ibid.; B. Niedziński, *Czy Mongolia powinna odejść…*.
1468 S. Radchenko, op. cit.
1469 M.Kaczmarski, *Russia-China Relations…*, p. 92.
1470 Ibid., p. 86.

able to manage their competition and create a kind of joint great powers' condominium. It remains to be seen, however, whether they are able to maintain this *status quo*.

International relations in Central Asia have induced many researchers to call the geopolitical realities there "a new Great Game."[1471] According to this narrative, this new great powers' competition started with the US incursion into the region in 2001. From the perspective of 2017, the US presence in the region proved to be temporary, while a more and more assertive Russia and China have remained on the battlefield and are bound to clash in the future. This narrative is challenged by an alternative one that claims that so far Moscow and Beijing are able to maintain compromise and that their cooperation outweighs competition – thus "a new *status quo* has emerged in Central Asia."[1472]

As long as the United States remained in the region, Sino-Russian interests were perfectly converged. With Washington's pulling out, however, contradictions became more and more visible. The economic crisis strengthened China's position in the region (Beijing became the region's largest trading partner) and showed Russia's inability to help Central Asians economically. This strengthened the potential for Russia-China competition: Russian regional dominance in security is difficult to reconcile with Chinese economic expansion in the long term. Energy is the most famous ground for competition: China was able to break the Russian monopoly on the delivery of oil and gas by constructing a pipeline from Kazakhstan in 2006 and the three spur Central Asia-China gas pipeline from Turkmenistan via Uzbekistan and Kazakhstan. Before the economic crisis, the region was locked in by Russia in the energy sector, after the crisis China was able to successfully launch "a full scale expansion in the energy sector" that had two effects on Russia-China relations: new pipelines deprived Russia of its monopoly on the transit of Central Asian gas and China "locked in Central Asian gas supplies for its own needs, replacing Russia in this role."[1473] Moreover, the growing trade volume between China and Central Asia, as well as Beijing's financial engagement there weakened Russia's position.

This all caused the intensification of Russian attempts to integrate the post-Soviet area, in Central Asia this is best illustrated by the strengthening of the security sphere (such as amendments to the CSTO's status that give Moscow the right of veto of a possible deployment of other states' armies in the region). Moreover, Moscow attempted to capitalize on anti-Chinese resentments in the

1471 A. Rashid, *The New Great Game – the Battle for Central Asia's Oil*, "Far Eastern Economic Review" 10.04.1997; M. E. Ahrari, *The New Great Game in Muslim Central Asia*, University Press of Pacific 2002; R. Mullerson, *Central Asia: A Chessboard and Player in the New Great Game*, New York, Columbia University Press 2007; A.Cooley, *Great Games, Local Rules: The New Great Power Contest in Central Asia*, Oxford University Press, 2012.

1472 M. Kaczmarski, *Russia-China Relations…*, p. 86.

1473 Ibid., p. 89.

region (resulting from settling the border issue – most of the countries had to concede to Beijing's wishes; and from fear of the long-term economic impact of Chinese influence and distrust of Chinese intensions) – as result elites and (even more) societies of Central Asia are still oriented towards Russia.

The most visible sign, however, was economic reintegration, best symbolized by the Eurasian Union: "Putin's flagship project"[1474], so far the most sophisticated – and successful – integration process in the post-Soviet area. It was motivated by pure political, not economic, ideas: intended to maintain Russia's great power status, counterweight the EU and China economic expansion, as well as loosening of the CIS-Russia ties.[1475] This is the best example of Russian "pseudomultilateralism", more subtle than in Soviet times (yet less effective from the Kremlin's point of view), where the "line between the bilateral and the multilateral effectively disappeared" and Moscow dominates: "formally, decisions are reached on the basis of consensus, but in practice the consensus that matters is the one in Moscow."[1476] In other words, this is the best example of attempts to secure a "Russocentric cultural sphere" in the post-Soviet area.[1477] The Eurasian Union, a hybrid of the European Union and the Soviet Union, in Russian plans is supposed to become the bridge that links Europe with Asia-Pacific. This was very bad news for China. Should the Eurasian Union achieve success, the consequences for Beijing would be negative: rising tariffs and institutional barriers to China's trade with Central Asia, threatening the plan to make Central Asia China's corridor to Europe (especially evident in case of Kyrgyzstan), obstacles for Chinese companies in doing business with Central Asia and possibly even limitation on access to the region's energy resources.[1478]

That is why China has different plans: its own integration idea called the "Silk Road Economic Belt" (later on called One Belt One Road), popularly called "the New Silk Road". This plan does not oppose Russian integration projects directly, but in reality it poses a challenge to them: Beijing at minimum does not want to be pushed out from the region; at most it wants to dominate the region.

Xi Jinping's visit to Central Asia in September 2013 inaugurated the New Silk Road plan, the best symbol of China's new assertiveness in the region. It ended the evolution of China's Central Asia policy – from calm, steady, conservative, hidden behind Moscow's backs in the 1990s through to more and

1474 I. Wiśniewska, *Eurasian integration. Russian attempt at the economic unification of the post-Soviet area*, OSW, Warsaw 30.07.2013; A. Jarosiewicz, K. Strachota, op. cit., pp. 21-30.

1475 *Концепция внешней политики Российской Федерации* [FR Foreign Policy Concept], Mid.ru, 18.02.2013.

1476 B. Lo, *Russia and the New World Disorder*…, p. 80.

1477 G. Rozman, *The Sino-Russian Challenge*…, p. 115

1478 M. Kaczmarski, *Russia-China Relations*…, p. 98.

more active: first directed at containing US influences and then towards liberating itself from Moscow in the energy sector, to Xi Jinping's "tour de force" in September 2013.[1479] Formally the Chinese initiative is not anti-Russian: Beijing as before tries to avoid direct confrontation with Moscow and still does not question Russia's political primacy over the region. China "respects traditional Russian interests in the region", and accepts – as Li Fenglin put it – that "Central Asia is Russia's backyard", but "one has to care about its own backyard, water the plants so that it does not get weedy."[1480] In accordance with this logic, China concentrates on gaining advantage via economic means instead: "having actively pursued its interests in the sphere of energy, Beijing showed tangible restraint with regard to the security realm and maintained its practical engagement in security issues at low levels (…) Beijing tacitly accepted Russia's security pre-eminence in Central Asia and Moscow's military posturing was not regarded as threatening by the Chinese; China did not object to Moscow building up its security and defence presence, nor did Beijing display any aspiration to play an independent role as region's security provider."[1481]

Nevertheless, the New Silk Road is against Russian interests, particularly against the Eurasian Union. The new Silk Road is its opposition: it does not require political integration, it is only a kind of political superstructure for numerous bilateral investments. China just wants to make Central Asia a geopolitical conveyor belt for Chinese goods to the West. This in turn requires developing ties, instead of creating barriers, like the Eurasian Union does.

The New Silk Road raises the risk of Central Asian republics "being annexed into the Chinese sphere of influence" which is the exact opposite to Russian interests. Moreover, development of economic relations between powerful China and weaker Central Asian countries is "inevitably leading to a situation where the Central Asian states are, to varying degrees, falling into political dependence on China, which in some cases is even taking on a neo-colonial character."[1482] The question whether China succeeds and whether it is able to accommodate Russia, remains open. Beijing has already showed that it has ways to bypass the Eurasian Union's regulations.[1483] On the other hand, Moscow proved that it can block Chinese plans in the region (by blocking the development of railways to China). Thus, a very complicated and nuanced political picture emerges in Central Asia. The followers of the "new Great Game" narrative would say that Moscow and Beijing under the presence of cooperation and convergence began a hidden competition to dominate Eurasia and that it will be Central Asia where their "strategic partnership" will finally break,

1479 A. Jarosiewicz, *Chinese tour de force …*

1480 Quoted in: А.В. Лукин, *Россия и Китай сегодня и завтра…*, p. 647.

1481 Marcin Kaczmarski, *Russia-China Relations…*, p. 94.

1482 A. Jarosiewicz, *Chinese tour de force…*

1483 A. Jarosiewicz, K. Strachota, op. cit., p. 62.

being destroyed by conflicting interests. Dramatic events in Ukraine have only added dynamism to this process. It is too early to estimate the final result – rivalry or cooperation are both possible with many interim options.[1484]

What is certain for now is that both Russia and China want to avoid confrontation and find a way to reconcile their interests. In accordance with this logic, "a peculiar division of influence has emerged"[1485] as Russia and China are striving to achieve "a stable division of labour."[1486] In other words, China and Russia have designated their zones of influences in the best concert of powers scenario: Moscow took security whereas Beijing economics. Moscow has been tolerating this new state of affairs, albeit with difficulties, since China's entry to region has unintentionally fulfilled Moscow's strategic goal of keeping the West in general and the EU in particular, away from Central Asia. Thus, Moscow decided that Beijing is a lesser evil. Russia has concealed its consent to a condominium in the region by evoking the Greater Eurasia concept which, in practical terms, equals to "Moscow's *de facto* abandonment of its attempts to block China's economic expansion in Central Asia."[1487] Russia, again, has made a virtue out of necessity and tried to use the OBOR project for its purposes: to place itself as "a bridge between Europe and Asia" that promotes a "dialogue between civilizations" in which "Russia plays a pivotal role by virtue of its geographical location, historical antecedents, and close ties with Europe, Central Asia, and China"; this tacticly "represents a form of soft balancing" which "serves the purpose of positioning Russia as the indispensable power."[1488] The results are, however, so far dissatisfying: despite attempts to link OBOR and Eurasian Union (e.g. create a trade agreement) "nothing really happened" in 2016: "the two sides were simply unable to find any mechanism to link the Chinese and Russian visions for Eurasian integration": Putin proposed a "broader economic partnership between the EAEU, the SCO, and the ASEAN" (Greater Eurasian Partnership), while the Chinese were busy at advocating OBOR; in the end the former remains a vision whereas the latter is still in its early stages.[1489] Despite an inability to link the OBOR and the EAEU (yet), according to Zhao Huasheng, the real value of the decision to link those projects is political.[1490] Consequently, Russia and China kept their relations stable.

1484 W. Rodkiewicz, *The Turn to the East…*, pp. 20-21.

1485 M. Kaczmarski, *Russia-China Relations…*, p. 92.

1486 A. Gabuev, *Friends with Benefits?…*

1487 M. Kaczmarski, W. Rodkiewicz, *Russia's Greater Eurasia and China's New Silk Road: adaptation instead of competition*, OSW, Warsaw 21.07.2016

1488 B. Lo, *Russia and the New World Disorder…*, p. 51.

1489 Yu Bin, *Politics of "Reluctand…* pp.129-144. On the other hand, Russian and Chinese dissedents are not rushing up to find a concrete agreement about functioning of the OBOR and the EAEU, I. Bond, op. cit.

1490 Zhao Huasheng, *Zhong'e guanxi zhibian le ma?* [Has there been a change in the nature of China-Russia relations?], 2016, Quoted in: M. Duchâtel, op.cit.

All these developments led to the "emergence of a new *status quo* in Central Asia; the new configuration has been far from optional from either Moscow or Beijing, but has nevertheless been satisfactory enough to remove Central Asia from the list of pressing problems"; so far "Russia and China have managed to steer their relations in Central Asia off a collision course and found a *modus vivendi*, despite fundamental shifts in the material distribution of power."[1491] It remains to be seen whether they can maintain this state of affairs.

1491 M. Kaczmarski, *Russia-China Relations…*, pp. 100-101.

Part Five: Asia-Pacific: Overshadowed by China

In the Asia-Pacific region politics has almost always been viewed through the bluntly realist lens of immediate material interests and military security. Perhaps it is because Asia-Pacific has traditionally been the arena of the clash of interests of great powers– "interactions between states have been characterized by constant competition and often outright hostility (…) zero-sum calculus and the balance of power have greater currency (here) than anywhere else on the planet" which, combined with the fact that there is no collective regional identity or tradition of cooperation, makes it "the ultimate geopolitical arena."[1492]

1. China's and Russia's Profile in Asia-Pacific

The positions of Russia and China in Asia-Pacific have been diametrically different. In Asia-Pacific, China has traditionally been "the Middle Kingdom", the central country for regional political, economic and cultural relations, the reference point for all major interests, hopes and anxieties, the regional power, which main interests are located here. It was here where Sinocentric world of tianxia existed before and dominated the pre-modern East Asian international relations.[1493] Nowadays, China considers itself an Asian country and the most important Asia player that is on the way to bringing the old system back.

Since the 1990s, Beijing has been building its position in Asia, usually by economic means which granted it pre-eminence.[1494] Beijing was able to convince Asia-Pacific states of its benign intentions, best illustrated by peaceful rise/development slogan.[1495] Since the late 2000s and the early 2010s, however, China has become more assertive, which led to growing tensions, particularly in the South China Sea and resulted in the US pivot to Asia, as well as hedging polices of China's neighbours (Burma/Myanmar, Vietnam, Philippines, Indonesia). Consequently, Beijing's achievements of the previous decades have been partly reversed.[1496] Nevertheless, China remains the most relevant Asia-Pacific country and the rise of China as the greatest regional power makes it the most important long-term political phenomenon in Asia-Pacific.

1492 B. Lo, *The Axis of Convenience…*, p. 117.
1493 M. Mancall, *China at the Center…*, pp. 3-38.
1494 D. Shambaugh, *China Goes Global: The Partial Power*, Oxford University Press 2013, pp. 108-113.
1495 *Full Text: China's Peaceful Development Road….*
1496 D. Shambaugh, *China Goes Global…*, pp. 113-114.

Against this background, Russia that "is in Asia, but is not of Asia", pales into insignificance.[1497] Russia has been "overshadowed by China" in Asia-Pacific.[1498] After the USSR's fall, Russia ceased to be an Asian power and since it has never been an important economic actor in Asia, its ways of influence (like military position) decreased further or even disappeared. The Russian position was handicapped due to two reasons: first by domestic weakness and inability to attract investments to the Asian part of Russia and second by lack of wider foreign policy in the region. Consequently, Russia's cooperation with Asia-Pacific was mainly limited to arms sales.

In the 1990s, Russia became secondary power not only to the USA, but also to China or to Japan. Moreover, Moscow traditionally considered Asia as a less important policy vector than Europe, particularly in the 1990s: "Kozyrev paid little attention to Asian affairs and almost everywhere in Asia receded into the background. As a result not only were ties with former Soviet ideological, political and military allies such as Vietnam or North Korea both changed in substance and severely curtailed in scope and intensity, but even relations with India, a major political and trade partner in Asia since the mid-1950s, went into decline."[1499] Russia itself in the 1990s has been perceived in Asia as a European state, worse – a colonial one.[1500] By looking for its place in Asia and dreaming the old dream of being a superpower, Russia has tried to play a role no longer possible; hence it became a regional outsider.

It begun to change after the nomination of Yevgeni Primakov, who increased the status of Asia-Pacific in Russian foreign policy conception from the 6th place to the 3rd one. Moscow has been trying to improve its position in the region by evoking methods of selective engagement on bilateral grounds, successful in the West, as well as by trying to join Asian integration economic and security processes.[1501] China was key in this strategy: privileged relations with China were intended to increase Moscow's possibilities of political maneuvering in Asia and beyond. China's choice, however, was not the result of a calculated strategy, but a logical consequence of failed attempts to initiate a closer cooperation with other countries or to formulate wider political strategy for the region – in the 1990s "China has been Russia's only real option for cooperation in Asia"[1502] as well as "a factor of strengthening Russian position against the USA."[1503]

1497 B. Lo, *The Axis of Convenience*..., p. 57.
1498 L. Buszynski, op. cit., p. 266.
1499 G. Chufrin, op. cit., p. 475.
1500 S. Bieleń, op. cit., p. 304.
1501 М. Л. Титаренко, *Россия лицом к Азии* [Russia Turns Its Face to Asia], Москва 1998, p. 304.
1502 S. W. Garnett, op. cit., p. 6.
1503 M. G. Nosov, *Russian-US Relations in Asia-Pacific*, [in:] *Russia and Asia*..., p. 353; S. Bieleń, op. cit., p. 305.

So again the "Western factor" appeared in the Russian policy: Moscow considered its Asian politics as a counterbalance to marginalization in the European affairs and to global dominance of the USA. It was best shown by initiatives such as Primakov's idea of Moscow-Beijing-Delhi triangle to balance US influences. Then, however, neither China nor India was enthusiastic about this proposal. Moreover, China in Russian plans was intended to help increase Russia's role in regional structures, such as the APEC, the ASEAN or the ASEM. Although, indeed, China backed Russia's bid to the APEC (1998) and to the ASEAN Regional Forum (1996) (Russia was accepted in the ASEM only in 2010), when it came to concrete, real support to strengthen Russian weak positions in Asia, China did little. Russian-Chinese rapprochement has not become a "Far Eastern Rapallo."[1504] For China, Russia in Asia-Pacific mattered only as an element of maintaining balance in the region and counterweight for US factor, but real Chinese and Russian interests in the region were contradicted. With the exception of hoping to avoid conflict in the Korea Peninsula, China and Russia had little in common in East Asia. China has not become Russia's "door keeper" in Asia: a country that helps Moscow to regain its power position in the region. China was doing little to help Russia in Asia: Beijing simply had no interests in this scenario.[1505] Beijing "does not want to 'share' Russia with others" – it wants Russian resources and not to assist a (re)entry of Russia to Asia-Pacific.[1506]

2. *Taiwan*

Taiwan is a different matter that needs to be described, yet it is difficult to be orderly placed within the structure of this book; thus, it will be, a bit separately, covered here. The rebellious island has always been a vulnerable point for Beijing: Taiwan issue has been the central and fundamental domestic and international point of reference for Beijing, while preventing Taiwan's declaration of independence remains top priority. Beijing tries to isolate Taiwan and demands from all its partners fulfilling basic requirement: accepting the "one China" policy[1507]. Russia was not different here, though initially there was a significant crack.

Yeltsin's new administration at the beginning was skeptical about China. Taiwan, on the other hand, was considered by some Russian politicians as a progressive, democratic country. The Taiwanese realized the opportunity and

1504 J. W. Garner, *A Far Eastern Rapallo: the post cold-war Russian-Chinese strategic partnership*, "Проблемы Далнего Востока" 1998, № 1, pp. 53-62.

1505 L. Buszynski, op. cit., p. 269.

1506 B. Lo, *The Axis of Convenience…*, p. 120.

1507 Wang Jisi, *China's Changing Role in Asia*, [in]: *The Rise of China and a Changing East Asian Order*, ed. Kokubun Ryosei, Wang Jisi, Tokyo 2004, pp. 3-21.

started lobbying for recognition. They won a supportive ally – Oleg Lobov, Yeltsin's old friend. Lobov used the structural chaos in the newly existing state as well as his old acquaintance with Yeltsin. On 2 September 1992 Lobov got from – a not quite aware – Yeltsin his consent to set up the Moscow-Taipei Coordination Commission on Economic and Cultural Cooperation, financed by Taipei, with diplomatic status, Russian civil servants and the right to issue visas.[1508] Beijing's reaction was excessively harsh: Chinese threatened to cancel the Russian-Chinese summit. This forced Yeltsin to announce a decree on 15 September where he confirmed the "one China policy."[1509] This counterplotted Lobov's plans – at that time he was already conducting a semi-official visit to Taiwan. Despite this failure, Lobov did not give in and continued lobbying for Taipei. In June 1993 he was able to open the Moscow-Taipei Coordination Commission on Economic and Cultural Cooperation in Moscow and Yeltsin called him up to serve as the head of Russian office in Taipei.[1510] In the meantime, however, Russian learned the Chinese rules of the game and understood that it was not worth it to sacrifice relations with the Big Dragon for relations with the Little Dragon.[1511] They postponed the opening of the Taipei office and started isolating the Moscow office.[1512] Due to these delays, Russian office in Taipei was opened only in December 1996, which was a clear sign of a change in the Russian agenda. In the mid 1990s, Russia and China finally worked out an unwritten understanding on the Taiwan issue: Russia would not make any steps in favour of recognizing Taiwain, whereas China would not oppose development of unofficial and economic relations.[1513]

In the mid 1990s, Taiwan found itself an extravagant ally in Russia – Vladimir Zhirinovski, the leader of the LDPR. Zhirinovski has tried to raise the Taiwain issue a few times, but it is uncertain whether that was a genuine political move or another public show. The latter is more probable, and it ended up this way.[1514] In the meantime the official Russian policy had been becoming more and more pro-Chinese. In November 1998, Yeltsin announced the "four no" policy towards Taiwan.[1515] A full pro-Beijing turn occurred in parallel with

1508 А. В. Лукин, *Китай: медьведь наблюдает…*, p. 431.

1509 *Указ Президента РФ об отношениях между Российской Федерацией и Тайванем* (FR President's Decree on Relations with Taiwan),Kremlin.ru, 15.09,1992.

1510 S. Rigger, *The Taiwan Issue and the Sino-Russian Strategic Partnership. The View from Beijing*, [w:] *The Future of China-Russia…*, p. 314.

1511 C. Tubilewicz, *The Little Dragon and the Bear: Russian-Taiwanese Relations in the Post-Cold War Period*, "Russian Review", no 61, 4/2002, p. 282.

1512 J. L. Wilson, *China, Russia…*, p. 296.

1513 А. В. Лукин, *Китай: медьведь наблюдает…*, p. 463.

1514 Ibid., p. 454.

1515 No for "two China" or "One China and one Taiwan"; no for Taiwan's independence; no for Taiwain's Entry to International Organization under the state name; no for arms sales to Taiwan, Российско-китайские отношения на пороге XXI века (*Совместное заявление по итогам российско-китайской встречи на высшем уровне*, [Russian-Sino Relations

equal Russian-Taiwanese disappointment. Taipei understood that there were no chances for Russian recognition and lost its interest in economic cooperation with Moscow. Russia on its side was unable to create favourable conditions for Taiwanese investments.[1516]

After the DPP's victory in the election in 2000, Taiwan became China's obsession. Russia drew conclusions from previous decade and supported Beijing's stance; Russian elites agreed on considering the Taiwan issue a "domestic Chinese family quarrel."[1517] Moscow supported Beijing in the 2001 treaty[1518] and by acknowledging the 2005 Anti-Seccesion Law: an "understanding between Moscow and Beijing means that Russia would not make any significant steps toward development of relations with Taiwan without Beijing's consent."[1519] In the 2000s, the influence of such individuals as Oleg Lobov diminished; while trade intensified (though without impressive results); despite some attempts from the DDP there was no breakthrough in Russian-Taiwanese relations; they improved only after the KMT came back to power in 2009 as it lowered down the political atmosphere over Taiwan Strait.[1520] Taiwan, despite minor relations with Russia, plays a subtle, though indirect role in Sino-Russian relations. As long as the island remains independent, Russia feels completely secure from China and may continue to sell arms to it.[1521] Moscow knows very well that Beijing's number one goal is to regain Taiwan. Until then, there will be no real or potential attempts to question Russia's sovereignty over the Russian Far East.

3. China-Russia Ambiguity in Asia-Pacific

Since Putin's first term in 2000, Russian foreign policy has been marked by a noticeable "Asianization" – he has pursued closer relations with China, Japan, North and South Korea, and Vietnam. The Kremlin wanted to return to the region neglected in the previous decade. Moscow wanted to "capitalize on the fact that not a single state regarded Russia as a potential threat" – it successfully established "a network of political and diplomatic contacts with all the

---

at the turn of 21th Century, Joint Declaration after High Level Russian-Chinese Meeting]) [in:] *Сборник российско-китайских договоров 1949-1999…* p. 453-457.

1516 А. В. Лукин, *Китай:медьведь наблюдает…*, p. 466.

1517 Ibid., p. 467.

1518 Article 5, *Договор о добрососедстве…*

1519 А. В. Лукин, *Китай: медьведь наблюдает…*, , p. 467.

1520 А.В. Иванов, *Без политики. Отношения России с Тайванем, Гонконгом и Макао* [Without Politics. Russia's relations with Taiwan, Hong Kong and Makao], [in:] *Россия и Китай: четыре века взаимодействия…*, pp. 550-567.

1521 J. L. Wilson, *Russia, China…*, p. 403.

relevant actors" as well as became a member-state of region's multilateral organizations and forums (APEC, EAS).[1522] Thanks to all this, "the slogan of multi-vectored foreign policy has acquired genuine substance."[1523] This was combined with hopes for attracting investments into the Russian Far East and integrating this region with the dynamism of Asia. Nevertheless, despite these efforts "geographical balance in Russian foreign policy remains elusive"; relations with major Asian powers have certainly grown in recent years, but from a very low base and Asia – despite ambitious attempt to re-orient Russia's foreign policy, such as the "turn to the East" – is still not the Kremlin's highest priority.[1524]As for Russia's approach to China, after several attempts to balance Beijing's influence in the 2000s, Moscow finally after 2014 gave up and decided to bandwagon with China.

From the very beginning of Putin's first presidential term, Moscow realized that China is the key to a come back in the Asian game. The Kremlin realized that without China, gaining back the great power status is impossible for Russia. On the other hand, Russian policymakers were afraid that once China becomes the leading power, it may no longer be so restrained.[1525] Anxieties about the Russian Far East aside, politically dominant China may undermine Russian attempts to play a more active role – this made Moscow ambiguous towards Beijing in relations to Asia-Pacific; there was understanding that to succeed in Asia, Russia must look beyond China.[1526] Basedg on this understanding, "the Russian elite worked out the consensus on basic ramifications for Russia's place in the East Asian order: politically as a balancing force between China and the US; economically as the supplier of energy resources and weaponry; and as a transportation link between East Asia and Europe".[1527]

China has responded to this calmly: Beijing has been fully aware of Russian plans, but decided to turn a blind eye on it. China knows perfectly well that "if there is one area where the great Asian powers (…) agree, it is that the region does not need the added complication of a state whose sense of entitlement greatly exceeds its real contribution."[1528] China does not support Russia's aspiration because firstly, this goes against Chinese interests, and secondly, this would damage the vulnerable image – already questioned after the disputes regarding the South China Sea – of a country that respects limitations, a one being a "responsible stakeholder" and a responsible subject of international

1522 M. Kaczmarski, *Russia-China Relations…*, p. 102.
1523 B. Lo, *The Axis of Convenience…*, pp. 115-116.
1524 Ibid., pp. 115-116.
1525 Ю. М. Галенович, *Россия-Китай-Америка. От сотрудничества к гармонии интересов?* [Russia-China-USA. From Competition to Harmony of Interests?], Москва 2006, pp. 269-302.
1526 B. Lo, *The Axis of Convenience…*, p. 118-120; Idem, *The New World Disorder…*, p. 143.
1527 M. Kaczmarski, *Russia-China Relations…*, p. 102.
1528 B. Lo, *The Axis of Convenience…*, p. 128.

law (Russia is not one). Finall,y it would undermine the fundamental concept of Chinese foreign policy – mutual benefits (what kind of benefit would Beijing get should Russia become more involved in Asia-Pacific?).

At the same time, China does not compete with Russia in Asia-Pacific as they are in different weights. The Chinese conduct a calm policy of awaiting and achieving maximum possible benefits because they know that "Russia remains a weak player in the region with few friends" and does not threat Chinese interests.[1529] Moscow, however, did not want to accept this situation and in the 2000s embarked on a series of attempts to upgrade its position and decrease overdependence on China.

4. *Russia's Balancing Attempts*

Russia sought to escape the isolation – and overdependence from China – through various ways. One was participation in the Asian regional multilateral structures.[1530] The awareness of its own marginalization and the need to liberate itself from an image of a country that considers Asia only a tool in geopolitical games made Russia suspend its typical policy of the predominance of bilateral ties. Moscow has tried to bandwagon to regional integration processes.[1531] Until 2015, Putin has attended nearly all major Asian multilateral summits (ASEAN, APEC, ASEM, EAS; later, after 2015 he lost his heart for it… to regain it in May 2016 while hosting the first Russia-ASEAN summit) and has visited most of the Asia-Pacific countries; Moscow organized the APEC summit in 2012 and started sending its high ranking representatives to influential forums such as the Shangri-La dialogue. Moscow's interest in the Asian organization was welcomed in the region – e.g. an invitation to the EAS was interpreted as "implicit balancing against China's rise".[1532] Russia has even tried convincing others that it shared the "Asian way"[1533] – built on Five Principles of Peaceful Coexistence and an emphasis on pragmatism, practical matters, discretion, consensus-building and non-confrontational attitude.

Despite these actions, Russia has been sending contradictory signals, while declarations disjointed with political practice. The best example was the arms sales to China. Moscow declares a peaceful approach and at the same time sells weapons to Beijing, which "does not sit well with its efforts to portray itself as

1529 Ibid., p. 131.

1530 J. L. Wilson, op. cit., p. 56.

1531 M. Титаренко, *Геополитическое…*, p. 409.

1532 M. Kaczmarski, *Russia-China Relations…*, p. 104.

1533 Naturally, the very concept of the Asian way is vague, non concrete, often used as a cliche and potentially controversial given the history with the "Asian values" (that turned out to be conservative European, or universal, values); nevertheless, with all reservations, I use this term in the "ASEAN way" meaning.

a good citizen of the Asia-Pacific."[1534] Pacific Asians cannot understand this approach: "What was the reason for this, the Indian wondered: are the Russians blind, stupid, or too obsessed with the United States?"[1535]. Moreover, Russians were not able to hide their distance for regional forums: they used these gatherings as opportunities for bilateral meetings with big players (USA, China) or for lobbying for investments; consequently, their interest for pan-regional affairs has been "superficial" and their contribution "lack substance": e. g. Putin "used the 2013 APEC summit in Bali not to detail what Russia could do for the Asia-Pacific region, but as a fishing expedition for outside investment in the Russian Far East."[1536] Finally, Russian resolution of Georgian and Ukrainian crises was a blow to the attempts of building an image of a "peaceful country that shares Asian values". It had little to do with the "Asian way" – it has broken probably all the major meta-principles of this philosophy, such as respect for territorial integrity, sovereignty, non-aggression, non-interference in domestic affairs, peaceful resolution of disputes, liberty from foreign intervention or renouncement of the use of force.

Worse still, Russia limited itself to words mostly. Moscow in the multilateral organization "was hardly active" – it "did not bring fresh ideas nor did it push forward the implementation of Moscow's regional designs", it stayed aside the core issue in Asia-Pacific, also the South China Sea disputes (and later it leaned towards China); thus "Russia's balance sheet in multilateral economic co-operation is equally limited (...) Moscow's failures are underpinned by the absence of any viable economic offer."[1537] Moscow wanted to use its traditional means: energy to reduce its dependence on China and improve its bargaining position *vis-à-vis* Beijing. Initially it worked to some extent: South Korea and Japan became major buyers of Russian LNG gas from Sakhalin-2 as well as its oil (Japan bough it from the ESPO terminal, too); Japan agreed with Russia for deliveries from the planned LNG plant in Vladivostok. However, "these plans did not boost energy co-operation with Japan to an extent that would balance Russia's energy relations with China", moreover, Russia failed to convince Japan to invest in the exploration of Siberian and Russian Far Eastern resources.[1538] With the Ukrainian crisis and its aftermath, hopes for closer cooperation with Japan were dashed, which was best symbolized by the postponing of the construction of the LNG plant in Vladivostok. Russia realized that East Asia will not replace China as major energy client and after 2014 decided to bandwagon to China. This too-close rapprochement with China after 2014 has, however, not been well-received in other Asian countries

1534 B. Lo, *The Axis of Convenience...*, p. 126.
1535 Д. Тренин, *Верные друзья?...*
1536 B. Lo, *Russia and the New World Disorder...*, p. 160.
1537 M. Kaczmarski, *Russia-China Relations...*, p. 105.
1538 Ibid., p. 105.

("a specter is haunting Asia—the specter of Sino-Russian collusion")[1539], which further diminished Russia's posture in Asia-Pacific.

Another Russia's attempt to balance China in the 2000s was its tacit acceptance of the US role in the region. According to this narrative, "much as the Kremlin would like to challenge American dominance, it does not really want to become China's junior partner. To spite Washington is one thing; to accept a junior position *vis-à-vis* Beijing is quite another."[1540] The understanding that the US presence may be beneficial, however, was never dominant – it was challenged by the anxieties that the US presence blocks Russia's possibilities in the security sphere. In the 2010s, the latter understanding prevailed in the Kremlin policymakers' thinking, which led to growing cooperation with Beijing – that in turn diminished chances for decreasing the Chinese dependence here. Moscow, despite having a potential to influence the security policy in the region, has not had a clear vision of its own presence. Consequently, its policy "has been erratic", and "lacked a clear-cut strategy", thus it "wavered between hedging against China's rise and defying the US position."[1541] Finally, the Ukrainian crisis diminished chances for establishing Russian military bases in the region, as most of Asia-Pacific countries are pro-US in the military sphere and cannot anger Washington by letting Russians in, at least for now.

That is why the Russian "beyond China" engagement with Asia-Pacific in security sphere was practically limited to short-lived attempts with Japan (see: below) and selling weapons to Vietnam and India. In Soviet times Hanoi has been its traditional balancer of China in East Asia and despite downturn in bilateral relations in the 1990s (Russia had been withdrawing from Cam Ranh Bay which culminated in 2002), in the early 2000s the relations were invigorated – Hanoi and Moscow established a strategic partnership in 2001 that was upgraded to "comprehensive strategic partnership" in 2012.[1542] In the 2000s the relations intensified thanks to weaponry sales and energy cooperation. Russia-Vietnam ties had been interpreted as a Russian way to resist dominance in East Asia; unfortunately Moscow-Hanoi rapprochement had its limits – Moscow distanced itself from China-Vietnam tensions over the disputed islands on the South China Sea, while Hanoi still did not agree on the return of the Russian fleet to Cam Ranh Bay (and is unlikely to do so given the present geopo-

---

1539 Akio Kawato, op. cit.

1540 Д. Тренин, *Верные друзья?*….

1541 M. Kaczmarski, *Russia-China Relations*…, p. 107.

1542 *Декларация о стратегическом партнерстве между Российской Федерацией и Социалистической Республикой Вьетнам* [Declaration of Strategic Partnership Between RF and Socialist Republic of Vietnam], Kremlin.Ru, 28.02.2001; *Совместное заявление об укреплении отношений всеобъемлющего стратегического партнерства между Российской Федерацией и Социалистической Республикой Вьетнам* [Joint Communique on Upgrading the All-Encompassing Strategic Partnership Between RF and Socialist Republic of Vietnam], Kremlin. Ru, 27.07.2012.

litical circumstances); this all showed the structural limitations of Russia-Vietnam cooperation.[1543] Besides that, to put in bluntly, Vietnam is not in the same category as China to be a real balancing option; the same can be said about other Southeast Asian states (Malaysia, Burma/Myanmar and Indonesia: important receivers of Russian arms); Southeast Asia still remains a backwater of Russian foreign policy.[1544]

India is a different story. India has always been Russia's traditional ally in Asia, its "strategic partner", or even "specially privileged strategic partner."[1545] Russia has much in common with India – traditional close ties in military relations; joint views on reforms of the UN Security Council, situation in Afghanistan or India's bid for presence in the SCO. Initially, after the USSR's fall, Moscow distanced itself from Delhi, but already in 1993 realism returned.[1546] Nevertheless, both sides did not consider each other the most important partners. India cared for relations with Russia – its main supplier of arms, but nothing more except this materialized. Delhi did not even notify Moscow about its planned nuclear attempt in 1998. This discontent (and India-China uneasy relations) explains the failure of Primakov's "strategic triangle" Moscow-Delhi-Beijing in the 1990s[1547] – this idea resurrected in the next decade but still has not gained much power – "it has become little more than a forum for exchanging polite views about the international situation."[1548] Throughout the 1990s, the main feature in Russian-Indian-Chinese relations has been Russian arms sales – Moscow's cooperation with Delhi went further than with Beijing (newer weapons, technology transfer) that frustrated China.[1549] Since the 2000s, Russian-Indian relations intensified on political level (much more contacts) and on economic level: trade volume grew (cooperation in oil, gas and exploitation of Russian deposits by Indian companies and civilian nuclear energy – Kudankulam power plant), though the bilateral trade remains low. Thus, arms sales remain the most important part of bilateral relations. The scale of this cooperation exceeded significantly cooperation with Beijing[1550], though slowed down in the late 2000s. This, combined with limited political cooperation made it impossible for Russia to balance China by India, let alone that New Delhi is more interested in economic cooperation with the USA than with

1543 M. Kaczmarski, *Russia-China Relations…*, p. 104.

1544 B. Lo, *Russia and the New World Disorder…*, p. 157.

1545 *Декларация о стратегическом партнерстве между Российской Федерацией и Республикой Индией* [Declaration of Strategic Partnership Between RF and Republic of India] "Независимая газета", 05.10.2000; W. Rodkiewicz, *The Turn to the East…*, p. 20.

1546 *Договор о дружбе и сотрудничестве между российской федерацией и республикой индией* [Russian Federation and Republic of India Friendship and Cooperation Treaty], Mid.ru, 28.01.1993.

1547 D. Trenin, *The China Factor …*, p. 53.

1548 B. Lo, *Russia and the New World Disorder…*, p. 155.

1549 G. Chuffrin, op. cit., p. 482; L. Buszynski, *Overshadowed by China…*, p. 280.

1550 L. Buszynski, op. cit., p. 280.

Russia. Furthermore, New Delhi has an "aversion to geopolitical games" and to forming any anti-US alliance, the lack of normative likemindedness between Russia and India, recent Russia-Pakistan rapprochement and lack of substance in bilateral agenda, all make Russia-India relations "relatively stable and trouble-free, but undynamic."[1551] Recent problems with Russian policy towards the Taliban and Russian willingness to participate in the China-Pakistan corridor (via India's claimed, Pakistani controlled, part of Kashmir)[1552] showed the limitations very well. Thus, India could not become Russia's balancer in Asia-Pacific, neither. For this role, however, another country has been better suited: Japan.

5. *Japan as the Balancer*

Russia's relations with Japan have showed clearly that Moscow had been ready to sacrifice the cooperation with China should a better opportunity appear. Thus Russian-Japanese relations underwent sinusoid throughout the 1990s, the 2000s and the 2010s. Tokyo remains the key in Russia's hopes to return "to the game in Asia": "Japan is an obvious candidate to become a strategic partner. A Russo-Japanese rapprochement, while not necessarily at Beijing's expense, would leave Russia less reliant on China."[1553] Japan, thus, is a perfect balancer for Russia in Asia-Pacific: "such a balance would greatly reduce the potential for Chinese aggression against the Russian Far East (…) it might offer Russia opportunities to act as the 'swing' power in East Asia."[1554] In the 1990s for many in Russian elites, mostly reformers, Japan was the partner of choice in Asia-Pacific[1555] and the Kremlin hoped for "parallel wheels" (the territorial question and economic cooperation) to be "discussed simultaneously but separately" which "appeared to offer a way forward."[1556] Furthermore, the elites and people of the Russian Far East in the 1990s were oriented towards Japan, not China.[1557] It was Japan, not China that remained the key in Russian hopes to renew relations with East Asia. Moscow had been dreaming of Japan becoming in Asia what Germany has been to Russia in Europe.[1558]

1551 B. Lo, *Russia and the New World Disorder…*, p. 155.

1552 *Мы пришли к вам с Кашмиром, Стратегическое партнерство России и Индии подверглось испытанию* [We came to you with Kashmir. Strategic partnership of Russia and India under question], Kommersant.Ru, 10.01.2017.

1553 Д. Тренин, *Верные друзья?…*

1554 B. Lo, *The Axis of Convenience…*, p. 121.

1555 N. Kuhrt, *Russian Policy towards China and Japan: The El'tsin and Putin Periods,* London, Routledge 2011, p. 60-100.

1556 B. Lo, *Russia and the New World Disorder…*, p. 150.

1557 А. В. Лукин, *Китай: медьведь наблюдает…*, pp. 312-318.

1558 D.Trenin, *Will Japan and Russia Escape the New Cold War?*Carnegie Moscow, 24.04.2014

Initially, after 1991, Moscow-Tokyo relations were worse than cold. The Japanese still considered Russia a threat and demanded it give back all four Kuril Islands. This cancelled any possibility of a compromise (Yeltsin apparently was prone to such). Moreover, Tokyo staunchly protested against Russia's inclusion into the G7. The relations reached the lowest level after the cancellation of Yeltsin's visit to Tokyo in autumn of 1992. Until 1997, Russian-Japanese relations remained in a stalemate. Only Moscow-Beijing rapprochement made Tokyo improve relations with Moscow and modified the "Russia policy". Under prime-minister Ryutaro Hashimoto who met with Yeltsin twice on "no ties" meetings (November 1997 and April 1998) Tokyo started its new approach. It was ready to invest in the Russian Far East before the returning of the Kuril Islands and withdrew its veto against Yeltsin's presence at the G7. Russia, in turn, supported new Japan-US agreement. This frustrated China, always sensible about the possibility of the encirclement by its neighbors.[1559] The culmination of the Russian-Japanese *détente* happened in November 1998 when Yeltsin and the new Japanese prime-minister Keizo Obuchi signed a "creative partnership" between Russia and Japan.[1560] Nevertheless, long-term Russian-Japanese relations did not materialize mostly due to structural reasons, such as chronic weakness of the Russian economy, hammered even further by economic crisis in 1998: "it was not the political obstacle (Kuril Islands) but rather a general perception among Japanese businessmen that Russia is a frustrating, inhospitable and generally unpromising place of investments that disenable a flow of Japanese capital"[1561] (this perception remains in place until today).[1562] The full benefits of ties with Japan would not emerge "unless Russian economy becomes more open, orderly, and predictable; China, however, needs not such changes."[1563] This is why Russian-Japanese breakthrough in the 1990s never materialized.

Putin upon becoming the president has tried to develop relations with Japan by expanding trade volume considerably and balancing China's influence with the ESPO pipeline – he hoped that a Chinese-Japanese competition for Russian resources between Japan and China would neutralize them and allow Russia to play them off against one another in a "resource competition."[1564] Putin's main goal has been to normalize relations with Japan on the Russian terms. This is based on "the method of 'strategic patience', a hope "that Tokyo will sooner

---

1559 H. Gelman, *The Changing Asia Area,* [in:] *Rapprochement or Rivalry…*, p. 424.

1560 *Moscow Declaration On Establishing A Creative PartnershipBetween Japan And The Russian Federation,* The Ministry of Foreign Affairs of Japan, 1998, 13 XI; Tsuyoshi Hasegawa, *Russo-Japanese relations and the security of North-East Asia in the 21 century,* [in:] *Russia and Asia…*, p. 318; G. Chuffrin, op. cit., p. 484.

1561 H. Gelman, p. 418.

1562 A. Габуев, *Вернуть нельзя сотрудничать…* ; *Results of JETRO's 2015 Survey on Business Conditions of Japanese Companies in Russia*, Jetro.Go.Jp, 21.12.2015.

1563 S. W. Garnett, op. cit., p. 29.

1564 B. Lo, *The Axis of Convenience…*, p. 121.

or later become ready to accept the compromise" on Russian terms (on Kuril Islands) and increase Japan's economic engagement in Russia.[1565] Kremlin has been operating "on the premise that it holds all the high cards in its dealings with Tokyo (…) and "feels under no particular pressure to surrender the disputed islands."[1566] Giving back (all) the Kuril Islands simply couldn't fit into Putin's vision of rebuilding Russia's great power status. Consequently, his stance has toughened in comparison with Yeltsin. Putin offered only Shikotan and Khabomai which was unacceptable for Tokyo (which underwent a series of domestic problems: a succession of weak and short-ruling prime-ministers). By 2006 the two sides reached an impasse that prolonged until 2012. After Japan parliament's declaration of sovereignty over all Kuril Islands in 2009 and Medvedev's visit there in 2010 Russian-Japanese relations "hit rock bottom."[1567] This led Russia to embrace China once again and act "in a way that both (Moscow and Beijing) know very well – symbolic manifestation" – Moscow and Beijing started using Japanese historical faults extensively.[1568] Both sides are to blame for this situation. The Russians believed they can separate economic relations from the "contaminating effect" of Kurile: they hoped that time "would either heal historical wounds or encourage forgetfulness"; the Japanese thought "the rise of China would make Moscow 'see sense' and agree to the return of the islands under certain conditions" such as 'Hong Kong option.'"[1569] Both sides operated on the assumption that the other side is in the weaker position and is going to give in soon.[1570] The result was stagnation.

Improved Tokyo-Moscow relations re-started after Shinzo Abe came back to power in December 2012. Abe set up an ambitious plan to gain Japan back economic power and the Asia-Pacific leader's position, lost to China. Normalization relations with Russia lied within this framework so he tried to improve relations with Moscow. That is why in 2013 a "fresh breeze started to blow" in Russian-Japanese relations – Abe visited Moscow in April 2013 and was supposed to find a common ground with Putin (they refer to each other by their first names, share a love for dogs and met four times in 2014).[1571] This is unsurprising, given the fact that they are both realists and share global ambitions

1565 W. Rodkiewicz, *The Turn to the East…*, pp. 6 and 26.

1566 B. Lo, *Russia and the New World Disorder…*, p. 152.

1567 Ф. Лукьянов, *Отношения России и Япония достигли дна* [Russian-Japan relations hit the bottom], Mail.Ru, 2011, 30 IV.

1568 M. Kaczmarski, *Russia-China Relations…* p. 103.

1569 B. Lo, *Russia and the New World Disorder…*, p. 151.

1570 A. Габуев, *Вернуть нельзя сотрудничать…*.

1571 Ф. Лукьянов, *Три к одному* (Three Against One), "Россия в глобальной политике", 2013, 21 II; *Премьер Японии приехал в Москву за весной* [Japan's PM Arrived to Moscow Seeking Spring], Окно в Россию 2013, 30 IV.

of regaining great power status for their countries and understood that a "Sino-centristic continent [is] not in their interests."[1572] Moscow and Tokyo agreed on establishing a 2+2 formula (meetings of foreign and defence ministries of Russia and Japan), joint maritime naval drills; moreover, Russia has granted Japan a status of observer in the Arctic Council (it ignored China's bid) and supported Tokyo bid for Olympic Games in 2020 in public.[1573] Finally, there were intensive plans of development of the economic relations – Japan was interested in a gas pipeline from Sakhalin and the LNG terminal in Vladivostok[1574] while Nissan and Toyota increased their presence in the Russian market and Tokyo imported "record volumes of Russian oil and LNG."[1575] In general it seemed as if Russia wanted to improve ties Japan in order to balancethe rising power of China.

Nevertheless, all these plans have been (so far) been dashed by Ukrainian crisis and its aftermath. Japan, forced by Washington, condemned Russia and introduced sanctions. As a result, Russia sided with China again by finalizing the gas contract in May 2014. This means that until relations with Japan improve, Putin is unable to fulfill his "strategic diversity" vision – this in turn benefits China. Judging by the recent perspective, "the ultimate impact of the 'Japanese card' on Moscow's relationship with Beijing remained insignificant."[1576] Although in September 2016, Russia and Japan achieved a "mini-breaktrough" at the Eastern Economic Forum in Vladivostok and thanks to Abe's "onsen diplomacy" Putin met with Abe in December 2016 and achieved signing of 80 documents (mostly non-biding memorandums) on Japanese investments to Russia without any concession on territorial issue[1577], it still remains to be seen whether this will transfer to any politically significant outcomes. For now, despite "a window of opportunity" between Moscow and Tokyo, unresolved Kurile issue and U.S.-Japan alliance "temper optimism for rapid improvements in the Japan-Russia relationship."[1578]

6. *The Dream of the Concert of Asia*

In the 2000s, Russia started dreaming of the "concert of Asia" – a kind of great powers' condominium supervising the region, where they would collectively

1572 Д. Б. Миллер, *Сближение России и Японии неминуемо?* [Is Rapprochement with Japan Inevitable?] 19 февраля 2014.D. Trenin, *Russia: Pivoting to Asia or Just to China?*, Carnegie Center Moscow, 2014, 24 III; F. Hill, op. cit.

1573 F. Hill, op.cit.

1574 Д. Б. Миллер, *Сближение*....

1575 B. Lo, *Russia and the New World Disorder*..., p. 152.

1576 M. Kaczmarski, *Russia-China Relations*... p. 104.

1577 A. Габуев, *Вернуть нельзя сотрудничать*....

1578 Shoichi Itoh, Ken Jimbo, Michito Tsuruoka, Yahuda Michael, *Japan and the Sino-Russian Strategic Partnership*, NBR special report #64|April 2017, pp. 3-10.

deal with the most important issues in Asia-Pacific.[1579] Moscow wanted to see "a strategic architecture of check and balances" in East Asia which would have two cardinal virtues: it would restrain the exercise of hegemonic influence of Beijing or Washington and it would allow secondary actors, such as Russia, a greater say in regional decision-making.[1580] The "Concert of Asia" is derived from a general vision of the "relations between powers in a new, polycentric international order" preferred by Moscow, that "should be based on an oligarchic consensus of great powers, civilisational pluralism, the de-ideologisation of interstate relations, the absolute non-interference in the internal affairs of 'great powers', respect for their spheres of influence, and the prioritization of business co-operation."[1581] Russia's policy towards Korea is the best example of this concept.

In the 1990s, Russia's position in the Korean peninsula lowered since Soviet times. Yeltsin continued late Gorbachev's redirection towards South Korea: he chose Seoul as the place of his first visit to the region and during his presidency Russia ceased to support North Korean economy due to its own bad condition.[1582] Moscow had hoped to get into the South Korean market (it turned out to be wishful thinking only, as this market has already been dominated by the USA and Japan, which was best illustrated by the history with Russian arms sales to Seoul).[1583] There were ambitions to mediate between the two Koreas, too, but these ended up in a failure due to weak contacts with South Korea. The most visible sign of Russia's weakness in the Korean Peninsula has been its exclusion from North Korean nuclear programme peace negotiations – Russia was not included in four-party talks and Pyongyang has rejected Russian offer of providing energy in return for abandoning the nuclear programme. The 1998 economic crisis has ruined Russian ambitions in the Peninsula completely. China, Russia's strategic partner was not supporting Moscow here. Beijing neither supported the idea of inclusion of Russia into four-party talks nor to help Russia to enter South Korea (where it could compete with Chinese investments). Thus, in the 1990s, China maintained its central position on the Peninsula, whereas Russia was not able to play the role of a balancer and lowered its position in the region when compared to Soviet times.

1579 A. Acharya, *A Concert of Asia?*, "Survival", vol. 41, no 3 (Autumn 1999), p. 89; B. Lo, *The Axis of Convenience…*, p. 124.

1580 B. Lo, *The Axis of Convenience…*, p. 123.

1581 W. Rodkiewicz, *The Turn to the East…*, p. 6.

1582 J. C. Moltz, *Russian Policy on the North Korean Nuclear Crisis*, Monterey Institute of International Studies, April 2003.

1583 Moscow claimed that it sels Seoul "defensive" arms, but tanks are hard to be consider as such; this enraged Pyongyang; Seoul at the same time announced that it accepts the weapons as a part of the repay of the depth; when Moscow offered South Korea rockets, USA intervened and blocked the fulfillment of this contract.

Responding to a sense of Korean "strategic regret"[1584], at the beginning of the 2000s, Putin decided to regain Russia's position on the Korean Peninsula. He knew he could not count on China.[1585] Russian and Chinese interests were contradictory here. China wanted to keep the North as a buffer against US influence and to keep Japan out, while Russians were be interested in Korea's unification. That is why China did not feel the need to invite Russia to the four-party denuclearization talks that collapsed due to Pyongyang's tough stance. Thus, Putin has opted for "personal diplomacy" to get Russia in the negotiation's table – and he was right. Thanks to his rapprochement with Kim Jong-Il in the early 2000s, North Korea (not China!) proposed to include Russia in six-party talks to keep the balance. Participating in the talks had been Russia's biggest success on the Korean Peninsula in the 2000s and showed how Russia perceives the idea of the "concert of Asia" – as a kind of great powers' condominium that deals collectively with regional problems (here: the North Korean nuclear programme); Russia, even being the weakest point, still remained in the talks which was important for Moscow for prestigious reasons.

Unfortunately, this beneficial status did not last long due to the actions of North Korea which in 2006 conducted nuclear weapons testing. All powers reacted toughly, even China which "lost face" – North Korea showed in public that China did not control it (nobody does; Pyongyang "has made a living of such blackmail for 20 years now, having successfully mastered the part of beggar with a stick.")[1586] Nevertheless, although Beijing's public stance toughened, Sino-North Korean relations intensified – China started investing heavily in North Korea. 2009-2013 saw a significant intensification of economic relations between the PRC and the DPRK.[1587] China therefore fulfilled its main goals – to vassalize North Korea and to prevent Korea from unification. As for Russian policy after the 2009 stalemate, it usually joined China in joint actions on North Korea and did not try to conduct an overly ambitious policy as it tacitly acknowledges its little importance there; consequently, Russia's Korean policy became "an extension of its partnership with Beijing."[1588]

After Kim Jong-il's death in 2011 and his son, Kim Jong-un's succession, Pyongyang has been trying to liberate itself from the Chinese dependence – it became Beijing's "rogue ally"[1589] – and at least partially diversify foreign influences in Korea. This opened the "window of opportunity" for Russia, which, in its "turn to the East" has tried to return to Korea. Moscow has cancelled 90%

1584 B. Lo, *Russia and the New World Disorder*..., p. 156.

1585 L. Buszynski, op. cit., p. 271.

1586 Yu Bin, *Pivot to Eurasia*...

1587 O. Pietrewicz, *Krewetka między wielorybami. Półwysep Koreański w polityce mocarstw* [A *Shrimp Between Whales. The Korean Peninsula in Great Powers' policies*], Warszawa 2016, p. 187.

1588 B. Lo, *Russia and the New World Disorder*..., p. 157.

1589 Yu Bin, *China-Russia Relations: Trilateral Politics*...

of North Korean debts (USD11 billion), offered to build a gas pipeline and a railway to North Korean SEZ Rajin, as well as trans-Korean railway linked with the Trans-Siberian Railway.[1590] Nevertheless, the Ukrainian crisis again dashed Russian hopes for playing a more active role in North Korea, out of a simple reason – Moscow squeezed by sanctions had no fonds to finance these ambitious projects (a nearly bankrupted Pyongyang could not finance it from the very beginning). Besides, there is a more important, structural obstacle to the Russian plans on the Korean Peninsula: Russia's main goals in Korea are contradictory with Pyongyang's and Beijing's. Russia hopes for grand inter-Korean projects, such as gas pipeline and railway which need unification to materialize. Moscow hopes that a unified Korea would turn to Russia to balance China, Japan and the USA.[1591] But the unification of Korea is against both Pyongyang's and Beijing's interests and is unlikely soon.

Moscow's plans for intensification with South Korea failed, too. In 2010, Russia and South Korea signed a memorandum on South Korean participation in the Russian Far East modernization.[1592] It was important then – "a strong political signal, as a similar memorandum with China was signed only a year later" – but proved to be a gesture only: "Russia has not achieved any breakthrough so far."[1593] The same applies to the idea of gas pipeline via the Korean Peninsula from 2011-2012. It was conceived as a potential leverage in negotiations with China, but small size of it (10-bcm) made it symbolic only, whereas political risks involved in it undermined the idea from the very beginning; finally when Gazprom signed the contract with Beijing, this made the "implementation of the project almost impossible."[1594] Although South Korean-Russian trade indeed improved (but not to important numbers), and recently Russia started selling oil to South Korea, but these are not game changers. Seoul has been more preoocupied in persuading Moscow to join anti-Pyongyang inititatives than in helping bilateral economic relations to flourish.

Thus, Moscow's success on the Korean Peninsula in the 2000s with six-party talks has proven to be short lived. Although Moscow for the past fifteen years succeeded in "maintaining an even-handed approach that made little political or moral distinction between North and South (...) by balancing growing economic cooperation with South Korea with closer political and security ties with North Korea", these "modest achievements hardly amount to game changers."[1595]

1590 *Russia, North Korea Sign Debt Pact*, "Wall Street Journal" 2012, 18 IX; Zachary Keck, *To Hedge Its Bets, Russia Is Encircling China*, The Diplomat, 05.11.2013.

1591 А.В. Лукин, *Россия и Китай* ...., p. 652.

1592 *РФ и ЮжКорея заключили ряд соглашений о сотрудничестве*, [RF and S. Korea concluded several cooperation agreements], Izvestia.ru, 10.11.2010

1593 M. Kaczmarski, *Russia-China Relations*..., p. 104.

1594 Ibid., p. 106.

1595 B. Lo, *Russia and the New World Disorder*..., p. 157.

In more general terms, the idea of the "concert of Asia" has not taken root out of two major impediments. The first is the continuing lack of a collective regional identity and tradition of transnational cooperation.[1596] The other one is that "concert of Asia" "presupposes a rough equivalence between the major powers" which is impossible in Asia-Pacific now.[1597] Because Moscow is unable to establish a "concert of Asia", its interest is exactly opposite to the majority of Asia-Pacific region. Pacific Asians strive for peace and prosperity, try to avoid conflicts – all this is the exact opposite of Russian politics whose favourite element is war.

7. *Russia's Pivot to Asia*

"Russia's pivot to Asia" or "Russia's turn to the East" has been Moscow's newest attempt to "return to Asia". It was born out of the realization that Russia must be strongly present in Asia and that "Asia matters in and of itself" – the Kremlin elite moved toward a "sharper, more sophisticated consciousness of Asia"; it was the changing geopolitical circumstances ("post-American world") forced the Kremlin "to make counterintuitive choices, including overcoming the prejudices and ignorance that have historically constrained Russia's approach toward Asia."[1598] Moscow hoped, too, to "make Russia a fully-fledged player in East Asian politics, a sui generis third party for the smaller states squeezed between the United States and China" and by becoming "attractive to East Asian states, Russia hoped to revive its own Far East."[1599]

Internationally it started with the APEC summit in Vladivostok in September 2012. Declarations were grand (with slogans like "Russia can pivot to Pacific, too"), and comparisons were full of pathos: "if Peter the Great were alive today, he would almost certainly leave behind the old Russian capital, Moscow, to establish himself (in) an already-built city, Vladivostok."[1600] Russia dreamed of becoming "a swing state" between USA and China thanks to its "turn to the East."[1601] The "turn to the East" was dreamed to "be a game changer, both for Russia's relationships with individual Asian countries and in terms of its broader influence in the Asia-Pacific region."[1602] Unfortunately, although there has been some progress in comparison to the pre-2012/2014 period, the results are far behind expectations and grandiose proclamations.

1596 N. Khoo, M. Smith, *A Concert of Asia?*, "Policy Review" 2001, no 108 (August); B. Lo, *The Axis of Convenience…*, p. 124.
1597 B. Lo, *The Axis of Convenience…*, p. 124.
1598 Idem, *Russia and the New World Disorder…*, p. 133 and 140.
1599 M. Kaczmarski, *Russia-China relations and the West…*
1600 D. Trenin, *Russia Can Pivot to the Pacific, Too*, The Globalist, 07.09.2012.
1601 I. Zevelev, *A New Realism for the 21st Century*, "Russia in Global Affairs", 27.12.2012.
1602 B. Lo, *Russia and the New World Disorder…*, p. 141.

Big investments in Vladivostok were supposed to be the proof of Russia's genuine interest in Asia. Although Putin was declaring the will to "catch up the Chinese wind"[1603], one of the implicit rationale of the turn was to reduce Russia's dependence on China. As before, the notion behind it was that over-dependence from China blocks Russian policy options. The initial response from Asia-Pacific countries that welcomed Moscow's decision with the hope of gaining an "additional hedge against Beijing's great powers ambitions", also offered good perspective for Moscow.[1604]

However, Russian policy from the very beginning was contradictory and half-hearted. Moscow wanted to maneuver itself into a better place in the region without harming relations with China at the same time – it wanted to "eat cake and have it, too". The Kremlin believes that "the road to a more secure and influential Russia ultimately runs through Beijing; no amount of improvement in ties with other Asian countries can compensate for a deterioration in relations with China."[1605] Thus, the Kremlin "was unsure whether to hedge against China's rise or to continue its Sinocentric policy", this ambiguity resulted in failure in capitalizing "the anxiety of smaller states" in both economic and security spheres (they turned to the USA instead), therefore "Moscow's failures to develop close political and economic ties with other Asian states have perpetuated the Sinocentric orientation of Russia's East Asian policy."[1606] Unsurprisingly, the "turn to the East" ended up in a "flawed diversification of Russian foreign policy."[1607] Perhaps because of this lack of success, the Kremlin soon lost interest in Asia. Vladivostok in the wider political and geopolitical sense has been forgotten and the Kremlin concentrated its effort on another grand enterprises – Sochi Olympics in 2014, football World Cup in 2018 and financing Crimea instead. As a result, until May 2014 nothing important happened. As one Russian researcher aptly summarized, the "Russian pivot to Asia" ended up… where it had begun, on Russky Island in Vladivostok (where the APEC summit took place).[1608]

However, after Putin's visit to Shanghai and the signing of the gas contract in 2014, voices about the "Russian pivot" reappeared. This pivot was supposed to "really begin"[1609] with the Ukrainian crisis as its catalyst[1610]. In this outlook,

1603 В. Путин, *Россия и меняющийся…*,

1604 M. Kaczmarski, *Russia-China Relations…*, p. 102.

1605 B. Lo, *Russia and the New World Disorder…*, p. 144.

1606 M. Kaczmarski, *Russia-China Relations…*, pp. 108-109.

1607 W.Rodkiewicz, *The turn to the East…*

1608 Private conversation with Prof. Oleg Tomofeev, Lodz 07.06.2014.

1609 *Поворот России в Азию. Реплика Федора Лукьянова* [Russia's Turn to Asia], Kavpolit 23.05.2014.

1610 *Логичное партнерство* [Logical Partnership], "Российская газета" 21.05.2014.

the gas agreement with China was supposed to become the real, long-term co-operation that is "acquiring truly strategic depth."[1611] The signing of gas contract with China, however, increased Russia's dependence on China instead of decreasing it, and distanced Russia from other Asian countries: "the crisis was not a game changer in the sense of introducing a new set of assumptions to Russia's relations with China and Asia. What it did was to reinforce long-established truths (...) the Ukrainian crisis has exposed the flimsiness of its attempts at diversification, the extent of Russia's strategic dependence on China, and the narrowness of the 'turn to the East.'"[1612] The Ukrainian crisis enhanced the already existant dominance of China in Russia's Asia policy and the narrowing place for maneuver: "Sinocentrism is by its very nature self-reinforcing and self-excluding. The more Moscow stakes on China, the closer it ties itself to Beijing's interests and priorities, and the harder it is to develop more fruitful relations with other Asian countries. Excessive Sinocentrism is the antithesis of a flexible and comprehensive Asian strategy."[1613] Instead of liberating from China's dependence, Russia became even more dependent – the "pivot to Asia" has transformed itself to "pivot to China".

2014 and afterwards events showed that Russia instead of focusing on Asia, concentrates its efforts on the consolidation of the "near abroad" (the Eurasian Union, Ukraine) – this is the priority combined with wrestlings with the West; "pivot to Asia" is far behind. Thus, again the practise of Russian foreign policy contradicts its rhetoric about pivoting to Asia. That is why the "turn to the East" has "failed to bring about the heralded fundamental change in relations between Russia and its Asian partners, nor has it significantly reinforced Russia's position in East Asia. It has also failed to create an effective mechanism for harnessing the economic dynamism of the Asia-Pacific region for the purpose of modernizing Russia's Far Eastern territories (...) Diversification has been restricted to the political and diplomatic dimensions, and does not extend to the economic realm."[1614] Due to the inability to address three most important obstacles of Russian policy in Asia (instrumentalism of its relations: "anti-relationship with the West", an excessive Sinocentrism and the disconnect between grandiose rhetoric and underwhelming achievement), Russia's economic integration with Asia-Pacific "is superficial at best", while "Russia's footprint on the Asian continent remains shallow, and few there believe that it has much to contribute beyond natural resources and weapons."[1615] Thus the Chinese dimension remains the main one in the Kremlin's Asian policy: "Sinocentrism is self-evident in Russia's Asian policy" and remains the "major structural obstacle to Russia's turn to the East", consequently, "Russia failed

1611 D. Trenin, *Gas deal entails China-Russia strategic depth*, "The Global Times", 25.05.2014.
1612 B. Lo, *Russia and the New World Disorder*..., p. 145.
1613 Ibid., p. 138.
1614 W. Rodkiewicz, *The Turn to the East*..., pp. 5-6.
1615 B. Lo, *Russia and the New World Disorder*..., p. xxi.

to do in East Asia what China managed to do in Central Asia: become an equal participant in regional politics."[1616] Despite diversification efforts "Russian policy in Asia has become more, not less, Sinocentric. And this was true even before the Ukraine crisis pushed the Kremlin further toward Beijing" (...) its relationships in Asia, with the exception of the Sino-Russian partnership, are weak and underdeveloped"; thus, Russian policy in Asia-Pacific equals to "China-plus", but China "matters above all because it is the next global power, not because it is Asian."[1617]

Thus, the outlook of Russian policy in Asia-Pacific is that it has tried (in vain) to liberate itself from Chinese domination. Nevertheless, all its attempts ended up in a partial or full failure and as a result, in the end, Moscow always leaned toward Beijing. The Kremlin considers cooperation with China on Chinese terms (with China benefiting from it most) better than nothing: Moscow has no choice but to lean toward China. That is why Russia's policy toward Asia-Pacific, despite attempts to balance, remains Sinocentristic. Beyond China it is mainly symbolism and arms sales.

1616 M. Kaczmarski, *Russia-China Relations...*, p. 108; Idem, *Russia-China relations and the West...*

1617 B. Lo, *Russia and the New World Disorder...*, pp. 137,143 and 164.

Summary: The Asymmetric Win-Win

Russia-China rapprochement has been one of the most spectacular phenomena in international relations in the last twenty-seven years. It is even more impressive when one takes into account bilateral historical problems, cultural and ideological differences, decades of psychological mistrust and general strangeness felt by the two countries towards one another. Lacking common identity or even mutual affinity, Moscow and Beijing have successfully built their contemporary relations on pure and simple interests. They proved the adequacy of Thucydides's maxim: "identity of interests is the surest of bonds whether between states or individuals".

The highly complex, complicated, ambiguous and yet truly successful relationship between Russia and China in the last twenty-seven years (1991-2017) is difficult to grasp theoretically. Russian and Chinese elites are hard-core realists in their foreign policies and neorealist school in international relations seems to be the most adequate one to research Sino-Russian relations. Realistically looking at Sino-Russian relations in the last twenty-seven years, one observes that throughout this period, China has achieved a multidimensional advantage over Russia: Beijing has made the Sino-Russian relations a growing asymmetry to its favour. Yet, at the same time, these two countries do not follow the patterns of power politics and are undergoing – as the constructivists would call it – a peaceful power transition. Beijing knows its limits and does not go to extremes by humiliating Russia or exploiting it completely. Rather, China successfully seeks to build a long-term stable relationship based on Chinese terms where both sides gain, but China gains more. Beijing gradually sets the agenda for Sino-Russian relations in accordance with Chinese needs, particularly the economic ones, and makes Russia a raw materials appendage to the Chinese economy. Russia in this agenda does not necessary lose (it gets money for its resources), but rather gains less from this asymmetric deal. Thus, a new model of bilateral relations emerges, a one that encompasses the paradox nature of Sino-Russian relations which may be called – paraphrasing the slogan of Chinese diplomacy – as "asymmetric win-win" formula.

The highly paradoxical and ambiguous nature of Sino-Russian relations enforces intellectual flexibility in researching it. Instead of proposing an all-encompassing theory that would dare to explain the complexity of international relations in the dimension of Sino-Russian relations (would such a theory be possible in the conditions of post-modern science?), this work sets itself a more modest aim of eclectically combining achievements of main schools in the field of Sino-Russian relations. Although some may find the theoretical approach proposed in this book a hazardous choice, this eclecticism is done on purpose. The specific nature of these countries that are states and/or civilizations at the same time, require going beyond the strictly realistic categories.

Moreover, this eclecticism is intended to be, at least in a way, intellectually healthy.

That is why this work uses tools of the neorealist school as well as that of the social constructivism school and asymmetry theory. In other words, it mixes neorealism with constructivism and with asymmetry theory and draws on several different influences. It emphasizes deeply rooted historical (Russian and Chinese imperial traditions – "collecting Russian lands" and Chinese Tianxia), cultural ("Russian idea" and Russia's great power syndrome; China's Sinocentricism and its trauma after colonial humiliation, Russian and Chinese approaches to war and peace and their perceptions in Asia) and psychological (punching above its weight for Russia, hiding behind a "strategic screen" for China) determinants of foreign policy that continue to shape Moscow's and Beijing's agenda. It shows the different global roles they play (throughout those twenty-seven years China has exchanged places with Russia as the West's most important interlocutor and partner) and the pragmatism derived from knowing geopolitical realities: both countries consider one another as safe rears (Russia represent "peace from the North" for China, China is equally safe rear for Russia in accordance with the "Alexander Nevsky paradigm"). The book describes common Russian and Chinese axiological approach to international relations, summarized by the phrase "democratization of international relations" which encapsulates their joint outlook that global matters should be resolved through collective decision-making of the great powers, not unilaterally by the strongest one (they dream, particularly Russia, of global concert of powers).

Russia and China share the worldview: they see the globe as the playground for great powers, through the prism of the 19th century power struggle, with the sole difference being that the USA constitutes a single hegemonic power, albeit weakening. They reject this state of affairs, albeit gently: they are "soft revisionists" of the current system which they consider unjust, a place where "organized hypocrisy" dominates and the logic of consequences prevails over the logic of appropriateness. They, too, reject democracy and human rights as Western instruments of enlarging the zone of influence and interfering in domestic affairs of other countries. Instead, they propose a world built on the Five Principles of Peaceful Coexistence.

Despite the similar approach, however, Russia and China represent two different forms of authoritarianisms: in general, there is more social freedom in Russia and less economic efficiency and the other way around in China. This does not exhaust the list of differences – these are present to such an extent that Russia and China are not normatively converged. What is common, however, in both countries, is that the authoritarian nature of Russian and Chinese political systems enforces concentration on the importance of individuals in politics (Yeltsin and Putin in Russia, Jiang Zemin, Hu Jintao and particularly Xi Jinping with his growing assertiveness under the "Chinese dream" slogan), in accordance with the well-known logic that the importance of individuals in politics increases in non-democratic countries. Particularly the role of personal ties between Putin and Xi and their "Bismarckian" style of policymaking should not be underestimated.

In general, this book follows the mainstream of Western academia in saying that Russia-China relationship is a "marriage of convenience", based on *Realpolitik* imperatives (national security, power projection, management of the strategic balance and emphasis on the primacy of state sovereignty), geopolitics, and common interests, but not on values or mutual affinity; Russia-China relationship is certainly a pragmatic relationship, as all marriage of convenience are. Yet at the same time, this book claims, following the constructivist school, that Russia-China relationship is stable and will remain so. It is, to use the international relations categories, a "normalized asymmetry" or "positive asymmetry". After all, bilateral relations are usually based on pragmatic interests and the pursuit of these interests is the very essence of foreign policy. And, as it often happens in life, the most long-lasting marriages are those based on convenience.

What is new in this book is presenting of what may be called a retrospective approach to Sino-Russian relations. It claims that the asymmetric win-win model of Russia-China relations is a kind of "return to the past" – it is a contemporary equivalent of the first, initial model of Russia-China relations: the *modus vivendi* from the 17th and 18th centuries.

For the first time in contemporary history, though not first time in their relations, Russia faces a China stronger and more dynamic than itself. The present model is a contemporary equivalent of the initial Sino-Russian relationship achieved after the Nerchinsk treaty. Moscow then, having lost the military duel with China, sacrificed its Far Eastern territorial gains for peace and trade with China, knowing that Russia had more important foreign policy dimensions to take care of. Qing court, on its side, having achieved dominance in bilateral relations, had granted Moscow a privileged – in comparison to the Western powers – position within the Sinocentristic *waifan* world in order to achieve a long-lasting peace and stability. In other words, Russia, although weaker and forced to withdraw from the Amur region, was nevertheless strong enough to be able to construct an acceptable *modus vivendi* with Beijing. China, though stronger, could not fully impose its will and had to restrain; the deal was broken on Chinese terms, but Russia did not become a tributary state, even though it was not equal to China. This model, indeed, proved to be very stable – it lasted until China's decline under colonial expansion in the mid 19th century. Thus, the retrospective approach presented in this book allows seeing striking comparisons with contemporary times.

Now, as before, China is stronger and Russia does not challenge it. Instead, Moscow quietly accepts this fact, as its most important interests are focused elsewhere, and it tries to maximize its options in the new situation. China sets the agenda of bilateral relations, as it was in the 17th and the 18th centuries (which leads to the predominance of the economic sphere of the relations), but Beijing does it with the long-term agenda in mind. Thus, China does not overuse its advantage over Russia; it does not exploit it completely. Moreover, as in the 17th and the 18th centuries, the system is again based on the contemporary equivalent of "cultural neutrality": an opposition against the Western values: Beijing does not enforce on its partners the expected patterns of political behavior, and neither does Moscow . Finally, there are, as in the 17th and the 18th centuries, narrow communication lines between the two societies (but not between the two elites) which help to minimize the potential for conflicts. All these features help to keep this system firm and stable and suggest optimistic prognoses for stable and peaceful bilateral relations, at least in the short-term period.

Naturally, so many things have changed, and it is a platitude to say that the 21st century is not the 17th or the 18th century – systematically speaking, the Sinocentristic world order in Asia and Westphalian state system in the West are gone; the scope of bilateral relations is much different, wider and more complex; Russia and China are completely different states than they were in the 17th and the 18th centuries, etc. – differences ale clear and obvious. But this does not falsify the proposed retrospective approach. All the mentioned differences are important, no doubt, but this is the external decorum around Russia-China relations only; the very essence of bilateral relations, the mechanism, or the systematic logic under which they operate, bears striking similarities to the initial, 17th and 18th century model of Sino-Russian relations.

As in the 17th century, when Sino-Russian relations started with disputes and clashes, so the contemporary (1991-2017) bilateral relations started with the negative heritage of Soviet-Sino hostility from the 1960s and the 1970s. Furthermore, the modernizing paths chosen by Russia and China after the demise of communism did not help either. Moscow and Beijing looked at each other with reservations, if not dislike. This has changed due to geopolitical realities – Russia's failed hopes to deliver equal relations with the West and Chinese pragmatism. Both countries understood the benefits of mutually friendly relations: strengthening their positions *vis-à-vis* the West being the most important one. So, again as in the 17th century Nerchinsk, the external factors made Moscow and Beijing negotiate, initiate rapprochement and work out a mutually beneficial model of relations. This model, started from a modest basis, turned out to be stable and long-lasting.

In the 1990s, it was the opposition against the West that became the engine of their relations. Moscow and Beijing shared a similar perception of global affairs: both opposed to the American unilateralism and disliked the Western values. The NATO's intervention in Kosovo, in particular, had far reaching consequences. It strengthened their belief in the US hegemonic attitude. Their opposition against the West united them and made their rapprochement in the

1990s possible. It was not, however, an alliance or a bloc. Russia and China simply strengthened their own positions against the West. In the 1990s, both Russia and China were quite ambivalent in attitudes to one another. Moscow took a dual approach – on the one hand it has proclaimed a strategic partnership with Beijing, while on the other it still considered China a threat to the Far Eastern provinces. Beijing was no better. The Chinese officially accepted the importance of relations with Russia, but when it came to concrete facts (choosing key investors in the country's modernization), they always preferred the Western ones (like in the case of the Three Gorges Dam contract). It can therefore be summarized that in the 1990s, Sino-Russian relations were not much more than an appendix to their ties with the West. Nevertheless, they achieved some significant success: the demilitarization and demarcation (though not full) of the border (for Russia giving back 720 km^2 was a difficult psycho-political task, but again, it was in Russian long-term interest: it postponed the threat of much serious Chinese territorial claims, at least for the time being), non-interference in domestic affairs (it may seem quite pale in comparison to other achievements, but given 400-year history of Sino-Russian relations, it must be considered a remarkable success, particularly from Beijing's position – China hates to be advised and generously rewards those who do not do it); arms sales, the "glue" of their relations in the 1990s, establishment of the mechanism of cooperation and even the economic relations and growing trade volume. The Chinese goods saved Far Eastern Russians from empty shelves whereas China's vast purchase of arms saved Russia's military-technical industry. Finally, Russia and China created an institutional and structural base for mutual contacts. This has proved to be fruitful within the new decade. Within the 1990s however, the partnership was more practical than strategic, and more limited than comprehensive. Where Russian and Chinese interests overlapped (Central Asia), there they gave support to one another. Where these interests were divergent or contradictory, Russia and China did not pay attention to one another (it was particularly evident in East Asia, where China did not become Russia's "door keeper") and were ready to sacrifice "strategic partnership" for better relations with the USA. The most important divergence, overshadowing most successes, or rather pushing them into background, was Russia's and China's main orientation towards the West. It always had priority over the "strategic partner" reaction: Washington had always been more significant for Moscow and Beijing.

In 1991, both countries were more or less equal in their international statuses. Russia, however, did not maintain its superpower status, was badly experienced by transformation to free market and fell to a secondary power status. China, with its pragmatism and lack of emotions in politics (with the exception of the Taiwan issue) steadily and consequently was striving towards its fundamental goal – rebuilding its central role in East Asia and beyond. This is why in the late 1990s, China's position was already stronger than Russia's one.

The 2000s brought forth significant changes (particularly on the Russian side where Vladimir Putin started strengthening the state) that helped to develop Sino-Russian relations further on. At the beginning of the decade, however, Sino-Russian relations repeated the 1990s scheme. Initial rapprochement with China (best symbolized by the 2001 treaty) was soon overshadowed by Putin's pro-Western turn after 11 September 2001. This rapprochement, however, ended in bitter disappointment. Moscow – strengthened by rising oil and gas prices – turned to Beijing again to balance Washington.

This time the Sino-Russian rapprochement had stronger fundaments. Their partnership became more multidimensional, substantial. It has normalized. The two sides were able to completely demarcate the border, which must be considered a historical breakthrough. Even the economic relations – which have always been the weakest point - have improved, with China becoming Russia's second trade partner. Russia and China were able to build a successful relationship. In a sense, this is one of their foreign policies' biggest achievements.

Despite strengthening and normalizing Russia-China relations, they have not stopped being prone to changeability. The rise of raw material prices allowed Russia to play a more ambitious role in the world, which in the case of China-Russian relations had consequences on Putin's Asian politics. He had tried to repeat his successful European politics of balancing the powers and playing them off against one another in order to carve a place for Russia on the Asian chessboard. The tool was energy and the main intended partners were China, Japan and South Korea. This worked out – Russia was repeating its usage of energy for geopolitical reasons with the ESPO pipeline – but only for a while. Around the late 2000s, Moscow understood that there was no chance for this grand scheme, as Japan and South Korea were unwilling and/or unable to present Russia with real alternative to China. When Russia was severely struck by economic crisis of 2008, it finally yielded and realized, in the Hegelian spirit, that "what is real is rational": there was no option for Russia in Asia but China. Thus, Moscow decided to deepen relations with China and to try to make use of its economic success. It other words, it tried to make a virtue out of necessity. As Asia-Pacific has never been the most important vector of Russian foreign policy (these have been "near abroad" and the West), it was easier for Moscow to accept the situation on the ground and take China as it is. Thus, the conditions forced Moscow to change its Asian policy from balancing China to bandwagon to it. This was best reflected in the ambitious, yet shallow slogan of Russian elites: the "Russian pivot to Asia" initially was intended to free Russia from overabundant domination of China, but in 2014 ended up as the "pivot to China" instead. Thus, China became the most important partner of Russia in Asia and the second most important in the world after the United States. Beijing became the biggest winner of this new reality: China was able to forge the agenda of the relationship in accordance with its own vision that reflected first and foremost the Chinese interests: making Russia a stable raw material base for the Chinese economy.

Sino-Russian relations intensified even further after 2012, when the fifth generation of Chinese leaders under Xi Jinping took the power. Responding to the geopolitical challenge from the United States which, with its pivot to Asia, tried to contain China's rise in Asia-Pacific, Beijing intensified relations with Russia. As in the 1990s or after 2003, the American factor contributed to the Sino-Russian rapprochement, but this time rather simply enhanced and intensified the existing political cooperation. The Ukrainian crisis intensified the relations even further – Moscow felt endangered in its core area of interest ("near abroad") and decided that in order to withhold the Western pressure, including sanctions, it needed China's support at all costs and yielded to China by accepting the gas contract which only deepened the already existent asymmetric model of bilateral relations. Moscow was aware of that, but chose to accept *nolens volens* this fact as a temporarily necessity that will be changed in the future. In doing so, the Kremlin's elites evoked the example of a medieval Ruthenia's prince Alexander Nevsky who successfully fought German invaders while remaining loyal to his suzerains: Mongol khans. According to this rationale, Ruthenia bent, but was not broken by the Mongols and later emerged as a powerful, sovereign state. Thus, this policy can informally be called the "Alexander Nevsky paradigm". It remains to be seen whether nowadays Russia will be able to emerge from the dependence on China. For now, the situation on the ground is that Sino-Russian relations are more and more asymmetric in favour of Beijing, yet stable at the same time.

China is more important to Russia, than Russia is to China. For Moscow, Beijing plays a psycho-political role of the West's equalizer - a strategic alternative, no matter if real or virtual (see: the crisis in Ukraine). More importantly, relations with the People's Republic of China touch upon many aspects of Russia's domestic (notably in the development of the Russian Far East) and foreign policy – only the United States are more important to Russia in this aspect. In the present day, Russia needs China, sometimes perhaps being dependent on it.

On the other hand, Russia carries much less importance to China: it is a useful, albeit not the only and not the most reliable, source of supplies. It is important as a partner that secures strategic rears, assures energy supplies and serves as the ideological opposition against the West. Russia is, too, an important tool for China's PR: that is, its claim that China is "peaceful". Russia for China is not, however, an ally in confrontation with the West (it is a convenient smokescreen behind which China can hide and win the interests of the Chinese quietly). China realistically assesses Russian possibilities and sees that Russian influences are shrinking globally and regionally. Russia is insignificant to the Chinese domestic policy and it is not central in Beijing's foreign policy. It is only a complement to the general strategy of "returning to the right place".

The asymmetry is best seen in the economic sphere. Despite an impressive increase in trade in the 2000s and the 2010s, Russia remains China's sixteenth trade partner only while China is Russia's second partner – after the EU. The structure of trade favors China and has an almost neo-colonial character: Russian resources in exchange for Chinese consumption goods and food (energy makes up around 70% of the value of Russian exports). Furthermore, two Russian attempts to engage actively with Asia through grand energy projects – oil pipeline ESPO and gas pipeline The Power of Siberia – instead of decreasing Russia's dependence on China, increased it and pushed Russia even further into becoming China's resource base. On the other hand, something is better than nothing: Russia gets money for its energy, has an alternative route and long-term, stable contracts for it. That is why this asymmetric model is in a way beneficial for both sides, not only for China, though naturally more for China.

The economic backwardness of the Russian Far East enhances the asymmetry in favor of China even further. Despite many declarations, some high-profile initiatives (the APEC summit in 2012 in Vladivostok), and the hope of development via grand energy projects (the ESPO), Moscow has been unable to reform the Russian Far East; it remains one of the most neglected regions of Russia. The sorry state of this strategically key-located place marginalizes Russia's role in Asia-Pacific and hinders Moscow's ambitions ("Russian pivot") to play an active role in Asia-Pacific. Realizing that, Moscow in the 2010s turned to China again in hope to develop the region via the increased cooperation with China ("catching Chinese wind"). In other words, Russia decided to like what it has, instead of hoping for something it likes: to make the best use of what is on the ground, by trying to work out benefits in the game played by the Chinese rules. So far, however, the results have not been impressive. China is more interested in importing the natural resources from the Russian Far East and turning this region into a material base for Chinese economy, than in participation in the Russian Far East's own development – China takes resources and other raw materials and sends commercial goods, food and IT products. This enhances the asymmetric win-win model: China gains more, but Russia at least gets something.

The low status of the Russian Far East, Russia's weak position there and Chinese *de facto* economic monopoly there, all translate into Russia's weak position in the whole Asia-Pacific region – this is another place where Sino-Russian asymmetry in favour of China is equally clearly seen. For Moscow, the region was almost non-existent in the 1990s; since the 2000s, however, Putin had been trying to find Russia a proper place in this most important economically region of the world and liberate itself from the overdependence from China. Moscow tried to use Japan as a balancer, dreamed of concert of Asia, increased its presence in regional multilateral organizations, developed relations with India, Vietnam and South Korea, and announced its own pivot to Asia. In the end, however, all Russian attempts ended up in partial or full failure, or were simply unable to balance China's dominance. Consequently, Moscow again decided that "what is real is rational" and leaned toward Beijing by considering cooperation with China on Chinese terms better than nothing. Thus, Moscow lost space to manoeuvre, but gained access, although secondary, to decisions in regional affairs. The Sinocentricism of Russian policy in Asia-Pacific is yet another strong proof of the asymmetric win-win logic behind Russia-China relations.

A more balanced situation takes place in Central Asia, where Russia and China now enjoy a more orless equal position (or, in the scenario more optimistic for Moscow, China is catching up with Russia). This situation itself, however, testifies to the extraordinary success of Beijing which was able to achieve this position from a very low basis. In 1991, Russia was everything for Central Asia while China was almost nothing – Chinese influences practically did not exist there. Yet Beijing, thanks to its wise policy of gradual and peaceful engagement and not provoking Russia at the same time, was able to gain stronghold there, particularly after the economic crisis in 2008. China broke Russia's monopoly on resources and transportation of energy there, became region's most important partner and announced unprecedented, ambitious New Silk Road (One Belt One Road) initiative. At the same time, however, Beijing is trying to appease Moscow and avoid confrontation. So far Moscow has been able to tolerate this new situation (though with difficulties), mainly because China's entry to the region has unintentionally fulfilled Moscow's strategic goal of keeping the West in general and the EU in particular away from Central Asia (in other words, the Kremlin decided that China is a lesser evil). Thus, a new status quo emerged in Central Asia, one that is far from the New Great Game logic. China and Russia have designated their zones of influence in the best concert of powers scenario: Moscow took security, whereas Beijing took economy, which effectively made Central Asia their joint condominium. This has worked out so far, it remains to be seen, however, how long they can maintain this state of affairs. The very fact that Russia must "share" Central Asia with China – albeit without major conflicts – proves the very asymmetry in their relations. Had Russia been stronger, this would have been impossible and Moscow would have been able to keep any other country, including China, away from Central Asia. On the other hand, this asymmetry is not so detrimental to Russian interests, as it keeps the West outside Central Asia, so situation in Central Asia again fits into the proposed asymmetric win-win model.

The only important sphere where it is Russia that still has significant advantage over China is the military sphere. Here the Russian army's fundamental advantage over the Chinese one – despite the impressive modernization and development achieved by the PLA in the last two decades – reassures Russian elites; as does the fact that the main vectors of China's foreign policy are directed to the east and southeast and that it is the United States, not Russia whom China wants to replace as a global hegemon. The understanding of this fact resulted in the intensification of arms sales in the early 2000s and again in the 2010s. Although Russia had been reserved for long over the idea of selling to China its most sophisticated weapons (contrary to the 1990s when arms sales to China was enforced by the dire situation of the Russian military-technological base, in the 2000s commercial anxieties were the dominant reason), this has changed in the 2010s, particularly in 2015 when the Kremlin finally agreed to sell the Su-35. Financial problems resulted from Western sanctions most probably have forced Russian elites to yield and accept increased arms sales. In general, the Sino-Russian military relations show what a long way those two countries have gone in the last twenty-seven years: from considering one another as almost a threat, to deep, multidimensional cooperation, beneficial for both sides, but more for the Chinese side (it gets most sophisticated weapons that it is unable to purchase anywhere else due to Western embargo, for a good price). Thus, military relations also show the general trend in Russia-China relations, emphasized in this book: asymmetric win-win in favour of Beijing. Although Russia is, indeed, stronger in the military relations, and it does not lose in cooperation with China, it is China that achieves more gain in these relations, as it gets a way to improve its military capabilities (so crucial given Sino-American competition in Asia-Pacific).

The Kremlin elites are aware of the asymmetry and the consequences behind becoming China's junior partner. Nevertheless, they choose to cooperate anyway. This happens for a few reasons. 1) They make a virtue out of necessity: they wanted to, but couldn't balance the Chinese influence, so they bandwagoned. 2) They are aware that so far Russia can stay calm: China's position is far from hegemony. The rise of China is not yet dangerous for Russia, because Moscow knows that – for now – the strategic ambitions of China are concentrated on East and Southeast Asia, not Northeast Asia. 3) China supports Russian actions in the post-Soviet area, at least rhetorically. 4) Although Russians acknowledge the success of the Chinese, they realize that the Chinese modernization is still unfinished; China still has a long way to go. 5) Contrary to the USA, China does not interfere in domestic affairs nor instruct others in public how they should conduct their own affairs (thus Beijing does not seek regime change; the opposite is true – China wants to have a stable partner and Putin fulfils this goal). Moreover, China knows Russian sensibilities: it shows Russia respect, praises Russia as the 'great power' (the Chinese learned how to tackle Russians: they know how to make use of the Russian megalomania) and knows its limits – the Chinese take advantage of their dominance in Sino-Russian relations but do not overuse it in order not to provoke Russia. This all makes China a much more bearable "senior" partner for Russia. 6) The rising

China weakens the United States and forms a more balanced international system, giving Moscow a place to manoeuvre. Russia, although anxious about China, knows that Chinese historical resentments are focused on the West rather than on Russia. Moscow also understands that it is the United States, not Russia, whom China wants to replace as a global hegemon. Henceforth, although Russia is dissatisfied with the growing asymmetry, it is not a basic, fundamental anxiety about the state and the regime's stability. Consequently, in spite of being asymmetric, the relations are strong and stable – it is the asymmetric win-win – and it will remain so in the near future.

This comprehensive win-win asymmetry for China is a stable relationship, because this asymmetry can be classified as "normalized asymmetry". Such asymmetry exists when the relations are not without strains, but both sides are confident of fulfilling their basic interests and expectations of mutual benefits. In other words, benefits outweigh the losses and both sides consider this situation worth keeping in accordance with the "acknowledgement-for-deference" logic. Russia-China relations can also be categorized as "positive asymmetry" where there is economic dependence, but not enmity: where the chief beneficiary (China) continuously deludes or coerces the lesser beneficiary (Russia), while the lesser beneficiary turns a blind eye on it by believing that this is a temporary necessity. Finally, Russia-China asymmetry may be described using "asymmetric option model", where both the stronger (China) and the weaker (Russia) state's approach is "open", which resolves bilateral issues cooperatively. China acts in accordance with this model – it promotes a stable asymmetric relationship, knowing that this is China's responsibility as the stronger partner to minimize misperception and increase involvement in its relations to the weaker partner, and to promote voluntary deference instead of facing resistance. This seems to be the success behind stable Sino-Russian relations.

Finally, having described the present state of affairs between Russia and China, one may dare to speculate and forecast about the future of Russia-China relations. If the historical experience evoked in this book – that the present asymmetric win-win is an equivalent to that of the 17th and the 18th centuries' Sinocentric model, with China at the apex and Russia in the subordinated position – is correct, then the future of their bilateral relations may unfold in accordance with the logic of this system. It would therefore be as before 1842, when the Sinocentric world order of tributary relations did not necessarily involve any significant political control carried out by China. It did require, however, the lesser political entities to recognize a hierarchical structure with China at the apex. In this scenario, Russia would have a chance to develop and even reintegrate the former USSR's area. This would occur, however, under one condition: the recognition of the Chinese primacy and becoming China's junior partner. If China were able to finish modernization and become a global hegemon – both at land and at sea – Russia would slip in to be its vassal state (though probably the most important one). And the relations with Russia might serve as a model for other, lesser, though important, entities. If this happens, then from the Chinese perspective it would not only be the return to the past, but also the return to what is natural.

This scenario is, however, roughly speaking, far from certain – China may stop on the development path due to domestic problems and/or American containment policy which would mean a chance for Russia to act beyond its power (which Moscow does brilliantly).

For here and now, however, one thing is sure. Historically speaking, the present, asymmetric win-win model of Sino-Russian relations means that Russia-China relations came back to the past: to the first, initial phase, when China was stronger and set the agenda of bilateral relations. Thus, the example of Sino-Russian relations shows what many Asians take for granted: that the world is spherical and historical periods come around in cycles.

References

Documents

Japan-Russia Action Plan, Ministry of Foreign Affairs of Japan, 2014, http://www.mofa.go.jp/region/europe/russia/pmv0301/plan.html (access: 03.09.2017).

Japan-U.S. Joint Declaration On Security – Alliance For The 21st Century, Ministry of Foreign Affairs of Japan, http://www.mofa.go.jp/region/n-america/us/security/security.html (access: 6.09.2017).

Joint Communiqué on the Meeting of BRICS Special Envoys on Middle East, 12.04.2017 Mid.ru, http://www.mid.ru/en/foreign_policy/news//asset_publisher/cKNonkJE02Bw/content/id/2725737 (access: 03.09.2017).

Moscow Declaration On Establishing A Creative PartnershipBetween Japan And The Russian Federation, Ministry of Foreign Affairs of Japan, 13.11.1998, http://www.mofa.go.jp/region/europe/russia/territory/edition01/moscow.html (access: 06.09.2017).

Permanent Neutrality of Turkmenistan, United Nations 17.04.1996, Resolutions Adopted by the General Assembly, A/RES/50/80, http://www.un.org/documents/ga/res/50/a50r080.htm (access: 03.09.2017).

Resolution 2094 (2013), United Nations Security Council, http://www.un.org/ga/search/view_doc.asp?symbol=S/RES/2094 (access: 03.09.2017).

Security Council Resolution 1973, UN Press Realese, 17.03.2011, http://www.un.org/News/Press/docs/2011/sc10200.doc.htm (access: 03.09.2017).

The Basic Provisions of the Military Doctrine of the Russian Federation, Federation of American Scientists, 02.11.1993, http://www.fas.org/nuke/guide/russia/doctrine/russia-mil-doc.html (access: 03.09.2017).

VII BRICS Summit: 2015 Ufa Declaration, BRICS Information Center, Toronto, 09.07.2015, http://www.brics.utoronto.ca/docs/150709-ufa-declaration_en.html (access: 03.09.2017).

Верховный Совет Российской Федерации постановление от 13 февраля 1992 г. п 2348-1о ратификации соглашения между ссср и кнр о советско-китайской государственной границе на ее восточной части [The Supreme Counsil of USSR decision on 13.02.1992 on Ratification of Agreement Between USSR and PRC on Soviet-Chinese State Border on its eastern part], Referent.ru, http://www.referent.ru/107/1981 (access:03.09.2017).

Внешняя политика России 1996. Сборник документов [Foreign Policy of Russia in 1996. The Collection of Documents], Министерство иностранных дел Российской Федерации, Е.П. Гусаров и др., Москва 2001.

Военная доктрина Российской Федерации [The War Doctrine of RF], Kremlin.ru, 21.04.2000, http://kremlin.ru/acts/bank/15386 (access: 03.09.2017).

Восточная газовая программа [Eastern Gas Programme], Газпром. http://www.gazprom.ru/about/production/projects/east-program/ (access: 03.09.2017).

Декларация глав государств-членов Шанхайской организации сотрудничества [Declaration of Heads of Member States of SCO], 05.07.2005, Sectsco.org.ru. http://rus.sectsco.org/documents/ (access: 03.09.2017).

Декларация о создании Шанхайской Организации Сотрудничества [The Declaration of Establishment of SCO], www.sectsco.org.ru, 15.06.2001, http://rus.sectsco.org/documents/ (access: 03.09.2017).

Декларация о стратегическом партнерстве между Российской Федерацией и Респуб ликой Индией [Declaration of Strategic Partnership Between RF and Republic of India], Независимая газета, 05.10.2000; http://www.ng.ru/world/2000-10-05/6_ind_rus.html (access: 03.09. 2017).

Декларация о стратегическом партнерстве между Российской Федерацией и Социалистической Республикой Вьетнам [Declaration of Strategic Partnership Between RF and Socialist Republic of Vietnam], Kremlin.ru, 28.02.2001, http://kremlin.ru/supplement/3283 (access: 03.09.2017).

Декларация пятилетия Шанхайской организации сотрудничества [SCO Fifth Anniversary Declaration], www.sectsco.org.ru, 15.06.2006, http://rus.sectsco.org/documents/(access: 03. 09.2017).

Договор между Российской Федерацией и Республикой Казахстан о добрососедстве и союзничестве в XXI веке [Treaty Between RF and Republic of Kazakhstan on Good Neighborhood and Alliance in 21th Century], Kremlin.ru 11.11.2013 http://kremlin.ru/supplement/1560 (access: 03.09.2017).

Договор о добрососедстве, дружбе и сотрудничестве между Российской Федерацией и Китайской Народной Республикой [The Treaty on Good Neighborhood, Friendship and Cooperation Between RF and PRC], Mid.ru, 18.07.2001, http://www.mid.ru/ru/maps/cn/-/asset_publisher/WhKWb5DVBqKA/content/id/576870 (access: 03.09.2017).

Договор о дружбе и сотрудничестве между российской федерацией и республикой индией [Russian Federation and Republic of India Friendship and Cooperation Treaty], Mid.ru, 28.01.1993, http://www.mid.ru/foreign_policy/international_contracts/2_contract/-/storage-viewer/bilateral/page-347/48462 (access: 03.09.2017).

Договор о коллективной безопасности [Joint-Security Treaty], Организация договора о коллективной безопасности, 15.05.1992, http://www.odkb-csto.org/documents/detail.php?ELEMENT_ID=126 (access: 03.09.2017).

Договор о союзнических отношениях между Российской Федерацией и Республикой Узбекистан [Treaty on Relations of Alliance between FR and Republic of Uzbekistan], MID.ru, 14.11.2005, http://www.mid.ru/foreign_policy/international_contracts/2_contract// storage-viewer/bilateral/page-143/45977 (access: 03.09.2017).

Душанбинская Декларация [SCO Dushanbe Declaration of Heads of State], Sectsco.org.ru, 28.08.2008, http://rus.sectsco.org/documents/ (access: 03.09.2017). *Заключительная сессия российско-китайской демаркационной комиссии* [Final Session of Russian-Sino Demarcation Comission], "Дипломатический вестник. Официальные материалы", 1999.

Концепция внешней политики Российской Федерации [FR Foreign Policy Concept], Министерство инностранных дел Российской Федерации, 18.02.2013, Mid.ru, http://www.mid.ru/foreign_policy/official_documents/-asset_publisher/CptICkB6BZ29/content/id/122186 (access: 03.09.2017).

Концепция национальной безопасности Российской Федерации, Независимая газета 14.01.2000, http://nvo.ng.ru/concepts/2000-01-14/6_concept.html (access: 03.09.2017).

Макенко Константин, *Военно-технические сотрудничество России и КНР в 1992-2002 годах:достижения, тенденции, перспективы* [Russian-Chinese Military-Technical Cooperation in 1992-2002 Successes, Tendencies and Perspectives], документ 2, Москва 2002

Меморандум между Правительством Российской Федерации и Правительством Китайской Народной Республики о сотрудничестве в области модернизации экономики [Memorandum between Goverments of RF and PRC on Cooperation in Modernization of Economy], Pravo.Ru, http://docs.pravo.ru/document/view/25735226/25471731/ (access: 03.09.2017).

Основные положения концепции внешней политики Российской Федерации в редакции распоряжения Президента Российской Федерации от 23 IV 1993 № 284-рп [The Basis Principles of Russia's Foreign Policy Concept] "Дипломатический вестник", 1993.

Основы государственной политики Российской Федерации в Арктике на период до 2020 года и дальнейшую перспективу [The Principles of RF Govermental Policy in Arctica in Period from 2020 Onwards], Совет Безопасности Российской Федерации. 18.09.2008, http://www.scrf.gov.ru/documents/98.html (access: 03.09.2017).

Пекинская декларация [The Beijing Declaration], Kremlin.ru, 12.07.2000, http://kremlin.ru/supplement/3181 (access:03.09.2017).

Письмо Путина европейским лидерам об урегулировании долга Украины за газ [Putin's Letter to European Leaders on Ukrainian Dept on Gas], Российская газета, 10.04.2014, http://www.rg.ru/2014/04/10/letter.html (access: 03.09.2017).

Постановление Правительства Российской Федерации от 15 января 2007 г. [Government of Russia Decision from 15.01.2007], Российская газета, 27.01.2007, http://www.rg.ru/2007/01/27/migranty-dok.html (access: 03.09.2017).

Программа сотрудничества между регионами Дальнего Востока и Восточной Сибири РФ и Северо-Востока КНР (2009 - 2018 годы) [Programme of Cooperation between RF Far East and East Siberia regions and Northeast China regions, 2009-2018], Политическое образование.Ru 18.07.2010, http://www.lawinrussia.ru/kabinet-yurista/zakoni-i-normativnie-akti/2010-07-18/programma-sotrudnichestva-mezhdu-regionami-dalnego-vostoka-i-vostochnoy-sib (access: 03.09.2017).

Распоряжение Президента Российской Федерации от 19 февраля 1996 г. № 77-рп «О мерах по завершению демаркационных работ на Восточной части российско-китайской государственной границы», Сборник законов законодательство Российской Федереаци [Presidential Decree on Terms of Ending the Demarcation Work on the Eastern Part of Russian Chinese State Border], Sbornikzakonov.ru, http://sbornik-zakonov.ru/217419.html (access: 03.09.2017).

Российско-Китайское совместное заявление [Russian-Chinese Joint announcement], Российская газета, 11.12.1999, http://www.rg.ru/oficial/from_min/mid_99/561.htm (access: 03.09.2017).

Россия и Китай: сборник документов 1991-2006 [Russia-China: the Collection of Documents], сост. И. И. Климин, СПБ 2007

Сборник российско-китайских договоров 1949-1999 [Collection of Russia-China Treaties], Москва 2000

Совместное заявление Российской Федерации и Китайской Народной Республики о взаимовыгодном сотрудничестве и углублении отношений всеобъемлющего партнёрства и стратегического взаимодействия [Joint Declaration of RF and PRC on Mutually Comfortable Cooperation and Deepening of All-Encompassing Partnership and Strategic Colaboration], Kremlin.ru, 22.03.2013, http://kremlin.ru/supplement/1423 (access: 03.09.2017).

Совместная Декларация Российской Федерации И Китайской Народной Республики О Международном Порядке в XXI Веке [Joint RR PRC Declaration on International Order in 21th Century], 27.02.2006, www.mid.ru; http://www.mid.ru/ru/maps/cn/-/asset_publisher/WhKWb5DVBqKA/content/id/412066 (access: 03.09.2017).

Совместная декларация Российской Федерации и Китайской Народной Республики [Joint Declaration of FR and PRC], Kremlin.ru, 02.12.2002, http://kremlin.ru/supplement/3546 (access: 03.09.2017).

Совместная декларация Российской Федерации и Китайской Народной Республики по основным международным вопросам [Joint RR PRC Declaration on International Issues], Kremlin.Ru, 23.08.2008, http://kremlin.ru/supplement/240 (access: 03.09.2017).

Совместное заявление об укреплении отношений всеобъемлющего стратегического партнерства между Российской Федерацией и Социалистической Республикой Вьетнам [Joint Communique on Upgrading the All-Encompassing Strategic Partnership Between RF and Socialist Republic of Vietnam], Kremlin.ru, 27.07.2012, http://kremlin.ru/supplement/1279 (access: 03.09.2017).

Совместное заявление Президента Российской Федерации и Председателя Китайской Народной Республики об укреплении глобальной стратегической стабильности [Joint Declaration of RF President and PRC Chairmant on Deepening Global Strategic Stability], Kremlin Ru, 26.06.2016, http://kremlin.ru/supplement/5098 (access: 03.09.2017).

Совместное заявление Российской Федерации и Китайской Народной Республики о новом этапе отношений всеобъемлющего партнерства и стратегического взаимо действия [Joint Declaration of RF and PRC on New Stage of All-Encompassing Partnership and Strategic Colaboration], Kremlin.ru, 20.05.2014, http://kremlin.ru/supplement/1642 (access: 03.09.2017).

Совместное заявление Российской Федерации и Китайской Народной Республики о дальнейшем углублении российско-китайских отношений всеобъемлющего равноправ ного доверительного партнерства и стратегического взаимодействия [Joint Declaration of RF and PRC on Further Deepening Sino-Russian Relations to All Encompassing, Equal, Trustful Partnership and Strategic Colaboration], Kremlin.ru, 05.06.2012, http://kremlin.ru/supplement/1230 (access: 03.09.2017).

Совместное заявление Российской Федерации и Китайской Народной Республики об углублении всеобъемлющего партнерства и стратегического взаимодействия и о продвижении взаимовыгодного сотрудничества [Joint Declaration of RF and PRC on Deepening of All-Encompassing Partnership and Strategic Colaboration and Moving Towards Mutually Beneficial Cooperation], Kremlin.Ru, 08.05.2016, http://kremlin.ru/supplement/4969 (access: 03.09.2017).

Совместное заявление Российской Федерации и Китайской Народной Республики о сотрудничестве по сопряжению строительства Евразийского экономического союза и Экономического пояса Шелкового пути [Joint Declaration of RF and PRC on Cooperation in Connecting Eurasian Union and Silk Road Economic Belt] , Kremlin.Ru, 08.05.2016, http://kremlin.ru/supplement/4971 (access: 03.09.2017).

Совместное коммюнике неформальной встречи глав МИД КНР, РФ и Индии [Joint Communique After Informal Meeting of Heads of MFA of PRC, RF and India], 03.06.2005, Генеральное Консульство КНР в г.Хабаровске, http://www.chinaconsulate.khb.ru/rus/xwdt/t199594.htm (access: 03.09.2017)

Совместное Российско-Китайское заявление об итогах встречи на высшем уровне в Москве [Joint Declaration on the Results of Meeting on the Top Level], Kremlin.ru, 17.06.2009 года, 2009, http://kremlin.ru/supplement/58 (access: 03.09.2017).

Соглашение между Министерством обороны РФ и Министерством обороны Китая о военном сотрудничестве 11.10.1993, Bestpravo.ru, http://www.bestpravo.ru/rossijskoje/rf-dokumenty/y0b.htm (access: 03.09.2017).

Соглашение между правительством Союза Советских Социалистических Республик и правительством Китайской Народной Республики о принципах создания и деятельности совместных предприятий (The agreement between USSR and PRC on terms of creation and action of joint-ventures), Пекин 08.06.1988, http://www.chinaruslaw.com/RU/CnRuTreaty/004/2011225222754_823742.htm (access: 03.09.2017).

Соглашение о принципах строительства и эксплуатации нефтепровода «Сковородино - граница с КНР» между Китайской национальной нефтегазовой корпорацией и ОАО АК «Транснефть» [Agreement of Principles of Building and Exploatation of Skorovodion-PRC border pipeline between CNPC and Transneft], Russian.China.Org.Cn, 29.10.2008, http://russian.china.org.cn/international/txt/2008-10/29/content_16681397.htm (access: 03.09.2017).

Стратегия развития России в АТР в XXI веке [Strategy of Russia's Development]. Аналитический доклад, Москва, Совет Федерации, 2000, http://archiv.council.gov.ru/inf_sl/bulletin/item/113/ (access: 03.09.2017).

Стратегия социально-экономического развития Дальнего Востока и Байкальского региона на период до 2025 года [Strategy of Socioeconomic Development of the Far East and Zabaykale region until 2025], Распоряжение Правительства РФ от 28 XII 2009 N 2094-р, Закон-Прост.Ru, http://www.zakonprost.ru/content/base/part/658676 (access: 03.09.2017).

Ташкентская декларация пятнадцатилетия Шанхайской организации сотрудничества [Tashkent Declaration of the 15th Anniversary of SCO], sectosco.ru, 24.06.2016. http://rus.sectsco.org/documents/ (access: 03.09.2017).

Ткаченко Борис И. (1999), *Россия-Китай: восточная граница в документах и материалах* [Russia China: the Eastern Border in Documents and Materials], Владивосток, «Уссури»

Указ Президента Российской Федерации о Ишаеве В.И. [RF President's Decree on Ishaev V.I.], 31.08.2013, Kremlin.ru, http://kremlin.ru/acts/bank/37592 (access: 03.09.2017).

Указ Президента Российской Федерации о структуре федеральных органов испольн тельной власти [RF President's Decree on structure of Federal Executive Organs], Российская газета 22.05.2012, https://rg.ru/2012/05/22/struktura-dok.html (access: 03.09. 2017).

Указ президента РСФСРО либерализации внешнеэкономической деятельности на территории РСФСР [FR SSR President's Decree on Liberaliztion of Foreign Economic Activity on the Territory of FR SSR), 17.11.1991, Consultant.ru, http://base.consultant.ru/cons/cgi/online.cgi?req=doc;base=LAW;n=12244 (access: 03.09.2017).

Указ Президента РФ об отношениях между Российской Федерацией и Тайванем (FR President's Decree on Relations with Taiwan), 09,1992, Kremlin. Ru, http://kremlin.ru/acts/bank/2010 (access: 05.09.2017)

Федеральная целевая программа «Экономическое и социальное развитие Дальнего Востока и Забайкалья на 1996-2005 и до 2010 года» [Federal Programme of Economic Development of the Far East and Zabaikale 1996-2005 and to 2010], NCS.ru, http://www.nsc.ru/win/sbras/bef/pos480.html (access: 03.09.2017).

Хартия Шанхайской Организации Сотрудничества [SCO Charter], www.sectsco.org.ru, 15.06.2002, http://rus.sectsco.org/documents/ (access: 03.09.2017).

Шанхайская конвенция [Shanghai Convention on Fight Against Terrorism, Separatism and Extremism], 15.06.2001, www.sectsco.org.ru, http://rus.sectsco.org/documents/ (access: 03.09. 2017).

Official Speeches, Articles, Interviews and Other Data

Feigenbaum Evan A. (2007), *The Shanghai Cooperation Organization and the Future of Central Asia*, Speech at Nixon Center, Washington D.C., 6.09.2007, https://2001-2009.state.gov/p/sca/rls/rm/2007/91858.htm (access: 05.09.2017).

Foreign Minister Wang Yi on Major-Country Diplomacy with Chinese Characteristics, World Peace Forum 27.03.2013, http://www.wpfforum.org/index.php?m=content&c=index&a=show&catid=15&id=92 (access: 03.09.2017).

Full Text: China's Peaceful Development Road, People's Daily Online 22.12.2005, http://english.peopledaily.com.cn/200512/22/eng20051222_230059.html (access: 03.09.2017).

Harmonious society, China Daily, 29.09.2007, http://english.people.com.cn/90002/92169/92211/6274603.html (access: 03.09.2017).
Hu Jintao, *Hold High the Great Banner of Socialism with Chinese Characteristics and Strive for New Victories in Building a Moderately Prosperous Society in All*, Report to 17th Party Congress, http://www.china.org.cn/english/congress/229611.htm (access: 03.09.2017).
President Xi Jinping Delivers Important Speech and Proposes to Build a Silk Road Economic Belt with Central Asian Countries, MFPRC, 07.09.2013, http://www.fmprc.gov.cn/mfa_eng/topics_665678/xjpfwzysiesgjtfhshzzfh_665686/t1076334.shtml (access: 03.09.2017).
Putin Vladimir (2013), *A Plea for Caution From Russia*, "The New York Times", 11.09.2013, http://www.nytimes.com/2013/09/12/opinion/putin-plea-for-caution-from-russia-on-syria.html (access: 05.09.2017).
Remarks by Vice President Biden at 45th Munich Conference on Security Policy, Office of the Vice President 07.02.2010, http://www.whitehouse.gov/the_press_office/RemarksbyVicePresidentBidenat45thMunichConferenceonSecurityPolicy (access: 03.09.2017).
Results of JETRO's 2015 Survey on Business Conditions of Japanese Companies in Russia, https://www.jetro.go.jp/en/news/releases/2015/44ccda712f1c9152.html (access: 07.09.2017).
Security Council Fails to Adopt Resolution Condemning Chemical Weapons Use in Syria, Following Veto by Russian Federation, UNSC, SC/12791, 12.04.2017, https://www.un.org/press/en/2017/sc12791.doc.htm (access: 07.09.2017).
Visiting Relatives and Friends to Discuss Cooperation Joining Hands to Develop a Better Future, MFPRC, 22.08.2014

Владимир Путин: между Москвой и Вашингтоном нет конкуренции за влияние на страны СНГ (2002), [Valdimir Putin: There is No Rivarly Between Moscow and Washington On the Influence over CIS], Интервью газете «Жэньминь Жибао» 04.04.2002. http://www.shanhai.rfn.ru/interviews/doc.html?id=392 (access: 05.09.2017)
Встреча с Председателем Китайской Народной Республики Ху Цзиньтао [Meeting with PRC Chairman Hu Jintao], Kremlin.ru, 07.09.2012, http://www.kremlin.ru/events/president/news/16408 (access: 05.09.2017).
Вступительное слово на совещании «О перспективах развития Дальнего Востока и Забайкалья» [Entry Word on Meeting 'Perspectives of Russian Far East and Zabaykale Development], Kremlin.ru, 21.06.2000, http://kremlin.ru/events/president/transcripts/21494 (access: 03.09.2017).
Выступление Ху Цзиньтао на торжественном вечере, посвященном 60-летию установления дипотношений между Китаем и Россией [Hu Jintao's Speech on Celebrated Gala Dedicated to 6oth Anniversary of Relations Between China and Russia], Russian.Xinhua.Com, 18.06.2009, http://www.russian.xinhuanet.com/russian/2009-06/18/content_894770.htm (access: 03.09.2017).
Выступление А.Чубайса "Миссия России" в Санкт-Петербургском государственном инженерно-экономическом университете [Lecture of A. Chubayis 'the Mission of Russia' in St.Petersbourg State University], vodaspb.ru, 26.09.2003, http://www.vodaspb.ru/archive/vp_sssr/knigi/liberalizm_vrag_svobodi_2003/chubais_missiya_rossii.pdf; access: 05.09.2017
Выступление и дискуссия на Мюнхенской конференции по вопросам политики безопасности [Speech and Discussion During Munich Conference on Security Policy], Kremlin.ru, 10.02.2007, http://kremlin.ru/events/president/transcripts/24034 (access: 03.09.2017).
Выступление Президента России на параде, посвящённом 70-летию Победы в Великой Отечественной войне [President Putin's Speech During 70th Anniversary of Victory in the Great Patriotic War], Kremlin Ru. 09.05.2015, http://kremlin.ru/events/president/transcripts/49438 (access: 03.09.2017).

Документы, подписанные в рамках официального визита Президента Российской Федерации В. В. Путина в Китайскую Народную Республику [Documents Signet During President Putin visit to PRC], Kremlin.ru, 20.05.2014, http://kremlin.ru/supplement/1643 (access: 05.09.2017).

Документы, подписанные по итогам российско-китайских переговоров [Documents Signed after Russian-Sino Talks], Kremlin.ru, 22.03.2013, http://kremlin.ru/supplement/1425 (access: 05.09.2017).

Заседание Международного дискуссионного клуба «Валдай» [Meeting of the Valdai International Discussion Club], Kremlin.Ru, 27.10.2016, http://kremlin.ru/events/president/news/53151 (access: 05.09.2017)

Заявления для прессы по итогам российско-китайских переговоров [Declarations for Press after the Russian-Sino Talks], Kremlin.Ru, 22.03.2013, http://www.kremlin.ru/transcripts/17728 (access: 03.09.2017).

Интервью Министра иностранных дел России С.В.Лаврова СМИ Монголии, Японии и КНР в преддверии визитов в эти страны [Foreign minister Lavrov's interview to Mongolian, Japanese and Chinese media], Москва, 12.04.2016, mid.ru, http://www.mid.ru/foreign_policy/news/-/asset_publisher/cKNonkJE02Bw/content/id/2227965?p_p_id=101_INSTANCE_cKNonkJE02Bw&_101_INSTANCE_cKNonkJE02Bw_languageId=ru_RU (access: 03.09.2017).

Козырев Андрей В., *преображенная Россия в новом мире* [Transformed Russia in the new world], "Международная жизнь". 1992. № 3–4.

Комментарий официального представителя МИД России А.А.Нестеренко в связи с инцидентом с судном «Нью Стар» [Commantaries of Official Representative of RF MFA Nesterenko Concerning the Incident with New Star Ship], Mid.ru, 20.02.2009, http://www.mid.ru/brp_4.nsf/newsline/8448A8FBF089FBC7C32575620057B8EE

Начало встречи с Президентом Узбекистана Исламом Каримовым [The Beginning of Meeting with President Islam Karimov of Uzbekistan], Kremlin.Ru, 06.06.2008, http://kremlin.ru/events/president/transcripts/336 (access: 03.09.2017).

Обращение Президента Российской Федерации [FR President's Adress], Kremlin.ru, 18.03.2014, http://kremlin.ru/events/president/news/20603 (access: 03.09.2017).

Ответы на вопросы журналистов [Putin's Answers to Journalists' Questions], Kremlin.Ru, 05.09.2016, http://kremlin.ru/events/president/news/52834 (access: 05.09.2017)

Председатель КНР поздравил Владимира Путина с победой на президентских выборах в России [Chairman of PRC Congratulated Putin on Winning the Presidential Elections in Russia], Итар-Тасс, 05.03.2012, http://tass.ru/arhiv/580522 (access: 05.09.2017).

Пресс-конференция по итогам российско-китайских переговоров [Press Conference after the Russian-Sino Talks], Kremlin.ru, 16.07.2011, http://kremlin.ru/events/president/transcripts/11594 (access: 03.09.2017).

Путин Владимир В. (2000) *Интервью китайской газете «Жэньминь жибао», китайскому информационному агентству Синьхуа и телекомпании РТР* [Putin's Interview to Chinese Media], 16.07.2000, Kremlin.Ru http://kremlin.ru/events/president/transcripts/24168 (access: 05.09.2017)

Путин Владимир В. (2012), *Россия сосредотачивается — вызовы, на которые мы должны ответить* [Russia Concentrates: Challenges We Should Answer], Известия 16.01. 2012.

Совместные документы, подписанные в ходе официального визита Президента Российской Федерации В.В.Путина в Китай [Documents Signed During President Putin's trip to China], Kremlin Ru, 26.06.2016, http://kremlin.ru/supplement/5101 (access: 05.09.2017).

Список документов подписанных в присутствии Президента России Владимира Путина и Председателя КНР Ху Цзиньтао [The List of Documents Signed During Meeting Between

President Putin and Chairman Hu], Kremlin.ru, 21.03.2006, http://kremlin.ru/supplement/2660/print (access: 05.09.2017).
Статья Министра иностранных дел России С.В.Лаврова «Историческая перспектива внешней политики России», опубликованная в журнале «Россия в глобальной политике» 3 марта 2016 года, MID.Ru, http://www.mid.ru/foreign_policy/news/-/asset_publisher/cKNonkJE02Bw/content/id/2124391 (access: 03.09.2017).
Статья Президента России Владимира Путина «Россия: новые восточные перспективы» [Article of FR President Putin "Russia: New Eastern Perspectives], Kremlin.Ru, 09.11.2000, http://kremlin.ru/events/president/transcripts/21132 (access: 03.09.2017).
Стенограмма выступления Министра иностранных дел России С. В. Лаврова в Совете Федерации Федерального Собрания Российской Федерации в рамках «правительственного часа» по теме: «Проблемы международно-правового обеспечения приоритетных направлений внешней политики», Москва, 13 мая 2010 года [Stenogramme of the Speech of the Minister of Foreign Affairs on 13th May 2010], Mid.ru, http://www.mid.ru/brp_4.nsf/newsline/4C257006D591F8F9C325772200591162 (access: 03.09.2017).
Фрагмент выступления С.В. Лаврова на Совете Федерации [Part of S.V. Lavrov's Speech in the Federation Council], Geshe.Ru, 17.05.2010, http://geshe.ru/node/435 (access: 03.09.2017).

Statistical data

Всеросийская перепись населения 2002 Том 4: Национальный состав и владение языками, гражданство (All Russia Census, Nationalities, Languages and Citizenship, 2002), http://www.perepis2002.ru/index.html?id=17 (access: 03.09.2017).
Всеросийская перепись населения 2010, Национальный состав населения (All Russia Census 2010), Федеральная служба государственной статистики, http://www.gks.ru/free_doc/new_site/perepis2010/croc/perepis_itogi1612.htm (access: 03.09.2017).
Население России 2009, Семнадцатый ежегодный демографический доклад [Population of Russia. 17th Yearly Demographic Account], отв. ред. А. Г. Вишневский, Demoscope.ru., http://demoscope.ru/weekly/knigi/ns_09/acrobat/glava5.pdf (access:03.09.2017).
Современная социално-демографическая ситуация и запатность населения России [Contemporary Sociodemographical Situation and Population of Russia], GKS.Ru, http://www.gks.ru/bgd/regl/b10_04/IssWWW.exe/Stg/d06/3-demogr.htm (access: 03.09.2017).

Reports

Annual Report to Congress. Military and Security Developments Involving the People's Republic of China (2013), Office of the Secretary of Defence, http://www.defense.gov/pubs/2013_china_report_final.pdf (access: 03.09.2017).
Bond Ian (2016), *Russia and China Russia and China Partners of choice and Partners of choice and necessity?* Centre for European Reform Report 2016, http://www.cer.eu/publications/archive/report/2016/russia-and-china-partners-choice-and-necessity

Carlsson Märta, Susanne Oxenstierna, Mikael Weissmann (2015), *China and Russia – A Study on Cooperation, Competition and Distrust*, Report, Stockholm: Swedish Defence Research Agency, 2015
Conventional Arms Transfer to Developing Nations 1988-2005 (2006), Congressional Research Service Report for Congress, 23.10.2006, http://www.fas.org/sgp/crs/weapons/RL33696.pdf (access: 03.09.2017).
Górecki Wojciech (2014), *Even Further from Moscow*, OSW, Warsaw 2014, http://aei.pitt.edu/58022/1/prace_48_ever_further_from_moscow_net.pdf (access: 05.09.2017).
Grant Charles (2012), *Russia, China and Global Governance*, London Centre for European Reform 2012, http://carnegieendowment.org/files/Grant_CER_Eng.pdf (access: 07.09.2017)
Jarosiewicz Aleksandra, Strachota Krzysztof (2013), *China vs. Central Asia. The achievements of the past two decades*, OSW, Warsaw 2013, https://www.osw.waw.pl/sites/default/files/prace_45_cina_vs_asia_ang-net.pdf (access: 05.09.2017).
Majid Munir (2012) Southeast Asia between China and the United States IDEAS reports - special reports, SR015, http://eprints.lse.ac.uk/47502/ (access: 05.09.2017)
Makienko Konstantin (2001), *U. S. Congressional Research Service Report on Russia's Place in the Arms Market*, "Moscow Defence Brief" 5/2001, http://mdb.cast.ru/mdb/5-2001/at/uscr/ (access: 03.09.2017).
Meick Ethan (2017), *China-Russia Military-to-Military Relations: Moving Toward a Higher Level of Cooperation*, U.S.-China Economic and Security Review Commission Report, 20.03.2017, https://www.uscc.gov/Research/china-russia-military-military-relations-moving-toward-higher-level-cooperation (access: 03.09.2017).
Petersen Alexandros, Barysch Katinka (2011), *Russia, China and the geopolitics of energy in Central Asia*, Centre for European Reform Report, 16.11.2011, http://www.cer.eu/publications/archive/report/2011/russia-china-and-geopolitics-energy-central-asia (access: 06.09.2017).
Preliminary findings on the events in Andijan, Uzbekistan, 13 May 2005, Organization for Security and Cooperation in Europe, 20.06.2005, http://www.osce.org/odihr/15653?download=true (access: 03.09.2017).
Short War, Long Shadow.The Political and Military Legacies of the 2011 Libya Campaign (2012), Royal United Service Institute Report 2012, https://rusi.org/publication/whitehall-reports/short-war-long-shadow-political-and-military-legacies-2011-libya (access: 05.09.2017)

Books and articles

Acharya Amitav (1999), *A Concert of Asia?*, "Survival", vol. 41, no 3 (Autumn 1999)
Ahrari Mohammed E., Beal James (2002), *The New Great Game in Muslim Central Asia*, University Press of Pacific
Ambrosio Thomas (2008), *Catching the 'Shanghai Spirit': How the Shanghai Cooperation Organization Promotes Authoritarian Norms in Central Asia*, "Europe-Asia Studies", Vol. 60, No. 8.
Anthony Ian, eds. (1998), *Russia and the Arms Trade*, Oxford, New York: Oxford University Press 1998.
Azrael Jeremy R, Payin Emil A., eds. (1996) *Cooperation and Conflict in the Former Soviet Union: Implications for Migrations*, Santa Monica California: Rand
Babones Salvatore (2016), *American Tianxia: Sovereignity in Millennial World-System*; IROWS papers, http://irows.ucr.edu/papers/irows102/irows102.htm (access: 05.09.2017).

Babones Salvatore (2017), *American Tianxia. Chinese Money, American Power and the End of History,* Bristol: Policy Press
Bäcker Roman (2007), *Rosyjskie myślenie polityczne czasów prezydenta Putina* [Russian political thinking during President Putin times], Toruń: Adam Marszałek
Ballington James H. (1970), *The Icon and the Axe: An Interpretative History of Russian Culture*, New York: Vintage Books
Bartosiak Jacek (2016), *Pacyfik i Eurazja. O wojnie* [Pacific and Eurasia. On War], Warszawa: Biblioteka Jedwabnego Szlaku
Basaldú Robert J. (2011), *Two Eagles, One Dragon: Asymmetric Theory and the Triangular Relations between the U.S., China and Mexico*, unpublished MA thesis, Baylor University
Beginning of the Bush Adinistration, "Tamkang Journal of International Affairs" 8-3/2003,
Bieleń Stanisław (2006), *Tożsamość międzynarodowa Federacji Rosyjskiej* [The international identity of Russian Federation], Warszawa: Oficyna Wydawnicza ASPRA-JR.
Bilateral Relations, and East Versus West in the 2010s, Woodrow Wilson Center: Stanford
Billington James H. (2004), *Russia in Search of Itself*, Woodrow Wilson Center and John Hopkins University Press 2004
Blank Stephen (1997), *The Dynamics of Russian Weapon Sales to China*, Washington D.C.: Brookings
Blank Stephen, eds. (2010), *Russia's Prospects in Asia*, Strategic Studies Institute, U.S. Army War College, Carlisle, PA,
Braekhus Kyrre E., Øverland Indra (2007), A Match Made in Heaven? Strategic Convergence between China and Russia, "China and Eurasia Quarterly" 2007, vol. 5, no. 2
Bryc Agnieszka (2004), *Cele polityki zagranicznej Federacji Rosyjskiej* [The Goals of Russian Federation's Foreign Policy], Toruń: Adam Marszałek
Cambodia, "The Journal of Strategic Studies", vol. 26, no. 2, June 2003
Chong-Pin Lin (2006), *Formująca się wielka strategia Chin: ku dominacji, ale bez walki* [The Formulating China's Grand Strategy: to dominate, but without fight], "Azja-Pacyfik" 9/2006
Chufrin Gennadi, eds. (1999) *Russia and Asia. The Emerging Security Agenda*, Oxford: Oxford University Press, 1999.
Cohen Ariel (2006), *After the G-8 Summit: China and the Shanghai Cooperation Organization*, "China and Eurasia Quarterly", Volume 4, no. 3.
Cooley Alexander (2012), *Great Games, Local Rules: The New Great Power Contest in Central Asia*, New York: Oxford University Press
de Haas Marcel (2007), *The Shanghai Cooperation and the OSCE: Two of a kind*, Helsinki Monitor 18.
de Haas Marcel (2007), *The Shanghai Cooperation Organization's Momentum Towards A Mature Security Alliance*, "Netherlands Institute of International Relations, 03.07.2007.
Dittmer Lowell (1981), *The Strategic Triangle: An Elementary Game-Theoretical Analysis*, "World Politics" 33, no. 4 (July 1981).
Dmochowski Tadeusz (2008), *Radziecko-chińskie stosunki polityczne po śmierci Mao Zedonga* [Soviet-Sino Political Relations After Mao Zedong's Death], Gdańsk: Wydawnictwo Uniwersytetu Gdańskiego
Does Chinese Migration Endanger Russian. Security? Moscow Carnegie Center Briefing Papers (1999), VIII, vol. 1, no 8
Fairbank John K. (1992/1998), *China: A New History*, Cambridge, MA: Belknap Press of Harvard University Press
Ferguson Chaka (2012), *The Strategic Use of Soft Balancing: The Normative Dimensions of the Chinese Russian 'Strategic Partnership'*, "Journal of Strategic Studies" 35, no. 2
Fitzgerald Charles P. (1950), *China: A Short Cultural History*, New York, 3rd ed: Cresset Press

French Howard W. (2017), *Everything Under the Heavens. How the Past Helps Shape China's Push for Global Power*, New York and Toronto: Alfred A. Knopf

Frost Alexander (2009), *The Collective Security Treaty Organization, the Shanghai Cooperation Organization, and Russia's Strategic Goals in Central Asia*, "China & Eurasia Forum Quarterly" 2009, Vol. 7 Issue 3.

Garner James W., *A Far Eastern Rapallo: the post cold-war Russian-Chinese strategic partnership*, "Проблемы Далнего Востока" 1998, № 1

Garnett Sherman W., eds. (2000), *Rapprochement or Rivalry? Russia – China Relations in a Changing Asia*, Washington D. C.: Carnegie

Gawlikowski Krzysztof, eds. (2000) Rosja-Chiny. Dwa modele transformacji (Russia-China. Two models of Transformation), Toruń: Adam Marszałek

Gelbras Vilya (2005), *Chinese Migration in Russia*, "Russia in Global Affairs", 2005, vol. 3, no 2 (April-June).

Gibson John, Hansen Philip, eds. (1995), *Transformation from Below: Local Power and the Political Economy of Post-Communist Transitions*, Cheltenham: Edward Elgar Publishing Ltd

Giplin Robert (1996), *No One Loves a Political Realist*, "Security Studies" 1996, vol. 5, Is. 3

Godement François (2016), *Contemporary China: Between Mao and Market*, Lanham, Boulder, New York, London: Rowman & Littlefield Publishers

Goldman Merle, MacFarquhar Roderick, eds. (1999) *The paradox of China's Post-Mao Reforms*, Cambridge Mass.: Harvard University Press

Góralczyk Bogdan (201), *Chiński feniks. Paradoksy wschodzącego mocarstwa* [The Chinese Phoenix. The Paradoxes of a Rising Power], Warszawa: Rambler

Góralczyk Bogdan (2013), *Chiński sen* [The Chinese Dream], "Komentarz Międzynarodowy Pułaskiego" 3/2013.

Góralczyk Bogdan (2016), *China under Uncle Xi*, "Aspen Review Central Europe" 2/2016.

Góralczyk Bogdan (2016), *W poszukiwaniu chińskiego modelu rozwojowego* [In Search of a Chinese Model of Development], "Sprawy Międzynarodowe" 2016, nr 1, pp. 40-61.

Hanova, Selbi (2009), *Perspectives on the SCO: Images and Discourses*, "China and Eurasia Quarterly" 2009, Vol. 7, no. 3.

Hill Fiona, Gaddy Clifford (2015), *Mr. Putin: Operative in the Kremlin*, Washington D.C.: Brookings, 2nd ed.

Huei-Ming Mao (2003), *The U. S. – China – Russia Strategic Triangle Relationship-Since the*

Huntington Samuel (1997), *The Clash of Civilization and the Remaking of World Order*, New Delhi: Penguin Books 1997.

IRPS, University of California Press, Spring 2006, Volume 5.

Iwashita Akihiro (2002), *The Influence of Local Russian Initiatives on Relations with China: Border Demarcation and Regional Partnership*, "Acta Slavica Iaponica", 2002, vol. 19.

Jakobsen Linda, Holtom Paul, Knox Dean, Jingchao Peng (2011), *China's Energy and Security Relations with Russia. Hopes, Frustrations and Uncertainties*, Stockholm: SIPRI policy paper no. 29

Jeffries Ian (2011), *Political Developments in Contemporary Russia*, London and New York: Routledge

Johnston Alastair I. (1998), *Cultural Realism: Strategic Culture and Grand Strategy in Chinese History*, Princeton: University Press Princeton.

Kaczmarski Marcin (2006), *Rosja na rozdrożu. Polityka zagraniczna Władimira Putina* [Russia at the crossroads. The foreign policy of Vladimir Putin], Warszawa: Spraw Polityczne

Kaczmarski Marcin (2017), *Chaos or Stability*, "New Eastern Europe", 2/2017

Kaczmarski Marcin, Konończuk Wojciech (2008), *Rosja-Chiny: umowa o ropociągu do Daqingu jako przejaw nowego kształtu stosunków dwustronnych* [Russia-China. Daqing Agreement as an Example of New Model of Bilateral Relations], OSW, Warsaw, 30.10.2008.

Kaczmarski Marcin, Konończuk Wojciech (2012), *Po obu stronach Amuru* [On both banks of Amur], Nowa Europa Wschodnia 5/2012.
Kaczmarski, Marcin (2015), *Russia-China Relations in the Post-Crisis International Order*, London and New York: Routledge,
Kagan Robert (2008), *The Return of History and the End of Dreams*, New York: Alfred A. Knopf
Kajdański Edward (2005), *Długi cień Wielkiego Muru. Jak Polacy odkrywali Chiny* [The Long Shade of the Great Wall; How Poles Were Discovering China], Warszawa: Oficyna Naukowa
Keohane Robert O., eds. (1986), *Neorealism and Its Critics*, New York: Columbia University Press
Kerr David (1996), *Opening and Closing the Sino-Russian Border: Trade, Regional Development and Political Interests in Northeast Asia*, "Europe-Asia Studies" 1996, vol. 48, no 6
Kerr David (1998), *Problems in Sino-Russian Economic Relations*, "Europe-Asia Studies", 7/1998
Keun-Wook Paik (2014), *Sino-Russian Oil and Gas Cooperation: The Reality and Implications*, Oxford: Oxford University Press.
Khanna Parag (2008), *The Second World. How Emerging Powers are Redefining Global Competition in the Twenty First Century*, New York: Penguin, Random House.
Khoo Nicholas, Smith Michael (2001), *A Concert of Asia?*, "Policy Review" 2001, no 108 (August 2001)
Kissinger Henry (2011), *On China*, New York: Penguin Press
Kokubun Ryosei, Wang Jisi eds. (2004), *The Rise of China and a Changing East Asian Order*, Tokyo: Japan Center for International Exchange
Konończuk Wojciech (2008), *Ropociąg Wschodnia Syberia – Ocean Spokojny (WSTO): strategiczny projekt – organizacyjna porażka?* [ESPO Pipeline: Strategic Project or Organizational Failure], OSW, Warsaw, 12.10.2008.
Konończuk Wojciech, eds. (2007) *Imperium Putina* [Putin's Empire], Warszawa: Instytut Batorego
Kozłowski Krzysztof (2011), *Państwo Środka a Nowy Jedwabny Szlak* [The Middle Country and the New Silk Road], Toruń: Adam Marszałek
Krasner Stephen D. (1999), *Sovereignty: Organized Hypocrisy*, New Jersey: Princeton University Press
Kuhrt Natasha (2011), *Russian Policy towards China and Japan: The El'tsin and Putin Periods,* London and New York: Routledge.
Kuhrt Natasha (2012), *The Russian Far East in Russia's Asia Policy: Dual Integration or Double Periphery?*, "Europe-Asia Studies", vol. 64, no. 3, May 2012
Kuryłowicz Michał (2014), *Polityka zagraniczna Uzbekistanu wobec Rosji* [Uzbekistan's Foreign Policy Towards Russia], Kraków: Akademicka.
Landes David (1998), *The Wealth and Poverty of Nations. Why Some are so Rich and Some so Poor*, New York: W. Norton
Larin Vladimir (2006), *Russia's Eastern Border: Last Outpost of Europe Or Base for Asian Expansion?* "Russian Expert Review", vol. 18, no. 4, October 2006.
Levin Michael. L. (2008), *The Next Great Clash. China and Russia vs. The United States*, Westport– London: Praeger Security International
Liu Mingfu (2015), *The China Dream: Great Power Thinking and Strategic Posture in the Post-American Era,* New York: CN Times Books.
Lo Bobo (2008), *Axis of Convenience. Moscow, Beijing and the New Geopolitics*, London: Chatham House
Lo Bobo (2015), *Russia and The New World Disorder*, London and Washington D.C: Chatham House and Brookings
Lo Bobo, Shevtsova Lilia (2012), *A 21th Century Myth. Authoritarian Modernization in Russia and China*, Carnegie Center Moscow 2012.

Łopińska Aleksandera (2012), *The "Yellow Peril" syndrome in contemporary Russia*, "Sensus Historiae. Studia interdyscyplinarne", vol. VIII, no 2012/3.
Lubina Michał (2014) *Niedźwiedź w cieniu smoka. Rosja-Chiny 1991-2014* [The Bear Overshadowed by the Dragon. Russia-China 1991-2014], Kraków: Akademicka.
Lukin Alexander (2009), *Russia's New Authoritarianism and the post-Soviet Polirtical Ideal*, "Post-Soviet Affairs" 25, no. 1/2009
Mancall Mark (1972), *Russia and China. Their Diplomatic Relations to 1728*, Cambridge Ms.: Harvard University Press
Mancall Mark (1984), *China at the Center: 300 Years of Foreign Policy*, New York: Free Press.
Matveeva Anna (2007), *Return to Heartland: Russia's Policy in Central Asia,* "The International Spectactor. Italian Journal of International Affairs", Volume 42, Issue 1.
Maung Aung Myo (2011), *In the name of Pauk-Phaw. Myanmar's China Policy Since 1948*, Singapore: Singapore University Press
Mearsheimer John (2001), The Tragedy of Great Power Politics, New York: W. Norton and Company
Menon Rajan (2003), *The Sick Man of Asia: Russia's Endangered Far East*, "The National Interest" 2003, no. 73
Miller Tom (2017), *China's Asia Dream. Empire Building along the New Silk Road*, London: Zed Books.
Moltz Clay J. (2003), *Russian Policy on the North Korean Nuclear Crisis*, Monterey Institute of International Studies: Center for Nonproliferation Studies, April 2003
Mote Frederick M. (1999), *Imperial China, 900-1800*, Cambridge, MA: Harvard University Press, 1999.
Mullerson Rein (2007), *Central Asia: A Chessboard and Player in the New Great Game*, New York: Columbia University Press
Nizioł Monika (2004), *Dylematy kulturowe międzynarodowej roli Rosji* [The Cultural Dilemmas of Russia's International Role], Lublin: Wydawnictwo UMCS
Nygren Bertil (2007), *The Rebuilding of Greater Russia: Putin's Foreign Policy Towards the CIS Countries*, Abingdon, New York: Routledge.
Olszewski Wiesław (2003), *Chiny. Zarys kultury* [China. The Outline of Culture], Poznań: Wydawnictwo UAM
Pierre Andrew J., Trenin Dmitri, eds. (1997), *Russia in the World Arms Sales*
Pietrewicz Oskar, *Krewetka między wielorybami. Półwysep Koreański w polityce mocarstw* [*A Shrimp Between Whales. The Korean Peninsula in Great Powers' policies*], Warszawa: Wydawnictwo Asian Century
Pipes Richard (2004), *Flight from Freedom. What Russians Think and Want*, "Foreign Affairs", vol. 83, no 3 May/June 2004.
Popova Liudmila (2006), *Recent Trends in Russian-Chinese Economic Cooperation*, "World Economic Papers" (special issue), no. 7 (2006).
Radzichowski Leonid (2007), *Traktat o szacunku* [The Treaty on Respect], Newsweek (Poland) 20.04.2007.
Ropp Paul, eds. (1990) *Heritage of China:Contemporary Perspectives on Chinese Civilisation*, Berkeley: University of California Press
Rozman Gilbert (1997), *Troubled Choices for the Russian Far East: Decentralization, Open Regionalism and Internationalism*, "Journal of East Asian Affairs" 1997, no 2.
Rozman Gilbert (2014), *The Sino-Russian Challenge to the World Order. National Identities,*
Rumer Eugene (2006), *China, Russia and the Balance of Power in Central Asia*, "Strategic Forum" 2006, No 223 (November).
Rumer Eugene, Trenin Dmitri, Zhao Huasheng (2007), *Central Asia: Views from Washington, Moscow and Beijing*, New York: M.E. Sharpe

Rumer Eugene, Wallander Celeste A. (2003), *Russia: Power in Weakness*, "Washington Quarterly", vol. 27, no 1 (winter 2003-2004)
Salin Pavel (2012), *Russia's Three Roads to Asia*, "Russia in Global Affairs", 27.12.2012.
Shambaugh David (2013), *China Goes Global. The Partial Power*, New York: Oxford University Press
Shambaugh David (2014), *Modernizing China's Military: Progress, Problems, and Prospects*, Berkeley: University of California Press
Shearman Peter, eds. (1995), *Russian Foreign Policy Since 1990*, San Francisco, Boulder: Westview Press
Shevtsova Lilia (2010), *Lonely Power: Why Russia Has Failed to Become the West and the West Is Weary of Russia*, Washington D.C.: Carnegie
Shi Ze (2005), *Relations Between China and Central Asian Countries Face Opportunity of All-Round Development*, "China International Studies" no 1, Winter 2005
Shinichiro Tabat, Akihiro Iwashita, eds. (2004) *Slavic Eurasia's Integration into the World Economy and Community*, Sapporo: Slavic Research Center, Hokkaido University
Shinichiro Tabata, Iwashita Akihiro, eds. (2004) *A New Dimension of 'Partnership' After the Post Cold War Period,* Sapporo: Slavic Research Center, Hokkaido University
Shlapentokh Vladimir (1995), *Russia, China and the Far East: Old Geopolitics Or a New Peaceful Cooperation?*, "Comunist and Post-Communist Studies", 1995, vol. 28, no 3.
Spence Jonathan (2001), *In Search for Modern China*, London: Norton.
Stewart Susan, Schröder Hans-Henning, Klein Margarete, Schmitz Andrea (2012), *Presidents, Oligarchs and Bureaucrats. Forms of Rule in the Post-Soviet Space*, London and New York: Routledge
Swanström Niklas (2005), *China and Central Asia: A New Great Game Or Traditional Vassal Relations?*, "Journal of Contemporary China" 2005, vol. 45, no 14 (November)
Sznajder Ariel P. (2006), *China's Shanghai Cooperation Organization Strategy*,
Terzani Tiziano (1997), *A Fortune Teller Told Me*, London: HarperCollins
Tolipov Farkhod (2005), *East vs. West? Some Geopolitical Questions and Observations for the SCO*, "China and Eurasia Quarterly" (July 2005).
Trenin Dmitri (2011), *Post-Imperium: Eurasian Story*, Washington D.C.: Carnegie
Troickiy Mikhail, Bailes Alyson J.K., Dunay Pál, Pan Guang, eds. (2007), *Shanghai Cooperation Organization*, SIPRI Policy Paper No. 17, May 2007
Tubilewicz Czeslaw (2002), *The Little Dragon and the Bear: Russian-Taiwanese Relations in the Post-Cold War Period*, "Russian Review", no 61, 4/2002
Wallander Celeste (2007), *Russian Transimperialism and Its Implications*, [in:] Washington Quarterly, vol. 30, no. 2.
Waltz Stephen (1979), *Theory of International Politics*, Reading, Mas.: Addison-Wesley Pub. Co.
Wardęga Joanna (2014), *Chinski nacjonalizm. Rekonstruowanie narodu w ChRL* [The Chinese nationalism. Reconstructing the nation in PRC], Krakow: Jagiellonian University Press
Watanabe Koji, eds. (1999), *Engaging Russia in Asia Pacific*, Tokyo: Japan Center for International Exchange
Weitz Richard (2012), *China –Russia Security Relations. Strategic Parallelism Without Partnership or Passion?*, Washington D.C.
Wendt Alexander (1995), *Constructing international politics*, "International Security", vol. 20, No. 1 (Summer, 1995)
Wendt Alexander (2000), *Social Theory of International Politics*, Cambridge: Cambridge University Press
Wilson Jeanne L. (2004), *Strategic Partners. Russian-Chinese Relations in the Post-Soviet Era*, London: M.E. Sharpe

Wishnick Elisabeth (2011), *Mending Fences. The Evolution of Moscow's China Policy from Brezhnev to Yeltsin*, Seattle: University of Washington Press
Wites Tomasz (2007), *Wyludnianie Syberii i rosyjskiego Dalekiego Wschodu* [The Depopulation of Siberia and Russian Far East], Warszawa: Wydawnictwo UW
Womack Brantly (2003), *Asymmetry and Systemic Misperception: China, Vietnam and*
Womack Brantly (2010), *China Among Unequals: Asymmetric Foreign Relations in Asia*, Singapore: World Scientific Publishing Company
Xi Jinping (2014), *The governance of China*, Beijing: Foreign Languages Press.
Xiaoming Huang, Robert Patman (2013) *China and the International System. Becoming a World Power*, London adn New York: Routledge
Yahuda Michael, Shoichi Itoh, Ken Jimbo, Michito Tsuruoka, eds. (2017), *Japan and the Sino-Russian Strategic Partnership*, NBR special report #64 (April 2017).
Yan Xuetong (2010), *Ancient Chinese Thought, Modern Chinese Power*, Princeton: Princeton University Press.
Yang Shu (2009), *Reassessing the SCO's Internal Difficulties: A Chinese Point of View*, "China and Eurasia Quartely", Volume 7, no. 3/2009.
Yu Bin (2001), *Crouching Missiles, Hidden Alliances*, "Comparative Connections" vol. 03, no 1.
Yu Bin (2002), *One Year Later:* Geopolitics or Geoeconomics? "Comparative Connections", vol.4 no.3.
Yu Bin (2004), *Presidential Politicking and Proactive Posturing*, "Comperative Connections", vol. 6,no 1.
Yu Bin (2005), *End of History. End of History, What Next?*, "Comperative Connections", vol. 6, no 4.
Yu Bin (2005), *Pollution, Politics and Partnership*, "Comparative Connections" vol. 7, no 4
Yu Bin (2005), *The New World Order According to Moscow and Beijing*, "Comparative Connections", vol. 7, no 3.
Yu Bin (2006), *China's Year of Russia and the Gathering Nuclear Storm*, "Comparative Connections", vol. 8, no 1.
Yu Bin (2006), G-8, *Geoeconomics, and Growing "Talk" Fatigue*, "Comperative Connections" vol. 8, no 3.
Yu Bin (2006), *What Follows China „Russia's Year"?* "Comperative Connections", vol. 8, no 4.
Yu Bin (2007), *Russia Says "No" to the West and "Sort of" to China*, "Comparative Connections" vol. 9, no 1.
Yu Bin (2007), *China-Russia Relations: Partying and Posturing for Power, Petro and Prestige*, "Comparative Connections" 2007, vol. 8, no. 2.
Yu Bin (2007), *Between Cooperation and Competition*, "Comparative Connections" , vol. 9, no. 3
Yu Bin (2008), *Living with Putin Unfading Glory and Dream*, "Comparative Connections", vol. 9, no. 4
Yu Bin (2008), *From Election Politics to Economic Posturing*, "Comparative Connections" 2008, Vol. 10, no 1.
Yu Bin (2008), *Medvedev's Ostpolitik and Sino-Russian Relations*, "Comperative Connections", vol. 10, no 2.
Yu Bin (2008), *Guns and Games of August: Tales of Two Strategic Partners*, "Comperative Connections", vol. 10, no 3.
Yu Bin (2009), *Between Crisis and Cooperation*, "Comparative Connections" vol. 11, no 1.
Yu Bin (2009), *Market Malaise and Mirnaya Missiya*, "Comparative Connections" vol. 11, no 3.
Yu Bin (2009), *Summitry: Between Symbolism and Substance*, "Comparative Connections" vol. 11, no 2.

Yu Bin (2009), *Mr. Putin Goes to China. Ten Years After*, "Comparative Connections", vol. 11, no 4.
Yu Bin (2010), *Reset under Medvedev: Zapad-Politik and Vostok 2010*, "Comparative Connections" 2010, vol. 11, no 2.
Yu Bin (2010), *Peace Mission 2010 and Medvedev's Visit to China*, "Comparative Connections" vo.11, no.3.
Yu Bin (2010), *Coping with Korea*, "Comparative Connections" vol. 11, no 4.
Yu Bin (2011), *Mounting Challenges and Multilateralism*, "Comparative Connections", vol. 12, no 1.
Yu Bin (2011), *Between Geo-Economics and Geo-politics*, "Comparative Connections", vol. 12, no 3.
Yu Bin (2011), *Politics of Two Anniversaries*, "Comparative Connections", vol. 12, no 2.
Yu Bin (2012), *Succession, Syria and the Search for Putin's Soul*, "Comparative Connections", vol. 14, no. 1.
Yu Bin (2013), *Pivot to Eurasia and Africa: Xi Style*, "Comparative Connections", vol. 15, no 1.
Yu Bin (2013), *Summer Heat and Sino-Russian Strategizing*, "Comparative Connections" vol.15, no 2.
Yu Bin (2013), *Putin's Glory and Xi's Dream*, "Comparative Connections" vol. 15, no 3.
Yu Bin (2013), *Tales of Different 'Pivots'* "Comparative Connections" vol.14, no 3.
Yu Bin (2014), *"Western Civil War" Deja Vu?"*, "Comparative Connections", vol. 16, no.1.
Yu Bin (2014), *Navigating Through the Ukraine Storm*, "Comparative Connections" vol. 16, no 2.
Yu Bin (2015), *Russia's Pride and China's Power*, "Comparative Connections" Volume 16, No. 3
Yu Bin (2015), *China-Russia, All Still Quiet in the East*, "Comparative Connections" vol.17 no.1.
Yu Bin (2015), *Tales of Two Parades, Two Drills, and Two Summits*, "Comparative Connections", vol. 17, no.2
Yu Bin (2016), *H-Bomb Plus THAAD Equals Sino-Russian Alliance?*, "Comparative Connections", Vol. 18, No. 1
Yu Bin (2016), *Into the Syrian Storm: between Alliance and Alignment,* "Comparative Connections", Vol. 17, No. 3, Jan. 2016.
Yu Bin (2016), *Politics of "Reluctant Allies"*, "Comparative Connections", vol. 18, No. 2.
Yu Bin (2017), *Trilateral Politics: Trump Style*, "Comparative Connections", vol. 19, No. 1.
Yu Bin (2017), *The Dawn of a Brave Trump World*, "Comparative *Trump World*, "Comparative Connections", Vol. 18, No. 3.
Zevelev Igor (2012), *A New Realism for the 21st Century*, "Russia in Global Affairs", 27.12. 2012.
Zheng Yongnian, eds. (2010), *China and International Relations. The Chinese view and the contribution of Wangu Gungwu*, London and New York: Routledge

Агранат Григорий А. (1992), *Возможности и реальности освоения Севера: глобальные уроки* [Possibilities and Realities of Colonizing Siberia: Global Lessons], Москва: Винити
Азиатско-тихоокеанское сотрудничество и место России в региональном развитии (2014), [AP cooperation and Russia's place in regional development], Москва 2014: РИСИ
Бажанов Евгений П. (1999), *Эволуция внешней политики России* 1991-1999 г. [The Evolution of Russia's Foreign Policy 1991-1999], Москва: Дипломатическая академия МИД
Бажанов Евгений П. (2002), *Актуальные проблемы международных отношений* [The Present Problems of International Relations], Москва: Научная книга
Бажанов Евгений П. (2007) *Китай: От срединной империи до сверхдержавы XXI века* [China: from Middle Empire to a Superpower of 21th Century], Москва: Известия

Бородавкин Алексей Н. (2009), *Россия и Китай: по пути добрососедства и сотрудничества* [Russia and China: Along the Road of Good-Neighbourliness and Cooperation] "Проблемы Дальнего Востока" 5/2009

Витковская Галина С., Тренин Дмитрий В., ред. (1999), *Перспективы Дальневосточного региона межстранное взаимодействия* [Perspectives of

Far Eastern Region, Interstate Joint Cooperation], Москва: Центр Карнеги

Воскресенский Алексей Д. (2004), *Китай и Россия в Евразии. Историческая динамика политических взаимовлиянии* [China and Russia in Eurasia. Historical Dynamism of Political Interactions], Москва: Муравей

Гайдар Егор Т. (1995), *Россия XXI века: не мировой жандарм, а форпост демократии в Евразии* [Russia: not a Gendarme of the World, but a Forepost of Democracy in Eurasia], Известия, 18.05.1995

Галенович Юрий М. (2006), *Россия-Китай-Америка. От сотрудничества к гармонии интересов?* [Russia-China-USA. From Competition to Harmony of Interests?], Москва: Наука

Галенович Юрий М. (2011), *История взаимоотношеий России и Китая, к. IV* [The History of Bilateral Relations of Russia and China], Москва: Восточная книга

Геллер Михаил Я. (1997), *История Российской империи. В трех томах*, Москва: МИК

Гельбрас Вилия Г. (2001), *Китайская реальность России* [Chinese Reality of Russia], Москва: Муравей

Глазачева Надежда Л., Залесская Ольга В., ред. (2013), *Россия и Китай: аспекты взаимодействия и взаимовлияния материалы IV Международной заочной научно-практической конференции* [Russia and China: Aspects of Interactions i Inter-Influence, Conference Proceedings], Благовещенск: БГПУ

Девятов Андрей П. (2002) *Китай и Россия в двадсать первом веке* [China and Russia in the 21th century], Москва: Альгорытм

Демидова Наталья Ф., Мясников Владимир С., ред. (1972), *Русско-китайские отношения в XVII веке. Материалы и документы* т. 2. 1686–1691 [Russo-Chinese relations in 17th Century. Materials and Documents], Москва: Наука

Деревянко Анатолий П. (1999), *Российское Приморье на пороге третьего тысячилетия (Russian Primore at the Turn of the Third Century)*, Владивосток: Дальнаука

Дьяченко Борис, ред. (1996), *Желтая опасность* [Yellow Peril], Владивосток: Ворон

Зайончковская Жанна А. (2005), *Перед лицом миграции* [Facing Immigrantion], "Pro et Contra", 2005, no 3 (30).

Звягельская Ирина Д. (2009), *Становление государств Центральной Азии. Политические процессы* [The Establishing of Central Asian States. Political Processes], Москва: Аспект Пресс

Зиновьев Георгий В. (2010), *Китай и сверхдержавы. История внешней политики КНР (1949–1991)* [China and Superpowers. History of PRC Foreign Policy 1949-1991], СПб: Изд. С.-Петербургского университета

Ивасита Акихиро (2006), *4000 километров проблем. Российско-китайская граница* [4000 kilometers of problems; Russian-Chinese border], Москва: Восток-Запад

Ивашов Леонид Г. (2003), *Хоронить не спешите Россию* [Don't Hurry Up to Burry Russia], Москва: Эксмояуза

Ишаев Виктор И. (2000), *Дальний Восток России: долговременные перспективы сотрудничества в Северо-Восточной Азии* [Russian Far East: long term perspectives of cooperation in Northeast Asia], Хабаровск: ДВО РАН

Какарев Константин А., ред. (2006), *Россия в Азии: проблемы взаимодействия* [Russia and Asia: The Problems of Interaction], Москва: РИСИ

Качинс Эндрю, Никонов Вячеслав А., Тренин Дмитрий В. (2005), *Российско-американские отношения. Как Добится лучшего?* [Russia-US Relations. How to Get it Better?], Москва: Карнеги 2005

Кулешов Валерий В., Атанов Николай И., Безруков Леонид А., Коржубаев Андрей Г. (2010), *О некоторых аспектах совершенствования российско-китайского межрегионального сотрудничества* [On several aspects on the existance of Russian-Sino interregional cooperation], "Проблемы Дальнего Востока" № 6/2010

Ларин Александр Г. (2009), *Китайские мигранты в России. История и современность* [Chinese Migrants in Russia. History and Contemporary Times], Москва 2009: Восточная Книга

Ларин Владимир Л. (1997), *Россия и Китай на пороге третьего тысячелетия: кто же будет отстаи вать наши национальные интересы?* [Russia and China at the Turn of Third Millenniu: Who Will Stand for our National Interets?], "Проблемы Дальнего Востока", 1997, № 1ю

Ларин Владимир Л. (1998), *Китай и Дальний Восток России в первой половине* 90-х: *проблемы регионального взаимодействия* [China and Russian Far East in the first half of 1990s: problems of regional cooperation], Владивосток: Дальнаука

Ларин, Владимир Л. (2006) *В тени проснувшегося дракона* [In the Shadow of the Waking Dragon], Владивосток: Дальнаука

Ларин Владимир Л. (2010), *Азиатско-тихоокеанский регион в начале XXI века: вызовы, угрозы, шансы Тихоокеанской России* [The region of AP in the beginning of 21th century: challenges, threats, chances of the Pacific Russia], Владивосток: Ииаэ НДВ До РАН

Ларин Владимир Л., Ларина Лариса Л. (1999) *Окружающий мир глазами дальневосточников (по итогам опроса населения 2008 г.)* [Surrounding World in Far Eastern Russian Eyes], " *Россия и АТР,*" 1/2009.

Лукин Александр В. (2007), *Китай: опасный сосед или выгодный партнер* [China: dangerous neighbour or convenient partner], "Pro et Contra", Ноябрь– декабрь 2007

Лукин Александр В. (2007), *Китай:медведь наблюдает за драконом. Образ Китая в России в XVII-XXI веках* [The Bear Watches Over the Dragon. The Image of China in Russia in 17-21th Centuries], Москва: Восток-Запад

Лукин Александр В., ред (2013), *Россия и Китай: четыре века взаимодействия. История, современное состояние и перспективы развития российско-китайских отношений* [RussiaChina Four Centuries of Interaction. History, Contemporary Situation and Perspectives of Development], Москва: Весь Мир

Макиенко Константин (1999), *Опасно ли торговать оружем с Китаем?* [Is it Dangerous to Sell Arms to China?], "Pro et Contra", Зима 1998. Т. 3, #1.

Малашенко Алексей (2012), *Центральная Азия: на что рассчитывает Россия?* [Central Asia: What Russia is Counting On], Москва: РОССПЭН

Миграционная ситуация на Дальнем Востоке и политика России (1996), [Migration Situation in Russian Far East], Москва: Центр Карнеги

Михаев Василий В., ред. (2005), *Китай. Угрозы, риски, вызовы развитию*, Москва: Центр Карнеге

Мясников Владимир С., ред. (1969) *Русско-китайские отношения в XVII в. т.1 1608-1683* [Russo-Chinese Relations in 17th Century, 1608-1683], Москва: Наука

Мясников Владимир С. (1985), *Сведения китайцев о России в XVII в.* [The Chinese People's Relations on Russia in 17th Century], "Вопросы истории" 1985, № 12

Мясников Владимир С. (1997), *Договорными статьями утвердили.Дипломатическая история русско китайской границы XVII-XX вв.*[The Treates Have Settled. The Diplomatic History of Russo Chinese Border in 17-20centuries], Хабаровск: ПГО

Рогачев Игорь А. (2005), *Российско-китайские отношения в конце XX — начале XXI века* [Russia-China Relations in Late 20th and Early 21th century], Москва: Известия

Рыбаковский Леонид Л., Захарова Ольга Д., Миндогулов Владимир В. (1994), *Нелегалная миграция в приг раничных районах Дальнего Востока: история, современность и последстия* [Illegal migration in the border regions of the Far East: History, Contempory and Consequences], Москва: ИСПИ РАН

Скачков Петр Е., Мясников Владимир С., ред. (1958) *Русско-китайские отношения 1689-1916. Официалные документы* [Russo-Chinese Relations 1698-1916. Official Documents], Москва: Наука

Стригин Евгений М. (2008), *Эра Дракона* [The Dragon's Era], Москва: Алгоритм

Титаренко Михаил Л. (1994), *Россия и Восточная Азия: Вопросы международных и межцивилизационных отношении* [Russia and East Asia. The Issues of International and Intercivilizational Relations], Москва: Фабула – Кучково поле

Титаренко, Михаил Л. (1998), *Россия лицом к Азии* [Russia Turn Its Face To Asia], Москва: Республика

Титаренко Михаил Л. (2003), *Россия. Безопасность через сотрудничество. Восточноазиатцкий вектор* [Russia: Security Via Cooperation; The East Asia Vector], Москва: Памятники ист. мысли

Титаренко Михаил Л. (2008), *Геополитическое значение Дальнего Востока. Россия, Китай и другие страны Азии* [The Geopolitical importance of the Far East. Russia, China and the other Asian countries], Москва: Памятники исторической мысли

Тихвинский Сергей Л. (2008), *Воспиятие в Китае образа России* [The Perception of Russia's Image in China], Москва: Наука

Тихвинский Сергей Л., ред. (1982) *Китай и соседи в новое и новейшее время* [China and Its Neighbours in the Modern and Contemporary Times], Москва: Наука

Тренин Дмитрий В. (1998), *Китайская проблема России* [Russia's China Problem], Москва: Карнеге

Тренин Дмитрий В. (2001), *Конец Евразии: Россия между геополитикой и глобализацией* [The End of Eurasia. Russia between Geoeconomics and Globalization], Москва: Интердиалект

Тренин Дмитрий В.(2006), *Интеграция и идентичность. Россия как «новый Запад»* [Integration and Indentity. Russia as a 'New West'], Москва: «Европа»

Тренин Дмитрий В. (2011), *Post-Imperium: Евразийская история* [Post-Empire: Eurasian History], Москва: Центр Карнеги

Тренин Дмитрий В., ред. (1996), *Россия в мировой торговле оружем: статегия, политика,экономика* [Russia in World Arms Sales: Strategy, Politics, Economy], Москва: Карнеге

Федотов Владимир П. (2005), *Полвека вместе с Китаем. Воспоминания, записы, розмышления* [Half Century with China. Memories, Nortes, Thoughts], Москва: РОССПЭН

Чубайс Игорь Б. (2014), *Как нам понимать свою страну. Русская идея и Российская идентичность. Прошлое, настоящее, будущее* [How should we understand our country. Russian Idea and Russian identity. Past, Present, Future] Москва: Арсисбоокс

Чуфрин Геннадий И.(1995), *Как перелезть через Великую китайскую стену?* [How to Climb Over the Chinese Wall], Московкое новости, 1995, 21-28 V, № 36.

Шаклеина Татьяна А. ред. (2002*), Внешняя политика и безопасность современной России. 1991-2002 Хрестоматия в четырех томах* [Foreign Policy and Security of the Russian Federation 1991-2002], Москва: Моск.гос.ин-т междунар.отношений

Яковлев Александр Г. (1995), *Международная политическая обстановка в СВА и положение России в регионе* [International political situation in East Asia and Russia's position in the region], "Проблемы Дальнего Востока" 1995, № 2.

Internet Sources

A New Anti-American Axis?(2013), "The New York Times", 06.07.2013, http://www.nytimes.com/2013/07/07/opinion/sunday/a-new-anti-american-axis.html (access: 06.09.2017).

Akio Kawato (2014), *Much Ado About Sino-Russian Axis*, Carnegie Center Moscow 10.06.2014, 10 VI, http://carnegie.ru/commentary/55870 (access: 06.09.2017).

Alexander Gabuev (2016), *Russia and China: Little Brother or Big Sister?*, Moscow Carnegie Center, 05.07.2016, http://carnegie.ru/commentary/64006 (access: 05.09.2017).

Behind China's $1 Trillion Plan to Shake Up the Economic Order (2017), "New York Times", 13.05.2017, https://www.nytimes.com/2017/05/13/business/china-railway-one-belt-one-road-1-trillion-plan.html (access: 06.09.2017).

Brown Kerry (2017), *Trump: The True New Maoist*, "The Diplomat", 19.01.2017; http://thediplomat.com/2017/01/trump-the-true-new-maoist/

Chasing the Chinese dream (2013), "The Economist", 03.05.2013, https://www.economist.com/news/briefing/21577063-chinas-new-leader-has-been-quick-consolidate-his-power-what-does-he-now-want-his (access: 05.09.2017).

China's Leader Tries to Calm African Fears of His Country's Economic Power (2013), "The New York Times", 25.02.2013, http://www.nytimes.com/2013/03/26/world/asia/chinese-leader-xi-jinping-offers-africa-assurance-and-aid.html (access: 06.09.2017).

Chinese Admiral: South China Sea 'Belongs to China', "The Diplomat", 16.09.2015, http://thediplomat.com/2015/09/chinese-admiral-south-china-sea-belongs-to-china/ (access: 05.09.2017).

Clinton Hilary (2011), *America's Pacific Century*, "Foreign Policy", 11.10. 2011, http://foreignpolicy.com/2011/10/11/americas-pacific-century/ (access: 05.09.2017).

Cohen David (2014), *China Maintains Studied Ambiguity On Ukraine As Russia Claims 'Concordance Of Views'*, "China Brief", Volume XIV, Issue 5, March 7, https://jamestown.org/wp-content/uploads/2014/03/China_Brief_Vol_14_Issue_5.pdf?x87069 (access: 06.09.2017).

Collins James, Trenin Dmitri, Shevtsova Lilia, Jensen Donald (2009), *Is Russia Ready for Change?* Carnegie Moscow Center 09.02.2009, http://carnegie.ru/2009/02/06/is-russia-ready-for-change-event-1258 (access: 05.09.2017)

Creutzfeld Benjamin (2011), *Qin Yaqing on Rules vs Relations, Drinking Coffee and Tea, and a Chinese Approach to Global Governance* (, Tsingua Theory Talk #45, https://www.files.ethz.ch/isn/155106/Theory%20Talk45_Yaqing.pdf (access: 05.09.2017)

Dmitri Trenin (2010), *Russia Hits the Reset Button*, Project Sindicate, 31.05.2010, https://www.project-syndicate.org/commentary/russia-hits-the-reset-button (access: 05.09.2017)

Dmitri Trenin (2015), *From Cooperation to Competition. Russia and the West*, Carnegie, 21.01.2015, http://carnegie.ru/2015/01/21/from-cooperation-to-competition-russia-and-west-pub-59436 (access: 05.09.2017).

Donald Trump attempting to play Nixon's 'China card' in reverse (2016), "The Guardian", 12.12.2016, https://www.theguardian.com/us-news/2016/dec/12/donald-trump-us-china-relations-taiwan-nixon (access: 07.09.2017).

Fischer Ewa, Kardaś Szymon, Rodkiewicz Witold (2014), *The rising cost of getting closer to Beijing: New Russian Chinese economic agreements*, OSW, Warsaw, 15.10.2014, https://www.osw.waw.pl/en/publikacje/analyses/2014-10-15/rising-cost-getting-closer-to-beijing-new-russian-chinese-economic (access: 07.09.2017).

Frustrated China seen getting no promises off Putin (2006), "The Star", 20.03.2006, http://www.thestar.com.my/news/world/2006/03/20/frustrated-china-seen-getting-no-promises-off-putin/ (access: 05.09.2017).

Fu Ying (2015), *How China Sees Russia: Beijing and Moscow Are Close, but Not Allies*, “Foreign Policy”, 14.12.2015, https://www.foreignaffairs.com/articles/china/2015-12-14/how-china-sees-russia (access: 05.09.2017).
Gabuev Alexander (2014), *Misreading Asia*, Moscow Carnegie Center, 03.06.2014, http://carnegie.ru/eurasiaoutlook/?fa=55776 (access: 10.10.2015).
Gabuev Alexander (2016), *China's Pivot to Putin's Friends*, “Foreign Policy”, 25.06.2016, http://foreignpolicy.com/2016/06/25/chinas-pivot-to-putin-friends-xi-russia-gazprom-tim chenko-sinopec/ (access: 05.09.2017).
Gabuev Alexander (2016), *Friends with Benefits? Russian-Chinese Relations After the Ukrainian Crisis*, Carnegie Moscow Center, 29.06.2016, http://carnegie.ru/2016/06/29/friends-with-bene fits-russian-chinese-relations-after-ukraine-crisis-pub-63953 (access: 05.09.2017).
Gabuev Alexander (2016), *Putin-Xi Friendship Driving Russia-China Ties*, Carnegie Moscow Center 03.06. 2016; http://carnegie.ru/2016/06/03/putin-xi-friendship-driving-russia-china-ties-pub-63733 (access: 05.09.2017).
Gabuev Alexander (2017), *Friends with Strategic Benefits*, Carnegie Moscow Center, 07.07.2017, http://carnegie.ru/2017/04/07/china-and-russia-friends-with-strategic-benefits-pub-68628 (access: 05.09.2017)
Gaddy G. Clifford, Ickes Barry W.(1998), *Russia's Virtual Economy*, “Foreign Affairs”, nr 77, 5/1998, https://www.foreignaffairs.com/articles/russia-fsu/1998-09-01/russias-virtual-econo my (access: 06.09.2017).
Godement François (2013), *Xi Jinping's China*, European Council on Foreign Affairs 17.07.2013, http://www.ecfr.eu/publications/summary/xi_jinpings_china212 (access: 05.09.2017).
Godement François and Duchâtel Mathieu, eds. (2016), *China And Russia: Gaming the West?*, European Council for Foreign Affairs, 02.11.2016, http://www.ecfr.eu/publications/summary/china_and_russia_gaming_the_west7166 (access: 05.09.2017)
Golden opportunity to hone world-defining China-Russia partnership (2013), “China Daily”, 22.10.2013, http://www.chinadaily.com.cn/china/2013-10/22/content_17050529.htm (access: 05.09.2017).
Goldstein Lyle J. (2017), *A China-Russia Alliance?* “The National Interest”, 25.04.2017, http://nationalinterest.org/feature/china-russia-alliance-20333 (access: 05.09.2017).
Goodrich Lauren (2011), *Russia: Rebuilding Empire While it Can*, “Stratfor”, 31.10.2011, https://worldview.stratfor.com/article/russia-rebuilding-empire-while-it-can (access: 05.09.2017)
Góralczyk Bogdan (2013), *Chińskie sny* [The Chinese Dreams], Obserwator finansowy, 21.07.2013, https://www.obserwatorfinansowy.pl/tematyka/makroekonomia/chinskie-sny/ (access: 05.09.2017).
Góralczyk Bogdan (2014), *Amerykański „naszyjnik" wokół Chin – USA zwiększają obecność w Azji* [American necklet on China. The Americans increase their presence in Asia], WP.PL, 07.05.2014, https://wiadomosci.wp.pl/amerykanski-naszyjnik-wokol-chin-usa-zwiekszaja-obecnosc-w-azji-6031569384788609a (access: 05.09.2017).
Góralczyk Bogdan (2015), *Twarda pobudka z chińskiego snu* [Tough Awakening from the Chinese Dream], Obserwator Finansowy, 28.12.2015, https://www.obserwatorfinansowy.pl/tematyka/makroekonomia/twarda-pobudka-z-chinskiego-snu/ (access: 05.09.2017).
Guilford Gwynn (2013), *What Is China's Arctic Game Plan?*, “The Atlantic”, 16.05.2013, https://www.theatlantic.com/china/archive/2013/05/what-is-chinas-arctic-game-plan/275894/?utm_source=feed (access: 05.09.2017).
Gushin Arthur (2013), *Understanding China's Arctic Policies*, “The Diplomat”, 14.11.2013, http://thediplomat.com/2013/11/understanding-chinas-arctic-policies/ (access: 05.09.2017).
Gvosdev Niklas (2004), *The Sources of Russian Conduct*, “The National Interest”, 2004, 1 IV, no 75, http://nationalinterest.org/article/the-sources-of-russian-conduct-647 (access: 05.09.2017).

Gvosdev Nikolas (2006), *Rival views of the thaw provoke another chill*, "The New York Times" 25.01.2006, http://www.nytimes.com/2006/01/25/opinion/rival-views-of-the-thaw-provoke-another-chill.html (access: 05.09.2017).

Hill Fiona (2013), *Gang of Two. Russia and Japan Make a Play for the Pacific*, "Foreign Affairs" 27.11.2013, https://www.brookings.edu/opinions/gang-of-two-russia-and-japan-make-a-play-for-the-pacific/ (access: 06.09.2017).

How Does China's Imperial Past Shape Its Foreign Policy Today? (2017), A ChinaFile Conversation, 15.03.2017, http://www.chinafile.com/conversation/how-does-chinas-imperial-past-shape-its-foreign-policy-today (access: 05.09.2017).

How long can Russia withstand the crisis?(2014), "Global Times", 22.12.2014, http://www.globaltimes.cn/content/897993.shtml (access: 07.09.2017).

In Reversal, Kyrgyzstan Won't Close a U.S. Base (2009), "The New York Times", 23.06.2009, http://www.nytimes.com/2009/06/24/world/asia/24base.html (access: 05.07.2017).

Jarosiewicz Aleksandra (2013), *Chinese tour de force in Central Asia*, OSW, Warsaw 18.09.2013, https://www.osw.waw.pl/en/publikacje/analyses/2013-09-18/a-chinese-tour-de-force-central-asia (access: 07.09.2017)

Jarosiewicz Aleksandra (2014), *Kazakhstan's attitude towards integration with Russia: less love, more fear*, OSW, Warsaw 26.05.2014, https://www.osw.waw.pl/en/publikacje/osw-commentary/2014-05-26/kazakhstans-attitude-towards-integration-russia-less-love-more (access: 05.09.2017).

Johnston Ian (2017), *Xi Jinping: The Illusion of Greatness*, "New York Review of Books", 17.03.2017; http://www.nybooks.com/daily/2017/03/17/xi-jinping-the-illusion-of-greatness-party-congress/ (access: 05.09.2017).

Kaczmarski Marcin (2012), *Russia's turn towards Asia: more words than actions*, OSW, Warsaw 09.09.2012, https://www.osw.waw.pl/en/publikacje/osw-commentary/2012-10-09/russias-turn-towards-asia-more-words-actions (access: 05.09.2017)

Kaczmarski Marcin (2012), *Russia's turn towards Asia: more words than actions*, OSW, Warsaw, 09.10.2012, https://www.osw.waw.pl/en/publikacje/osw-commentary/2012-10-09/russias-turn-towards-asia-more-words-actions (access: 06.09.2017).

Kaczmarski Marcin (2017), *How China and Russia avoided the Thucydides trap*, Iowy Institute, Iowy Institute,11.04.2017, https://www.lowyinstitute.org/the-interpreter/how-china-and-russia-avoided-thucydides-trap (access: 05.09.2017)

Kaczmarski Marcin (2017), *Russia-China Relations and the West*, Working Paper Series Russia and the West: Reality Check, GDAP, March 2017, https://transatlanticrelations.org/publication/russia-china-relations-west-marcin-kaczmarski/ (access: 05.09.2017).

Kaczmarski Marcin, Jakóbowski Jakub (2016), *China on Russia's intervention in Syria*, OSW, Warsaw, 19.01.2016, https://www.osw.waw.pl/en/publikacje/osw-commentary/2016-01-19/china-russias-intervention-syria (access: 07.09.2017).

Kaczmarski Marcin, Rodkiewicz Witold (2016), *Russia's Greater Eurasia and China's New Silk Road:adaptation instead of competition*, OSW, Warsaw 21.07.2016, https://www.osw.waw.pl/en/publikacje/osw-commentary/2016-07-21/russias-greater-eurasia-and-chinas-new-silk-road-adaptation

Kaczmarski Marcin, Szymon Kardaś, Ewa Fischer (2015) *Russia-China. Ritual Demonstration Against the West*, OSW, Warsaw, 13.05.2015, https://www.osw.waw.pl/en/publikacje/analyses/2015-05-13/russia-china-ritual-demonstrations-against-west (access: 07.09.2017).

Kaczmarski, Marcin (2011), *Russia/China: energy cooperation is the biggest challenge*, OSW, Warsaw,12.10.2011, https://www.osw.waw.pl/en/publikacje/analyses/2011-10-12/russia/china-energy-cooperation-biggest-challenge (access: 05.09.2017)

Kagan Robert (2006), *League of Dictators?*, "Washington Post", 30.04.2006, http://www.washingtonpost.com/wp-dyn/content/article/2006/04/28/AR2006042801987.html (access: 07.09. 2017)

Karaganov Sergey (2011), *Lucky Russia*, "Russia in Global Affairs", 29.03. 2011, http://eng.globalaffairs.ru/pubcol/Lucky-Russia-15154 (access: 05.09.2017)

Kardaś Szymon (2014), *The eastern 'partnership' of gas. Gazprom and CNPC strike a deal on gas supplies to China*, OSW, Warsaw, 16.04.2014, https://www.osw.waw.pl/en/publikacje/osw-commentary/2014-06-16/eastern-partnership-gas-gazprom-and-cnpc-strike-a-deal-gas (access: 06.09.2017).

Kardaś Szymon, Rodkiewicz Witold (2013), *The Chinese leader in Moscow: geopolitical harmony, moderate progress on energy cooperation*, OSW, Warsaw, 27.03.2013, https://www.osw.waw.pl/en/publikacje/analyses/2013-03-27/chinese-leader-moscow-geopolitical-harmony-moderate-progress-energy (access: 06.09.2017).

Keck Zachary (2013), *To Hedge Its Bets, Russia Is Encircling China*, "The Diplomat", 05.11.2013, http://thediplomat.com/2013/11/to-hedge-its-bets-russia-is-encircling-china/ (access: 05.07. 2016).

Keck Zachary (2014), *Why Did BRICS Back Russia on Crimea?*, "The Diplomat" 31.03.2014, http://thediplomat.com/2014/03/why-did-brics-back-russia-on-crimea/ (access: 05.09.2017).

Korejba Jakub (2014), *Putin wali głową w mur (chiński)* [Putin bangs his head against (Chinese) Wall], "Nowa Europa Wschodnia" 11.06.2014, http://www.new.org.pl/1905-putin-wali-glowa-w-mur-chinski (access: 07.09.2017).

Krutikhin Mikhail (2014), *A Mystery, Wrapped in Puzzle*, Carnegie Center Moscow 23.05.2014, http://carnegie.ru/eurasiaoutlook/?fa=55680 (access: 10.10.2015).

Laumulin Murat (2006), *The Shanghai Cooperation Organization as 'Geopolitical Bluff'? A View From Astana*, "Russie.Nei.Visions" 12.06.2006, https://www.ifri.org/sites/default/files/atoms/files/laumullinenglish.pdf (access: 07.09.2017)

Laumulin Murat (2012), *Virtual Security of Central Asia*, "Russia in Global Affairs", October 7, 2012, http://eng.globalaffairs.ru/number/Virtual-Security-of-Central-Asia-15694 (access: 05. 09.2017).

Lo Bobo (2017), *A Wary Embrace. What the China-Russia relationship means for the world*,

Lukyanov Fyodor (2011), *Vigor, Toughness and Tolerance*, "Russia in Global Affairs", 27.03. 2011, http://eng.globalaffairs.ru/number/Vigor-Toughness-and-Tolerance-15152 (access: 05. 09.2017)

Lynch Elisabeth (2017), *America's Mao Zedong*, "Foreign Policy", 01.02.2017, http://foreignpolicy.com/2017/02/01/americas-mao-zedong-trump-chaos-is-deliberate/ (access: 07.09.2017).

Menkiszak Marek (2016), *Moscow chooses Trump. Russia on the US presidential elections*, OSW, Warsaw, 09.11.2016, https://www.osw.waw.pl/en/publikacje/osw-commentary/2016-11-09/moscow-chooses-trump-russia-us-presidential-elections (access: 07.09.2017).

Minxin Pei (2013), *China and Russia: Best Frenemies Forever?*, "Fortune", 28.03.2013, http://www.gmfus.org/commentary/china-and-russia-best-frenemies-forever (access: 05.09. 2017)

Minxin Pei (2016), *Vladimir Putin's China Visit Put His Weakness on Full Display*, "Fortune" 29.06.2016, http://fortune.com/2016/06/29/vladimir-putins-china-visit-put-his-weakness-and-desperation-on-full-display/ (access: 07.09.2017).

Mitchell Derek J. (2007), *China and Russia*, CSIS, 2007, https://csis-prod.s3.amazonaws.com/s3fs-public/090212_07china_russia.pdf (access: 05.09.2017)

Niedziński Bartłomiej (2014), *Czy Mongolia powinna odejść od balansowania między Rosją a Chinami?* [Should Mongolia leave its balancing policy between Russia and China], polska-azja.pl, 27.06.2014, http://www.polska-azja.pl/b-niedzinski-czy-mongolia-powinna-odejsc-od-balansowania-miedzy-rosja-a-chinami/ (access: 05.07.2017).

Opinion: Russia's attitude over Syria is significantly affected by West's deception over Libya (2013),Left Foot Forward 09.09.2013, https://leftfootforward.org/2013/09/opinion-russias-attitude-over-syria-is-significantly-affected-by-wests-deception-over-libya/ (access: 05.09. 2017)

Orwell George (1946/2015), *Politics and the English Language*, www.orwell.ru, http://www.orwell.ru/library/essays/politics/english/e_polit/ (access: 05.09.2017)

Paal Douglas H. (2014), How *Does the Ukraine Crisis Impact China*, Carnegie Center Moscow, 24.03.2014, http://carnegieendowment.org/2014/03/24/how-does-ukraine-crisis-impact-chi na-pub-55077

Paramonov Vladimir, Stolpovski Oleg (2008), *Russia and Central Asia: Multilateral Security Cooperation*, Advanced Research and Assessment Group, Defence Academy of the United Kingdom, March 2008, https://www.files.ethz.ch/isn/92584/08_March_Russia_Central_Asia.pdf (access: 06.09.2017).

Putin Hits on China's First Lady, Censors Go Wild (2014), "Foreign Policy", 10.11.2014,

Pyffel Radoslaw (2009), *Chiny-Rosja: Kto kogo?* [China-Russia Who will Beat Whom], polska-azja.pl, 16.10.2009, http://www.polska-azja.pl/chiny-rosja-kto-kogo-komentarz-wizyty-premiera-putina-w-pekinie/ (access: 05.09.2017).

Pyffel Radosław (2014), *Po Boeingu w objęcia smoka* [After Boening into Dragon's Embrace], polska-azja.pl, 31.07.2014, http://www.polska-azja.pl/r-pyffel-po-boeingu-w-objecia-smoka/ (access: 07.09.2017).

Pyffel Radosław (2014), *Siedem powodów dla których Chiny nie włączą się w wydarzenia na Ukrainie i pozostaną w ukryciu* [Seven Reasons Why China Will Not Join The Events In Ukraine And Will Stay In The Shadow], polska-azja.pl 04.04.2014, http://www.polska-azja.pl/2014/03/04/r-pyffel-siedem-powodow-dla-ktorych-chiny-nie-wlacza-sie-w-wydarzenia-na-ukrainie-i-pozostana-w-ukryciu/ (access: 10.10.2015).

Qingguo Jia (2001), *The Success of Shanghai Five: Interests, Norms and Pragmatism*, Commonwealth Institute, http://www.comw.org/cmp/fulltext/0110jia.htm (access: 06.09.2017).

Radchenko Sergey (2013), *Sino-Russian Competition Competition in Mongolia*, "The Asian Forum" 22.09.2013, http://www.theasanforum.org/sino-russian-competition-in-mongolia/ (access: 05.07.2017).

Russia Seeks Food-Export Boom With China But Obstacles Abound (2017), "Bloomberg", 10.02.2017; https://www.bloomberg.com/news/articles/2017-02-08/russia-seeks-food-export-boom-with-china-but-obstacles-abound (access: 06.09.2017).

Rodkiewicz Witold (2014), *Putin in Shanghai: a strategic partnership on Chinese terms*, OSW, Warsaw, 21.05.2014, https://www.osw.waw.pl/en/publikacje/analyses/2014-05-21/putin-shanghai-a-strategic-partnership-chinese-terms (access: 10.10.2015).

Rumer Eugene (2014), *China the Winner*, Carnegie Center Moscow, 16.06.2014, http://carnegie.ru/eurasiaoutlook/?fa=55614 (access: 10.10.2015).

Russian Business Interests in China (2016), "New Eastern Outlook", 05.10.2016, https://journal-neo.org/2016/10/05/russian-business-interests-in-china/ (access: 06.09.2017).

Security Council Fails to Adopt Draft Resolution on Syria as Russian Federation, China Veto Text Supporting Arab League's Proposed Peace Plan (2012), UN Security Council Press Release 04.02.2012, http://www.un.org/press/en/2012/sc10536.doc.htm (access: 05.09.2017)

Shambaugh David (2014), *China's Identity as a Major Power*, George Washington University 09.07.2014, https://www2.gwu.edu/~sigur/assets/docs/major_powers_091407/Shambaugh_on_China.pdf (access: 05.09.2017)

Shen Dingli (2016), *Russian cooperation with China is tactical, not strategic*, "Global Times", 27.06.2016, http://www.globaltimes.cn/content/990867.shtml (access: 05.09.2017)

Shevtsova Lilia (2013), *Russia's "Pivot" to China: Is It Real or Fake?* Carnegie Center Moscow,28.03.2013, http://carnegie.ru/2013/03/28/russia-s-pivot-to-china-is-it-real-or-fake-pub-51654 (access: 05.09.2017).

Sino-Russian bond more than expediency (2014), "Global Times", 14.10.2014; http://www.globaltimes.cn/content/886081.shtml (access: 05.09.2017).

Stakelbeck Frederick W. Jr. (2005), *A New Bloc emerges?*, "The American Thinker", 05.08.2005, http://www.americanthinker.com/articles/2005/08/a_new_bloc_emerges.html (access: 07.09.2017)

Stokes Jakob (2017), *Russia and China's Enduring Alliance*, "Foreign Affairs", 22.02.2017, https://www.foreignaffairs.com/articles/china/2017-02-22/russia-and-china-s-enduring-alliance (access: 07.09.2017).

Strachota Krzysztof (2004), *Tadżykistan: czas próby* [Tajikistan: Test Time], Warsaw, OSW working paper nr 15, October 2004, https://www.osw.waw.pl/pl/publikacje/prace-osw/2004-10-15/tadzykistan-czas-proby (access: 05.09.2017).

Strzelecki Jan (2017), *Painful adaptation. The social consequences of the crisis in Russia*, OSW, Warsaw, 06.02.2017, https://www.osw.waw.pl/en/publikacje/osw-studies/2017-02-06/painful-adaptation-social-consequences-crisis-russia (access: 05.09.2017)

Swaine Michael D. (2014), *The 18th Party Congress and Foreign Policy: The Dog that Did Not Bark?*, The Hoover Institution, 14.01.2014, http://media.hoover.org/sites/default/files/documents/CLM40MS.pdf (access: 05.09.2017).

Swanström Niklas (2008), *Georgia: The Split that Split the SCO*, CACI Analyst, 03.09.2008, https://akipress.com/news:12791/ (access: 07.09.2017)

The Geopolitics of Russia: Permanent Struggle (2012), "Stratfor",15.04.2012, https://worldview.stratfor.com/article/geopolitics-russia-permanent-struggle (access: 05.09.2017)

Trenin Dmitri (2006), *Russia Leaves the West*, "Foreign Affairs" 87, no. 4 (July/August 2006), https://www.foreignaffairs.com/articles/russia-fsu/2006-07-01/russia-leaves-west (access: 05.09.2017)

Trenin Dmitri (2007), *Russia's Strategic Choices*, Carnegie Moscow Center, Policy Brief no. 50, May 2007, http://carnegieendowment.org/files/pb50_trenin_final.pdf (access: 05.09.2017)

Trenin Dmitri (2012), *Russia Can Pivot to the Pacific, Too*, "The Globalist", 07.09.2012, https://www.theglobalist.com/russia-can-pivot-to-the-pacific-too/ (access: 07.09.2017).

Trenin Dmitri (2014), *China's Victory in Ukraine*, Project Syndicate, 31.07.2014, https://www.project-syndicate.org/commentary/dmitri-trenin-says-that-only-one-major-country-stands-to-gain-from-russia-s-conflict-with-the-west (access: 05.09.2017).

Trenin Dmitri (2014), *Gas deal entails China-Russia strategic depth*, "The Global Times" 25.05.2014, http://epaper.globaltimes.cn/2014-05-26/53339.htm (access: 07.09.2017).

Trenin Dmitri (2014), *Russia Faces Tough Road to Success*, 19.05.2014, Carnegie Center Moscow, http://carnegie.ru/2014/05/19/russia-faces-tough-road-to-success-pub-55642 (access: 06.09.2017).

Trenin Dmitri (2014), *Russia: Pivoting to Asia or Just to China?*, Carnegie Center Moscow, 24.03.2014, http://carnegie.ru/commentary/55062 (access: 05.07.2016).

Trenin Dmitri (2014), *Russia-China. The Russian Liberals Revenge*, Carnegie Center Moscow, 19.05.2014, http://carnegie.ru/commentary/55631 (access: 05.07.2017).

Trenin Dmitri (2014), *Sochi: The Game of Politics*, Carnegie Center Moscow, 27.01.2014, http://carnegie.ru/commentary/54317(access: 06.09.2017).

Trenin Dmitri (2014), *Will Japan and Russia Escape the New Cold War?* Moscow Carnegie Center, 24.04.2014, http://carnegie.ru/commentary/55384 (access: 05.07.2016).

Trenin Dmitri (2015), *From Greater Europe to Greater Asia? The Sino-Russian Entente*, Carnegie Moscow Center, 09.04.2015, http://carnegie.ru/2015/04/09/from-greater-europe-to-greater-asia-sino-russian-entente-pub-59728 (access: 05.09.2017)

Trenin Dmitri (2016), *Russia, China Can Help Kashmir Tensions*, Carnegie Moscow Center, 10.10.2016, http://carnegie.ru/2016/10/10/russia-china-can-help-kashmir-tensions-pub-64824 (access: 05.09.2017)

US pressure spurs closer Sino-Russian ties (2016), "Global Times", 27.06.2016, http://www.globaltimes.cn/content/990616.shtml (access: 05.09.2017).

Weitz Richard (2011), *Is BRICS a Real Bloc?* "The Diplomat", 21.04.2011

Why Russia needs the BRICS (2013), "Global Public", 03.09.2013, http://globalpublicsquare.blogs.cnn.com/2013/09/03/why-russia-needs-the-brics/ (access: 05.09.2017).

Willy Wo-Lap Lam (2002), *Moscow Tilts West, Beijing Worries*, "China Brief" 2, Issue 12, Jameston 6 June 2002, https://jamestown.org/program/moscow-tilts-west-beijing-worries/ (access: 05.09.2017).

Wiśniewska Iwona (2013), *Eurasian integration. Russia's attempt at the economic unification of the Post-Soviet area*, OSW, Warsaw 30.07.2013; https://www.osw.waw.pl/en/publikacje/osw-studies/2013-07-30/eurasian-integration-russias-attempt-economic-unification-post

Wojny (chyba) nie będzie (2016) [There won't be, probably, a war], "Krytyka Polityczna", 30.11.2016, http://krytykapolityczna.pl/swiat/wojny-chyba-nie-bedzie/ (access: 05.09.2017).

Wołoska Anna (2004), *Kazakhstan: the regional success story*, OSW, Warsaw 15.10.2004, https://www.osw.waw.pl/en/publikacje/osw-studies/2004-10-15/kazakhstan-regional-success-story (access: 05.09.2017).

Wu-ping Kwo, Ahiau-shyang Liou (2005), *Competition and Cooperation Between Russia and China in Central Asia and 'Shanghai Cooperation Organization: Analytical View from International Regime*, National Chengchi University, 18.04.2005, https://iir.nccu.edu.tw/hjourn/is_c/is_c_9403.htm (access: 10.10.2015).

Yan Jiann-Fa (2012), *Vladimir Putin's Deepening Rapprochement with China in the Tangled China Russia-US Triangle*, NCCU, 20.05.2012, http://rustudy.nccu.edu.tw/download.php? (access: 05.09.2017).

Yan Xuetong Urges China to Adopt a More Assertive Foreign Policy (2016), New York Times, 09.02.2016, https://www.nytimes.com/2016/02/10/world/asia/china-foreign-policy-yan-xuetong.html (access: 05.09.2017)

Zhao Huasheng (1998), *Security Building in Central Asia and the Shanghai Cooperation*, Slav.hokudai, 04.07.1998, src-h.slav.hokudai.ac.jp/coe21/publish/no2_ses/4-2_Zhao.pdf (access: 06.09.2017).

Zhao Kejin (2014), *China Turns to Southeast Asia*, Carnegie-Tsinghua Center 28.03.2014, http://carnegietsinghua.org/2014/03/28/china-turns-to-southeast-asia-pub-55099 (access: 05.09.2017)

«Не понимаю, почему Россия не настаивает на формировании альянса с Китаем» (2017) [I Don't understand why Russia is not pushing for forming an alliance with China],interview with Yan Xuetong, Kommiersant.Ru, 17.03.2017, https://www.kommersant.ru/doc/3243633 (access: 05.09.2017)

«Китайцы понимают, что Россия деградирует из-за коррупции и неэффективного управления» (2015) [The Chinese understand that Russia degradates due to corruption and mismanagement], Lenta.Ru, 30.04.2015, https://lenta.ru/articles/2015/04/29/gabuev/ (access: 05.09.2017)

Габуев Александр (2015), *Поворот в никуда: итоги азиатской политики России в 2015 году* [A Turn to Nowhere. The Results of Russia's Asia Policy in 2015], Carnegie.Ru, 29.12.2015, http://carnegie.ru/commentary/62369 (access: 05.09.2017)

Габуев Александр (2016), *Вернуть нельзя сотрудничать: чем важны новые договоренности России и Японии* [Cooperate, Cannot Give Back; why New Russia and Japan Agreements are important], Carnegie Moscow, 19.12.2016, http://carnegie.ru/commentary/66491 (access: 05.09.2017)

Габуев Александр (2017), *Шелковый путь в никуда* [Silk Road to Nowhere], Ведомости, 14.05.2017; https://www.vedomosti.ru/opinion/articles/2017/05/15/689763-shelkovii-put (access: 05.09.2017)

Гильбо Евгений В., *Перспективы китаизации России* [Perspectives of Sinization of Russia], Русское Дело, http://www.russkoedelo.org/mysl/gilbo/kitaizatsija.php (access: 05.09.2017)

Где-то в Китарктике. Пекин подбирается к полярным богатствам (2013) [Somewhere in Chinoartika. China Attempts to Take Polar Riches], Lenta.Ru, 14.06.2013, https://lenta.ru/articles/2013/06/14/chinarctic/ (access: 05.09.2017)

Ельцин напомнил Клинтону и миру: Россия остается ядерной державой (1999), [Yeltsin Reminded Clinton: Russia Remains a Nuclear Great Power], "Независимая газета", 10.12.1999, http://www.ng.ru/world/1999-12-10/1_pekin.html (access: 05.09.2017)

Караганов Сергей А. (2013), *Зачем нужна национальная идентичность* [Why a national identity is needed], Ria Novosti, 23.09.2013, https://ria.ru/valdaiclub_anniversary_comment/20130819/957213227.html (access: 05.09.2017)

Коморов А. (2002), *О российской националной идее* [On Russian national idea], "Духовное наследе. Аналитика", http://old.nasledie.ru/oboz/N04_01/4_02.HTM (access: 05.09.2017)

Лекторий СВОП: Почему Россия никак не может попасть в Европу (2016) [Why Russia Cannot Land in Europe], SVOP.Ru, 24.05.2016, http://svop.ru/проекты/lectorium/20272/ (access: 05.09.2017)

Лукьянов Федор А. (2010), *Поворот на восток* [Pivot to the East], SVOP, 15.02. 2010, http://svop.ru/news/2649/ (access: 05.09.2017)

Лукьянов Федор А. (2013), *Мы и новая Азия* [We and the New Asia], SVOP. Ru, 11.11.2013, http://svop.ru/news/7661/ (access: 05.09.2017)

Лукьянов Федор А. (2013), *Три к одному* (Three Against One), "Россия в глобальной политике", 21.02.2013, http://globalaffairs.ru/redcol/Tri-k-odnomu-15854 (access: 05.09. 2017)

Лукьянов Федор А. (2014), *Логичное партнерство* [Logical Partnership], Российская газета 21.05.2014, http://svop.ru/news/11455/ (access: 05.09.2017)

Мы пришли к вам с Кашмиром, Стратегическое партнерство России и Индии подверглось испытанию (2017), [We came to you with Kashmir. Strategic partnership of Russia and India under question], Kommersant.Ru, 10.01.2017, https://www.kommersant.ru/doc/3187318 (access: 05.09.2017)

Поворот России в Азию. Реплика Федора Лукьянова (2014) [Russia's Turn to Asia], Вести.ру 23.05.2014, http://www.vesti.ru/doc.html?id=1607387 (access: 05.09.2017)

Прощание с «азиатскими Балканами» Восприятие китайской миграции на Дальнем Востоке России (2014) [Farwell with Asian Balkans. The Perception of Chinese Migrantion to Russia Far East], SLON.ru, https://republic.ru/russia/kitayskaya_kolonizatsiya_dalnego_vostoka-1101179.xhtml (access: 05.09.2017)

Путин и Си Цзиньпин сошлись характерами (2013) [Putin and Xi Jinping Share Characters], Столетие 24.03.2013, http://radiovesti.ru/news/530520/ (access: 05.09.2017)

Путин о газовом контракте с КНР: китайцы – надежные партнеры (2014) [Putin on Gas Contract with PRC – Hopeful Partners], РИА Новости, 21.05.2014, https://ria.ru/economy/20140523/1009068014.html (access: 05.09.2017)

Путин привел Александра Невского как пример патриота (2011) [Putin Showed Alexander Nevsky as an example of patriot], Gazeta.Ru, 23.05.2011, https://www.gazeta.ru/news/lenta/2011/05/23/n_1851753.shtml (access: 05.09.2017)

Ради дружбы Путина и Си Цзиньпина (2016) [Concerning the Friendship of Putin and Xi Jinping], Inosmi.Ru 17.03.2016, http://inosmi.ru/politic/20160317/235747288.html (access: 05.09.2017)
Разуваев Александр (2015), *У России есть два достойных союзника* [Russia Has Two Noble Allies], Vzglyad.Ru 10.07.2015, https://vz.ru/columns/2015/7/10/755520.html (access: 05.09. 2017)
Россия и Китай «навеки друзья и никогда – Враги» (2001) [Russia and China"Forever Friends Never Enemies"], Pravda.Ru, 16.07.2001, https://www.pravda.ru/politics/16-07-2001/803 406-0/ (access: 05.09.2017)
Россия прорубила "газовое окно" в Азию – благодаря, но не назло Европе (2014) [Russia has broke open a gas window into Asia, thanks to, not against Europe], РИА Новости, 21.05.2014, https://ria.ru/economy/20140521/1008746496.html (access: 05.09.2017)
Тренин Дмитрий В. (2012), *Верные друзья? Как Россия и Китай воспринимают друг друга*, Carnegie, 01.06.2012, http://carnegie.ru/2012/02/29/ru-pub-47390 (access: 05.09.2017)
Фёдор Лукьянов: «Азия – это не периферия» (2014) [Asia is not periphery], Городские новости 12.03.2014, http://gornovosti.ru/tema/delovoy-chetverg/fedor-lukianov-aziya-eto-ne-periferiya51548.htm (access: 05.09.2017)

News Agencies, Newspapers and Online Journals

PAP (Polish Press Agency), Reuters, AP, CNN, BBC; The New York Times; The Guardian; The Times; The Diplomat; The Sydney Morning Herald The Moscow Times; English.People.Com; Bloomberg; China.Org.Cn; CCTV.Com; China Daily; Xinhua.Com; Xinhuanet; Forbes; Want China Times; The Jakarta Post; The Wall Street Journal Asia; Global Times; St. Petersbourg Times; Russia Today; Tass; Far Eastern Economic
Review; Satrapia. The Gazette of Central Asia; Tass; Moscow News; Bloomberg; The Diplomat
Эхо Сибири; РИА Новости; Московский комсомолец; News.Ru; Russian.People.Cn; Газета.ry; Tajik News; Фергана.News; Вести.Ru; Окно в Россию.ru; Polit.Ru; Известия; Lenta.Ru, ИА REGNUM; РИА Новости; Радио Голос России; BFM.RU; Коммерсанть; Взгляд; Российская газета; Ведомости(Vedomosti); Газпром.ru; Oil Capital.Ru; Business-Gazeta.Ru; Известия; News.ru; Tumangan.ru

Index

CPSIA information can be obtained
at www.ICGtesting.com
Printed in the USA
LVOW07*0148090118
562324LV00002B/4/P